The Vikings

ROBERT FERGUSON

The Vikings

A History

VIKING

VIKING
Published by the Penguin Group
Penguin Group (USA) Inc., 375 Hudson Street,
New York, New York 10014, U.S.A.
Penguin Group (Canada), 90 Eglinton Avenue East, Suite 700,
Toronto, Ontario, Canada M4P 2Y3
(a division of Pearson Penguin Canada Inc.)
Penguin Books Ltd, 80 Strand, London WC2R 0RL, England
Penguin Ireland, 25 St. Stephen's Green, Dublin 2, Ireland
(a division of Penguin Books Ltd)
Penguin Books Australia Ltd, 250 Camberwell Road, Camberwell,
Victoria 3124, Australia
(a division of Pearson Australia Group Pty Ltd)
Penguin Books India Pvt Ltd, 11 Community Centre, Panchsheel Park,
New Delhi − 110 017, India
Penguin Group (NZ), 67 Apollo Drive, Rosedale, North Shore 0632,
New Zealand (a division of Pearson New Zealand Ltd)
Penguin Books (South Africa) (Pty) Ltd, 24 Sturdee Avenue,
Rosebank, Johannesburg 2196, South Africa

Penguin Books Ltd, Registered Offices:
80 Strand, London WC2R 0RL, England

First published in 2009 by Viking Penguin,
a member of Penguin Group (USA) Inc.

10   9   8   7   6   5   4   3   2   1

Map illustrations by Jeff Edwards

LIBRARY OF CONGRESS CATALOGING IN PUBLICATION DATA

Ferguson, Robert, 1948-
The Vikings : a history / Robert Ferguson.
p. cm.
Includes bibliographical references and index.
ISBN 978-0-670-02079-9
1. Vikings. 2. Civilization, Viking. 3. Europe—History—476–1492. I. Title.
DL65.F467 2009
948.022—dc22
2009026818

Printed in the United States of America

'Get off this estate.'
'What for?'
'Because it's mine.'
'Where did you get it?'
'From my father.'
'Where did he get it?'
'From his father.'
'And where did he get it?'
'He fought for it.'
'Well, I'll fight you for it.'
Carl Sandburg, *The People, Yes*

The activity of being a historian is not that of contributing to the elucidation of a single ideal coherence of events which may be called 'true' to the exclusion of all others; it is an activity in which a writer, concerned with the past for its own sake and working to a chosen scale, elicits a coherence in a group of contingencies of similar magnitudes. And if in so new and delicate an enterprise he finds himself tempted into making concessions to the idiom of legend, that perhaps is less damaging than other divergences.
Michael Oakeshott, *The Activity of Being an Historian*

Contents

List of Illustrations

1 The Oseberg ship, excavated in 1904. (Museum of Cultural History, Oslo)
2 The reconstructed Oseberg ship being transported through the streets of Oslo. (Museum of Cultural History, Oslo)
3 Gotland picture stone showing a Viking longship. (photograph: author's collection)
4 The Oseberg ship on display in the Bygdøy museum. (Museum of Cultural History, Oslo)
5 A wooden bearing dial used for navigation, found at Wolin. (photograph: Blazej Stanislawski. The object is in the collection of the Institute of Archaeology and Ethnology, Polish Academy of Sciences)
6 Lindisfarne Island, Northumberland. (photograph: Skyscan Balloon Photography)
7 The Lindisfarne Stone. (photograph: Skyscan Balloon Photography)
8 Carving of Odin.
9 Bronze figurine of Odin from Skåne, southern Sweden. (photograph: Christer Åhlin/Museum of National Antiquities Stockholm, Sweden)
10 A bronze statue of Thor, from the tenth century. (photograph: The National Museum of Iceland)
11 Thor represented in the form of a hammer-shaped amulet. (photograph: Christer Åhlin/Museum of National Antiquities, Stockholm, Sweden)
12 A bronze statue of Frey, the god of fertility. (photograph: Museum of National Antiquities, Stockholm, Sweden)

List of Maps

A Note on the Language

I regret I have been no more successful than most other Scandinavian-
ists in finding a method of rendering names, terms and phrases from
Old Norse and modern Norwegian, Swedish and Danish into English
in a way that adequately conveys their pronunciation to English
readers. I have settled for a fairly thoroughgoing anglicization that
involves removing most of the diacritics and ligatures, leaving in just
a few as a reminder of the exotic nature of the original forms. Both *á*
and *å* are pronounced long (*aw*), and ð is voiced 'th' as in 'the'.

Introduction

In a recommendation from 1806 on the conditions and needs of a planned Danish National Museum the Danish historian Rasmus Nyerup wrote this on the nature of pre-Christian history:

Everything stemming from ancient times and before the introduction of Christianity to these lands can properly be described as infinitely old. With the coming of Christianity we acquired better writing materials than rocks and trees, and faster scribes than the runemasters of old . . . All that happened before, everything from ancient heathen times we see swirling before our eyes as though in a thick fog, in a vast space. We know that it is older than Christianity, but if it be a few years, or a few hundred years, or maybe even a few thousand years, is all a matter of conjecture.[1]

When in 1816 the Danish government went ahead with its plans for a national museum, responsibility for ordering the large collection of finds stored in the loft of Copenhagen's Trinitatis Church was given to Christian Jürgensen Thomsen, the son of a wealthy city merchant who in his youth had become interested in archaeology. Thomsen decided to try to bring some order to this vague and diffuse idea of a public past. On entering the loft for the first time, he reported, his general impression was of items randomly scattered in 'dust and disorganized disarray, hidden away in chests and baskets, among bits of material and paper. It was total chaos.'[2] He began by grouping the articles according to composition and function. They included tools and weapons made of stone; weapons and other items associated with combat made of bronze; articles made of iron; household items; ornamentation; urns containing incinerated remains; and a class of sundry other items. With the exhibits sorted into these three basic groupings of stone, bronze and iron, an exhibition opened to the public in the Trinitatis Church loft in 1819. This was the first time the tripartite division of the past into Stone, Bronze and Iron Ages was used.

Thomsen's original aim had been merely to solve the practical problem of exhibiting the finds coherently. When he began to study the implications of his own system, however, he realized that it almost certainly described a forward movement in time from an older to a younger period and began to refine it accordingly, introducing sub-divisions within each of the three groups. A full presentation of his ideas appeared in book form in 1836. Translated into English as *A Guide to Northern Antiquities* in 1848, its principles were quickly accepted and adopted throughout Europe. Further sub-divisions in the groupings have been made by each of the Scandinavian countries. In Sweden the Later Iron Age is divided into Wendel and Viking Ages, the former covering the period c.550–800 AD and taking its name from a number of ship burials excavated near Vendel in northern Uppland, the latter beginning with the raids by Heathen Scandinavians on Christian targets in the British Isles in 793. The Danes prefer the term Germanic Iron Age for the earlier period, and in Norway it is known as the Merovingian Period, after the Frankish Merovingian dynasty that was the dominant power in Europe from about 460 to 751. The warrant for the creation of a particular 'Viking' Age within the Iron Age was the number of finds from the later part of the period associated with seafaring and returning warriors. So familiar has Thomsen's tripartite division of the past into a Stone, a Bronze and an Iron Age become, so complete the authority it has acquired, that we easily forget its comparatively recent vintage and attribute to it a degree of reality that it scarcely has a right to. If astronomers can deprive Pluto of its status as a planet then it is possible that future historians will become so frustrated by the constrictions of inherited periodization that the whole system of archaeological time will one day be overhauled, with attendant redefinitions, promotions and demotions.

And in such an event, the Viking Age would probably occasion an unusual amount of headscratching, for it eludes almost every attempt at packaging and labelling. The British start their 'insular' Viking Age cleanly with the raid on Lindisfarne in 793 and end it as cleanly with the Battle of Hastings in 1066. The Irish would close theirs with the Battle of Clontarf in 1016. Harald Hardrada's failed attempt to invade England in 1066 is significant in Norwegian history, but the date has no special resonance for the Danes or the Swedes. And was the large fleet under Håkon IV that was defeated by the Scots at the battle of Largs in 1263 a Viking fleet, or a Norwegian fleet? Historians of the Baltic island of Gotland would end their Viking Age in about 1020. Wales seems scarcely to have had a Viking Age, though this may reflect only the poverty of the written record.[3] Some historians take the narrative up to the extinction of the Norse colony on Greenland in about 1500; but were the colonizations of Iceland and Greenland even Viking enterprises at all?[4] In the 1970s the Uppsala-based British historian Peter Sawyer divided the insular Viking Age into two, with a first period extending from 793 to the fall of the Viking kingdom of York in 954 and a second from the resumption of Viking raiding in about 980 to the conquest of England in 1013 by the Danish King Sven Forkbeard and his son Cnut. As a general survey of the whole field of Viking activity this book does not take the insular perspective. The multiple beginnings and wide choice of endings mean that its parameters are fluid, but based on the unmoving fact that, at the start of the period, *roughly speaking* all the Scandinavian peoples were Heathens; and by the time it ends, *roughly speaking* all the Scandinavian peoples thought of themselves as Christian. Sometimes red and dramatically visible, at other times grey and hard to spot, the long, slow process of religious and cultural change runs like a thread throughout the Viking Age.

One might suppose the etymology of the word would tell us at least how the Vikings viewed themselves. But its origins are obscure and there is little agreement about it. It is not even certain that the word is Scandinavian in origin. It occurs several times in the Old English poem *Widsid*, usually dated to the end of the seventh century, and in the eighth-century Old English poem *Exodus*, where the tribe of Reuben are described as 'sæwicingas', meaning 'sea-warriors', as they cross the Red Sea on their way out of Egypt. But the *Anglo-Saxon Chronicle*, that great compendium of historical records begun in the time of Alfred the Great, uses the term only four times before 1066, in the native English forms *wícenga* or *wícinga*, in 879, 885, 921 and 982.[5]

The rigidity of the structural rules governing the creation of the Viking Age court poetry, known from its makers or 'skalds' as 'skaldic poetry', means that those examples of it handed down, usually embedded within sagas written down in the Christian era, are regarded by linguistic scholars as authentic documents from the early years of the Viking Age in both content and language. Surviving examples of skaldic poetry contain some thirty references to 'vikings' meaning 'long-distance sea-warriors' in contexts which are positive and approving. In the anonymous collection of poems from the Viking Age known as the Edda that forms part of the thirteenth-century manuscript *Codex Regius*, now in the Árni Magnusson Institute in Reykjavik, four references have this sense. A handful of appearances on runestones from Sweden and Denmark seem to confirm the heroic and manly usage, often in some form of the phrasal verb *fara í víking*, 'to go on a Viking expedition'.[6] A stone at Hablingbo church in southern Gotland was erected by two of his sons in memory of their father Hailka – 'who went west with the Vikings'. As a personal name it occurs on a score of Swedish runestones, and also enjoyed some popularity in those parts of England settled by Scandinavians. This might explain why the English language, which at different times has adopted 'vandal', 'barbarian', 'thug' and 'hooligan' to denote violent and dangerous people, never made similar use of 'viking'. But as Christianity began to make serious inroads on Scandinavian culture towards the end of the Viking Age, negative connotations begin to appear. A runic inscription on the Bro stone, some forty kilometres north-west of Stockholm, was raised by his widow in praise of a certain Assur for the diligence with which he had 'kept watch for Vikings'.[7]

Some linguists believe the word derives from the Latin *vícus*, meaning a 'town' or 'camp' or 'dwelling-place'. Others suggest that the noun comes from an Old Norse verb *víkja*, meaning 'to travel from place to place'. A simple and persuasive theory is that it originally denoted people from the Vik, the name for the bay area of south-eastern Norway around the Oslo fjord that also denoted the inland

4

coastal region, and possibly included the coast of Bohuslän in present-day Sweden. There is support for the suggestion in the frequency with which the waters of the Vik appear in saga literature, suggesting it was the most heavily trafficked maritime area in the region at the time.[8]

To some extent the Norwegian, Danish and Swedish historians who constructed the Viking Age in Scandinavia did so for ideological reasons. Each nation was, for differing reasons, in need of a lost golden age of greatness. Denmark needed to reassure itself after being overpowered by Prussia in 1864 and forced to give up control of the duchies of Schleswig-Holstein. The peace settlement meant that she also lost the right to carry out further excavations at Nydam, a bog site that offered a wealth of well-preserved sacrificial materials from the third to the fifth centuries. It was in response to this sort of reverse that the nineteenth-century Danish historian Johannes Steenstrup urged the specifically Danish elements in the 'European' colonizations carried out by the Vikings in England and Normandy, asserting that Normandy's founder Ganger Rolf ('Rolf the Walker') was a Dane and not, as the Norwegians claimed, a native of Møre og Romsdal on the west coast of Norway. To bolster a separate Norwegian cultural identity as part of the drive towards the independence from Sweden that came in 1905, the Norwegian Gustav Storm vigorously promoted the fact that it was essentially his countrymen who had colonized Iceland, Greenland, and established the short-lived settlement in North America in 1000. The Swedes too looked for the compensations of nationalist nostalgia to make up for the painful loss of Finland to Russia early in the nineteenth century.

Historians from all three communities adapted the evolutionary theory of the English biologist and philosopher Herbert Spencer, originator of the phrase 'survival of the fittest', to their own studies to discover an 'evolution' of peoples and cultures over historical time that led to technological and moral progress. It enabled them to place their Viking forefathers somewhere in the chain of their own development as 'noble savages', living out a violent period of their destiny as they moved inexorably towards the higher stage of development represented by the Christianity to which they all, eventually, subscribed. So while there were obligatory words of censure for the ferocity of the conversion campaigns of both Olaf Tryggvason and Olav Haraldson at the turn of the tenth century in Norway, there was never any doubt in Victorian eyes but that these excesses were committed for the best of reasons.

The cultural relativity of our own times makes this kind of assertion problematic. No longer able to view the violence characteristic of the Vikings as a sort of brisk adolescent workout before the onset of maturity, we prefer instead to describe and analyse their achievements as traders, travellers, explorers and founders of towns, and to extol the beauties of their poetry and jewellery. But, while all of these are entirely valid perspectives, the pendulum may have swung too far: as one modern historian puts it, the revisionist view has come close to giving us an image of the Vikings as a group of 'long-haired tourists who roughed up the locals a bit'.[9] Among the aims of this book is to restore the violence to the Viking Age, and to try to show why our understanding is incomplete without it.

Uncertainty about the proper dimensions of the Viking Age is reflected in a very conditional acceptance of the literary sources that once formed the bedrock of what historians thought they knew about the period. The main objection to the use of the histories and sagas is that they were written in most cases some 300 years after the events they describe. It is absolutely possible to show under close analysis that the objectivity of the central literary source for the settlement of Iceland at the end of the ninth century, *Islendingabok* or *The Book of the Icelanders* by Ari Thorgilsson, known as 'the Learned', completed by about 1130, is prejudiced by the author's inclination to exaggerate the importance of members of his own family in the commission of important deeds. Much of what we think we know about the beliefs and doings of Viking Age Scandinavians derives from *Heimskringla or The Lives of the Norse Kings* by the thirteenth-century Icelandic poet, historian, novelist and politician Snorri Sturluson. Snorri's distinction as a sort of cultural Noah who provided for the preservation of pre-Christian beliefs, ideas and events in prehistoric and early historical Scandinavia is beyond dispute; but it is not an ideal dependence, for in an era in which claims to political power were intimately bound up with family and genealogical background, Snorri was, like Ari, concerned to promote the claims to significance of his own ancestors in the shaping of Norwegian and Icelandic history. Earlier than either Ari or Snorri is Adam of Bremen's *Gesta Hammaburgensis* or *Deeds of the Archbishops of the Church of Hamburg*, completed by about 1070 and the major source of our knowledge of events in northern Europe and Scandinavia from the end of the eighth to the thirteenth century. Writing at a time when relations between the archbishopric of Hamburg-Bremen and the papacy were in crisis, Adam is prone to simplifying the conversion of the peoples of the north to Christianity by attributing it almost exclusively to the efforts of his own church and ignoring the role played by English missionaries in the process. *The Anglo-Saxon Chronicle*, originating in Wessex, may well have overplayed the role of Wessex in organizing resistance to the Viking armies. The French monk Dudo of St Quentin wrote a history, *De moribus et actis primorum normanniae ducum*, or 'On the manners and deeds of the first Norman dukes'. Completed by about 1015, it is a hugely entertaining work that is compromised as history by Dudo's desire to flatter the ancestors of the ducal patrons who had commissioned him to write it.

But beyond a certain point conditionality defeats its own ends. Writing in 1912, at a time when modern source criticism first entered the field of Viking studies, the Danish historian Ebbe Hertzberg entered some pertinent observations against too much deconstructive rigour, warning that it would lead to a state of affairs in which the clear and connected sense of history offered by the sagas would be replaced by hypotheses on events and their causes that were at best less than convincing and at worst lacked all context and cohesion.[10] Archaeology and the sophisticated research techniques of numismatic analysis, dendrochronology which permits highly accurate dating of wooden objects by tree-ring analysis, archaeozoology, palaeobotany, DNA analysis, ice crystallography and climate analysis have compensated considerably for the losses sustained to modern source criticism; but even here there are cautionary tales to be told. In 1222 Saxo Grammaticus, the Danish cleric and historian, author of the *Gesta Danorum* or *History of the Danes*, recorded his belief that a long series of enigmatic markings on the Runamo rock in Blekinge contained a runic account of the deeds of the pre-historical King Harald Hildetand. A later king, Waldemar the Great, exercised himself in the attempt to decipher the message, and in the seventeenth century the priest and runologist Jon Skonvig succeeded in deciphering the name of the Swedish town 'Lund' among the inscriptions, at that time part of Denmark. The rock was cleaned, several more runes emerged and an attempt at a full transliteration was made in the 1830s by the Icelander Finn Magnusen. A study in 1844 then revealed conclusively that the whole 'inscription' was a phenomenon of nature, a wonder in its own way certainly, but historically irrelevant.[11] Runes on a stone found at Byfield, Massachusetts, were likewise once 'translated' to give the exciting message *Overland route, Øn set the stone*. If confirmed, it would have opened a whole new chapter in the history of the Vikings in America. Alas, on closer examination these too turned out to be glacial striations.

It is inappropriate to call these observations on the nature of Viking Age sources 'problems'. They are simply the conditions of the study. They make the pattern of Viking Age history hard to trace, and I am only too well aware that in trying to trace it anyway I may have produced in this book my own share of such phantoms, and along the way made any number of what Michael Oakeshott once called 'concessions to the idiom of legend'. But my aim has been to provide the intelligent general reader who has an interest in the Viking Age with a study that might satisfy his or her interest without burdening it with an account of the innumerable controversies that cover every field of study of the period. I have accordingly tried to limit the number of 'perhaps's and 'possibly's which would otherwise overwhelm almost every paragraph. I hope the reader who desires them will supply these unconsciously. I am, of course, profoundly indebted to the work of innumerable expert archaeologists, translators, linguists, geneticists, runologists, topographical analysts and earth scientists whose work I hope I have not travestied too much in trying to give what is in most cases an all too brief summary.

I

The Oseberg Ship

The identification, about 180 years ago, of a 'Viking Age' in Scandinavia fired the creative imaginations of novelists and painters alike. The Swedish novelist Esaias Tegnér's *Fridtjofs Saga* became a bestseller throughout Europe on its publication in 1820 and inspired a wave first of antiquarian and then of literary and historical interest in the large body of Old Norse saga literature. Artists such as Johannes Flintoe, P. N. Arbo and Anker Lund based their careers on illustrations of scenes and characters from the sagas. Their efforts gave a strong but still only tentative legitimacy to the idea of a 'Viking Age'. For the less romantically inclined, however, something more was needed to confirm 'the Viking Age' as a culture or civilization so distinct as to warrant separate naming.

When confirmation came it did so dramatically in the form of a short series of archaeological discoveries made in Norway in the late nineteenth and early twentieth centuries. The first of three Viking Age longships which emerged from more than 1,000 years of obscure anchorage inside burial mounds in the rural south-east of Norway was the Tune ship, unearthed at Rolvsøy in Østfold in 1867 and dated to about 900. A rectangular grave-chamber behind the mast housed the remains of a man, along with a horse, sword, spears and the remnants of a saddle. The discovery caused much excitement and provided significant new information about the construction of the Viking longships, already familiar from saga literature and tapestries, and soon to become the defining symbol of the Viking Age. Thirteen years later another ship discovered inside a mound at Sandar in Vestfold, known as the Gokstad ship, overshadowed the Tune find. A medical examination, carried out in 2007 by Professor Per Holck of the University of Oslo's Anatomy Department, of the remains from the ship's grave-chamber revealed a very different picture from that presented by a study carried out shortly after the initial discovery, which had suggested a man of between fifty and seventy, so badly afflicted by rheumatism that he was probably bed-ridden and scarcely able to feed himself. Professor Holck's results show that the occupant was an extremely powerful and muscular man in his forties. At about 181 cm in height, he would have towered some 15 cm above the average man of his time. His thigh bones alone weighed 30 per cent more than the average for men of a similar height in modern times, a development suggesting that he spent much of his time on horseback, with his thigh muscles in constant use as they pressed in against the flanks of his mount. Neurologists at the Oslo National Hospital also found that he had a pituitary adenoma, or tumour of the pituitary gland, that led to an increased production of growth hormone and probably gave him the physical characteristics associated with gigantism. Appropriately enough, this first real Viking had died a violent death. Professor Holck suggests a sequence of events in which the Gokstad chieftain was ambushed by two or perhaps three assailants. A blow with a sword to the left leg, just below the kneecap, would have left him unable to stand. The left knee was then attacked a second time with some kind of club-hammer, and the outer part of the right ankle was sliced off in the heat of the struggle. A stab wound in the right thigh struck perilously close to the main artery, and these four wounds from three different weapons were enough to kill him.[1] A dozen horses had been buried with him, along with six dogs and a peacock, five beds, three small boats, a bronze pot with suspension chain, a barrel, buckets, and sixty-four shields with traces of yellow and black paint on them that had been fastened to the outside of the ship's rail. The tent-shaped grave-chamber containing the skeleton had been built using notched logs (*lafteteknikken*); it remains the only physical proof that this particular woodworking technique was known to the Vikings.

The Gokstad ship itself was overshadowed by the discovery of the even more richly furnished and exquisite Oseberg ship, at Slagen in Vestfold in 1904. Unlike other mounds in the area on the western bank of the Oslo fjord, like those at Borre and Farmannshaugen near

Tønsberg, there was no tradition associating the mound on Oskar Rom's farm with a burial site. It was known locally as 'Revehaugen', meaning a place where foxes were to be found. In the wake of the huge national and international interest aroused by the Gokstad find, there had been a certain amount of active looking for ship-burial sites in Norway. Rom had done some desultory digging in Revehaugen and found something he thought might be interesting, and on 8 August 1903 he travelled to Oslo (Kristiania, as it was then known) to show it to Professor Gabriel Gustafson, the curator of the University's Museum of Antiquities.

Gustafson was initially sceptical of Rom's claim, but the moment Rom showed him the small sample of carved wood he had brought along with him from the mound his scepticism vanished. Two days later he visited the site himself and dug a provisional shaft which persuaded him of the importance and size of the discovery. It was too late in the year to begin a full excavation so he closed the shaft to protect the find from frost and spent the winter making practical and financial preparations for carrying out the work of unearthing it. Less than a year later, on 13 June 1904, with all the necessary financial support in place, excavation of the mound began.

The mound was some 40 metres in diameter and rose to a height of 2.5 metres above the surrounding field, having collapsed from an estimated original height of about 6.5 metres.[2] The summer turned out to be a dry one, which was good news for the excavating team. It made the digging easier, and justified a decision to dam the nearby stream and run hosepipes from it to keep the ship watered. The first significant find came within a few days, when the ship's intricately carved sternpost emerged. It was a harbinger of how crucial the discovery of this grave and its contents would be for the creation of the Viking Age, for here was artwork that complemented and instantly expanded existing conceptions of Viking art which, until then, had been based on small finds of jewellery, the carvings on Swedish runestones, the Gotland picture-stones, and the designs and illustrations used by carvers on the doors of Norwegian stave churches which were from a later, post-Christian period.

It was soon clear that the vessel was broken and much distorted from the pressure of the piled earth. This had forced the lower part of it down into the soft clay beneath, breaking the keel in the middle and forcing up the grave-chamber – positioned, like that of the Gokstad chamber, behind the mast – until it was higher than the railing. Inside it were two beds in which the two female occupants of the grave had originally been placed. At an unknown date the grave had been entered and their remains removed from the beds by intruders who had left the bones scattered in the entry-shaft. The smaller finds, too, were fragile, often in pieces, and saturated with moisture. Each item that emerged was packed in wet moss and sent to Oslo by weekly shipment. A wooden chest that had lain undisturbed for 1,000 years opened smoothly on its hinges at the first attempt. There was rope all over the deck of the ship.

With these smaller items out of the way, it was time to raise the ship itself. Nikolay Nikolaysen, the archaeologist in charge of the Gokstad excavation, had been lucky: apart from a clean, central break, his ship had been in one piece and cutting through the break had made it an easy, if laborious, task to transport the ship to Oslo in two manageable halves. The Oseberg ship, by contrast, had retained its basic shape but in shattered form. It was like a giant jigsaw puzzle. A marine engineer was given the task of identifying and marking each of the 2,000 or so pieces as they came up. By 5 November the digging was completed and the ship followed the smaller finds up the fjord to Oslo, where the task of reconstruction began.

The most urgent need was to preserve the individual parts of the find from decay. Much of the oak used to build the ship had survived in reasonable condition and could be treated with linseed oil and carbolic acid during a slow process of drying out. Other types of wood were preserved in water. Objects made of iron were dried and then cooked in paraffin to prevent rusting. Bronze articles were dried and then lacquered. Rope was treated with glycerine, leather was oiled. Textile finds presented particular difficulties: the wool and silk had kept fairly well in the clay, but the linen had coagulated into a layered cake which proved almost impossible to separate.

Gustafson, meanwhile, had embarked on a fact-finding tour of European museums, visiting his colleagues and consulting them on the latest techniques of preservation. He returned with the idea of saturating the wood in a solution of alum and water. Afterwards the alum was washed off the outside and the wood allowed to dry. The alum inside crystallized and bulked out the wood, giving it structure and preventing shrinkage. Once dry it was coated with linseed oil and a layer of matt lacquer applied. The technique was the best then available to Gustafson. With the passage of time, however, the alum has assumed a wafer-like consistency that leaves the wood delicate and difficult to handle and highly sensitive to variations in temperature and humidity. If change occurs too rapidly the crystallization process in the alum will reverse and the wood burst.

After treatment it proved possible to use over 90 per cent of the original oak in the reconstructed keel, as well as over half the iron nails used by the builders of the ship. Both fore and aft ship-posts and the tiller had been twisted out of shape and there were anxious moments for the restorers as these were steamed and subjected to pressure from the braces, but these techniques, too, proved successful. The sternpost, the upper part of which was found in a break-in shaft dug at an unknown time by grave-robbers, did not survive exposure to the air. The only wholly new part of the restored ship, it was designed as a dragon's tail to match the dragon's head of the forepost, using as a guide images such as the invasion ships depicted on the Bayeux Tapestry.

From discovery in 1904 to completed reconstruction in 1926, the restoration project took twenty-two years. A new museum was purpose-built for the three ships on the Bygdøy peninsula a mile or so from the centre of Oslo, and on 27 September 1926 the Oseberg ship was packaged in a frame of iron and wood before being mounted on a specially adapted railway wagon to begin its slow journey from the university workshops at Fredriksgate 3 to the docks at Pipervika. The wagon was dragged through the streets of Oslo on railway tracks laid by a team of soldiers. After every 100 metres the cortège came to a halt as the tracks were retrieved from behind the wagon, carried forward and re-laid in front of it. Large crowds of sightseers turned out to watch. Security precautions were high owing to fears of vandalism from the disturbed or drunken. At Pipervika the ship was transferred on to a barge for the short distance over the water to Bygdøy. There the rail-laying process continued as the ship was dragged up the slope of Huk Aveny to the museum, where she joined the Tune and Gokstad ships. In 1948, as a gesture of respect and in the presence of the king of Norway, the bones of the two women whose deaths had started the whole train of events over 1,000 years previously were ceremonially reinterred in granite sarcophagi in the reconstructed mound at Slagen.

If the Oseberg ship-coffin and its contents were all the archaeological evidence we had of the Viking Age and its culture we would still be fortunate, for the range and quality of the items buried with the two women far outstrip the grave-goods found in the other burials for sheer artistic merit and in terms of the amount of practical information they provide about the lives, ways and beliefs of the Vikings. Gustafson and his team of archaeologists, diggers, engineers and restorers left a compendious record of every detail of the excavation. In combination with modern techniques of scientific analysis it provides enough information to permit a reconstruction of the possible sequence of events surrounding the burial.[3]

Dendrochronological analysis shows that the Oseberg ship was built from trees felled in 820. Her hull was 22 metres long and 5 metres broad, and made of twelve overlapping oak planks, secured to each other with iron nails, a technique known to boat-builders as 'clinker-building'. Nine timbers formed the hull, the larger tenth marked the waterline, and the two upper timbers the sides. Tiller, oars and mast were of pinewood. The narrow and elegant lines of her bow originally led to an assumption that she was probably some sort of royal yacht used for travelling locally in the sheltered waters of the Oslo fjord. A recent electronic scan has revealed, however, that the horizontal ribs on either side of the reconstructed keel should have been curved and not straight. At the cost of elegance the broader bow would have made her quite capable of sailing on the open seas.[4] Dendrochronological analysis has established that her active life ended in the spring of 834, when her presumptive owner died.

Some historians believe that the Viking practice of burying their dead leaders in large mounds that were close to the family home reflected the significance of the mounds as a visible broadcast of the family's power. In that case the Oseberg mound is an exception, for

its location has been described as almost actively 'anti-monumental'.[5]
Possibly in a deliberate attempt to exploit the preservative properties
of the clay, low-lying ground to the east of the stream at Slagen was
preferred to the higher ground just a couple of hundred metres north
of it. And unlike the complex of mounds at nearby Borre, for example,
which functioned as a burial ground from about 600–650 until well
into the Viking Age, this was an isolated construction. At that time
the fjord lay about 1 kilometre further south than it does today, and
the ship had to be dragged from the boathouse up the stream until
that became too narrow, then hauled up on land and dragged on
wooden rollers (how little had changed by the time of the journey to
Pipervika) the rest of the way across the field to the long furrow which
had been dug to receive it. The clay-type soil from the furrow was
heaped up nearby on the grass, incidentally preserving the meadow
flowers beneath it, from which it has been deduced that the furrow
was cut in the spring. Once the ship was in position, facing south and
toward the fjord, a tent-shaped oak shelter was built behind the mast
to house the dead women. The whole community must have been
engaged in the process at this time, craftsmen working on the ornaments and household objects that were to accompany them into the
grave (though many showed signs of use in daily life), others digging
the peat with which the mound was to be covered, still others breaking
and transporting boulders from the rocky outcrop that lay north-east
of the mound. The after part of the ship, between the grave-chamber
and the sternpost, was loaded with what the passengers would need
on their voyage: small axes and knives (no weapons were found in
this female grave), cooking equipment and a whole ox – 'the kitchen',
this part has been called – and the whole then covered by a layer of
boulders. Beds, white woollen blankets with red patterns, down quilts,
clothing, pots and buckets of various sizes, a weaving tablet with a
half-woven piece of cloth in it as well as other pieces of weaving
that perhaps originally hung as strip decorations on the walls of the
chamber, and many other items were carried into the burial chamber
behind the mast. The ship was then partially buried, starting from the
stern, continuing up to and framing the triangular entrance to the
grave-chamber behind the mast, at which point soil analysis shows

that work stopped. If one of the two women was a slave fated to serve her mistress in the next life as in this then now was perhaps the point at which she would have been sacrificed.[6] The two were ceremoniously carried on board and placed on the beds inside the chamber, and the entrance boarded up with surprising carelessness and lack of attention to detail, perhaps a hint that the consumption of alcohol in quantity may have formed part of the ritual.

More valuable and ornate gifts were then loaded on board, again seemingly haphazardly, including a beautifully carved ceremonial wagon and three sledges with shafts indicating that they were to be drawn by two horses, a gangway, oars, rigging (but no sail), rope, bailer, five metal rattles, of which one was attached to one of the animal-head posts inside the burial chamber, a beechwood saddle (the only complete surviving example of a saddle from the Viking Age), combs and wooden buckets. The handle of one bucket, the 'buddha bucket', was decorated with two beautiful bronze figures seated in the lotus position with eyes closed and four yellow enamel swastikas decorating their chests. The tops of their skulls had been neatly sliced off. Originally thought to hint at trade relations with Asia, a recent theory suggests they may be representations of seventh-century Celts who had been ritually sacrificed, desiccated and then buried to function as tribal messengers to the gods.[7] All in all, the wealth of material buried with this ship – to say nothing of the ship itself – was such as to make it hard to imagine the loss was not felt in the community sponsoring the burial.

Now, with the chamber boarded up, came what was probably the heart of the proceedings. Four or five dogs and two more oxen were slaughtered, as well as fifteen horses that had first been run to exhaustion. The furniture, tools and carriages scattered across the foredeck were bathed in their blood. Stones were then piled over the ship, breaking many of the grave-goods and rendering them unusable. The sights and sounds accompanying such an orgy of blood-letting we might perhaps be able to imagine, the atmosphere conjured by it probably not. As the mourners then set about completing the mound, the sight before them must have been eerie and awe-inspiring, the blood-spattered ship with its cargo of dead women seeming to lurch forward across the field in a last attempt to shake off the engulfing wave of dark earth rising behind it. The meadow flowers preserved from this stage of the proceedings were autumnal, showing that the whole process from the opening of the furrow to the closing of the mound must have taken about four months. Clearly at least one of the women had died long before the burial took place.

It is hardly possible to conceive of a society that is not curious about the possibility of a life after death. The *Saga of the Jomsvikings*, a story first written down about 1200, contains a scene in which a number of warriors sit on the beach awaiting their turn to be executed after defeat in a sea-battle at Hjórungavág, off the coast of Norway, in about 986. One recalls with his neighbour their conversations on the subject of life after death, and tells him he intends to use his execution as the occasion of an experiment to find out if such a thing exists. When his turn comes he grasps a knife in his hand and tells the executioner that, if he is able to, he will hold up the blade after his execution as a signal that he is still conscious. 'Thorkel hewed,' the sagaman relates remorselessly, 'the head flew off, and the knife dropped.'[8]

On the other side of the Viking world from Oseberg and the Norwegian Vestfold and about a century later, the Arab diplomat and Islamic teacher Ibn Fadlan noted down his detailed description of the rites surrounding the cremation of a Viking chieftain on the banks of the Volga which he witnessed in 921. A slave girl had been chosen to join her master in his death:

They led the slave girl to a thing that they had made which resembled a doorframe. She placed her feet on the palms of the men and they raised her up to overlook this frame. She spoke some words and they lowered her again. A second time they raised her up and she did again what she had done; then they lowered her. They raised her a third time and she did as she had done the two times before. Then they brought her a hen; she cut off the head, which she threw away, and then they took the hen and put it in the ship. I asked the interpreter what she had done. He answered, 'The first time they raised her she said, 'Behold, I see my father and mother.' The second time she said, 'I see all my dead relatives seated.' The third time she said, 'I see my master seated in Paradise and Paradise is beautiful and green; with him are men and boy servants. He calls me. Take me to him.'[9]

Saxo Grammaticus in the *Gesta Danorum* described a similar use being made of a cockerel as a medium or spirit messenger during a journey through the kingdom of death undertaken by a hero named Hading with a female companion:

Moving on, they found barring their way a wall, difficult to approach and surmount. The woman tried to leap over it, but to no avail, for even her slender, wrinkled body was no advantage. She thereupon wrung off the head of a cock which she happened to be carrying and threw it over the enclosing barrier; immediately the bird, resurrected, gave proof by a loud crow that it had truly recovered its breathing.[10]

Was it the observed tendency of hens to run around in a wild parody of continued existence after decapitation that lay behind their role in such situations? Was something similar done in connection with the Oseberg burial? We can hardly know. Because Viking Age Scandinavians had only a rudimentary written culture, in the form of terse runic inscriptions on stones and sticks, and because knowledge of Heathen rites and beliefs was actively suppressed by the Church after the triumph of Christianity, our ignorance of what these people believed about first and last things, and of how these beliefs manifested themselves in practice, is considerable. Here at last, in the form of the Oseberg ship, was a time-capsule from the Viking Age, free from the taint of the 'creative imagination' of the novelists, dramatists, painters and composers who had previously tried to describe it. But how was its wealth of material to be interpreted? What did it all mean? Stones were piled on to the ship: was this to prevent the dead from walking again, or to sink the ship to a level at which the voyage to the next world might begin? And if the ship was to start out on such a voyage, why then anchor her by a doubled rope at the bow to a very large boulder? Who was to cast her off? Who was to sail her, and where to? Why were many of the oars on board bundled and unfinished? What logical or magical purpose was served by the decapitation of all fifteen horses that went into the grave? Why had a shaft been cut into the mound not long after it was closed? Was there in fact a ritual purpose behind the apparently haphazard disordering of the women's bones that were found in the shaft? A disappointment for the first students of the Oseberg discovery was that only two samples of runic writing appeared among the artefacts. One was a faint label carved on the outside of a pinewood bucket that has been interpreted as meaning 'Sigrid owns me.' The other was on a cylindrical piece of wood, tentatively identified as part of an oar and inscribed *litiluism*, interpreted by some runologists as *litilvíss (er) maðr* or 'man is little wise'.[11] If correct, the interpretation is apt, for while the find conveyed an extraordinary amount of new information about the Vikings, the very richness of it took away the certainties of ignorance, and raised as many questions as it answered about the nature of Heathen spiritual beliefs and the larger culture of which they formed a part. Our task in the next chapter must be to try to reconstruct a general outline of this culture of northern Heathendom, which was in so many essentials distinct from the Christianity that had become, by the end of the eighth century, the dominant culture across mainland Europe.

2

The culture of northern Heathendom

Our main sources of information for Viking Age Heathendom are the four poems of cosmological and mystical content known as 'The Seeress's Prophecy', 'The Sayings of the High One', 'Vafthrudnir's Sayings' and 'Grimnir's Sayings', which form part of the collection called the *Poetic Edda*; and the use made of these as illustrative material by Snorri Sturluson in the *Prose Edda*, a manual for the understanding of poetry which he wrote in Iceland in about 1220. As a lover of literature and a man with a strong sense of the importance of maintaining a respectful relationship to his cultural tradition, Snorri had become concerned that, after 200 years of active suppression of Heathen culture by the Christian Church, the survival of the large body of Old Norse poetry known as skaldic verse was threatened. The understanding of it depended to such a high degree on a knowledge of the myths and legends of the Old Norse gods and heroes that, unless something were done about it, they would shortly become incomprehensible to future generations of Icelanders. The chief problem was the use made by skaldic poets of elaborate figures known as *kennings*, periphrases which used details from the mythological stories of the adventures of the Norse gods and heroes to create names for familiar places, objects and people from other contexts that pushed them three or four metaphorical steps away from the original referent. The greater the distance, the greater the skill of the poet. The game for the listener was to untangle this dense thicket in order to reach the meaning of the poem. Though wildly anachronistic, the adjective 'baroque' suitably conveys the degree of their complexity.

It was always recognized that Snorri must have worked from a specific collection of poems, and in 1643 a vellum manuscript containing what turned out to be this collection came into the hands of an Icelandic bishop and scholar named Brynjolfúr Sveinsson. Dating from about 1270, it was itself a copy of an original dating to the early years of the same century. A few years later the bishop presented the collection to the king of Denmark, apparently as a way of restoring his own reputation and that of an unmarried daughter who had severely embarrassed them both by getting pregnant by a young priest.[1] Since that time the manuscript has been known as the *Codex Regius*. Many of Snorri's references in the *Prose Edda* were to details of Old Norse cosmology and myths that had remained obscure for later scholars, and the emergence of the *Poetic Edda* proved the key to unlocking many of them. The cosmological poems are difficult to date. Unlike skaldic poetry, which is by named poets, their creators were unknown. The unhurried devotion of 'Vafthrudnir's Sayings' might suggest that it was composed well before its author perceived any threat to Heathendom from Christianity, perhaps early in the tenth century, while the urgent intensity of 'The Seeress's Prophecy' suggests it may have been composed as an act of liturgical defiance much later on in the same century, when the threat was more clearly perceived.

The *Prose Edda* opens with a section called *Gylfaginning*, or the 'Beguiling of Gylfi', that describes how a legendary Swedish King Gylfi visited three Heathen gods in order to question them about the origins of the world. Snorri uses the replies King Gylfi receives to lay out the creation myth and cosmological structure of northern Heathendom. Gylfi learns that everything began in an empty chaos that contained a world of heat and light called Muspelheim, and an opposing dim, dark and cold world called Nifelheim. The two worlds were separated by a chasm, Ginnungagap. In the extreme physical forces that operated across Ginnungagap a giant named Ymir came into being. He was nourished by milk from the udders of a primordial cow, Audhumla. Audhumla next licked the salty stones around her into the shape of another giant, Buri. By an unspecified process Buri fathered a son, Bur, who wed a giantess, Bestla. The couple produced three sons, one of whom was Odin. Odin and his brothers created the physical world by killing Ymir and, in an act of prodigious violence, tearing the body apart and flinging the pieces in all directions. The giant's blood became the sea, his flesh the land, his bones the mountains and cliffs, his skull the vault of the heavens. Later, as Odin and his brothers were walking by the sea, two logs washed up on the sands, and from these the gods created the first human beings by breathing life and consciousness into them. They named the first man Ask and the first woman Embla. Ask means 'ash', the meaning of Embla remains obscure.

Snorri's further history of earliest things proceeds in a detailed and poetic vein, and to a modern mind unfamiliar with his world and his mindset it rapidly becomes confusing. Our confusion is compounded by the fact that in the *Ynglingasaga* with which he opens *Heimskringla* he provides a completely different, euhemeristic account of the origins of Odin and the Aesir, as Odin's family of gods was known, in which Odin features as the chieftain-priest of a tribe living in the area around the Black Sea in the days of the Roman empire. This tribe migrated northwards through Russia and finally settled near Uppsala, on the coast of south-central Sweden, where Odin rewarded his followers in the traditional way by dealing out land to them.[2] Rather than attempt to resolve these paradoxes, our aim here will be simply to try to abstract from *Gylfaginning* and the cosmological poems a general outline of the world-view that underpinned Viking Age Heathendom.

The cosmological world was conceived of as a flat circle divided into three distinct regions, each with its own characteristic set of inhabitants, and sharing a common centre.[3] The innermost world was Asgard, where the Aesir lived, each in his or her own home. Odin lived in Valhalla, Thor in Trudheim, Freyja in Folkvang. As the god of war and warriors, poetry and hanged men, Odin's work was to inspire poets, wage war and give fighting men courage in battle. Thor was responsible for natural phenomena such as wind, rain, thunder and lightning. These two were the most important male gods. In general terms Odin was the aristocratic god, worshipped by the dedicated warrior and the poet, while Thor was the god of the farmer and common man, especially popular in Iceland, Norway and Denmark. The eddic poem 'The Lay of Harbard' summarizes the distinction thus:

> Odin claims the earls who fall on the field,
> Thor only thralls.[4]

Freyja was skilled in sorcery and was the embodiment of female sexual power. Her brother Frey was the god of male potency, good weather, good harvests and fertile beasts. The image of him that stood in the great Heathen temple in Uppsala sported a large, erect phallus, and the 7 cm-high bronze figurine found at Rällinge in Södermanland, priapic as he sits cross-legged and naked save for a pointed cap, one hand holding his braided beard in a gesture of self-control, is almost certainly a depiction of him. Another god that looms large in the myths and the eddic poems was Loki, a son of giants adopted into the family of the Aesir. He was also Odin's troubled – and troubling – half-brother whose amoral and chaotic fickleness and lack of discipline introduced a dangerous unpredictability into many of the Aesir's enterprises.

Beyond this inner region was Midgard, domain of the humans. The word meant 'home or farm in the middle' and conveyed clearly the humans' sense of being located midway between the gods in Asgard and Utgard, or 'the outer place', the outer rim of the disc-world, a region inhabited by giants and other elemental beings associated with untamed chaos. Between Midgard and Utgard lay a sea, home to an enormous serpent which encircled the world and kept it bound together by biting on its own tail.

The vertical axis of the flat, round world was an ash-tree named Yggdrasil, connected to the sky at its crown, and at its roots penetrating to a subterranean realm that included a well, known as Urd's Well, where the gods held their assembly meetings and where three females, known as Norns, spun out the destinies of humans and gods alike. The role of Yggdrasil in this cosmology was to assure the inhabitants of Midgard that there was a centre to the world, and that all things were connected, appearances to the contrary, despite the ceaseless struggle between a will to order, represented by the gods of Asgard, and the entropic lure of chaos, represented by the giants and creatures of Utgard. The tree symbolized the cycle of life, drawing water from the well at its roots and returning it to the world as nourishment in the form of dew.

Though Utgard was a threatening and frightening place to be, even for the gods, it was understood that in the chaos within its borders lay the raw materials necessary for the learning of new skills and the creation of valuable treasures that the Aesir could hand on to the humans of Midgard. The story of how Odin forced the secrets of the art of writing runes from the reluctant terrain of this mental region is a dramatic illustration of the view that learning, knowledge and progress had to be fought for and suffered for. In a famous interlude in the long wisdom poem 'The Sayings of the High One', Odin describes how he hung from the branches of Yggdrasil:

> I know that I hung on a windy tree
> nine long nights,
> wounded with a spear, dedicated to Odin,
> myself to myself,
> on that tree of which no man knows
> from where its roots run.

Despite his status as the god of Hanged Men, it may be that on this occasion he is to be imagined as dangling upside down by the foot, as the 'Hanged Man' of the medieval Tarot is depicted.[5] This simplifies the logistics of the theft that follows:

> No bread did they give me nor a drink from a horn,
> downwards I peered;
> I took up the runes, screaming I took them,
> then I fell back from there.

Proudly Odin relates the advances that his suffering has paid for:

> Then I began to quicken and be wise,
> and to grow and to prosper;
> one word found another word for me,
> one deed found another deed for me.[6]

These skills were duly passed on to the inhabitants of Midgard. The story emphasizes the thirst for knowledge that was one of the most striking of Odin's characteristics, and the lengths he would go to in order to get it. In another story Odin requested a drink from a well of wisdom maintained by a mysterious giant named Mimir. When Mimir suggested an eye as the price of his assent Odin did not hesitate to pay. Odin's curiosity about the world, and his willingness to take enormous risks to satisfy it, are among the characteristics that distinguish him most sharply from the omniscient and omnipotent God of

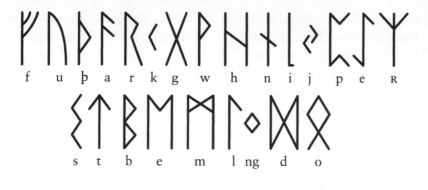

f u þ a r k g w h n i j p e R

s t b e m l ng d o

f u þ ã r k h n i a s t b m l R

Above: The older futhark, consisting of 24 runes, was in use for
about 700 years after the birth of Christ.
Below: A rationalized form using only 16 runes was in use by the
end of the eighth century.

the Christian conception. Another is that the Aesir knew they were
mortal. Odin's search for knowledge was very often a driven curiosity
aimed at finding out more about how their deaths would occur.

In some cases these tales of the gods on their forays into Utgard to
outwit the giants and wrest secrets and treasures from them also give an
insight into the lost astronomy of the Viking Age. Odin's sacrifice of an
eye is likely the remnant of a story once told to explain why the sky only
has one eye, in the form of the sun. The sibyl in this verse from 'The
Seeress's Prophecy' seems to be referring to the rising of the morning sun:

> I sat outside alone; the old one came,
> The lord of the Aesir, and looked into my face:
> 'Why have you come here? What would you ask me?
> I know, Odin, how you lost your eye:
> It lies in the water of Mimir's well.'
> Every morning Mimir drinks mead
> From Warfather's tribute. Seek you wisdom still?[7]

25

More directly explanatory is a story of the constellation known to the Vikings as 'Thiazzi's Eyes'. As a result of a piece of intemperate behaviour by Loki, the gods' apples of eternal youth fell into the hands of a giant named Thiazzi, whom they had to kill in order to recover them. When Thiazzi's daughter Skadi turned up at Asgard looking for revenge for the killing, Odin offered her compensation in the form of celestial immortality for her father, throwing his eyes into the night sky where they became stars to which he gave the name 'Thiazzi's Eyes'. These two stars are probably to be identified with Castor and Pollux in the constellation Gemini of our own astronomy.[8] The tale of Thor's duel with the giant Hrungnir is another myth with astronomical content. Following his success in the duel, Thor helped out a dwarf named Aurvandil by carrying him across the primordial river Élivagar in a basket on his back. When Aurvandil complained of frostbite in one of his toes Thor broke it off and threw it into the sky, where it became the star known as 'Aurvandil's Toe', corresponding in our astronomy to Alcor in Ursa Major.[9] Thor told the story to Aurvandil's wife Groa as she worked to remove a splinter of broken whetstone lodged in Thor's head after the duel. Groa became so excited at his news that she abandoned the job and never returned to it, leaving poor Thor with a chronic headache. This whetstone splinter in his head was said to be the nail that held Yggdrasil fixed to the sky. Its modern astronomical correspondent is probably our Polaris, the North Star in Ursa Minor, then as now the star around which the whole of the northern night sky seems to revolve. Viking Age Scandinavians must have had many more such explanatory tales, but the early scribes of the Christian era who had occasion to mention the stars and constellations in their writings preferred to use the Latin names, with the result that the native names disappeared, all but those few which survived down into Snorri's time, securely embedded in the Eddic poetry.

Probably as a result of his pre-eminence as the god of poets, Odin had over 150 names, but the most significant of them was simply 'All-Father'. Most of the gods were his children by various mothers. Some of them were Aesir, like himself. Others, like Thor's mother Jord ('Earth'), were giantesses from Utgard. That the gods of Asgard were willing to engage in such fraught unions with their enemies underscores Midgard's perception that social and technological advances could only be achieved by risk-taking. Among Frey's significant earthly progeny was his son by the giantess Gerd, who became the first king of the Yngling dynasty that ruled over the Swedes and, in later, historical time, over the Norwegians of the Vestfold region in the south of the country; Sæming, founding father of the long line of powerful chieftains who ruled over the Lade district in the region of Trondheim in present-day Norway, was likewise the son of a union between a god and a giant, as was Skjold, the legendary first king of the Danes. This genealogical link back to divinity was important because it legitimized the claims to power of the Scandinavian kings who ruled in later, historical times.[10]

This world of Asgard, Midgard and Utgard, with Yggdrasil at its centre, can be seen as a macrocosmic image of the world of a typical, Viking Age homestead. At the centre stood the main farmhouse building and outhouses, ringed around by a belt of cultivated land and pasture. Beyond this lay the rimmed horizon of uncultivated wilderness. Close by the main house stood a tree, known in Sweden as a *vårdträdet* and in Norway as a *tuntreet* or 'house-tree'. Each family cultivated a mystical association with its 'house-tree' that served as a symbol of continuity through the generations.[11] The circle in the physical form of a ring had particular significance in Viking Heathen culture. As a symbol of loyalty and honesty it appears in an entry in the *Anglo-Saxon Chronicle* for 876, noting a settlement between the Christian King Alfred of Wessex and three Viking chieftains. The *Chronicle* tells us that the chieftains 'swore him oaths on the sacred ring' that they would leave his kingdom at once, and that this was 'a thing which they would not do before for any other nation'.[12] A verse in 'The Sayings of the High One' expresses in negative fashion the binding gravity of such an oath:

> Odin didn't honour his oath on the ring
> What good is any pledge he gives?
> Suttung died of a poisoned drink,
> And Gunnlod grieves.[13]

The reference here is to the story of how Odin obtained the mead of poetry from the giant Suttung, having seduced his daughter Gunnlod, to whom Suttung had entrusted the mead. This, like the secret of the runes, is another example of a treasure stolen by an inhabitant of Asgard from the hazardous mental region of Utgard for the benefit of the humans of Midgard. Odin broke his word to Gunnlod because the consuming need for poetry justified any means to gain possession of it. This ruthlessness in pursuit of his own ends made Odin feared and admired among his followers and, as we shall see, Viking warriors abroad would very often take their cue from him in their dealings with the Christian kings of England and Francia.

The ring seems also to have been a symbol of eternal recurrence, illustrated by one of Odin's magical treasures, the ring Draupnir, made for him by the dwarves of Utgard, that dripped eight new rings every ninth night. The ring also played an important role in the sanctification of Heathen gatherings. According to the *Book of the Settlements*, a ring was to lie on the altar of every Icelandic chieftain and he was obliged to wear it on his arm at every assembly meeting over which he presided as chieftain-priest. The same obligation is also referred to in a description of a chieftain-priest's temple contained in the *Eyrbyggja Saga*.[14] This is a late source, probably composed about the middle of the thirteenth century, and though the usual reservations about reliability have to be made it is evidently the work of an author with a great interest in the early history of his own country. He mentions a table in the centre of the temple with a ring lying on it. Sacrifice, varying in intensity from fruit to the offering of a life, was a central means of communication between followers and gods, and beside the ring stood a bowl in which the blood of a sacrificed animal would be collected. Next to it lay a twig that may have been dipped into the bowl and shaken over the gathering as a way of binding it together, much as Moses is said to have done in the Old Testament.[15] It may also have been used to create a random pattern of blood-spots in which the chieftain-priest might read the oracular response to an important question.

The sites of two major festivals are known, one at Leire in Zealand, in Denmark, and the other at Uppsala in Sweden. Both were enneadic events, announcing a mystical attachment to the number nine. At the festivals at Leire ninety-nine humans and as many horses, dogs and roosters were sacrificed. Though he did not see the building himself,

Adam of Bremen reported a description of the temple at Uppsala in his *Gesta Hammaburgensis* as a sumptuous palace, richly decorated in gold, where people gathered to make sacrificial offerings before a trio of images, with Thor at the centre, flanked on either side by Odin and Frey. Each day for nine days the males of nine species, including humans, were sacrificed by hanging from trees in a small copse not far from the temple. One of the textile remains from the Oseberg burial appears to show such a scene, with numerous bodies dangling from the branches of a large tree. From Saxo's passing reference to 'the clatter of actors on the stage' it seems the rituals also involved the performance of some kind of cult drama.[16] Songs were chanted at the Uppsala festivals which were reported to Adam of Bremen by his informant but which the cleric found so obscene he declined to record them.[17] 'Haustlong', by the late ninth-century Norwegian Tjodolf of Hvin, is a rare example of a skaldic poem that incorporates lines of spoken dialogue which may have been part of such a cult drama.[18] Of the actual formalities of worship, however, we know little. The only prayer of direct address to the gods is the brief invocation in 'The Lay of Sigrdrifa':

> 'Hail to the Aesir! Hail to the goddesses!
> Hail to the mighty, fecund earth!
> Eloquence and native wit may you give us
> And healing hands while we live!'[19]

Archaeological evidence that human sacrifice was practised does exist, but is not extensive. Much depends on the interpretation of the finds. In the 1990s excavations were carried out by a team under Lars Jørgensen of the National Museum of Denmark on what was originally thought to be the rubbish dump of a chieftain's farm on a site at Lake Tissø, in Western Zealand. The team unearthed an increasingly confusing mixture of buried silver, gold, and animal and human bones, which eventually, along with the illogical location of the dump on a hilltop, persuaded them to reinterpret the site as a place of sacrifice.[20] At Lillmyr in Barlingbo, on Gotland, close to the modern town of Roma and near to where the island's main assembly formerly met, an excavated pit that contained the mingled remains of humans, horses and sheep has been tentatively identified as a place of human sacrifice.[21] There is more potential evidence in scenes depicted on the Hammars picture-stone from Lärbro on Gotland, dated to 700–800.[22] A man carrying a shield seems to be tied by his neck to the branch of a tree which has been tethered down. When the tree is released he will be jerked from his feet. The main focus of the scene, however, is the small figure, perhaps a dwarf or child in the centre of the panel, who lies face downward upon a platform of some kind. Above the figure hangs a *valknut*, three triangles that mark the victim as dedicated to Odin, bound in the same impossible perspectual framework that so fascinated the Dutch graphic artist M. C. Escher.

A separate category of human sacrifice involved the killing of slaves to serve their dead masters in the afterlife. Ibn Fadlan's account of the funeral on the Volga to which we referred earlier included a description in pathetic detail of the fate of such a slave, cajoled into volunteering to join her owner in his funeral ship with the promise of a few days of special treatment and a great deal of alcohol. After her ritual rape by the chieftains' companions she was handed over to an old woman known as the 'Angel of Death' to be strangled and stabbed before being carried on to the funeral ship beside him, along with his shoes, his weapons and the other items he would need in his next life. Most double graves from the Viking Age which show an apparent inequality in the status of the dead are interpreted as being those of master or mistress and slave. Of two male skeletons found in a single grave at Stengade, in Langeland in Denmark, one was buried with a spear and the other, bound and decapitated, has been identified as his slave. The Viking Age grave at Ballateare, on the Isle of Man, also contains two bodies, one a male buried with his sword, shield and three spearheads, the other a female with the top of her head sliced off, the mark of a ritual death.[23] Sacrifice was so central to the practice of Heathendom that the law codes of the Christian-era culture that eventually displaced it in the Scandinavian lands found it necessary expressly to forbid the practice: 'Nor may we sacrifice,' said the Norwegian Gulathing Law, 'not to Heathen gods nor to mounds nor piles of stones.'[24] The Gotland Gutalagen was similarly trenchant: 'All sacrificing is strictly forbidden as are all practices formerly connected with Heathendom.'[25] Equally dogmatic was the Uppland Law of the eastern Swedes: 'No one shall sacrifice to false gods, nor worship groves nor stones.'

These greater and smaller feasts were important social and religious institutions that bound communities together under their chieftain-priests in symbolic acts of feasting, eating and worshipping. They were also occasions on which the important matter of the law was dealt with. The Old Norse gods were not ethical beings. Ethics were the province of man and the law. The word 'synd' (sin) does not appear in any Viking Age literary source until as late as about 1030, when the poet Torarin Lovtunge in his 'Glælognskvida' described the Norwegian saint-king Olav Haraldson as having died a 'sinless death'.[26] Viking Age ethics were based on the opposition of shame and honour. Openness was the keynote of the oldest surviving codes, and though these were written down in post-Heathen times there is no reason to doubt that they convey the spirit of the ages that preceded them.[27] Whether it be a business deal or a divorce, the requirement of the law for a large number of witnesses was always present, under-scoring the role of shame in discouraging anyone inclined to go back on an agreement entered into so publicly. The distinction drawn between crimes committed openly and in secret marks an even clearer example of the use of shame to maintain social order. That bad actions are not always the work of bad people was recognized by the requirement that manslaughter be declared in front of witnesses within a specific time after the killing. The law obliged the killer to report the deed to the first person he or she met afterwards, although they could, if they wished, avail themselves of an exemption that allowed them to pass by two houses – but not a third – if they suspected that relatives of the dead person lived there, before making their con-fession. If the proper procedures were followed, the killing could be atoned for by compensation.[28] Murder, on the other hand, was a dis-honourable act, committed in secret, unacknowledged and liable to set in train a cycle of revenge killings. An Old Norse proverb delivered the legal distinction poetically: náttvíg eru morðvíg ('killing by night is murder'). Unannounced killings were, by definition, murder.

Communal responsibility was further promoted by laws that made personal involvement mandatory in certain circumstances: any persons who witnessed an accidental death and failed to report it to the family and heirs of the deceased were likely to find themselves facing an accusation of murder. One section of the law of the west-Norwegian Gulathing, whose writ ran from Stad in the north to Egersund in the south, dealt with a killing done in an ale-house. Whether it happened by daylight or by firelight, all those present were obliged to join in apprehending the culprit. Failure to do so entrained a compensation payment to the relatives of the victim, making it in the financial interests of all present to ensure the killer was caught. A thief surprised in the act of stealing might legally be killed, but not a robber, whose crime was committed face-to-face. The rationale, in this culture of self-reliance, was that the victim of a robbery had in principle at least a fair chance of preventing it. Under the laws of both the Gulathing and the Frostathing, at which the people of the Trøndelag region gathered to do business, the punishment of criminals was likewise a communal responsibility. A thief convicted of a petty offence had to run a gauntlet of stones and turf. The thirteenth-century Bjarkøyretten that regulated local affairs in Trondheim even stipulated the fine to be paid by anyone who failed to throw something at the thief.

The practice of oath-taking in courts of law likewise showed the strong natural inclination towards the involvement of the whole community. Depending on the seriousness of his or her crime, an accused person might be asked to give one of four grades of oaths requiring the support of, respectively, one, two, five or eleven compurgators or supporters, with a twelve-fold oath being used in the extreme case of murder. They were not necessarily swearing to anything that had a bearing on the facts of the case in hand. Essentially they were character witnesses, affirming their belief in the honesty of the person giving the oath. Strict rules governed the process of oath-taking, and any breach of them made the oath invalid.

The most striking deviation from this adherence to communal responsibility involved kings. The price paid by some early Yngling kings for claiming descent from the gods was to be blamed when the gods turned against their followers and blighted the crops, emptied the seas of fish or in some other way brought famine and ill-luck on the tribe. Snorri tells us that in the reign of the legendary King Domaldi in

Sweden an enduring famine occurred that occasioned a hierarchy of sacrifices. It began with oxen, proceeded to men and, when none of this had any effect, culminated in the sacrifice of the king himself. Nor were substitutes acceptable: *Gautrek's Saga*, preserved in a number of manuscripts dating from the early fifteenth century, tells the remarkable tale of an attempt to regain Odin's favour by the mock-sacrifice of a certain King Vikar, whose name in Norwegian means 'substitute'. The guts of a slaughtered calf were looped around his neck instead of rope, and tethered to a twig. Instead of the point of a spear, a blade of straw was jabbed against his side. The dedication was announced: 'Now I give you to Odin.' Instantly the straw turned into a spear that penetrated the king's side, the tree-stub he was standing on turned into a stool that tumbled over, and the intestines became a stout rope. The twig flexed and thickened and the king was dragged high into the air. The similarities to the scene described in pictures on the Hammars stone are striking.

Domaldi's son Domar was luckier than his father. Snorri tells us Domar

ruled for a long time, and there were good seasons and peace in his days. About him nothing else is told, but that he died in his bed in Uppsala, was borne to Fyrisvold, and burned there on the river bank where his standing-stone is.[29]

For a king to die peacefully in this way was the sign of a happy and prosperous reign. This explains the apparent anomaly in Snorri's biography of the euhemeristic Odin, in which this greatest of all warriors is reported to have died in his bed.

As these stories show, Scandinavian Heathens were fatalists who nevertheless believed that the gods might be prepared to change their fates if only the gifts offered were rich enough. This belief that fate might be changed also manifested itself at the day-to-day level, where the sorcerer's art of *seid* was much prized as a way of trying to influence the working of fate in the personal sphere. *Seid* was a form of divination closely related to shamanism that sought access to secret knowledge of hidden things, whether in the mind or in the physical world. In its 'white' form it could be used to heal the sick, control the weather and call up fish and game before the hunter. Its 'black' form had the power to raise the dead, curse an enemy and blight his land, raise up storms against him and destroy his or her luck in love and in war. In both his euhemeristic and his divine manifestations Odin was a master of the art. His skill as a shape-changer enabled him to transform himself into a fish, a bird, a beast or snake and transport himself over vast distances. It gave him knowledge of the future and the power to enter grave-mounds, bind the dead and take from them whatever treasures he wanted. He could control fire with it and order the wind to change direction. *Seid* gave him the power to strike his enemies in battle blind or deaf, blunt their weapons and freeze them in terror. He could imbue his followers with such strength and courage in battle that they turned into raging berserks, wild men able to kill with one blow, as strong as bears and as savage as wolves, disdaining the use of armour and in their ecstatic fury impervious to all harm. In Snorri's words:

From these arts [Odin] became very celebrated. His enemies dreaded him; his friends put their faith in him and relied on his power and on himself. He taught most of his arts to his priests of the sacrifices, and they came nearest to him in sorcery. Many others, however, occupied themselves much with it; and from that time sorcery spread far and wide, and continued long.[30]

'He and his temple priests were called song-smiths, for from them came that art of song into the northern countries,' Snorri adds, and perhaps these songs were the chants that Adam of Bremen judged too shocking to repeat in his history. Their importance in Heathen ritual is reflected in the prohibition in the post-Heathen Gulathing law against *galdresang* or 'spell-chanting', which was punishable by banishment.

Despite the powers *seid* conferred on its user, Snorri tells us that in time it was felt to compromise masculinity so profoundly that it presently became the province of women, and possibly of homosexual men. In a disapproving reference in the *Gesta Danorum* to the ceremonies at 'Uppsala in the period of sacrifices', Saxo Grammaticus writes of the 'soft tinkling of bells' and the 'womanish body movements' of the participants. Like Adam he too mentions the role of chanting. In one of the Eddic poems, 'Loki's Quarrel', in which Loki ritually heaps insults upon each of the Aesir, it is for his feminizing practice of *seid* that Loki attacks Odin when his turn comes:

> But you once practised *seid* on Samsey,
> and you beat on the drum as witches do,
> in the likeness of a lizard you journeyed among
> mankind,
> and that I thought the hallmark of a pervert.[31]

An account in the twelfth-century *Historia Norwegie* of a shaman-istic seance among the Lapps may shed some light on the sexual ambiguity of the sort of performance Loki was mocking:

Once when some Christians were among the Lapps on a trading trip, they were sitting at table when their hostess suddenly collapsed and died. The Christians were sorely grieved but the Lapps, who were not at all sorrowful, told them that she was not dead but had been snatched away by the *gandi* of rivals and that they themselves would soon retrieve her. Then a wizard spread out a cloth under which he made himself ready for unholy magic incantations and with hands extended lifted up a small vessel like a sieve, which was covered with images of whales and reindeer with harness and little skis, even a little boat with oars. The devilish *gandus* would use these means of transport over heights of snow, across slopes of mountains and through depths of lakes. After dancing there for a very long time to endow this equipment with magic power, he at last fell to the ground, as black as an Ethiopian and foaming at the mouth like a madman.[32]

The great power attached to being a sorcerer is one possible expla-nation for the sumptuous nature of the Oseberg ship-burial.[33] Among the arguments advanced for identifying one of the women as a sorcer-ess are the find of a peculiarly ornate kind of staff associated with witchcraft, and four seeds of *cannabis sativa*. Such an identification might also shed light on the hitherto unexplained function of the iron wrangle or rattle found in the grave – four iron hoops threaded on to a barred handle that might have been vigorously shaken to drive away malignant spirits. Medical tests carried out on the remains of the women in 2007 and 2008 showed that the older of the two suffered from a hormonal imbalance which probably rendered her sterile, at the same time promoting a strong growth of hair, including facial hair. At the age of about fifteen she appears to have sustained severe damage to her left knee, perhaps as the result of a bad fall, from which she emerged a semi-invalid who must have walked with a heavy limp. Professor Per Holck's analysis has shown a striking over-development of the musculature of her upper arms consistent with the long-term use of crutches. Perhaps this set of physical abnormalities, combined with a striking personality, defined her status as a sorceress for a community that saw them as the visible signs of her rare and magical ability to inhabit the worlds of both male and female.[34]

As part of the ritual of worship, as transport, as beast of burden, as food and as companion, the importance of the horse in the culture of northern Heathendom can hardly be overestimated. Viking Age cosmology fancied the sun drawn across the sky by two of them, Alsvinn, 'the Speedy', and Arvakr, 'the Wakeful'. Odin rode on an eight-legged grey named Sleipnir that was as quick over sea as land, and the identification of the ship as 'the horse of the sea' was one of the staple metaphors used by skaldic poets. Much like the modern car, the horse was a status symbol. A verse in 'The Sayings of the High One' made the point in negative fashion:

> Don't be hungry when you ride to the Thing,
> be clean though your clothes be poor;
> you will not be shamed by shoes and breeches,
> nor by your horse, though he be no prize.[35]

The Viking Age horse had a shorter back and thicker neck than the modern horse, and with an average height of just under 2 metres it was not much bigger than a large pony of today. The modern Icelandic horse is its direct and almost unchanged descendant, with its characteristic thick mane and tail and five gaits: walking, trotting, galloping, flying, and the unique fifth gait known as *tolting*, a sort of running walk with a low knee-action which enabled horse and rider to cover long distances without tiring. This was particularly useful in Iceland, where the lack of timber for ship-building meant that riding rather than sailing was the preferred method of travelling along the coast. The horse played a large part in the sporting life of these people. In the *Saga of Sigurd the Crusader and his brothers Eystein and Olaf*, Snorri describes, with his usual gusto, a series of races run for a wager between King Harald Gille of Norway on foot and his nephew Magnus Sigurdsson on horseback. The fact that Harald emerged as winner tells us that, for all its strength, good nature and endurance, the horse was small and not especially quick.[36] Horse-fighting was a popular sport and the drama of one of the most frequently anthologized short stories from Iceland, *Thorstein the Staff-struck*, derives from tempers lost following an incident during a horse-fight. Horses were raced against each other too. In England the names Hesketh Grange, in Thornton Hough, and Heskeths at Irby, in the Wirral, both derive from Old Norse *hestur*, 'horse', and *skeid*, 'track', and both preserve the memory of Viking Age racetracks at these locations.[37]

As a mount in battle the horse was less favoured. The bridle-bits found in Viking Age graves are of the type known as snaffle-bits, with a jointed central mouthpiece and rings on either side, which made them unsuitable for use in battle. Riders on the Gotland picture-stones are depicted without stirrups, which again would have made fighting from horseback difficult. The horse might be used as a means of transport to reach the field of battle, but once there the warriors would dismount and engage with the enemy on foot. The Oseberg tapestries that originally probably hung on the walls of the burial chamber featured multiple depictions of horses, and horses' heads were carved into the bedposts and on the ends of the burial-chamber crosspieces. A literary reflection of this degree of devotion is found in the late thirteenth-century masterpiece *Hrafnkels Saga*, which describes the special relationship between the farmer-chieftain Hrafnkel and his stallion, Freyfaxi. Hrafnkel declares Freyfaxi sacred to Frey and forbids any man to ride him. Though we learn no further details of the arrangement it binds Hrafnkel sufficiently to kill a shepherd boy who one day disobeys the ruling.

The taboo exercised by Christian writers on matters relating to the cult of the horse will have obscured a great deal of material on the subject, but strewn across the literature are stray reminiscences of the status of the horse as an image of potency and fertility. The short story known as the *Völsa tháttr* describes how the Norwegian King Olav Haraldson and two of his men arrived at a remote farm while out travelling.[38] As they sat to dine with their hosts the farmer's wife took a stallion's penis from the linen wrapping in which she stored it, using an onion as a preservative. This object, which she called Volsi, was passed from hand to hand among the guests to the accompaniment of a repetitive chanting. When the king's turn came he brought proceedings to an abrupt halt by throwing Volsi to the family dog, which promptly ate it. Some form of phallic horse-worship also appears to be referred to in a poem of the purposefully offensive type known as *nid*, in which the poet, the Norwegian King Magnus the Good, mockingly accused his Heathen opponent, Sigurd syr, of having built 'a ring of stakes around a horse's penis'.[39]

One of the most remarkable testaments to the importance of the horse in Heathen culture is found in a passage in *The Topography of Ireland*. Here the Welsh historian Giraldus Cambrensis describes a king-making ceremony among the Heathens of Kenel Cunill, in a remote part of northern Ulster.[40] At a gathering of the tribe a white mare is brought into the ring of people and an act of bestiality involving the king and the mare takes place at which the king becomes, by association, a stallion. The mare is then killed and dismembered and a broth made of her blood and flesh. After the king has bathed in it, he and the other members of the tribe eat the flesh and drink the broth. The account derives from the extreme end of the spectrum of what Christians might believe about Heathens; but if it represents only an isolated case it might yet be enough to explain the degree of horror felt by Christians at the practice of eating horse-meat. As we shall see, on two occasions in particular the part played in the hallowing of the Heathen assemblies by the ritual preparation and consumption of horse-flesh marked a dramatic highlight in the religious tensions between followers of the old faith and adherents to the new, the first involving an early attempt by King Håkon the Good to impose the Christian faith on his fellow-Norwegians, and the second as part of the dramatic series of events surrounding the acceptance by Icelanders of Christianity as their official religion in the year 999.

So great is our debt to Snorri Sturluson for the insight he gives us into how Viking Age Heathens explained the facts of life and death to themselves that there is a danger of our assuming that he has, in fact, told us all there is to know on these subjects. He gives us something approaching a coherent narrative, and that fact alone ought to make us a little wary. Grave-mounds are commonplace to him, but there is nothing in either *Heimskringla* or the *Prose Edda* to suggest that he was aware that the dead inside them may have been buried in ships. None of his landscapes of Heathen death involves a place that must be reached by water, and in terms of understanding the thought that lay behind them, what he tells us sheds little light on the specific cases of the Oseberg and Gokstad burials. The great wealth of these two burials might be in conformity with one of the laws Snorri attributes to the euhemeristic Odin, that those who joined him in Valhalla should enjoy there what they had buried in the earth with them; but both burials are then in defiance of an injunction in the same set of laws to cremate the dead and their possessions.[41] The choice of inhumation rather than cremation may have been a sign that the dead person had been a particularly successful leader. So successful was the reign of King Frey, the founder of the Yngling dynasty, who ruled in Uppsala shortly after the death of Odin, that when he died his closest followers kept the death a secret, buried his body in a mound and told people that he was still alive and looking after them.[42] Ultimately the lack of consistency only comfirms the futility of expecting it. As Anthony Faulkes, the translator and editor of Snorri's *Prose Edda* puts it, the Heathen religion was probably never understood systematically even by those who practised it. From the *Saga of the Jomsvikings* we know that people cultivated supernatural personal helpers whose powers they placed above those of any of the Aesir. In a desperate attempt to change the course of the crucial sea-battle at Hjörungavág in about 986, Håkon the Bad, a Norwegian Earl of Lade, sacrificed his nine-year-old son Erling to a personal goddess, Thorgerdr Holgabrudr, who rewarded him with a hailstorm that turned the tide of battle in his favour.[43] The tenth-century Icelandic priest-chieftain, Thorgeir Ljosvetningagodi, practised an informal worship of the sun, and when he felt death approaching asked to be carried out into its light. There were probably other forms of worship, other objects of devotion of which we know nothing.

Even with all these uncertainties, however, one thing is abundantly clear: whatever else it was, northern Heathendom was not the absence of a culture. Viking Age Scandinavians had their own cosmology, their own astronomy, their own gods, their own social structure, their own form of government and their own notions of how best to live and die. By the middle of the eighth century, regional power centres had grown up on the south-west and south-east coasts of Norway, around the kings and chieftains of Avaldsnes on the island of Karmøy, near Haugesund in Rogaland, and those kings of Vestfold in the Tønsberg area who claimed descent from the Yngling dynasty.[44] Confirmation that there was high-level communication between these regions came in 2009 with dendrochronological analysis which showed that the timber used to build the Oseberg ship in 820 came from the same south-west coastal region as that used for the three ships found at the end of the nineteenth century in the Storhaug and Grønnhaug mounds at Karmøy. Tree-ring dating also indicates that the ship in the Grønnhaug mound was built in 720, and both large and small ships in the Storhaug mound in 771.[45] All three were propelled exclusively by oars. The Storhaug ship was interred in late 779 and is the youngest large, man-powered rowing-ship we know of. The Oseberg ship remains the oldest known example of the classic, sail-powered Viking longship. The conclusion is that at some point in the forty years that separate the building of the two, a remarkable technological breakthrough occurred in the construction and use of sail, which greatly increased the speed longships were capable of reaching and removed much of the physical burden of rowing from their crews. The breakthrough would have a dramatic effect on the development of European history over the next three centuries.

3

The causes of the Viking Age

The *Anglo-Saxon Chronicle* reports that extraordinary weather conditions preceded the raid on Lindisfarne in 793, high winds and lightning flashes that were afterwards understood to have been portents – 'and a little after that in the same year on 8 January the harrying of the heathen miserably destroyed God's church in Lindisfarne by rapine and slaughter'.[1] Experiments with modern reconstructions have shown that in good visibility a Viking longship at sea could be seen some 18 nautical miles away. With a favourable wind, that distance could be covered in about an hour, so that is perhaps all the time the monks had to prepare themselves for the attack.[2] It is unlikely they did anything at all, for the written records of the raid present it as completely unexpected:

We and our fathers have now lived in this fair land for nearly three hundred and fifty years, and never before has such an atrocity been seen in Britain as we have now suffered at the hands of a pagan people. Such a voyage was not thought possible. The church of St Cuthbert is spattered with the blood of the priests of God, stripped of all its furnishings, exposed to the plundering of pagans – a place more sacred than any in Britain.[3]

The extract is from a letter, written in the wake of the attack, to King Ethelred of Northumbria by Alcuin, one of the leading Christian figures of the age. Born in Northumbria, Alcuin had been a monk in York before accepting an invitation in 781 to join Charlemagne at his court in Aachen, where he soon played a prominent role in the revival of learning known as the Carolingian renaissance. He knew both the monastery at Lindisfarne and many of its leading figures well.

A third account of the atrocity by Simeon of Durham, the early twelfth-century English chronicler, adds detail that may come from a lost Northumbrian annals:

In the same year the pagans from the northern regions came with a naval force to Britain like stinging hornets and spread on all sides like fearful wolves, robbed, tore and slaughtered not only beasts of burden, sheep and oxen, but even priests and deacons, and companies of monks and nuns. And they came to the church at Lindisfarne, laid everything waste with grievous plundering, trampled the holy places with polluted steps, dug up the altars and seized all the treasure of the holy church. They killed some of the brothers, took some away with them in fetters, many they drove out, naked and loaded with insults, some they drowned in the sea . . .[4]

A fourth document, of unknown date but possibly near-contemporary, is the Lindisfarne stone. This shows seven marching men in profile. Perhaps in response to the constraints of the semi-circular stone, those at the front and the rear of the column are unarmed. Of the central five the first two are carrying axes, the three behind them swords. The axes are distinct from one another in shape and are held about halfway up the handle. The men wear tunics that reach to about midway down the thigh and seem to have some kind of padding or reinforcement around the midriff. They wear tight-fitting leggings and heavy shoes that appear to be ankle-high. They march with stiff necks and chests out, their weapons raised one-handed above their heads as though about to sweep down. The stylization is strikingly similar to the image of warring men depicted on a panel of the Gotland Hammars picture-stone. The Hammars stone is the more accomplished work of art, but there is a telegrammatic crudeness about the Lindisfarne stone that seems to convey more directly and urgently the brutality of face-to-face violence. Unlike the men on the Hammars stone, the Lindisfarne warriors are not carrying shields. It is as though they were not expecting to encounter resistance.

'Such a voyage was not thought possible,' Alcuin wrote. And in a long poem on *The Destruction of Lindisfarne* he once again conveyed the impression that the attackers were an unknown quantity. His lute groans sadly, he writes, at the appearance of this 'pagan warband arrived from the ends of the earth'. And yet, in that same letter, he rebuked Ethelred and his people in terms that wholly contradict the impression that the raid came as a surprise: 'Consider the luxurious dress, hair and behaviour of leaders and people,' he urged the king. 'See how you have wanted to copy the pagan way of cutting hair and beards. Are not these the people whose terror threatens us, yet you want to copy their hair?'[5] The sentiments are similar to those expressed in a letter, fragmentary and incomplete, from an unknown sender to an unknown recipient or recipients, criticized for

loving the practices of Heathen men who begrudge you life, and in so doing show by such evil habits that you despise your race and your ancestors, since in insult to them you dress in Danish fashion with bared necks and blinded eyes. I will say no more about that shameful mode of dress except what books tell us, that he will be accursed who follows Heathen practices in his life and in so doing dishonours his own race.[6]

Much as the sixth-century British monk Gildas, some 300 years before him, had interpreted the invasion of Alcuin's own Anglo-Saxon and Heathen forebears as God's punishment on Britons for their lax observance of the Christian way of life, so did Alcuin discover in the Vikings God's scourge on a lax and degenerate Northumbrian clergy and court. In several letters written after the attack he painted a dismaying picture of contemporary monastic life, inveighing against drunkenness and the practice of inviting 'actors and voluptuaries' to dine at the monastery tables instead of the poor, and condemning the practice of entertainment at mealtimes. In place of the sounds of the harp, accompanying 'the songs of the heathens', he suggested readings from the Bible and the Church fathers. 'For what has Ingeld to do with Christ?' he added, incidentally condemning the popularity in monasteries of *Beowulf*, a cultural betrayal which must have struck him as even more dismaying than the fashion at King Ethelred's court for Heathen hairstyles.[7] The unavoidable conclusion of all this is that at the time of the Lindisfarne raid Alcuin and the people of Northumbria were already quite familiar with their Scandinavian visitors. What was new was the violence.

Attempts to provide a single aetiology for the beginning of the Viking Age soon run across difficulties similar to those posed in trying to set its parameters. The suggested causes are numerous and often cancel each other out. The sheer geographical spread of the Scandinavian homelands means that a suggested cause for the activities of Norwegians on the west coast of the peninsula across the North Sea in the British Isles may have little or no relevance to the impulses that drove the Swedes to cross the Baltic and, in due course, navigate their way down the Russian rivers to the Black Sea. The persistent Danish and Norwegian interest in the territories of the Frankish empire may not be illuminated by either explanation. Braving these difficulties – which are in truth insurmountable – we might suggest that the possible causes can be divided into two basic groups. The first consists of mainly abstract reasons that have a general applicability across the Scandinavian peninsula and the island territories of the Danes; the second deals with a set of more clearly defined causes, each with a specific and regional applicability. The divergences in the latter group are so great that I make no attempt to include possible reasons for the onset of a Swedish Viking Age here, saving those for a later chapter that deals with Viking activity east of the Baltic.

Adam of Bremen considered that the original cause of the Viking phenomenon was a simple one: poverty in the Scandinavian homelands. In *De moribus et actis primorum normanniae ducum*, Dudo of St-Quentin found a similarly straightforward explanation. In his résumé of the early life of Rollo, founder of the duchy, Dudo wrote of family quarrels over land and property at home that were resolved by 'the drawing of lots according to ancient custom'. The losers in these lotteries were condemned to a life abroad, where 'by fighting [they] can gain themselves countries where they can live in continual peace'. The drawing of lots as a way of solving urgent social problems is echoed in the Gotland *Gutasaga*, where a rapid increase in population and a subsequent famine were dealt with by a lottery as a result of which one in three families were obliged to leave the island with all their property.

Adam and Dudo both saw the movement of Viking bands about mainland Europe as what modern historians might identify as a late manifestation of the Age of Migrations. As the name implies, this was a period of intense restlessness that characterized mainland Europe for some 400 years, between 300 and 700. For reasons not yet properly understood but which it might seem natural to ascribe, as Adam and Dudo did, to poverty, shortage of land and natural disaster, successive waves of Germanic peoples began pouring across the Danube and moving westwards across Europe until they reached the frontiers of a crumbling Roman empire. The Ostrogoths, Visigoths, Alans, Burgundians, Langobards, Jutes, Angles, Saxons, Alemanni and Vandals were among them. These tribes rapidly brought about the fall of the empire in the west, adapted and adopted its political structures as they took over, and redrew the cultural and political map of Europe.

Roman intellectuals such as the first-century politician and historian Tacitus had long seen this as one likely fate for the empire. Tacitus' ethnographic study *De Origine et situ Germanorum*, known as the *Germania*, was written partly to explain to his fellow citizens why the might of Rome had failed to conquer the Germanic tribes on their northern borders, despite their lack of Roman civilization and Roman discipline. The main reason was that Germanic males were naturally attracted to violence and enjoyed fighting. Leaders among them formed warbands and maintained the loyalty of their men by the practice of constant warfare. The commitment to their leader of members of such a warband or *comitatus* was personal: while the chieftain fought for victory, his men fought for him. Reward came in the form of feasts, entertainment and the proceeds of violence. Disdainful of trading and farming, such young men thought it 'tame and stupid to acquire by the sweat of toil what they may win by their blood'.[8] Within such a culture, 'the bravest and most warlike do no work; they give over the management of the household, of the home, and of the land to the women, the old men, and the weaker members of the family, while they themselves remain in the most sluggish inactivity'. Arrogant idleness of the kind described by Tacitus is also a hallmark of some of the most notable heroes of the Icelandic sagas, men like Grettir the Strong and Egil Skallagrimsson, known in their youth as 'coalbiters' from their habit of idling away the days between adventures at home by the family longfire, irritably gnawing at lumps of coal, annoying themselves and annoying those around them. Tacitus' description of the *comitatus* warband remains a valid account of the way Viking raiders organized themselves throughout the Viking Age, a loyalty-for-rewards structure that carried over even into the tenth and eleventh centuries and the establishment of rudimentary versions of Danish, Norwegian and Swedish monarchies.

The late Richard Fletcher offered, with due reservations, a coherent short narrative that linked together the main features of the case for a local crisis in early ninth-century Scandinavia that led so large a number of young men to depart their native lands in search of wealth and, eventually, respectability as the colonizers of new territories:

The diffusion of the use of iron in Scandinavia gradually made possible more intense agricultural exploitation. This in turn permitted demographic growth that would in time press upon the limited resources of the Scandinavian environment. Technical advances in shipbuilding, which would produce such masterpieces of strength and elegance as the Gokstad ship, opened the sea-ways of the North Sea and the Atlantic to Viking enterprise. The influx of silver bullion from the Islamic Middle East, well-attested archaeologically and attracted by trade in slaves, furs and timber with the distant lands of the caliphate in Iran, may have had far-reaching consequences for Scandinavian society. It provided capital for shipbuilding, weaponry and trading ventures. It drove a wedge between those who were its beneficiaries and the rest. An elite of wealth and status emerged, competitive and acquisitive, whose members attracted retinues of unruly young warriors on the make; and these men, in their turn, had to be rewarded. The emergence of stronger kings in Denmark and Norway, for reasons not unconnected with this new wealth, could make life at home difficult for these turbulent nobilities. It is to some such cluster of factors as these that we should attribute the beginnings of Viking age activity in western Europe.[9]

Inevitably, other interpretations of the material exist. By comparison with immediately preceding periods, the relative frequency of grave-finds from the Viking Age has been seen as evidence in support of a population explosion that began around 800. Yet the excavations at Forsandmoen in the Ryfylke district of Rogaland on the south-west coast of Norway which show that thriving settlements had existed there for over a thousand years between the Bronze Age and the Age of Migrations have failed to unearth a single grave from the period. It suggests that the incidence of graves found is not a reliable barometer of either the duration of a settlement or its intensity.

Norwegian archaeologists have also registered a consistent decrease in the amount of iron produced in the forest and mountain regions of southern Norway during the early Viking period, and in the intensity of elk- and reindeer-trapping in the interior, and interpreted both as inconsistent with a theory that Norway was over-populated at the time.[10] Another important component of the traditional theory is that the large number of Norwegian settlement names containing the element '-*stadir*' (meaning 'place') originated in about 800, and that these too underscore a scenario in which a population explosion at about that time occurred with severe social consequences that included a Scandinavian diaspora. More recent interpretation of the archaeological data has shown, however, that these place-names should instead be associated with a wave of settlements that started in Norway as early as the fifth century.[11] Ottar, a Norwegian merchant whom we shall meet again later, visited the Wessex court of Alfred the Great towards the end of the ninth century and told the king that he lived 'furthest north of all the Norsemen' and made his living by reindeer farming, whaling and exacting tributes from the nomadic Lapps. The discovery in 1981 of an enormous Viking Age farm at Borg, on the Lofoten Islands off the northern coast of Norway, confirms that the area north of the Arctic Circle was considered habitable by Viking Age families willing to look beyond conventional animal husbandry for their subsistence. The population density in the whole Scandinavian peninsula during the early Viking Age has been estimated at one to two people per square kilometre. The figure is an educated guess, but one that certainly does not support a theory of over-population.[12]

On the question of why raiding on northern Britain began in 793, and not fifty years earlier or forty years later, Norwegian historians and archaeologists have been increasingly attracted in recent years to an idea that looks outside Scandinavia for an explanation and takes into account the political tensions in northern Europe at the close of the eighth century.[13] The three major political powers in the world at that time were the Byzantine empire in the east, which had survived the break-up of the Roman empire and its disappearance in the west; the Muslims, whose expansion during the years 660 to 830 under the Umayyad and Abbasid caliphates had taken them eastward as far as

Turkistan and Asia Minor to create an Islamic barrier between the northern and southern hemispheres; and the Franks, who had established themselves as the dominant tribe among the successor states after the fall of the Roman empire in the west. The Byzantine empire, with its capital Constantinople, was remote from the Scandinavian lands and would be more or less able to dictate the terms of its encounters with the Viking phenomenon. The Islamic expansion into Europe via the Iberian peninsula in the first half of the eighth century pushed European trade routes northwards, a development which increased trading opportunities for the Scandinavian lands and also created ideal conditions for piracy in the North Sea area. Of the three major powers it was the Franks who would be most profoundly involved with the Vikings.

By the middle of the eighth century most of Europe between the Elbe in the east and the Pyrenees in the west was under Merovingian Frankish – and Christian – control. In 751 Pippin became the first king of the dynasty known as the Carolingians. On his death in 768 he was succeeded jointly by his sons Charles and Carloman. With Carloman's death in 771 Charles became sole ruler and presently set about the long series of expansionist gestures in the name of the Christian faith which characterized his reign and would gain him, within fifty years of his death, the appellation of Charlemagne, Charles the Great. His western-Europe territory was greater even than that of the Romans, who never ventured beyond the Rhine after the disaster of the Battle of the Teutoburg Forest in AD 9. Charlemagne took seriously the religious obligations imposed on him by his position as the most powerful ruler in western Christendom. He halted the Muslim expansion into Europe, drove the Arabs back across the Pyrenees, and established Frankish dominance in Spain and Gaul. The Lombards were driven from power in Italy, and the Slavs on the eastern border of his empire were compelled into tributary status. His authority, and that of the Christian Church, reached its limits at the Saxon marches in the north-east of the Frankish kingdom. Beyond lay the territories of the Danes and the Granii, the Augandzi, the Rugi, the Svear and Gautar in Sweden and the other more or less obscure Heathen tribes of the lower Scandinavian peninsula.

From about 772 onward Charlemagne's chief preoccupation

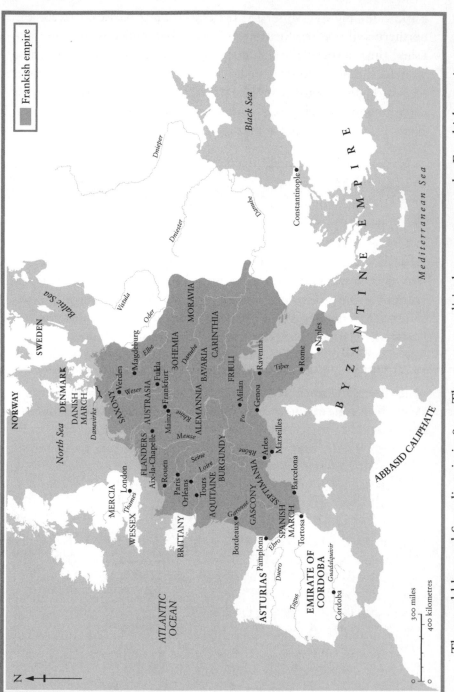

The world beyond Scandinavia in 813. The 3 great political powers were the Frankish empire, the Byzantine empire, and the Muslim caliphates of the Ummayads of Cordoba and the Abbasids.

became the conversion to Christianity of the Saxons on his north-eastern border. In that year his forces crossed the rivers Ediel and the Demiel and destroyed Irmensul, the sacred wooden pillar or tree that was the Saxons' most holy shrine, and probably their version of the 'world-tree' Yggdrasil of Scandinavian cosmology. The emperor's determination to achieve his purpose is evident from an entry in the *Royal Frankish Annals* for 775:

While the king spent the winter at the villa of Quierzy, he decided to attack the treacherous and treaty-breaking tribe of the Saxons and to persist in this war until they were either defeated and forced to accept the Christian religion or entirely exterminated.[14]

Another invasion of Saxon territory in 775 involved 'severe battles, great and indescribable, raging with fire and sword'.[15] In 779 Widukind, the Saxon leader, was defeated in battle at Bochult. Saxony was taken over and divided into missionary districts. Charlemagne himself conducted a number of mass baptisms, for the close identification of Christian missionary churches with Charlemagne's military power was always made clear to the Saxons. A young English missionary, Lebuin, built a church at Deventer on the banks of the Ysel from which to lead his mission. When the Heathens burnt down his oratory, Lebuin made his way to the tribal gathering at Markelo and addressed the crowd:

Raising his voice, he cried: 'Listen to me, listen. I am the messenger of Almighty God and to you Saxons I bring his command.' Astonished at his words and at his unusual appearance, a hush fell upon the assembly. The man of God then followed up his announcement with these words: 'The God of heaven and Ruler of the world and His Son, Jesus Christ, commands me to tell you that if you are willing to be and to do what His servants tell you He will confer benefits upon you such as you have never heard of before.' Then he added: 'As you have never had a king over you before this time, so no king will prevail against you and subject you to his domination. But if you are unwilling to accept God's commands, a king has been prepared nearby who will invade your lands, spoil and lay them waste and sap away your strength in war; he will lead you into exile, deprive you of your inheritance, slay you with the sword, and hand over your possessions to whom he has a mind: and afterwards you will be slaves both to him and his successors.'[16]

The 'nearby king', of course, was Charlemagne. Once they had recovered from their surprise the Saxons seized Lebuin and would have stoned him to death had not an elder intervened to save his life. In 782 the Saxons rebelled again and defeated the Franks in the Süntel hills. Charlemagne's response was the infamous massacre of Verden on the banks of the river Aller, just south of the neck of the Jutland peninsula. As many as 4,500 unarmed Saxon captives were forcibly baptized into the Church and then executed.[17] Even this failed to end Saxon resistance and had to be followed up by a programme of transportations in 794 in which about 7,000 of them were forcibly resettled. Two further campaigns of forcible resettlement followed, in 797 and in 798. A final insurrection was put down in 804 and Einhard the Monk, Charlemagne's biographer, articulated the fate of the defeated tribe. The Saxons were to 'give up their devil worship and the malpractices inherited from their forefathers; and then, once they had adopted the sacraments of the Christian faith and religion, they were to be united with the Franks and become one people with them'.[18] Charlemagne's capitulary for Saxons, *De Partibus Saxoniæ*, operative by the mid-780s, listed the punishments for those who tried to reject the imposition of Christian religious culture:[19] death for eating meat during Lent; death for the cremating of the dead in accordance with Heathen rites; death for any 'of the race of the Saxons hereafter, concealed among them, [who] shall have wished to hide himself unbaptized, and shall have scorned to come to baptism, and shall have wished to remain a Heathen'. Heathens were defined as less than fully human so that, under contemporary Frankish canon law, no penance was payable for the killing of one.[20] By way of comparison, under the 695 law code of the Kentish King Wihtred, Christians caught 'sacrificing to devils' were punishable merely by fines and the confiscation of property.[21]

Charlemagne and his missionaries set the terms of the encounters between Christians and Heathens, destroying the religious sanctuaries and cultural institutions of those who refused to embrace Christianity exclusively, and the Heathens saw no reason not to respond in kind.

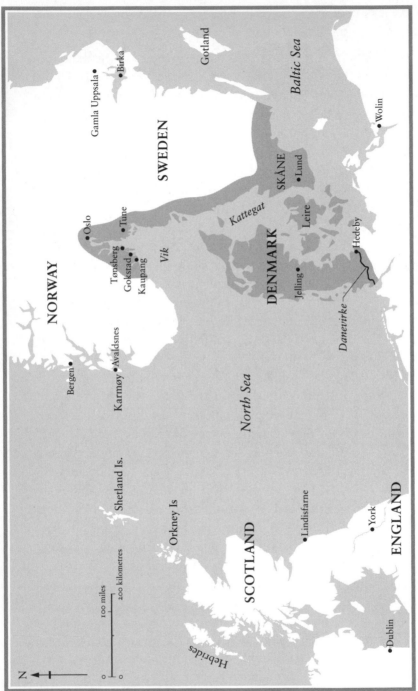

The first Viking raids on north-eastern Britain were launched from the Norwegian west coast. The shaded area shows Denmark and the sphere of influence of Danish Kings in about 800.

When Saxons attacked and burned Christian churches, an element of reciprocated cultural hostility lay behind their attacks. In the *Royal Frankish Annals* account of the attack on a church at Fritzlar in 773 the sole aim of the Heathens was to set fire to the church:

The Saxons began to attack this church with great determination, trying one way or another to burn it. While this was going on, there appeared to some Christians in the castle and also to some Heathens in the army two young men on white horses who protected the church from fire. Because of them the pagans could not set the church on fire or damage it, either inside or outside. Terror-stricken by the intervention of divine might they turned to flight, although nobody pursued them. Afterwards one of the Saxons was found dead beside the church. He was squatting on the ground and holding tinder and wood in his hands as if he had meant to blow on his fuel and set the church on fire.[22]

Charlemagne's vast empire ran from the Ebro in Spain to the Elbe in northern Germany, and the line between it and the Saxons' small pocket of territory in the north-east corner of Europe passed through more or less open country. Once Charlemagne had made up his mind to crush his neighbours there could have been, in Einhard's confident phrase, 'only one possible outcome'.[23] Even so, the great English historian Edward Gibbon expressed surprise at the degree of effort the emperor put into the war, reflecting on 'three-and-thirty campaigns laboriously consumed in the woods and morasses of Germany' which would have brought easier and greater glory had they been directed against the Greeks in Italy, and a further reduction in Muslim power in Spain. To Gibbon, the political significance of Charles's treatment of the Saxons was clear:

The subjugation of Germany withdrew the veil which had so long concealed the continent or islands of Scandinavia from the knowledge of Europe, and awakened the torpid courage of their barbarous natives. The fiercest of the Saxon idolaters escaped from the Christian tyrant to their brethren of the North; the Ocean and the Mediterranean were covered with their piratical fleets; and Charlemagne beheld with a sigh the destructive progress of the Normans, who, in less than seventy years, precipitated the fall of his race and monarchy.[24]

Gibbon was echoed in 1920 by the English novelist and man-of-letters H. G. Wells in his widely read *The Outline of History*:

Most of our information about these wars and invasions of the Pagan Vikings is derived from Christian sources, and so we have abundant information of the massacres and atrocities of their raids and very little about the cruelties inflicted upon their pagan brethren, the Saxons, at the hands of Charlemagne. Their animus against the cross and against monks and nuns was extreme. They delighted in the burning of monasteries and nunneries and the slaughter of their inmates.[25]

Lucien Musset, the greatest French scholar of the Viking Age in the twentieth century, is another who insisted that the violence that is its most outstanding characteristic must have had its origins in a cultural and religious conflict of the most dramatic sort.[26]

Several times in the course of his doomed campaign of resistance, Widukind had sought refuge across the border with his brother-in-law Sigfrid, a Danish king. His tales can have left Sigrid in no doubt as to the passion with which his powerful Christian neighbour in the south lived out the missionary imperative of Christianity. News of the Verden massacre must have travelled like a shock-wave through Sigfrid's territory, crossing the waters of the Kattegat and the Vik and on into the Scandinavian peninsula, arousing fear, fury and hostility towards both Charlemagne and Christianity. An incident that took place in 789 on the south coast of England at Portland, involving 'the first ships of Danish men which came to the land of the English', may well reflect the tensions aroused by this incident.[27] The chronicler Æthelweard provides a scene-setting description of the incident, with people 'spread over their fields and making furrows in the grimy earth in serene tranquillity' when the ships arrived. The king's reeve, a man named Beaduheard, rode to the harbour and confronted the sailors, admonishing them 'in an authoritative manner' before ordering them to be taken to 'the royal town'. The men, who had identified themselves as natives of 'Hörthaland', the modern Hordaland on the west coast of Norway, must have refused, for a fight broke out and Beaduheard and his men were killed. With no mention of subsequent plundering or attacks on churches or monasteries it looks like a case of fatal mistrust, routine perhaps, were it not for the raid on the monastery at Lindisfarne four years later to which it now seems a prelude. Perhaps the men were afraid they might be forcibly baptized and then executed. The Danes were certainly on the Church's list of peoples to be converted. Bede mentioned them, along with the Frisians, the Rugini, the Huns, the Old Saxons and the Boructvari, among a number of Germanic peoples still observing pagan rites in the early eighth century.[28] In about 710, during the time of King Ongendus, a fearsome Heathen 'more savage than any beast and harder than stone', Bede's contemporary, St Willibrord, carried out his mission among the Danes and returned to Utrecht with thirty boys whom he intended to instruct in Christianity. Clearly nothing had come of this, for in the year of the Portland raid Alcuin had written to a friend, proselytizing among the Saxons, 'Tell me, is there any hope of our converting the Danes?'[29]

Our pluralistic twenty-first century tries to encourage respect for the cultures of others and an acceptance of them on their own terms. The position would have baffled men like Bede and Alcuin, effortlessly certain of their right to impose the new and superior values of one culture upon another perceived as inferior and backward. We see Heathen ninth-century Scandinavians not as the horde of savages they were to these early churchmen but as a people who had evolved a social and spiritual culture of their own. Certainly it was very different from that of the Christians, but it was their own and we must assume they were content with it.[30] The Norwegian archaeologist Bjørn Myhre has suggested that for a period of perhaps three or four hundred years there had been a relatively stable North Sea community of peoples enjoying normally peaceful contact across the water with each other as traders, in technological and artistic exchange, in marriage and in the fostering of each other's children.[31] Alcuin's letter to the Northumbrian King Ethelred, quoted at the beginning of this chapter, is evidence for this kind of contact. So too are the grave-goods and shield and helmet from the East Anglian Sutton Hoo ship-burial from the middle years of the seventh century, which bear striking stylistic resemblances to Swedish artefacts of the same period found in royal graves at Vendel and Valsgärde. Ironically, this posited stability may in part have been due to the emergence of the Merovingian Franks as the dominant power in mainland Europe during the sixth and seventh centuries, one result of which had been to encourage trade around the North Sea and the development of a string of coastal trading towns like Dorestad at the mouth of the Rhine, Hamwic on the site of present-day Southampton, London by the Thames, Ribe on the west coast of South Jutland from about 700 and Kaupang in the Norwegian Vestfold a few years later.

As the degree of tension caused by Charlemagne's activities grew more marked, so too, in accordance with a familiar anthropological response to outside threat, did the intensity with which the Scandinavians began to mark their artefacts as a way of asserting their cultural identity. Burial practices, personal ornamentation like brooches, clothing styles and the design of houses all show, on this interpretation, a heightened degree of intensity in ethnic self-identification.[32] The threat may even have affected Viking Age poetry. As we noted earlier, many scholars believe that the Viking Age's greatest spiritual monument, 'The Seeress's Prophecy', was composed comparatively late in the history of northern Heathendom as a direct response to the threat of militant, expansionist Christianity and the dramatic and seductive Judaic creation myths of the Bible.[33] The local Scandinavian cultures that felt the first stirrings of this threat were neither compact nor centralized enough to organize themselves into anything like a structure that could have mounted a military campaign against Frankish Christendom. A more feasible goal, closer at hand, easier of reach, undefended and, in the parlance of modern terrorist warfare, 'a soft target', was the monastery at Lindisfarne. In Alcuin's phrase, it was 'a place more sacred than any in Britain'. With an indifference to the humanity of their Christian victims as complete as that of Charlemagne's towards the Saxons, a psychopathic rage directed at the Christian 'other' was unleashed, expressing itself in infantile orgies of transgressive behaviour that offered the same satisfactions whether the taboos transgressed were their own or those of their victims.[34] Simeon of Durham tells us that monks were deliberately drowned in the sea by the raiders: perhaps some travesty of baptism was intended. They dug up the altars, presumably because someone had revealed to them, under torture, that some of the monastery's greatest treasures lay buried there – but aware, too, of a blasphemous offence to their victims that was every bit as great as that suffered by the Saxon Heathens at the destruction of Irmensul. A feature of the raiding and church-burning that ensued was the Vikings' penchant for cutting up stolen items, like Bible clasps and crosses, and reshaping them into items of personal ornamentation. 'Ranvaik owns this box', its new owner had inscribed in runes on a beautiful, house-shaped box found in Norway in the seventeenth century. Graffiti depicting the prows of longships had been carved on its base. Made in Scotland towards the end of the eighth century, its original purpose had been to house the bones of a Christian saint. Useful enough for Ranvaik no doubt, but also an active expression of cultural dis-respect.[35]

Non-literate Viking culture has nothing to say to us on this difficult subject, but from the time the Vikings first came to the attention of the annalists in England, the view of their victims was insistently that they were engaged in an ongoing religious war. Though they were sometimes their place of origin, with 'Danes' serving as a generic term for all Scandinavians, sometimes 'foreigners' and sometimes 'flotman', 'sæman', 'sceigdman' and 'æscman' – all terms referring to their being seaborne raiders – with overwhelming frequency the Vikings were referred to in terms of their religion.[36] One hundred years after the first Lindisfarne raid, the Welsh bishop Asser, in his biography of Alfred the Great, continued to refer to those much larger bands of Scandinavian aggressors who had by then established themselves along the eastern seaboard of England as 'the pagans' (*pagani*), and to their Anglo-Saxon victims as 'the Christians' (*christiani*). Alcuin had sensed at once the real consequences of the 793 raid. 'Who does not fear this?' he had asked in his letter to Ethelred of Northumbria. 'Who does not lament this as if his country were captured?'

4

'The devastation of all the islands of Britain by the Heathens'

However we rank the reasons for the Vikings' sudden and dramatic eruption into the written records of England and Ireland at the turn of the eighth century, there is little debate about the importance of the longship, with its large sail, in making such raiding possible. The story of the introduction of sail into Scandinavia as told by the Gotland picture-stones is of a slow evolution, taking place from the sixth to the eighth centuries, in which a rudimentary piece of cloth fastened high on a pole gradually turned into a sophisticated, full-sized sail, with a tall mast and ropes that gave a high degree of control over its tension and orientation to the wind.[1] Some might argue that the mere possession of a technological wonder like this, and the desire to exploit it fully, must be counted among the reasons for the onset of the Viking Age.

It is thought that boat-builders worked in pairs, perhaps with a master craftsman on one side and an apprentice on the other, who was able to watch and mirror his techniques. Tools used were mainly chisels, hammers, axes and a type of drill that rested against the breastbone as the handle was turned. Most of the work was done using the long-handled cutting axe, heavier than a hand-axe and with a short, almost straight edge. Builders of reconstruction boats report that the most arduous and time-consuming part of the work was the shaving and shaping of the boards, a job that called for the broad-edged 'bearding-axe'.

Logs for ship-building were split with a club and wedge along the central pith rays that gave further splits into four, eight, sixteen and sometimes thirty-two parts. The advantage of this was that the integrity of the wood-fibre system was preserved, minimizing the penetration of water and providing good resistance to rot. It also made for a boat that was light in weight but flexible and strong, qualities that were perfect for the Viking raiding tactic of beaching in locations thought to be inaccessible to warships. The mild climate of those times produced huge oak forests, and the very large number of trees from which the boat-builder could choose meant that for those parts, such as the keel and hull of the boat, where a curve was needed, he was able to pick out a tree in which such a curve occurred naturally. This ability to 'see' the shape of a plank inside a growing tree must have been an essential part of the Viking Age boat-builder's skill. A builder of reconstruction boats found that the use of naturally curving planks gave up to twenty times more resilience in the timber than planking that had been sawn to shape.[2] The keel could not be jointed, so the length of the timber dictated the length of the boat. A socket construction called the 'mast-fish' held the mast, which could be lowered and removed when not required, and the rectangular sails were made of wool reinforced with leather bands.

A characteristic of the longship was a steering-oar mounted at the rear on a small shaft on the starboard side (from the Old Norse *styrbord*, meaning 'steering side') of the ship. The familiar stern-mounted rudder of the modern boat is a more efficient navigational device, and since the Vikings had the technology to make the iron hinges on which to hang a sternpost rudder it is natural to wonder why they did not do so. The strongest advantage seems related to the shallowness of the draft, in that it enabled navigation in almost any type of water, from the open North Sea to the rivers and streams of Ireland, Francia, England and the lands east of the Baltic. Fully extended at sea, the oar hung vertically below the level of the ship itself in a leather strap and could be easily adjusted up or down to allow for differences in the depths of the water. It could also be loosened from the strap and stored horizontally when navigating in shallow waters, or prior to landing on a beach. It enabled ships to load or unload cargoes from a river bank, or when beached at low tide. The ease of removing it would enable boats to be dragged deep inland up narrow rivers and towed backwards to open water where there was no possibility of turning round, a manoeuvre that would be impossible for a ship with a rudder mounted on the sternpost.[3]

The longship, high at both ends, with the large keel that was essential to maintain stability when crossing an ocean and its retractable side-oar that functioned as a rudder remains, for most people, the symbol of the Viking Age. The idea of the purpose-built vessel, in particular one designed for use as a merchant ship, does not seem to have arisen until a time somewhere between the building of the Gokstad ship in about 900 and of the five ships discovered at Skuldelev,[4] built around the middle of the eleventh century, that had been filled with boulders in their old age and scuttled to protect the approaches to the harbour at Roskilde, then the capital of Denmark. These were discovered and raised in the 1960s.[5] Taken together they offer a fairly representative selection of the range of ships in use in the Viking Age.

Each vessel revealed a different functional design: Skuldelev 1 was an ocean-going trading vessel, possibly a *knarr*, with decks fore and aft and open holds amidships. She would have been crewed by six to eight men. Regardless of size, ships were not fitted with benches and men would use their sea-chests to sit on when rowing. Skuldelev 2 was a longship that would have had a crew of about seventy men. It has been estimated that with sixty men manning the thirty pairs of oars (by way of comparison, Oseberg had fifteen) Skuldelev 2 would have been able to maintain a speed of about six knots for long periods of time. Under sail and in favourable wind conditions she could probably have reached twenty knots. Dendrochronological analysis shows that Skuldelev 2 was built from trees felled in a forest at Glendalough, north of Dublin, in about 1042. Skuldelev 3 was a small, oak-built trading and transport ship. She had an open hold with space for about four tons of cargo. Skuldelev 5 (Skuldelev 4 turned out to be part of Skuldelev 2) was a small longship of the type known as a *snekke* with thirteen pairs of oars and room for thirty warriors on board. Tests with a replica showed that, even when fully manned, she drew no more than 50 centimetres of water. Skuldelev 6 was a high-sided fishing vessel that probably also saw service as a ferry boat.

The Skuldelev ships were built mainly of oak, with ash and pine also being used, and in the 'clinker-built' style, working from the outside in, with each board overlapping the one below it and fastened to it with iron rivets. By contrast with the Oseberg ship, on which the fibres, up to 3 metres long, used by whales to filter the seawater for their food,[6] were used to bind her shipboards to the interior struts – something that gave her hull a remarkable flexibility – the Skuldelev ships were jointed with nails.[7] Caulking was done with moss and tar, and they all showed signs of having been repaired or adapted at some point in their lives, with rotten or damaged planks being replaced. Among the tools employed would have been a two-pronged iron 'nail-seeker' used to locate and cut rivet heads of the type found at the excavations of a Viking Age ship-building site at Paviken on Gotland.[8]

No rigging has survived in any of the ship-graves discovered so far, and for our knowledge of the sails and rigging of Viking ships we are dependent on the picture-stones from Gotland, some of which, like the Alaskog stone and the Stora Hammars stone from Lärbro, show remarkable detail. A stone of unknown provenance shows a relatively rare representation of a longship with her sails reefed. Coins from the later Viking Age sometimes display longships, like the coin found in 2000 near Lake Tissø. The coin and a number of picture-stones show shields mounted on a 'shield-rail' running round the railing of the ship, like the sixty-four yellow and black shields buried with the Gokstad chieftain on his ship. Ship-building as an industry throughout the Viking Age must have been a major part of the daily life of very large numbers of a great many communities, and the foresters, carpenters, blacksmiths, sail-makers, rope-makers and labourers in-volved must have been legion; yet the sagas convey nothing of this. Perhaps it was the very ubiquity of its sights and sounds that left the industry unremarked, unless it were that their authors hailed mostly from treeless Iceland where little ship-building was done and old ships patched up and kept afloat for as long as possible.

The wealth of incidental detail concerning navigation scattered across *Heimskringla* and in the sagas suggests the use of techniques ranging from the simple plumbline to avoid shallows and the countless tiny and rocky *skjær* that form a natural barrier to so much of the Norwegian coastline, to the sophistications of a sun-compass. When crossing the open sea the Vikings would use 'dead-reckoning', a method of navigation that involved observing the latitude and estimating the longitude to give some idea of the total distance travelled. Latitude sailing necessitated the use of a navigational aid called a 'sun-shadow board'. This was a wooden disc with a pin or gnomon at the centre that could be adjusted up or down according to the time of year. It was floated in a bowl of water and the shadow of the sun at noon noted. If the ship was on course then the shadow would reach a circle marked on the board. If it passed beyond, the ship was north of this latitude. Should it fail to reach the circle she was south of it and the skipper could make the necessary adjustments. A cauldron of the type found in the aft or 'kitchen' section of the Oseberg ship, when not in use for on-board cooking, could have been used to float the device. There is archaeological evidence in the form of a partial wooden disc, found in 1948 at Uunartoq fjord, near the Eastern Settlement, one of the two colonies established by the Vikings in Greenland in about 985.[9] It is marked with hyperbolas and sixteen small cuts crossing a long line that seems to indicate north. Dated to about 1000, in its complete form it would have measured about 7 cm in diameter, with thirty-two carved triangular points cut around its circumference. The shadow cast by the tip of a gnomon in the centre of the disc described different hyperbolas at different times of the year. In the few weeks of the year around the summer solstice, at latitude 62° north of the equator, rotating the disc until the shadow of the tip fell on the curve would give the general directions with sufficient accuracy to sail a bearing. A second and more complete sun-compass, dated to the eleventh century, was found at Wolin in Poland in 2002.[10]

A reference in a late and literary source describes the use of a 'sun-stone', a mineral that occurs in several forms in Iceland with the property of polarizing light when held up in the direction of the sun. *Raudulfs tháttr*, a short story preserved in a manuscript from the early fourteenth century, describes the visit of the Norwegian King Olav Haraldson to the home of a rich farmer named Raudulf. Olav asked his host's son Sigurd if he had any special talents, and the youth replied that indeed he did – he was able to tell the time, day or night, even when no celestial body was visible. The king was interested and on the following day, which was overcast, he challenged the youth to demonstrate his skills. Once Sigurd had done so, Olav ordered a sun-stone to be brought out and held up to the sky in the general direction the sun was thought to be. In the story the light streams through the prism and Sigurd's remarkable talent is confirmed to the king's satisfaction.

In general, there is uncertainty about the degree of astronomical knowledge the Vikings had. Oddi Helgason, a twelfth-century Icelander known as Star-Oddi for his knowledge of astronomical phenomena, kept an almanac with precise calculations of the occurrence of the summer and winter solstices and diverse other mathematical observations, but it is not known whether Oddi merely noted down knowledge that had been common in the far north since the ninth century, or was a genius responsible for the calculations himself.[11] Another enigma involves thirty lenses of rock crystal that are part of the collection of the Visby Museum on Gotland. Dating from the very late Viking period, and at first assumed to be ornamental trinkets, tests conducted on the lenses revealed that they had imaging powers as good as those of modern optics.[12] They had obviously been made on a turning lathe and were of such high quality that they could have been used as magnifiers, as fire-starters, to cauterize wounds, or even to make up the light-chain in a telescope. Their rarity has led to the supposition that they were not the work of a Viking Age craftsman but came originally from the more advanced workshops of Constantinople or ancient Persia. To all such speculations we can only add the further presumption that efficient and safe long-distance navigation involved for the Vikings a knowledge of the major landmarks observable on the longer voyages; of the direction and strength of currents at sea; of birds – particularly sea-birds – and of their environments and habits of flight; of cloud formations; of the use of both day and night sky as an almanac; as well as a developed sensitivity to the subtleties of sea, sky and weather well in excess of anything we possess now.

Simple dead-reckoning would have sufficed to cross the sea to northern Britain from the west coast of Norway, and there was a second raid in Northumbria in the year after Lindisfarne, when Vikings 'ravaged in Northumbria, and plundered Ecgfrith's monastery at *Donemuthan*'.[13] Alcuin, with his local knowledge, had warned the religious communities at nearby Wearmouth and Jarrow to be on their guard – 'You live by the sea from whence this plague first came.' Simeon of Durham identified the site of the monastery at the mouth of the Don as Jarrow, and reported with satisfaction that its great protector St Cuthbert had not allowed the Heathens to go away unpunished,

for their chief was killed by the English with a cruel death, and after a short space of time the violence of a storm battered, destroyed and broke to pieces their ships, and the sea overwhelmed many of them. Some were cast on the shore, and soon killed without mercy. And these things befell them rightly, for they had gravely injured those who had not injured them.[14]

The thirteenth-century historian Roger of Wendover referred to a raid on Northumbria a few years later in 800, by 'the most impious armies of the pagans [who] cruelly despoiled the churches of Hartness and Tynemouth, and returned with its plunder to the ships', after which the focus of the raiding turned to religious sites in Ireland and in the Western Isles of Scotland, a region which the Irish Christian scribes of the *Annals of Ulster* regarded as falling within their sphere of interest and of whose sufferings at the hands of the Vikings they duly opened an account.[15] The annals for 794 note the 'devastation of all the islands of Britain by the Heathens', the following year that the Isle of Skye was 'overwhelmed and laid waste'. Iona, a religious site that was, if anything, more sacred to Christians even than Lindisfarne, was attacked for the first time in 795, and again in 802. In 806 the monastery was burned down and the community of sixty-eight people killed. The monastery was attacked again the following year.

There are no records of raids on Orkney or Shetland, sixty miles to the north of it, but with a fair wind Shetland lay only twenty-four hours' sailing west of Bergen and we may be sure they took place. Finds of combs made from the antler of reindeer, an animal not indigenous to the islands, have been taken as likely evidence of contact between Norwegians and the aboriginal Pictish inhabitants of the island from the time before things turned violent.[16] A degree of activity that the annalists saw fit to describe as the 'devastation of all the islands of Britain'[17] probably implies the existence as early as the 790s of a base in the north from which the raiders could easily reach targets further west round the coast of Scotland, and to which they could return without risking a North Sea crossing each time. The Northern Isles would have been the most obvious location of such a base. The date given by the *Anglo-Saxon Chronicle* for the Lindisfarne raid is 8 January (the ides of January). Following Simeon of Durham in the *History of the Church of Durham*, written some 300 years later, historians have conventionally altered this to 7 June (the ides of June), on the grounds that a crossing of the North Sea in an open boat in the dead of winter would have been unthinkable.[18] The objection would be less compelling had the raiders started their journey not from Norway but from some such local base to the north. There is increasing acceptance of the likelihood that part of this first manifestation of Viking violence involved the colonization of the Orkneys, and shortly afterwards of the Western Isles of Scotland, and that before the middle of the ninth century a de facto Viking kingdom, referred to by the Irish annalists as Lothlend, Laithlinn or Lochlainn, had come into being and ruled over both, as well as over the Caithness and Sutherland regions of north-east mainland Scotland, and was independent of the power structure in Norway.[19]

The *Orkneyinga Saga*, a narrative history of the Norwegian presence on the islands written down in Iceland in about 1200, does not begin its tale until much later, with the establishment of the islands as a Norwegian earldom in the last two or three decades of the ninth century. The Norwegian King Harald Finehair crosses the North Sea as part of his campaign to unify the inhabited territories of Norway under his kingship. His immediate purpose was

to teach a lesson to certain vikings whose plunderings he could no longer tolerate. These vikings used to raid in Norway over summer and had Shetland and Orkney as their winter base. Harald conquered Shetland, Orkney and the Hebrides, then sailed all the way to the Isle of Man where he laid its settlement in ruins. During his campaign he fought a number of battles, winning himself territories further west than any King of Norway has done since. In one of these battles Earl Rognvald's son Ivar was killed. On his way back to Norway, King Harald gave Earl Rognvald Shetland and Orkney in compensation for his son, but Rognvald gave all the islands to his brother Sigurd, the fo'c'sle-man on King Harald's ship. When the King sailed back east he gave Sigurd the title of earl and Sigurd stayed on in the islands.[20]

Details involving their own ancestors are what seemed important to the storyteller and his audience in the early thirteenth century; who or what preceded them on the islands was of lesser interest. At the time the Viking Age began in the west, a community of Picts had been living on the islands since the fourth century, as part of a larger kingdom comprising the Northern Picts in what is now the Caithness area, and the Southern Picts in the area known as 'The Mounth'.[21] Little is known of their society, but it seems to have been Christian. According to Adomnán, an abbot of Iona in the late seventh century and the biographer of Columba, the community's founder, the saint visited the Picts in the course of his missionary work and made some converts at the court of their king, Bridei. A Bishop Cuiritán is reported to have preached the gospel to them from a base at the head of the Moray Firth, and a congregation of Pictish memorial stones in the area seems to confirm the existence of a Christian centre there.[22] Adomnán also writes that monks from Iona were living in a hermitage on the Orkneys during the sixth century, and there may have been a church on St Ninian's Isle by the eighth century.[23]

The size and ferocity of the Viking warbands that began to appear towards the end of the eighth century severed the links of these Orcadian Picts to their fellows on the mainland and left them to their fate. The toponymists tell us that names of all the towns, settlements, farms, rivers and natural features of the landscape of the Shetland and Orkney Islands are, with the obvious exception of modern names, of Norse origin. Only the name Orkney itself, which means 'seal-island', is pre-Scandinavian. This is a very unusual state of affairs and the interpretation of it is controversial. It may mean only that, within a fairly short space of time around the turn of the eighth and ninth centuries, practically all native Picts were wiped out. Such a campaign would have been in the spirit of the Vikings' well-documented slaughter of whole communities of Christian ecclesiastics in the surrounding regions at about the same time. A parallel has been drawn with the situation in nineteenth-century Tasmania, where the combination of disease and a colonial campaign of slaughter by the British resulted in the disappearance of not only the aboriginal peoples but also of all the aboriginal place-names.[24] The oldest farm-names in the Orkneys show that the Vikings brought their

Heathendom west with them. Mill Bay on the eastern side of Stronsay has the Norwegian coast as its nearest landfall in the east, and among the names of Norse origin found there are Odness, also known as Odin Ness, and an Iron Age dry-stone wall structure of the type known as a 'broch', which acquired the name God-Odina. Below the broch is a beach named Dritness. In the *Book of the Settlements* Ari tells us that 'Dritsker' was the name of the skerry appointed for use as a public toilet by those attending the Assembly site at Thorolf Mostrarskegg's temple-farm at Hofstadir in Iceland. The geographical proximity of two so resonantly named sites on an Orkney island may well have been typical of Heathen Viking settlements, identifying this particular site as a place at which assemblies were held. Another farm-name that reinforces the association with south-west Norway is Avaldsay on Rousay, just north of Orkney's Mainland island, was probably named from Avaldsnes in Karmøy, in Rogaland, the place from which, in the later years of the ninth century, Harald Finehair began his campaign to unify Norway.[25]

A second explanation for the missing Pictish names may be that the arrival of a Viking warrior aristocracy occasioned only a transfer of power from the ousted Pictish leaders of the native community. For these the consequences might be very dramatic, for those lower down the social scale less so. The latter would simply orientate themselves towards a new set of leaders to whom to pay their taxes and from whom to request protection. Finds in 1970 and 1971 at a Norse farm built on top of a Pictish house on the Point of Buckquoy, at Birsay in Orkney, have been used to support this theory, interpreting the presence of Pictish bone pins and bone combs at the Norse cultural level as a sign that the Vikings had obtained these and other items of domestic equipment from a surviving but subjugated native population. A third possibility is that the Picts who survived a first wave of conquest simply fled the islands in fear and left the Vikings with no local naming culture to relate to at all.

A lean linguistic survival from pre-Norse times in the Orkneys and Shetland sheds little light on these matters. Effectively this consists of a single inscription, that on the Bressay stone found at Cullbinsgarth in Shetland in the early 1850s. A number of theories concerning the script and its meaning have been adopted and discarded since its discovery. Some linguists interpret the writing as a mixture of Old Norse runes and a linear form of script called *ogham*, which was developed in the south-east of Ireland during the fourth century and is known to have been used by the Picts. They interpret the mixture as evidence of contact, communication and cultural continuity between Picts and Vikings, and even as evidence that some Vikings had adopted Christianity by the time the stone was cut.[26] Commemorative inscriptions in mixed languages of a later period, from the Isle of Man, provide a theoretical justification for this type of interpretation. The problem is that there is no general agreement about what the inscription on the Bressay stone means, and interpretation is hindered by its decayed and damaged state.[27]

The archaeological record is similarly a case of sparse material remains that give rise to conflicting interpretations. The discovery of Pictish artefacts, usually pottery, in Norse-style houses, and of Viking artefacts in Pictish houses, might indicate peaceful continuity between the two cultures, or it could indicate that the Vikings killed the Picts and took over their houses and buildings. Geneticists, precise in their measurements, can give no unequivocal answer to these riddles. In a survey carried out in 2000 for the BBC television series *Blood of the Vikings* by Professor Daniel Goldstein and a team from University College, London, 60 per cent of the male population of Shetland and Orkney were found to have DNA of Norwegian origin. One condition of the testing was that the island volunteers were able to trace back their male lineage in the same area for at least three generations.[28] A study that limited testing to men with surnames going back to the end of the earldom in the Orkneys in 1469 found an even higher percentage correlation with Norwegian DNA, indicating a genetic deposit from Vikings of somewhere between 60 and 100 per cent.[29] This could equally be the result of a gradual process over time, or of the summary extinction of the indigenous local population over a very short period of time.

The unknown author of the *Historia Norwegie*, a synoptic twelfth-century history of Norway, includes in his account a brief and half-mythological history of the Orkneys at about the turn of the eighth century. At that time, he tells us, the islands were occupied by Irish priests and Picts. A fleet of Norwegians arrived and 'totally destroyed these people of their long-established dwellings and made the islands subject to themselves'.[30] He describes the Picts as an industrious people whose strength would mysteriously desert them in the middle of the day, so that they would run away and hide themselves 'for fear in underground chambers'.[31] Such timidity, and the fact that he described them as a half-mythical race of goblins, 'only a little taller than pygmies', might be the vestiges of a Viking Age dehumanization of the Picts that was a psychologically necessary precondition for killing them easily, rather as Charlemagne's capitularies of about the same time ruled that no compensation was payable for the killing of a Heathen, on the grounds that the unbaptized were not fully human.

Where the evidence is so flimsy and ambiguous, its interpretation will tend to reflect the view of human nature of the interpreter. The optimist finds evidence of a saturation degree of Scandinavian immigration that led to a new social synthesis. The pessimist, with a glance over his or her shoulder at recent events in Nazi Germany, Yugoslavia, Rwanda, and aware of the record of Viking atrocities carried out in the region at the same period, will conclude that the only realistic explanation for the riddle of the missing Orcadian place-names and the DNA of the islands' current inhabitants is a genocide. In his early eleventh-century *Chronicle*, Adémar of Chabannes, the French Benedictine, imputed a genocidal 'thought' to Viking encroachments upon Ireland:

At this time the aforesaid Normans invaded the Hibernian island of Ireland with a large fleet, something their fathers had never dared to do, together with their wives and children and the Christian captives, whom they had made their slaves, with the intention that with the Irish wiped out, they themselves could inhabit this very prosperous country.

Anomalies of place-naming in the Outer Hebrides suggest a scenario similar in most respects to that involving Shetland and the Orkneys: the killing or capture and sale as slaves of the original inhabitants, in a process so swift and complete as to leave behind only fragmentary traces of the place-names used by those original inhabitants.[32] By the middle of the ninth century the Irish annalists had started to refer to the Hebrides as 'Na hInnsi Gall' or 'the islands of the foreigners'. A second genetic survey of the populations of the Northern and Western Isles, carried out by scientists from the University of East Anglia and published in 2005, looked at both the female mitochondrial DNA as well as the male Y-chromosomal and found that the figure for overall Scandinavian ancestry among inhabitants of the Northern Isles was about 44 per cent for Shetland and 30 per cent for the Orkneys, with roughly equal genetic contributions from Scandinavian males and females.[33] Scandinavian ancestry for inhabitants of the Outer Hebrides was lower, at about 15 per cent, and the findings showed a much higher contribution to the gene pool from Scandinavian males than females. The likely explanation is that the patterns of settlement were different. In the geographically closer Northern Isles, Viking settlers brought their Scandinavian families over with them from Norway, while the typical Hebridean settler was a young Viking who took from among the local girls, whether they were willing or not. Males among the local population were deprived of even this melancholy option. The 'hostage stone', a slate found in separate pieces and on separate occasions on the Hebridean island of Inchmarnock in 2001 and 2002, shows a crude drawing that probably symbolizes the fate of those who were not killed: three men wearing chain mail, one wild-haired, another armed with a spear, appear to be conducting a shackled man to a waiting longship. He holds what may be a reliquary and his head is bowed as he contemplates the life of slavery that awaits him over the seas.[34]

After the raids of 806 and 807 the remains of the community at Iona crossed the North Channel to Ireland to begin work on a safe refuge at Kells in Ireland, a retreat that marked a first tangible effect of Viking terror directed against Christian targets. But as we have seen, Ireland itself had already become a target. In 795 the monastery at *Rechru* was burnt, and in 798 St Patrick's Island was attacked and the Vikings 'took the cattle-tribute of the territories and broke the shrine of Do-Chonna'.[35] The country had been Christian since the fifth century, and it was from Ireland, and the monastery centres of the Western Isles founded by Irishmen, that Christianity was exported to northern Britain in the succeeding centuries. The cultivation of monastic life over three centuries led to the establishment of communities

Map of Ireland showing the locations of some of the early raids and the
longphort bases established by the Vikings.

in the vicinity of monasteries with many of the features of trading towns. A seventh-century account of the community that had evolved around the monastery at Kildare refers to the 'multitudes who live there', in a place where 'no man need fear any mortal adversary or any gathering of enemies'. 'And who could number the varieties of people who gather there in countless throngs from all provinces? Some come for the abundance of its feasts; others, in ill-health, come for a cure; others come simply to watch the crowds go by.' 'A great metropolitan city', a contemporary historian called it.[36] By the time of the first Viking raids the practice of working precious metal into altar-vessels, book-covers and shrines had become part of the religious culture of these Irish monastic centres. As a result of the legal functions that fell to them, such as the pledging of agreements, each monastery probably disposed of a collection of valuable objects like brooches.[37] Beyond their walls the picture that emerges from the law codes of the political organization of early ninth-century Ireland is of a hierarchy of kings. Chieftains with authority over local areas recognized the authority of a group of about five more powerful regional kings, who in their turn acknowledged the superiority of a yet more powerful 'king of overkings', an office associated with the kingdom of Tara on the central east coast of the island, who claimed precedence over them all.[38]

The main literary sources for this field of Viking activity are the *Annals of Ulster*, a fifteenth-century compilation from earlier sources, the *Annals of the Four Masters*, a seventeenth-century compilation from medieval monastic sources that uses the *Annals of Ulster* for some of its later entries, and the late *Fragmentary Annals of Ireland* which, as the name implies, is a collection of the fragmentary survivals of lost annals that ranges from 573 to 914. Preceding and then accompanying the descriptions of Viking activity in Ireland in these sources are references to a close association between the political and religious authorities that fostered rivalries between the neighbouring monasteries and often led to pitched battles in which large numbers of people were killed. In 807 the *Annals of Ulster* report 'a battle between the community of Corcach and the community of Cluain Ferta Brénainn, among whom resulted a slaughter of a countless number of ordinary ecclesiastics and of eminent men of the community of Corcach'.[39] In

831 the fair at Tailtiu turned into a riot that began in some unspecified dissension over holy relics, 'and many died as a result'.[40] By a
well-established tradition, family was the crucial factor in succession to church office in Ireland. Feidlimid, son of Crimthann, of the
Eoghanacht dynasty of Munster, was both king and cleric who seized
power in 820, interfered in the politics of Armagh in 823 and 836 to
take the side of a favoured candidate in a succession dispute, feuded
endlessly with the Clonmacnoise, carried out the 'smashing of the
southern Uí Briúin' in 830 and took by force the abbacy of Cork in
836.[41] And yet there is just a hint that the parties in such fighting tried
in principle to observe certain behavioural limits. In 833 the chieftain
Feidlimid executed members of the community of Clonmacnoise 'and
burned their church-lands to the very door of the church'. The community of Dairmag suffered similar treatment, we are told. They, too,
had their lands burnt, 'to the very door of the church'. The annalist
seems to be making a point here, that the burning of churches was a
transgression unique to the Vikings, and one that was in defiance of
a logic that must have told them it would make better economic sense
to leave them standing, for their store of replenishable treasures would
have been available to steal again that much more quickly. Sanctuary
was respected. Where breaches of sanctuary by fellow-Irishmen
occurred, compensation was paid to the monasteries involved.[42] At
the very least there would be formal pronouncement of a curse on the
intruders. Nor did the Irish aristocrats who waged war against each
other's monasteries count, among the spoils of victory, the right to
sell the defeated into slavery. Viking cruelty was regarded as being in
a class of its own. Implying that this was no normal hunting practice,
the annal for 828 reports 'a great slaughter of porpoises on the coast
of Ard Cianachta by the foreigners'.[43] The Vikings had discovered,
either through torture or treachery, the Christian custom of housing
the remains of their revered dead in sumptuous containers like the
'shrine of gold and silver' which contained the bones of a certain
Conlaed; or the 'gold and silver casket' in which the remains of Ronan,
son of Berach, were placed.[44] In 824 they plundered the monastery at
Bennchor (Bangor), 'destroyed the oratory and shook the relics of
Comgall from their shrine'. Blamac was an Irish chieftain's son who
had chosen life as a monk of Iona. His martyrdom in 825 at the hands

of the Vikings became the subject of a lament by Walafrid Strabo, a scholar at the Frankish court of Charlemagne's son, Louis the Pious. Blamac had gone to Iona knowing well that the Vikings had already attacked the island several times, and when they did so yet again he took it upon himself to warn other monks to flee for their lives, but stayed behind himself to bury the holy relics of St Columba. Strabo relates that he was tortured to death by Vikings trying to discover their whereabouts. In a raid on Étar (Howth) in 821, at which they 'carried off a great number of women', the raiders showed that they had discovered the potential of these territories for the slavery which was to fund so much of their activity over the next two centuries. And they had quickly learnt the significance for Christian communities of the Church calendar, and the advantages to be had from raiding on feast days, when the crowds of people who flocked to the monasteries to trade and buy could themselves be stolen away and traded on.

As the relentless nature of the new threat became apparent, some among the approximately 150 kings of Ireland, great and small, began to engage the Vikings in battle. A militarized Church leadership joined in, putting abbots into the field at the head of their own monastery armies. In 811 there was 'a slaughtering of the pagans at the hands of the Ulaid' that came to the admiring attention of the *Royal Frankish Annals* in the following year, and Viking forces were beaten twice more in 812. The annalists continue to note sundry atrocities and encounters: in 821 the Vikings occupied the islands of Wexford Harbour, in the same year as the annalist reported the abduction into slavery of the women of Étar. In 823 and 824 they invaded Bangor, and in 824 raided the remote hermitage of Skellig Michael, off the Kerry coast, carrying off a hermit named Éitgal who shortly afterwards died of hunger and thirst, whether from deliberate maltreatment or in self-denial the annals do not say. Indeed, by contrast with the makers of the *Anglo-Saxon Chronicle*, the Irish annalists are almost conventionally reticent, though that very reticence conveys the fate of a harmless individual like Éitgal, and of all those taken away into slavery, perhaps better than outrage would. When he tells us that the captives were 'led away', or that they were 'brought to the ships' or 'taken away' and sometimes 'taken away to the ships', we realize that these are stoicisms and not euphemisms. In 831 the Vikings raided

Conaille in County Louth, captured the king and his brother and took them back to their ships as prisoners. In 832 they discovered the wealth of the Armagh monastery and attacked it three times in one month. Churches at Mucnám, Lugbad, Uí Mécth and elsewhere were plundered, more monasteries and churches burnt, more people abducted into slavery. Just occasionally one of those 'led away' makes a reappearance in the annals. In 845 Forannán, abbot of Armagh, with his collection of relics, was captured by the Heathens 'and brought to the ships of Luimnech'. The following year, without further explanation from the annalist, the same Forannán returns 'from the lands of Mumu [Munster] with the halidoms of Patrick'. He resumed his previous post but retired two years later and a final entry records his peaceful death in 852. Probably only a very few of the abducted were as fortunate.

Thus far the Vikings had confined their attacks to coastal targets. From about the 830s onwards they began forcing their way ever deeper inland as a prelude to larger and more organized raiding that was probably also an investigation of the possibilities of settlement and/or colonization. In 837 two fleets of sixty ships each arrived on the Boyne and the Liffey, a likely raiding force of between 3,000 and 4,000 men. They 'plundered the plain of Life and the plain of Brega, including churches, forts and dwellings' and brought 'havoc in all the lands of the Connachta'. The death at the hands of Cianacht of a chieftain named Saxolb (Old Norse *Saxulfr*) is noted in that year, the first Viking name to appear in the written record after some forty years of incessant raiding. It was progress of a sort, a sign that the two sides were at least in communication with each other. But with no monarch seeking the tangible prize of a coherent kingship to take over, the sides seemed doomed to decades of intermittent and inconclusive warfare.

If the fragmented nature of secular power in Ireland and the ad hoc nature of the chieftains' military organization made a territorial takeover of Ireland an impractical goal, these conditions did provide an opportunity for Viking leaders to become involved in regional conflicts between the great families that could help them force a legitimate way into the native power structures. In the late 830s a Viking army was defeated at Derry by a force whose leaders included Murchad mac Máele Dúin, a deposed king of Ailech. This Murchad was father to a son named Erulb. Linguists suggest this may be an Irish version of the Norwegian name *Herulfr*, indicating that the child may have been the result of a marriage alliance. And with intermarriage came bilingualism, religious flexibility and all the subtle yet profound effects that follow when cultures that collide violently wheel, like colliding galaxies, into accommodation with each other.[45] In due course Olaf, the first king of Dublin, is said to have married a daughter of an Irish high-king, Aed Finlaith. When a later king, Ivar, died in 873 the annalist wrote that he 'rested with Christ', though whether this was merely formulaic or not is impossible to tell. Marriage between a Heathen and an Irish princess must have involved the Viking in some kind of conciliatory gesture towards Christianity. At the least he was probably asked to submit to the ceremony of the *prima signatio* or 'prime-signing', the 'first marking with a cross' that became, throughout the Christian world, an important tool of correspondence for those on both sides who were determined not to let religious belief stand in the way of business and power politics. Prime-signing was a preliminary to baptism. In one of its fuller forms the priest would lay his hand upon the catechumen's head, breathe on him to drive out evil spirits, make the sign of the cross on his forehead and place a corn of salt on his tongue to symbolize his purification in Christ. With this provisional ceremony out of the way Christians might trade and interact with Heathens as they wished.[46]

Another change that evolved out of the confusion and violence of the first decades of raiding was the appearance from about the middle of the century of a new group of warriors whom the annals call the *Gall-Gædhil* or 'Foreigner-Celts'. They were a mixed group, some being Irish renegades who had opportunistically adopted the lifestyle of the invaders, others the products of the union of Norwegian and Irish, still others Irish raised by Viking foster-fathers. Between 830 and 880 the annals record eighty-three incidents of Norse burnings and plunderings in Ireland. The record of similar assaults by Irish forces during the same period is modest by contrast, a mere ten. Three more were attributed to these *Gall-Gædhil*.[47] Their loyalties were to themselves and they fought now on the Viking side against the Irish, now for the Irish against the Vikings. In this they were, in truth, no different from either the Irish or the Vikings themselves. Cinaed, king of North Brega, rebelled in 850 against the high-king Mael Sechnaill and, joining forces with a Viking band, ravaged the lands of the southern Úi Néill. Inevitably the frail ethical code that had protected Irish clerics and church buildings from the worst of the secular violence gave way and it was the raw brutality of the Vikings that prevailed. During the attack on the church at Trevet 260 people who sought refuge in the oratory were burnt alive. Cinaed was finally captured and executed by drowning, 'in a dirty stream', according to a source, though the quality of the water can scarcely have mattered to him.

The available archaeological evidence reinforces the commonsense notion that the raiders during the first fifty years of the Irish Viking Age came, in the main, from the south-west coast of Norway. Viking Age graves excavated in the region at Gausel, near Stavanger in northern Jæren, contain the highest concentration of artefacts of Irish origin found outside Ireland.[48] These include the grave of a female discovered in 1883 by a local farmer, which was lost and subsequently rediscovered in 1997. Among over forty items buried with her were an Irish hanging bowl and two Irish bronze mounts from a reliquary shrine. An analysis of the 500 or so items of insular metalwork found in Scandinavia led to a similar conclusion: most of the graves identified as being from the decades around 800 were in the Sogn og Fjordane and Møre og Romsdal areas of western Norway, and in most of them the grave-goods were of Irish ecclesiastical origin.[49] Linguists are also able to tell us that the forty or so loan-words absorbed by Irish during the Viking Age point to the south-west of Norway as their place of origin.

A significant development occurred in 848 with the arrival in Ireland of a fleet bearing another large number of Scandinavian warriors, these so distinct from their original tormentors that the annalists called them 'the dark Heathens' or 'the black foreigners'. They were Danes. They attacked and overwhelmed their rivals, the *Finngall* or 'fair foreigners' of Norway at their base in what would later be Dublin, killing a great many of them and robbing them of their possessions. The Norwegians re-grouped and in 852 a fleet of 160 ships engaged the Danes in a ferocious sea-battle at Snám Aignech that lasted three days and nights before the Danes emerged triumphant. Even for violent times these were exceptionally violent years. In four separate battles fought in 848 a total of precisely 2,600 men are said to have been killed. Among the dead at the battle at Sciath Nechtain was the Earl Tomrair, described as a 'tanist of the king of Lochliann'. This mysterious king seems to have decided that now was the time to impose his authority on an increasingly chaotic situation. He sent his son Amlaíb, or Olaf, to Ireland at the head of a fleet of 140 ships for the purpose of exacting obedience from the various Norse bands operating there. 'The foreigners of Ireland submitted to him,' the annalist tells us, 'and he took tribute from the Irish.'[50] This marked the start of the Norse kingdom of Dublin, one of several enclosed Viking colonies that developed out of the creation of permanent bases known as *longphorts* to service their ships. The most notable other *longphort* sites were at Hlymrekr (Limerick), Vethrafjörth (Waterford), Veigsfjörth (Wexford) and at Vikingalo (Wicklow). In time these evolved into Ireland's first proper towns, superseding the rudimentary trading centres associated with the monasteries. Dublin may have remained a very insular kingship. The University College, London, genetic survey mentioned above also carried out tests in search of Viking DNA among the Irish, and while the complete absence of any in the samples taken from Castlerea, in the rural heart of the country, came as no surprise, since there has never been any suggestion that the Vikings established inland settlements of any size, the researchers were surprised at the similarly complete absence of any Scandinavian DNA in material taken within a 20-mile radius of Rush in north County Dublin that just swept the northern outskirts of the city. One of a number of possible explanations is that they did not settle much beyond the confines of the original site on the Liffey.[51]

The Viking takeover included the Isle of Man, in the Irish Sea. Over thirty grave-finds from about 850 to 950 indicate Viking settlements on some of the best agricultural land on the island, in the north-west and south-east.[52] As on the Orkneys, the names of a large number of features of the natural landscape, like the Snæfell peak and the Laxey river, are of Scandinavian origin. The Point of Ayre was formerly Eyranes, the Calf of Man, Manarkalfrinn. Saving Douglas and Rushen, no Celtic settlement names seem to have survived the arrival

N

CAITHNESS

Lewis

St Kilda   Harris

North Uist

South Uist   Skye   Raasay
                      Scalpay

Barra   Canna

Rhum   Eigg

Muck

Coll

Tiree

Iona   Mull

ATLANTIC   ARGYLL
OCEAN

Colonsay

Jura

Bute

Islay   Inchmarnock

Arran

Kintyre

North Sea

Lindisfarne

GALLOWAY

ULSTER

Man

York •

Irish Sea

• Dublin

0   50 miles
0   50 kilometres

The Kingdom of Man and the Isles at its greatest extent in about 1095.

of the Vikings. Were it not for the fact that the Norwegian DNA signature from the UCL survey was about 15 per cent, declining in reciprocal proportion to the distance from Norway, the assumption might be that the island's population suffered a fate similar to that of the Orcadian Picts. Evidence of a more harmonious encounter may be the mingled inscriptions on one of the crosses at Old Kirk Braddan, a late tenth-century tapering pillar with a small pierced ring at the cross head and a characteristically Scandinavian design of tiny dragon-like creatures with intricately twined limbs, tails and top-knots cut down one side. Along the other side a runic inscription announces that the cross was raised by a father with the Norwegian name of Thorleif, in memory of a son with the Celtic name of Fiac.[53] The island benefited from its proximity to Dublin and coin hoards from about 960 to about 990 show connections with England and Ireland, later hoards from about 1020 to 1080 indicating that the connections with Ireland had grown stronger. Because it is not confirmed in any of the Irish sources, historians are inclined to doubt the statement in the *Orkneyinga Saga* that King Harald Finehair got as far as the Isle of Man during his campaign to discipline unruly Vikings in the Orkneys; but, as part of the expansion of the earldom of Orkney in the late tenth and early eleventh centuries under Sigurd the Stout that brought the Western Isles of Scotland under his control, it is likely that Man entered the earldom's sphere of influence. Later still, under Godfred Crovan in the eleventh century, it had its own kings who also ruled the Western Isles. A relic of this island kingdom survives today in the name of the bishopric, Sodor and Man – sodor being *Súthreyjar* or 'the southern islands', which the Hebrides were to these northern Vikings.

In Dublin, the intervention of the king of Lochlainn had brought a degree of stability to the region for the next few decades, a period referred to in the Irish annals as the 'Forty Years Rest'. In 902 the Vikings were driven out of the city, but in 914 a huge fleet appeared off Waterford under the leadership of Ragnald and Sihtric Cáech. Already its Viking identity is compromised, for Sihtric was a member of the powerful Celtic-Norse Uí Ímhair dynasty and whose personal name was a gaelic rendering of the Scandinavian 'Sigtrygg'. The nickname Cáech was a Celtic word meaning 'squint' – put together they show further evidence of the continuing process of acculturation. He defeated the O'Neill king of Tara, captured Dublin in 917 and took control of the other *longphort* settlements at Waterford, Wexford and Limerick. With Man in the middle of the Irish Sea as a bridgehead, this was one of several opportunities that fell to Viking leaders in the ninth and tenth centuries to unite the kingdom of Dublin with York in the north-east of England, which, as we shall shortly see, had been a Viking kingdom since 866. In the hands of an ambitious and capable ruler a kingdom bridging the whole of northern Britain like this would have been very difficult for the English to resist and might have led to their conquest a full century before this was achieved by Sven Forkbeard and his son Cnut. But these Viking kingdoms were not monarchies, their kings not military visionaries, and the attractions of assimilation proved greater. Sihtric's grandson Olaf married an O'Neill princess, was baptized in 943 and died in monkish old age on the island of Iona, which his forefathers had so often tried to destroy. The twelfth-century history known as the 'War of the Irish with the Foreigners' dramatized the Battle of Clontarf in 1014 and immortalized Brian Boru as a national, Christian and Irish 'king of kings', who finally triumphed over the barbaric and Heathen Vikings; but Brian's principal opponent in the battle was the king of Leinster, Brian himself is said to have been too old to fight in the battle and, in truth, the Vikings had ceased to pose a threat to Irish society and its Christian culture some fifty years earlier.

The Orkney earl, Sigurd the Stout, was among those who died fighting at Clontarf for the Leinster king. His son Thorfinn, later called the Mighty, was five years old at the time of his father's death and became the first Orkney earl to be raised a Christian. He continued the expansion of the earldom begun by his father and, after a successful career as a raider in the prime of his life, devoted himself in his later years to the conversion of a population still largely Heathen. After a pilgrimage to Rome where, the *Orkneyinga Saga* tells us, he received absolution from the pope for all his sins, he returned to his capital at Birsay and established a bishopric there.[54]

Too remote to have formed part of Orkney, or any other kingdom or earldom, the Faroes are nevertheless linked to the islands south of them in reflecting the cultural assimilation going on there. According to the collection of texts gathered as the *Færeyinga Saga*, the first settler bore another Celtic-Norse combination of names, Grímur Kamban, and probably came from Man, Ireland or the Hebrides.[55] The saga, anxious to glorify his name, credits the Norwegian King Olaf Tryggvason with bringing Christianity to the islands at the end of the tenth century, though it seems tolerably certain he did not.[56] Someone certainly did: finds from excavations carried out during the late 1980s near the town of Leirvík on Eysturoy included, besides bronze pins in a recognizably Irish-Scandinavian style used for fastening a man's cloak, two quite large wooden crosses made of larch that had probably arrived as driftwood from Siberia before being carved in a characteristically Irish ring-cross style.[57]

5

The Vikings in the
Carolingian Empire

Notker the Stammerer, one of Charlemagne's biographers, has left us in his 'Life' with a remarkable image of distressed greatness. Charlemagne arrives in an unnamed seaside town in Southern Gaul. As he sits eating his supper a fleet of pirates makes an attack on the harbour. At first there is confusion about their identity. Some take them to be Jewish merchants, others believe them to be traders from Africa or Britain. Charlemagne, however, from the build of the ships and their speed through the water, at once recognizes them as Northmen. 'Those ships are not loaded with goods' he tells his men, 'they are filled with savage enemies.' As the Vikings make their getaway after the lightning attack, the emperor's men take up the chase but are soon outsailed. Afterwards, writes Notker,

Charlemagne, who was a God-fearing, just and devout ruler, rose from the table and stood at a window facing east. For a long time the precious tears poured down his face. No one dared to ask him why. In the end he explained his lachrymose behaviour to his warlike leaders. 'My faithful servants,' said he, 'do you know why I wept so bitterly? I am not afraid that these ruffians will be able to do me any harm; but I am sick at heart to think that even in my lifetime they have dared to attack this coast, and I am horror-stricken when I foresee what evil they will do to my descendants and their subjects.[1]

The story is perhaps too good to be true and may only have been Notker's way of announcing the emperor's early perception of the dreadful havoc the Northmen would wreak on his legacy. Charlemagne will have been abetted in his pessimism by his close associate Alcuin, for whom the assault on Lindisfarne remained a catastrophic watershed in the history of civilization. Well before his death in 814

Charlemagne had plentiful experience of the new and troubling neighbour on his northern border following the subjugation of the Saxons and occupation of their territory in the 780s. The Danes were, in the judgement of the contemporary eastern Frankish *Annals of Fulda*, 'the most powerful people among the Northmen'.[2] Of the three Viking peoples it is they who, at all times, most resemble a coherent military power. As the references in the Irish annals to conflicts arising in the middle of the ninth century between the 'fair' and the 'dark' foreigners make clear, beyond the fact of a shared Heathendom (or more pertinently a shared non-Christianity) and a common language, Vikings from the various regions of Scandinavia were often rivals for territory and property. We know very little about the governmental and social structures of Norwegian society at the time, but of Danish society the comparative thoroughness of the Frankish annalists conveys the impression that towards the close of the eighth century it was ruled by a strong monarchy and extended over a stable region not unlike that of present-day Denmark, with the addition of that part of southern Sweden known as Skåne and the shore of the Vik in the vicinity of the Oslo fjord. Prior to the Carolingian expansion the Danes seem also to have claimed tributary rights over a number of other peoples in their region, including the Saxons and a tribe of Polabian Slavs or Wends known as the Obodrites. This in itself was an indication of local cultural superiority, for like most other Slav peoples the Obodrites were an egalitarian and clan-based society without tribal leaders which, in times of crisis, elected leaders at assemblies known as *veche* for the duration of the crisis only.[3] The comparatively late arrival of the Danes in Ireland may in part have been due to the fact that they were engaged elsewhere, in the first instance watchful and anxious of Charlemagne and his expansionist Christianity.

The *Royal Frankish Annals*, which chronicle events involving Frankish rulers from 741 to 829, record a number of diplomatic contacts between the Franks and the Danes as they struggled to keep track of the changing status quo. In 782, the year of the massacre at Verden, the Danish King Sigfrid, who was then sheltering his Saxon brother-in-law Widukind from the Franks, sent an emissary named Halptani (Halvdan) to Charlemagne for formal political discussions at which a number of other Saxon leaders were also present.[4] Sigfrid is noted as receiving an envoy from Charlemagne in 798 but then disappears from the record. In 799 the first Viking raid within Frankish territories was recorded, an attack on the monastery of Noirmoutier in the Vendée, in the Loire region of western France. It is likely the raiders were Norwegians who had taken the *vestrveg* from Ireland. In response Charlemagne ordered the building of a fleet specifically to counter the attacks of the Northmen. The ships were to be built and berthed 'near to the rivers which flow out of Gaul and Germany into the North Sea'. Ports and the mouths of all rivers large enough to give access to foreign ships were also reinforced.[5]

Sigfrid was succeeded by King Godfrid, who in the course of a short reign developed what often seems like a personal rivalry with Charlemagne. He makes his first dramatic appearance in the *Royal Frankish Annals* in 804, arriving in Schleswig on the border between Danish and Saxon territory in 804 with his fleet and his entire cavalry for an apparently straightforward exchange of envoys with the emperor. In 808 he attacked his wayward tributaries the Obodrites to punish them for allying with Charlemagne, and destroyed their trading settlement of Reric. Reric's traders were forcibly relocated within his own territory at Hedeby, a nascent trading settlement at the neck of the Jutland peninsula. The Franks reacted, and in the subsequent fighting Godfrid's relative Reginold was killed. Still fearing the potential threat from a military alliance between Saxons and Danes, or even a direct attempt to take Saxony by Godfrid, Charlemagne had all the Saxons living close to the Danish border transported into Francia.

Godfrid continued to make his presence felt in the region. Well aware that it was a provocation, at about this time he ordered the reinforcement on his southern border of the Danevirke, a massive rampart some 14 kilometres long that straddled the Jutland peninsula from the marches of West Jutland to the town of Schleswig. Raised some seventy years earlier as a protective measure against Obodrite and Saxon raids, and linked to the horseshoe-shaped defence surrounding Hedeby, its very size remains a witness to the organized nature of Danish society at this time.

According to Einhard, Godfrid was 'so puffed up with empty ambition that he planned to make himself master of the whole of

Germany. He had come to look upon Frisia and Saxony as provinces belonging to him; and he had already reduced the Obodrites, who were his neighbours, to a state of subservience and made them pay him tribute.'[6] Einhard even claims that his plans to march on the imperial capital at Aachen with a large army were at an advanced stage when, in 810, he was murdered by one of his own followers.

Godfrid's joint successors were the brothers Harald, known as Klak-Harald, and Reginfrid, who may initially have been regents for the late king's young son.[7] In 813 an army under these two made its way to the Norwegian Vestfold, 'an area in the extreme north-west of their kingdom whose princes and people refused to submit to them'.[8] It sounds as if the purpose of this expedition was to re-impose a tributary status that had been neglected. The Norwegian archaeologist Bjørn Myhre has advanced a theory that the ritual damage done to the grave-mounds in the great Heathen burial centre at Borre in Vestfold may have been carried out by these two kings on this occasion, to punish the local people and reassert Danish power.[9] The rebellion itself may have been another result of the general breakdown in regional stability caused by Charlemagne's war against the Saxons. A further result may have been the emergence, as a coastal power centre a few decades later, of Avaldsnes on Karmøy, the regional home of the first wave of Vikings who raided west across the North Sea in England and the islands of Scotland and Ireland.

It was unwise to be long away from home in such unstable times. When the brothers returned they faced a large army raised by the sons of the late King Godfrid and were easily driven from the land. Reginfrid was killed in 814 trying to regain the throne, leaving Harald as a diligent and persistent pretender. With the death of Charlemagne a few months later, in January 814, the stage was set for a chaotic century during which his empire slowly disappeared, lashing and plunging like some great leviathan as it sank beneath the waves, goaded towards extinction by the ceaseless jabbing and thrusting of those seaborne northern warriors whose manifestation in southern Gaul had so distressed him. The chaos was compounded by the fact that the Danish royal families too were, for much of the time, engaged in dynastic struggles of their own, in the course of which it becomes very difficult to keep track of a meaningful distinction between, on the one hand, violent activity that might have been part of a coherent 'foreign policy' decided upon by a legitimate monarch and his advisers and carried out by a 'national' army; and, on the other, those actions – often the work of the same kings – which were nothing more than privateering on the grand scale.

In his attempts to reclaim the Danish crown after the coup by the sons of King Godfrid, Harald began a long association with the Franks. The Obodrites, apparently once again under Frankish control, were ordered by Charlemagne's successor Louis the Pious to help him, and in 819 the sons of Godfrid – always a corporate identity in the annals – allowed him to join them on the throne. The unstable arrangement lasted only until 823, when the brothers once more drove Harald out. Again Harald applied to Louis for help.

Louis' response was to send Harald back to Denmark, accompanied by emissaries who were to investigate the nature of the dispute, 'as well as the condition of the whole kingdom of the Norsemen', and report back to him.[10] The sequence of events thereafter forms the first important narrative thread of Rimbert's *Vita Anskarii*, his 'Life' of St Anskar, the 'Apostle of the North' and the missionary most closely associated with early attempts to curb Viking violence by bringing their Scandinavian communities into the fold of Christian peoples. Encouraged by the successes of Ebbo of Reims, who had preached among the Danes 'and baptized many converts to the faith during the previous summer', Louis suggested to Harald that he convert to Christianity.[11] Such a move, he assured him, would lead to 'a more intimate friendship between them, and a Christian people would more readily come to his aid and to the aid of his friends if both peoples were worshippers of the same God'.[12] The offer of the political benefits of the adoption of Christianity was one that would be repeated many times by rulers in the Christian world who found themselves under attack by Vikings.

Like his father Charlemagne, Louis used the Church as an instrument of government. At a ceremony in Rome, on Christmas Day in 800, Charlemagne had been crowned first emperor of what would later be called the Holy Roman Empire. Contemporaries perceived this 'empire' as identical with western Christendom, though no such geographical entity existed. The symbolic significance of the ceremony was that Charlemagne became the pope's designated partner in the promotion of Christianity, and the protector of the Church; and that he shared the Church's vision of Christendom as a single community, ruled, under God, by a single spiritual ruler, with a single temporal ruler as his right hand. The arrangement has been called a dyarchy of pope and emperor.[13] The political implications of this were well understood in the Europe of the time, by Viking leaders in their Scandinavian homelands as well as by tribal leaders in territories to the east of the empire. In the course of the ninth and tenth centuries the dynasties of Great Moravia, Bohemia and Hungary all requested a missionary presence to help their applications to join what was, in effect, a primitive form of European cultural union, with Christianity as its common spiritual currency. In 821 the exiled Obodrite prince Slavomir submitted to baptism prior to embarking on a campaign to claim his crown, no doubt for the same reasons as Harald signalled his agreement to Louis' suggestion.[14]

Anxious not to be outmanoeuvred, the sons of Godfrid sent envoys to Louis in 825 requesting a peace agreement, and this was duly arranged in October. The following year envoys from the Danish kings attended the imperial assembly at Ingelheim to ratify the agreement. But now Harald, in the company of his wife, brother, 'and a large number of Danes', arrived at St Alban's in Mainz and on 24 June submitted to baptism.[15] The immediate political rewards for his conversion included a gift of the coastal county of Rüstringen in Frisia, between the rivers Ems and Aller, which was intended as a safe haven for him in times of trouble, and Louis' renewed promise of friendship and help to recover the throne.

Louis' political aim had been the pacification of his Danish neighbours under the rule of his Christian ally, Harald. If, as a pious man himself, he secretly hoped for genuine conversion and not merely the cultural accommodation of Christianization then he presently had good cause to doubt the likelihood. Having promised the emperor that they would 'obey him always and everywhere and in all matters', Harald's newly christened Danes found themselves adopted by the nobles of the royal palace, 'almost as if they had been children' as Notker writes, a line that recalls the strange enchantment worked by the pre-Lindisfarne pagans on the Northumbrian aristocrats at Athelstan's court. Each catechumen received a white robe from the emperor's wardrobe, and from his sponsors a full set of Frankish garments, with arms, costly robes and other adornments. This happened repeatedly, says Notker:

More and more came each year, not for the sake of Christ but for mundane advantages. They used to hurry over on Easter Eve to pay homage to the Emperor, more like faithful vassals than foreign envoys. On one occasion as many as fifty arrived. The Emperor asked them if they wished to be baptized. When they had confessed their sins, he ordered them to be sprinkled with holy water.

On one occasion when there were not enough linen garments to go round, Louis ordered some old shirts to be cut up and stitched together. Confronted with his, one old Dane regarded it suspiciously for some time before complaining to the emperor that he had gone through the procedure some twenty times now and always before been given a splendid white suit for his troubles. This was just an old sack. It made him feel like a pig-farmer, not a soldier. Having taken away his own clothes they'd left him with the choice of wearing this or else going about naked. As far as he was concerned they could keep their Christ, and their old rags too.[16]

Obviously some rudimentary notion of what it meant to be Christian would have to be conveyed if Christianization were to work as an effective political tool. Anskar was detailed to accompany Harald on his journey back to Denmark, to be his Christian conscience and help him bring the rest of the Danes to Christ. Extreme danger attached to the venture: the *Vita Anskarii* reports that Anskar and his companion Autbert had to make the journey without servants because none dared accompany them.[17] Louis provided the mission with writing cases and tents.

Treated by his Danish travelling companions with indifference or contempt at first, Anskar's status rose after the bishop of Cologne made him a present of a fine boat with its own comfortable sleeping quarters. It is not clear from Rimbert's account whether or not the party was actually allowed to enter Denmark. He writes that Harald was stopped at the Danish border, but goes on to describe two years spent by Anskar preaching among the Danes. If Harald did return to power it was a brief and conditional return and not the Christian wedge into Denmark that Louis had been hoping for.

At this point Klak-Harald drifts out of Rimbert's narrative and his later career is uncertain. The *Annals of St-Bertin* mention a certain 'Harald, who along with other Danish pirates had for some years been imposing sufferings on Frisia and other coastal regions of the Christians', and appear to identify him with Harald, a king without a territory, bound to a cycle of eternal raiding so that he could reward his men for their loyalty to him, so that they would follow him on his next raid, so that he would reward them for their loyalty.[18] If this identification is correct, then he is also the apostate leader whose Viking activities in the region around what are now the Netherlands proved so disruptive to Louis' son Lothar that he tried to buy him off with the gift of the province of Walcheren, in the mouth of the Scheldt estuary, a move that seemed to the annalist

an utterly detestable crime, that those who had brought evil on Christians should be given power over the lands and people of Christians, and over the very churches of Christ; that the persecutors of the Christian faith should be set up as lords over Christians and Christian folk have to serve men who worshipped demons.[19]

Saxo Grammaticus, in the *Gesta Danorum*, is more generous in his assessment. Only after describing what looks like a sincere but failed attempt on Klak-Harald's part to introduce Christianity to the Danes does he turn to condemning him as a 'notorious apostate'.[20] The *Annals of Fulda* carried a notice of his death on the Danish border in 852 at the hands of a Frankish border patrol, in which he is recalled as a 'person of doubtful loyalty and a potential traitor'.[21] In his pragmatic acceptance of baptism for political ends, Klak-Harald set an example that other leaders would follow for much of the Viking Age, to the endless frustration of their Christian godfathers.

The last decade of Louis the Pious' life brought him many dis-appointments, though he was in many ways the author of his own misfortunes. In 814, the year of his father's death, Louis had made a division of the imperial territory among his sons that favoured Lothar with Bavaria and Pepin with Aquitaine. Three years later he confirmed

Pepin in his possession of Aquitaine, gave Bavaria to another son, Louis, known as 'the German', and invited his eldest son Lothar to join him as co-emperor. His own father had been seventy years old and within months of his death before Louis had been similarly elevated; for Louis to have followed suit while his son was still only twenty-three was to prove a disastrously precipitate move. His anxious haste to secure the future of the empire was cruelly exposed when his second wife, Judith of Bavaria, bore him a son Charles, later 'the Bald', in 823. Under Judith's influence Louis revoked the agreement of 817 and in 829 brought the child into the equation of his inheritance by giving him Alemannia. The immensely complex civil wars known as 'the wars of the three brothers' ensued. Lothar rebelled, and with the support of his brothers by Louis' first wife, Irmengard, deposed his father. Louis was restored in 830 and attempted to mollify Lothar by giving him Italy in 831. In 832 he took Aquitaine from Pepin and gave it to young Charles, at which his older brothers revolted. Once more the emperor was deposed. Restored in 834, he made his peace with Pepin and Louis the German. Later that same year Lothar, who nursed the greatest grievance against his father, again rebelled. He stood alone this time, and his failure obliged him to retreat to Italy. Louis' gifts of more territory to Charles in 837–8 were grudgingly accepted by the older brothers. Pepin's death in 838 should have simplified matters but did not. Louis offered the three surviving sons a fourth partition in 840, dividing the empire between Lothar and Charles and leaving Louis the German with Bavaria. Dissatisfied, Louis rose against his father, but the challenge came to nothing. In an attempt to put an end to the chaos Louis summoned his sons to an assembly at Worms in July 840, but died before it could take place. At Verdun in 843 the brothers signed a treaty intended to bring order to his problematical legacy. Western Francia went to Charles, Eastern Francia to Louis the German, and a middle kingdom, Lotharingia, was created and named for Lothar. Western Francia may be identified roughly with the territory of present-day France, Louis' share with modern Germany, and Lothar's unnatural slice of territory, extending from the North Sea to Italy, with almost nothing at all. The arrangement did not put an end to the wars between the brothers.

As well as he was able, Louis had carried on the pursuit of his

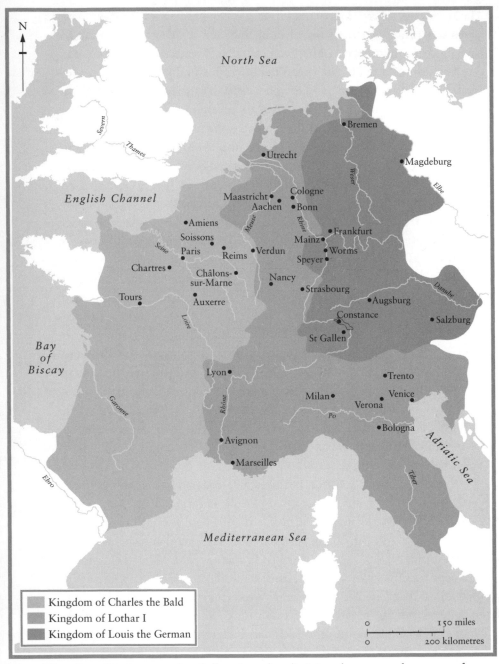

N

North Sea

English Channel

Bay
of
Biscay

Mediterranean Sea

Adriatic Sea

Bremen
Utrecht
Magdeburg
Maastricht
Cologne
Aachen
Bonn
Amiens
Frankfurt
Soissons
Mainz
Paris
Reims
Verdun
Worms
Chartres
Speyer
Châlons-
sur-Marne
Nancy
Tours
Auxerre
Strasbourg
Augsburg
Constance
Salzburg
St Gallen
Lyon
Trento
Milan
Venice
Verona
Avignon
Bologna
Marseilles

Severn
Thames
Seine
Meuse
Rhine
Weser
Elbe
Loire
Danube
Rhône
Po
Garonne
Ebro
Tiber

Kingdom of Charles the Bald
Kingdom of Lothar I
Kingdom of Louis the German

0   150 miles
0   200 kilometres

The Carolingian empire following the division between the sons of
Louis the Pious after 843.

father's goal of a Europe united under one, Christian culture. The creation of an episcopal see at Hamburg for the specific purpose of promoting missionary activity among the Scandinavians in the far north was, in this respect, his most significant achievement. In 829, with Anskar and Klak-Harald encamped on the Danish borders pending Harald's hoped-for return to power among the Danes, messengers had arrived at Aachen from the trading town of Birka in the Mälaren district of Sweden requesting that Christian missionaries be sent to instruct the local people.[22] Anskar was recalled and asked to undertake the mission. On the way his party was attacked by pirates and robbed of all their possessions, including a library of some forty books. Anskar continued on his journey and was well received at Birka by the local leader, King Bjørn.

Rimbert's near-contemporary account describes Anskar's mission to the Swedes as successful. He mentions in particular a man close to King Bjørn, a certain Herigar, who was baptized and presently built a church on his own property.[23] After two winters in Birka, Anskar returned to submit a report to the emperor. Louis thereupon 'began to enquire by what means he might establish a bishop's see in the north within the limits of his own empire', a place that might be used as a centre for the bishop appointed to make 'frequent journeys to the northern regions for the sake of preaching the gospel, and from which all these barbarous nations might easily and profitably' come to Christianity.[24] His advisers replied that his far-sighted father had already made plans for such a see. When Charlemagne

had subdued the whole of Saxony by the sword and had subjected it to the yoke of Christ, he divided it into dioceses, but did not commit to any bishop the furthest part of this province which lay beyond the river Elbe, but decided that it should be reserved in order that he might establish there an archiepiscopal see from which, with the Lord's help, the Christian faith might successively spread to the nations that lay beyond.[25]

In 831 the see of Hamburg was duly created, with Anskar as its first bishop. Already the time had passed when a Frankish emperor might have been able to impose Christianity on the Scandinavians by force, and the imperial decision to place the monastery of Turholt, in the presumed security of Flanders, at the disposal of Hamburg, 'inasmuch as this diocese [Hamburg] was situated in dangerous regions, and it was to be feared that it might come to an end in consequence of the savagery of the barbarians by which it was threatened', shows a recognition of the fact that a dark and dangerous future loomed:[26] Walafrid Strabo, the scholar who wrote the verse account of Blamac's martyrdom on Iona in 825, was a court favourite of Louis, just as Alcuin had been a favourite of his father, and the dreadful story of Blamac's death would have been familiar enough at Aachen.

For much of the period during which the Frankish empire suffered 'the wars of the three brothers', effective power among the Danes seems to have been in the hands of the astute King Horic. He was probably the last surviving of the 'sons of Godfrid', and held on to the crown more or less consistently from 814 until his death in 850. He turned out to be considerably more successful than Klak-Harald in juggling the double role of Viking and legitimate king.

A lull in Viking raiding after the 799 attack on the monastery at Noirmoutier was broken in 820 by thirteen Danish ships that attacked the coastal settlements of Flanders. Driven off, they had turned their attention to the mouth of the Seine, where they were once again repelled, with the loss of five of their men. From here they sailed up the coast of Aquitaine, successfully plundered the village of Bouin and returned home 'with immense booty'.[27] The Frisian trading town of Dorestad near Nijmegen, despite the protection of water, palisades and a fortress, was attacked and burnt in 834. So was Antwerp. When Dorestad was devastated for a third time two years later Horic sent envoys to the imperial assembly at Worms soliciting peace and friendship with the emperor. At the same time he formally complained about the murder near Cologne of a previous group of his envoys.

In 837 the exposed territory of Frisia was again attacked and the island of Walcheren plundered, the Vikings appearing 'with their usual surprise'. Like his father Godfrid before him, Horic was unwilling to abandon the power exercised by Danes in the region before the advent of Charlemagne and in 838 he sent emissaries to Louis the Pious requesting recognition for his overlordship of the Obodrites and the

Wilzes.[28] His presumption seemed to Louis so inappropriate that the emperor simply ignored it. Yet the same emissaries also brought the emperor news that as a sign of King Horic's friendship and good will he had captured and killed most of the pirates who had lately been troubling Louis' territory. Horic's gesture asked Louis to make a distinction between the activities of a legitimate royal house, and the embarrassing and entirely private doings of a large and unruly group of his subjects.

In 841, with the fortifications built by Charlemagne at the turn of the century to protect his rivers against just such raiding probably destroyed long before by his sons' and grandsons' warring, a fleet led by a Norwegian named Asgeir sailed up the Seine and captured and burnt Rouen. Asgeir's army plundered its way up the Seine and burnt the wealthy monastery at Jumièges. Nearby Fontenelle was also attacked, sixty-eight monks taken prisoner and ransomed. Nantes was hit in 843 by a fleet of sixty-seven Norwegian Viking ships which probably set out from a *longphort* base in Ireland. The bishop of Nantes was among those killed, in one account while taking Mass. Others were captured to be sold abroad as slaves. From their experiences in Ireland the Vikings had learnt that Church festivals were among the most profitable times to attack, and Nantes was terrorized in late June, on the feast day of St John the Baptist. Nearby Noirmoutier – Francia's Iona – had been attacked so often that in 830 the emperor gave his permission for it to be fortified. For a while the monks abandoned the island in the summer and returned in the winter when the danger of attack was less. In 836 the monks were forced to abandon the monastery altogether, taking with them the relics of the founder, St Philibert, and retreating further inland. Some thirty years later, the monk Ermentarius described their fear of the wilful blasphemy of the Vikings:

But in truth this is what they feared most: that the faithless men would dig up the grave of the blessed Philibert and scatter whatever they found in it hither and yon, or rather throw it into the sea. This was known to have happened in the region of Brittany to the remains of certain holy men; this we were told by those who had seen it and had fled before the most oppressive rule of these men.[29]

The Nantes Vikings, meanwhile, made camp on the island and used it as a base from which to terrorize the regions of the Loire and Aquitaine.

In late March of 845 a fleet of 120 ships appeared in the Seine, 'laying waste everything on either side and meeting not the least bit of opposition', and presently threatening Paris.[30] *The Annals of St-Bertin* name its leader as Reginfred, a figure sometimes identified with the Danish chieftain, Ragnar Lodbrok, meaning 'Hairy-Breeches', whose role as a Viking Age legend we shall examine in more detail later. The army of Charles the Bald fled before this force and in desperation Charles offered them 7,000 pounds of silver to leave. This is the first recorded example of the danegeld payment, a money-with-menaces tactic that the Vikings would later employ with great success in England. In their own way these Vikings kept their word, heading 'back down the Seine to the open sea', raiding, looting and burning as they went. As they were heading for home, their ships laden with booty, the annalist recorded a divine retribution that struck them in the form of a severe illness, very likely dysentery.

In the same year, King Horic sent an enormous fleet of ships up the Elbe to attack the eastern Frankish territories of Louis the German. This sounds like a 'legitimate' royal enterprise, one king waging war on another; but once the fleet was repulsed the soldiers donned Viking caps and turned their fury on Hamburg. Again there was the familiar slaughter of monks, the burning of churches and monasteries, and the inescapable sense of *overkill* that characterized Viking violence against manifestations of institutional Christian culture. Anskar was in Hamburg at the time and with characteristically obstinate courage tried to persuade people to resist until reinforcements arrived. But perceiving the futility of it, he gathered what relics he could and fled. Alas for the monks of Hamburg, at the division agreed between the three brothers at Verdun in 843 the see had lost possession of their 'safe haven' monastery at Turholt and the monks were left with nowhere to go. Eventually a benefactress gave them a property about fifteen miles from Hamburg, and it was from here that Anskar gradually began the work of reviving the community. Horic, meanwhile, after the failed raid up the Elbe, turned himself back into a legitimate king again. He sent envoys to Louis the German with an offer to release all the captives taken by the invaders of 845, and promised he would try to recover the stolen treasure and return it to its rightful owners.

Some revision of Charlemagne's original plan would have to be made if the campaign to Christianize the north were to continue. The devastations of 845 made it clear that the Hamburg site was simply too vulnerable. The solution approved by Anskar's new patron, Louis the German, was to appoint him to the vacant see of the more easily defensible Bremen. After some bureaucratic manoeuvrings, Bremen was presently joined to Hamburg in 847–8 to create the archbishopric of Hamburg-Bremen, though papal ratification of the joint see was not forthcoming until 864. Anskar was its first archbishop; Rimbert, his biographer, was his successor.

Birka, the island town where Anskar seemed to have given Christianity a first frail foothold among the northern Heathens, was for much of the Viking era one of the most important trading centres in northern Europe. Situated in the Mälaren region of south-central Sweden between the territories of the Goths and the Svear, it was founded on royal initiative sometime in the middle of the eighth century and subsequently patterned after the trading centres of the Carolingian empire. One theory is that it came into being after the Islamic expansion of the seventh century had disrupted traditional trade routes between east and west in the south via the Mediterranean. From Birka it was only five days' sailing across the Baltic to Russia and the great southbound rivers that gave access to markets all the way down to Constantinople. Adam of Bremen tells us that it was also only a five-day journey by sea from Hedeby, the market town created by Godfrid from the remnants of Reric.

Birka's location on the island of Björkö made it an attractively safe harbour, but its developing importance and wealth rapidly made it a natural target for pirates. A hill-fort and a semi-circular rampart 350 metres long and 3 metres wide was built, crowned by a wooden walkway and turrets that gave a commanding view of the surrounding waters. Similar semi-circular ramparts have also been found at Hedeby, Århus in Denmark, and Ipswich in England. Adam tells us that among its other defences was an enormous underwater stone wall, and archaeologists have found the remains of a barrier of wooden stakes anchored in the clay bed of the lake that forced ships into a narrow approach lane and made it hard to approach the town unseen. Excavations undertaken in the 1930s of the area north-west of the hill-fort and the finds of very large numbers of arrow- and spearheads, chain mail and shield bosses, as well as a section of lamellar armour, thin, flat and layered, confirm that this was a vibrant centre that required the protection of a sizeable military presence. A population of somewhere between 700 and 1,000 was concentrated in the harbour area, living and working in small, square timber-framed buildings with wattle-and-daub walls, and wooden, thatched or turf roofs, two to a plot on each side of a system of plank-laid tracks. The so-called Warriors' Hall built on the upper terrace of the garrison area was huge by comparison, 19 metres long and 9.5 metres wide, with two entrances and double-vaulted walls which provided good insulation. This hall-house was divided into two tall rooms with a fireplace in each. Locks, keys and chest fittings, spearheads and shield bosses were found along the walls. In the western part of what was almost certainly the town's main hall, at which the king would be received when visiting, were found, among other things, a dragon's head made of bronze, slivers of glass from goblets and two sword handles. Some forty comb-cases were also found for the combs that warriors would wear suspended from their richly decorated belts.[31]

The garrison warriors and probably many of the craftsmen were resident in Birka all year round. Others used the town only during the summer trading months. Raw materials such as iron, furs and horn were worked by craftsmen for local use as well as for export, jewellers had workshops there, as did smiths who made swords for export to the east. Much of the huge quantity of silver from the Islamic world was brought by merchants into the west via Birka. The town was also the centre for a slave-trade that was probably the most lucrative Viking Age business of all. When we reflect that the later African slave-traders made a profit of 600 per cent on the purchase price of slaves in Africa, and that the Vikings did not even buy their slaves but simply captured them, the proceeds of the trade must have been enormous. The islands of Britain were one source, the Slavic regions of eastern and eastern-central Europe another. Mainly the prey of the eastern-orientated Vikings of Sweden, these populations were captured for sale and dispersal on such a scale that their ethnicity became synonymous with their fate and the word 'slave' passed into the English language as the generic term. Rimbert writes of the joy of those Christians among the Birka slaves when Anskar's arrival there in 829 gave them chance to celebrate again the proper rites of their religion. Anskar may even have bought their freedom for them, something Rimbert tells us he did whenever he was able.

The wealth attainable by the town's most successful inhabitants is obliquely reflected in finds from some of the 3,000 or so graves located on the site. The richest of them, dated to the early years of the ninth century, was the last resting place of an aristocratic woman whose grave-gifts included gold- and silver-plated bead necklaces, silver clasps in the shape of horse heads, bowls, beakers and a glass funnel, and a glass smoother and whalebone plaque for her to iron her clothes with. A key opened a small chest that contained an exquisitely decorated comb.[32] A literary reflection of the town's wealth is found in a story of uncertain date that Rimbert tells in the *Vita Anskarii* about a deposed Birka king named Anund, who had taken refuge among the Danes. Anund made a deal with a local band of Vikings that he would leave Birka and all its merchants and silver open to them, if they would place their ships at his disposal and help him regain power. The town would be more or less undefended, he said, and at very little personal risk they would become very rich indeed. A fleet of thirty-two ships then descended on Birka, forcing the inhabitants to flee to the safety of nearby Sigtuna. From here they sent a message to Anund, asking his price to return Birka to them. Anund's demand of 100 pounds of silver was met, and in turn he agreed to keep his part of the bargain. He thus crossed the line again and was a king once more, not a Viking. His Danish allies were furious at this sudden access of decency. They scorned the ransom he had demanded, claiming that 'each individual merchant in the place had more than had been offered to them'. They threatened to pillage and burn Birka to the ground, and then do the same to Sigtuna. Anund played his double role well. Persuading the Vikings that there was some doubt about their chance of success he suggested they cast lots to see the will of the gods. The results were interpreted, the attack was doomed to fail, and the Vikings departed. So that their journey would not have been entirely in vain they sacked a town on the Slav border as they made their way back to Danish territory. Anund afterwards returned the ransom money to the Birka merchants.[33]

Birka lay not far from the temple centre of Uppsala, where Heathen culture was at its strongest, and it is no surprise that, at about the same time as Anskar and the other Hamburg exiles were wandering with their relics in search of a new home, the inhabitants of Birka should have turned against Gautbert, the bishop he had left behind to guide them in the ways of the new faith. They killed his chaplain Nithard and several others with him, robbed the bishop and drove him out of the country 'with insults and abuse'. On this point Rimbert is insistent: 'This was not done by command of the king, but was brought about by a plot devised by the people.'[34] The reaction left the Church without a presence in Birka for some seven years, until 851. Rimbert learnt later of the hostility endured by the converted Herigar. During a general discussion about religion at an Assembly meeting, defenders of the old faith had reproached him for having accepted, alone, a creed that seemed to the rest of them worthless. His greatest crime was cultural treason, that in choosing Christianity he had 'separated himself from them all'.[35]

All the sweeter, then, for Anskar to have finally baptized a reigning Danish king. In a rare moment of unity Lothar, Louis and Charles had sent envoys to Horic in 847 ordering him to stop his people from attacking Christians and threatening him with war should he fail to do so.[36] But Adam of Bremen tells us that the Danish Vikings paid what amounted to a licence fee to their king for the right to raid, and the profession of seaborne violence was by now so profitable that control of it was no longer in Horic's hands. Pragmatist and survivor that he was, he submitted instead to baptism by Anskar as the missionary was passing through his territories on the way back to Birka. Horic later built a church in Schleswig and permitted the practice of Christianity throughout his territory, without making it compulsory.[37]

With Horic's conversion, the Danish dynastic conflict that flared up again not long afterwards acquired, if only incidentally, a religious dimension when it pitted him against his Heathen nephew, Guttorm. Both were killed in circumstances which are unclear and the throne passed to another Horic, known as the Younger. This youth at once began to persecute those who had converted to Christianity under the liberal regime of his predecessor, driving out the priests and closing down the churches.[38] The charismatic Anskar travelled to see him, struck up an immediate rapport with him and presently converted him. Rimbert credits Horic the Younger with the building of a church at Ribe, the second in Denmark after the Schleswig church.

Anskar died of natural causes in Bremen in 865 and was canonized a few years later. It was, Rimbert tells us, a matter of regret to him that he had not died the death of a martyr. But, as the record of his fearless engagement shows, the failure was no fault of his. The archaeological record makes no unequivocal statement about the success of his Birka mission. Mere burial and the fact of the east-facing orientation of the buried individual are no longer regarded as an infallible indication that he or she was a Christian, buried thus for a first sign from the east of the Second Coming. Indeed, as the Oseberg and Gokstad burials show, inhumation was practised as often as cremation by Heathen Vikings. In general it would seem that the syncretism characteristic of most cosmopolitan centres typified the funerary practice of the inhabitants of Birka. A richly furnished double burial containing the familiar weapons, jewellery, tools, food and bowls, as well as a single cross pendant and a single Thor's hammer pendant, is one example.[39] The fact that Rimbert singles out two Birka women, Frideborg and Katla, as being notably good Christians may hint that Christianity was especially attractive to Heathen women. The possibility is reinforced when we consider that all ten cross pendants found in Birka, including the one in the double grave, were located in graves in which women had been buried.

It might seem as though Christianity had made little headway in Scandinavia in the ninth century, despite the efforts of Anskar, Ebbo, Gautbert, Herigar and the other priests, missionaries and converts who preached among the Danes and Swedes.[40] But, just as the early, sporadic Viking raids prepared parts of the British isles and northern France for future colonization, so might Anskar's missionary activity have prepared the ground in the Scandinavian homelands for a coming sea-change in religious belief.

*

When, as part of the baptism deal of 826, Louis the Pious handed territory over to Klak-Harald he set a volatile and unpredictable precedent for his sons. Lothar had employed the tactic again in 841 to buy off (probably) the same Harald with Walcheren, though the annalist calls that a gift 'to secure the services of Harald'. Rorik, a nephew of Harald, inherited the gift and the relationship. In 850 he broke it off and with an enormous number of ships attacked Frisia and the Betuwe region of what is now the Netherlands, between the Waal and the Rhine. Unable to deal effectively with him, Lothar made him a gift of lands including Dorestad, in effect washing his hands of it. Like other trading towns, it had become a favourite target for Viking raiders.

Charles the Bald had made payments to Reginfred to buy off a force besieging Paris in 845 and, as we have seen, other payments in 857 or 858 to a Viking named Bjørn who had fortified himself on the island of Oissel and was using it as a base for raiding in the surrounding countryside.[41] Bjørn's army seems not to have honoured its side of the bargain on this occasion, for in 861 Charles had to pay another 5,000 pounds of silver to a fleet of Vikings, led by Weland, to dislodge them. This they did; but the success of the tactic was only apparent, for the displaced Oissel army then attacked Meaux in an attempt to win back what they had lost. A large part of one or both of these armies then became directly involved in Charles's dispute with King Salomon of Brittany over the possession of Anjou. Salomon was already using an army of Viking mercenaries, and Robert the Strong, the Frankish commander in Neustria, now offered an army of Seine Vikings 6,000 pounds of silver to join him in fighting against them. The upshot was that, by the Treaty of Entrammes in 863, Charles the Bald recognized Anjou as part of Brittany. He resorted to payments again in 866 and 877, on both occasions because his army proved incapable of matching the Viking armies on the Seine.

A thread that runs through most of the ninth century links some of these Frankish concessions of money, and sometimes land, to the ambition originally attributed by a mocking Einhard to Godfrid, king of the Danes, that he wished to challenge the Carolingian empire itself. Louis the Pious' support for Klak-Harald, and the intermittent acceptance of his claims by the sons of Godfrid to be joint ruler of the

Danes, suggest there was a genuine basis to his claim. Information in the sources about Danish dynasties is sparse from the death of Godfrid until the rule of Gorm the Old over 100 years later. We know that Klak-Harald had a son whom he named Godfrid. If he was following a dynastic naming practice in this, it may imply that the Godfrid whom he succeeded in 811 was his father, so that he was an older and perhaps illegitimate half-brother of the 'sons of Godfrid' and that this was the basis of his claim. His son, the second Godfrid, was paid by Charles the Bald in 853 to defect from an alliance with Lothar. Afterwards he raided in Frisia in the area around the Scheldt, and finally threatened the lands around the Seine. An entry in the *Annals of Fulda* says that Charles also gave him 'land to live on'.[42] He in turn had a son, also named Godfrid, who became heavily involved in the Carolingian power struggle in the 880s that followed the death in 882 of Louis III, a grandson of Charles the Bald and king of the western Franks, and the crowning of Charles the Fat, brother of a grandson of Charles the Bald, as emperor. In the notably chaotic year of 882 a Frankish army was defeated by a force under this third Godfrid. The *Annals of Fulda* tell us that the Vikings followed after the retreating Franks 'and burnt with fire all that they had previously left intact, as far as the castle of Koblenz, where the Moselle enters the Rhine'.[43] They attacked Trier, drove off or killed the inhabitants, and on 5 April burnt it to the ground. They took control of the monasteries nearby, and also the monasteries at Liège, Prüm and Inden. The greatest insult came when they took 'even the palace at Aachen and all the monasteries of the neighbouring dioceses', most of which they burnt.[44] The end of the Carolingian dynasty could not be far away when Charlemagne's capital, the seat of power in what had once been an unassailable empire, could not be protected against the invaders. Charles the Fat appeared willing to head a major attempt to get rid of the menace before it was too late. An army of Franks, Bavarians, Alemans, Thuringians and Saxons, large enough 'to be feared by any enemy, if it had a suitable leader and one it agreed on', marched on the Vikings' fortification of Asselt.[45] Things seemed to be going the way of this besieging force when, to the annalist's disgust, Charles was persuaded to offer terms to Godfrid – 'the emperor received him as if he were a friend and made peace with him; and hostages were exchanged'. To show their sincerity the Vikings gave what was obviously a familiar signal and 'hoisted a shield on high after their fashion and threw open the doors of their fortress'. Curious, probably hoping to do some trading, Charles's soldiers entered the camp, at which the Vikings 'reverted to their usual treacherousness', lowered the shield, closed the gates and killed or captured the trapped soldiers. Charles's position may have been weaker than the annalist knew. Instead of avenging the slaughter the emperor then 'raised the aforementioned Godfrid from the baptismal font, and made the man who before had been the greatest enemy and traitor to his kingdom into a co-ruler over it'. Godfrid was given the territories and benefices previously handed over to Klak-Harald and his brother Rorik by Louis the Pious. Using money obtained from Church funds Charles also paid his army a large sum of money. To complete their humiliation, the Franks had to look on as the Vikings loaded their ships with booty and hundreds of captives for sale as slaves. Charles's desperation, the sheer military power of this Viking force, and Godfrid's high ambition are all reflected in a marriage agreement that formed part of the settlement in which Godfrid was given Gisela, a daughter of Lothar II, king of Lotharingia. But in what looks like a last attempt to realize in full the dreams of power attributed to the first in this line of ambitious Godfrids he threw it all away in 885, renounced his faith and set off up the Rhine at the head of a great army on a campaign of major conquest. He too, however, like that first Godfrid, was murdered before he had made a real start on his campaign.

It seems obvious now that policies of appeasement and alliance with individual Viking leaders only encouraged them to push harder. The tactics employed by Louis the Pious, Lothar, Charles the Bald and Charles the Fat established clear precedents for the gift of lands around Rouen and the lower Seine made to the Viking leader Rollo in about 911, which eventually led to the creation of the duchy of Normandy. Even so, it is hard not to sympathize with them, in particular with the two Charleses who made the most active use of the policy, or to see what alternatives they had. From about 840 onwards Paris was under more or less constant threat from Viking armies of a size that dismayed Frankish observers into what may sometimes have been exaggeration but what must always have been, on any account, terrifying manifestations. The monk Abbo de St Germain, in his epic Latin verse *De bellis Parisiacae*, written in the early 890s, gives us a vivid literary reflection of what the Parisians were up against, trebuchets or 'engines of war' and all. It also shows how much the western Franks needed a hero and how, with the great siege of Paris in 885, they got one in Count Odo. Prior to the attack, writes Abbo, 700 sailing ships and an undisclosed number of smaller ships packed the Seine for a distance of more than two leagues, 'so that one might ask in astonishment in what cavern the river had been swallowed up, since it was not to be seen'.[46] The engagement that followed was regarded by contemporaries as crucial. In his letter to Charles the Fat, Archbishop Fulk of Reims wrote of Paris as the 'head and key' of the western Frankish kingdoms of Neustria and Burgundy. If it fell to the Danish invaders, he predicted, it would spell the end of France.[47] The Danes, under the command of Sigfrid, arrived on 25 November and made their demands for tribute. According to Dudo of St Quentin, Rollo, the founder of the duchy of Normandy, was another of the leaders, though most historians doubt this. The demand was rejected. After a scene-setting prelude, Abbo's account of what followed places us memorably at the very heart of a Viking Age battle:

The second day after the fleet of the Northmen arrived under the walls of the city, Sigfrid, who was then king only in name but who was in command of the expedition, came to the dwelling of the illustrious bishop. He bowed his head and said: 'Gauzelin, have compassion on yourself and on your flock. We beseech you to listen to us, in order that you may escape death. Allow us only the freedom of the city. We will do no harm and we will see to it that whatever belongs either to you or to Odo shall be strictly respected.' Count Odo, who later became king, was then the defender of the city. The bishop replied to Sigfrid, 'Paris has been entrusted to us by the Emperor Charles, who, after God, king and lord of the powerful, rules over almost all the world. He has put it in our care, not at all that the kingdom may be ruined by our misconduct, but that he may keep it and be assured of its peace. If, like us, you had been given the duty of defending these walls, and if you should have done that which you ask us to do, what treatment do you think you would deserve?' Sigfrid replied. 'I should deserve that my head be cut off and thrown to the dogs. Nevertheless, if you do not listen to my demand, on the morrow our war machines will destroy you with poisoned arrows. You will be the prey of famine and of pestilence and these evils will renew themselves perpetually every year.' So saying, he departed and gathered together his comrades.

In the morning the Northmen, boarding their ships, approached the tower and attacked it. They shook it with their engines and stormed it with arrows. The city resounded with clamour, the people were aroused, the bridges trembled. All came together to defend the tower. There Odo, his brother Robert, and the Count Ragenar distinguished themselves for bravery; likewise the courageous Abbot Ebolus, the nephew of the bishop. A keen arrow wounded the prelate, while at his side the young warrior Frederick was struck by a sword. Frederick died, but the old man, thanks to God, survived. There perished many Franks; after receiving wounds they were lavish of life. At last the enemy withdrew, carrying off their dead. The evening came. The tower had been sorely tried, but its foundations were still solid, as were also the narrow bays which surmounted them. The people spent the night repairing it with boards. By the next day, on the old citadel had been erected a new tower of wood, a half higher than the former one. At sunrise the Danes caught their first glimpse of it. Once more the latter engaged with the Christians in violent combat. On every side arrows sped and blood flowed. With the arrows mingled the stones hurled by slings and war-machines; the air was filled with them. The tower which had been built during the night groaned under the strokes of the darts, the city shook with the struggle, the people ran hither and thither, the bells jangled. The warriors rushed together to defend the tottering tower and to repel the fierce assault. Among these warriors two, a count and an abbot, surpassed all the rest in courage. The former was the redoubtable Odo who never experienced defeat and who continually revived the spirits of the worn-out defenders. He ran along the ramparts and hurled back the enemy. On those who were secreting themselves so as to undermine the tower he poured oil, wax, and pitch, which, being mixed and heated, burned the Danes and tore off their scalps. Some of them died; others threw themselves into the river to escape the awful substance . . .

Meanwhile Paris was suffering not only from the sword outside but also from a pestilence within which brought death to many noble men. Within the walls there was not ground in which to bury the dead . . . Odo, the future king, was sent to Charles, emperor of the Franks, to implore help for the stricken city. One day Odo suddenly appeared in splendour in the midst of three bands of warriors. The sun made his armour glisten and greeted him before it illuminated the country around. The Parisians saw their beloved chief at a distance, but the enemy, hoping to prevent his gaining entrance to the tower, crossed the Seine and took up their position on the bank. Nevertheless Odo, his horse at a gallop, got past the Northmen and reached the tower, whose gates Ebolus opened to him. The enemy pursued fiercely the comrades of the count who were trying to keep up with him and get refuge in the tower.[48]

The siege went on for about eight months. By the time it ended Sigfrid had already accepted a paltry ransom in silver and led his men away. Twice Odo had managed to slip through the Viking lines and urge Charles the Fat to come to the rescue of the Parisians. In the summer the remaining Vikings, weary of the wait, their morale ebbing, made another desperate attempt to breach the walls. When it failed, still more of them gave up, dispersed and set about looting the surrounding countryside. Charles arrived in October with the imperial army and surrounded the remaining force. The stand-off lasted until the spring of the next year, when Charles's offer of 700 pounds of silver was accepted. Deposed in 887 and dead in 888, Charles was replaced as king of the western Franks by the heroic Odo and for the first time the crown passed out of the hands of the Carolingian dynasty. Over the next century it would pass back and forth between the Robertians, named for Odo's father Robert the Strong, and the Carolingians, but with the accession of the Robertian Hugh Capet in 987 the great dynasty finally and permanently lost its hold on power. The Vikings did not cause this break-up of Charlemagne's empire and the demise of his dynasty. Responsibility for that lay squarely on the ceaseless disagreements between Louis' sons, 'the three brothers', but Viking military activity made these disagreements hard to resolve, and the presence, throughout the long crisis, of mercenary groups of skilled warriors, prepared to fight alongside whoever made them the best offer, was a temptation the brothers too often failed to resist.

6

Across the Baltic

An entry in the *Annals of St-Bertin* tells us that, on 18 May 839, a group of envoys from the Byzantine Emperor Theophilus arrived at Ingelheim and presented themselves at the court of Louis the Pious. Their purpose was to confirm a treaty of 'peace and perpetual friendship and love' between the two emperors. Attached to their party were a number of men who described themselves as belonging to a group or tribe that called itself 'Rhos' or Rus. They presented a message of friendship from their own leader and a letter from Theophilus requesting that Louis give them safe conduct through his territories on their homeward journey north. The letter explained that the reason these men were taking such a roundabout route was that on their outward journey to Constantinople they had encountered a number of dangerous and threatening tribes whom they wanted to avoid on the way back.

Louis distrusted these Rus. He suspected them of spying. On closer investigation, the annalist tells us, the emperor learnt 'that they belonged to the people of the Swedes'. Since Anskar's first mission to Birka in 829, the Franks had learnt enough about travelling Swedes to distrust them, and to associate them with the attacks on their territories by other northern pirates. With these in mind, Louis may well have found their claim to be seeking protection from 'primitive tribes that were very fierce and savage' an ingenuous one. In his reply to Theophilus he said that he would detain the men at his pleasure, pending a further investigation of them. Should this prove satisfactory he would give them the help requested. Should they fail to pass his tests he would send them back to Theophilus for the emperor to deal with as he saw fit. Disappointingly the story ends there and we learn nothing more about the fate of these travellers. A particular frustration is that we do not know whether they were making their way back to Birka and Sweden, or whether their goal was a settlement already established on the far side of the Baltic, possibly at Gorodische at the northern end of Lake Ilmen.[1]

This is the first reference in the written sources to that group of Vikings from the eastern side of the Scandinavian peninsula who crossed the Baltic in search of wealth, trading opportunities and new lands to settle. Several explanations have been advanced for the name by which they became known, the Rus. One is that their tribal home was Roslagen, an old name for the coastal stretch north of Stockholm.[2] Another relates it to *ruotsi*, a name by which Finns refer to present-day Sweden and which, in former times, meant 'men who row'. The early history of the Rus is shrouded in mystery, for the tribes they encountered in these regions were as little literate as themselves, and the scholars and historians of the Islamic caliphate and of the Byzantine empire met them too infrequently to provide a coherent record of their provenance and their doings. But from the material in Snorri Sturluson's *Ynglingasaga* it is clear there was a long tradition among Scandinavian kings of piracy and land-taking across the Baltic dating back to a time long before the appearance of the Rus at Louis' court in 839. Snorri summarizes Sweden's legendary past as a series of power struggles that usually ended with the flight of the defeated candidate. Some of these dispossessed or landless leaders went west into Norway and became kings there. Others became the kind of hybrid he calls 'sea-kings'. 'At that time,' he writes, 'kings, both Danes and Norsemen, were harrying in Sweden. There were many sea-kings, who had great armies but had no land.' One he names was Salve, son of a king from the Naumdal district of Norway, who began his career harrying in the Baltic before an attack on Sigtuna won him the kingship of the Swedes on land.[3] The enterprise of such leaders often led them east, to try their luck on the far side of the Baltic. The long and partly legendary succession of the Yngling kings was finally ended by Ivar the Far-Travelled, whose territories, according to Snorri, included all of Sweden and Denmark as well as parts of Saxony and the Baltic provinces. Snorri's belief that the Caucasus was the ancestral home of the Swedes seems to have derived, in part at least, from stories that connected certain of these early and legendary kings with the region, to which he afterwards added the homophonic 'proof' of *Aesir* and *Asia*. He tells us of a Swedish king named Svegdir who crossed the Baltic on a sort of pilgrimage in search of 'the Godheims and Odin the Old', the home of the gods and Odin.[4] He stayed away five years and eventually reached 'the land of the Turks and Sweden the Great, and found there many kinsmen'. Tjodolf of Hvin described in verse the result of his search. Very drunk and on his way to bed one evening, he saw a dwarf sitting under a large stone. The dwarf lured him inside with a promise that he would meet Odin. Svegdir accepted and was never seen again.

The site of Svegdir's supposed disappearance was a town in Estland called Stein, and this strip of Baltic coastline between Estland on the Gulf of Finland and the territory of the Couronians bounded in the west by the river Niemen became, for obvious geographical reasons, the first focus of interest for Swedes travelling east. A series of excavations, begun in 1929 by the Swedish archaeologist Birger Nerman near the Latvian city of Grobin, some 15 kilometres inland from the coast, showed that a Scandinavian colony had existed in the Couronian region of the Aland river for some 200 years, from about 650. Nerman associated this colony with the expulsion of one-third of the inhabitants of Gotland, as a result of the famine described in the *Gutasaga*. Three burial grounds in particular show signs of Scandinavian burial customs. Many of the graves in level ground were those of women, whom their belt-buckles and so-called disc-on-bow brooches identified as natives of Gotland. Women in such numbers are unlikely to have crossed the sea alone, and it seems probable they were members of a community which had settled in the area. The grave-mounds housed predominantly men, very often accompanied by typically Scandinavian weaponry. In one grave a picture-stone depicting two duck-like birds was found. These picture-stones were unique to Gotland, and evolutions in their shapes and motifs over the centuries date this Grobin stone to the sixth or seventh century. The importing of picture-stones was not unheard of; one that has since been lost was recorded in the churchyard at Norrsunda, Uppland, in 1632. Two others turned up on the island of Öland.[5]

Saxo Grammaticus, in the *Gesta Danorum*, describes Viking raids across the Baltic in about 840 and 850 and gives the names of the leaders as Ragnar Lodbrok and Hasting. Hasting is another, like Ragnar, who looms large in the treacherous marches that divide legend from credible fact in Viking Age history.[6] His activities may lie behind a series of events described by Rimbert in the *Vita Anskarii*, in which he may also be referring to the Grobin colony. According to Rimbert, people inhabiting the Courland regions of Latvia rebelled after a long period as tributaries of Swedish rulers. In about 854 a fleet of Danes – conceivably led by Hasting – attempted to reimpose the tribute on their own behalf but was heavily defeated and suffered the ignominy of having its own ships plundered. The Swedes then raised an army to win back the former colony, in the process destroying an army of 7,000 men and devastating the trading centre at a place Rimbert calls 'Seeburg', usually identified as Grobin.[7] From Seeburg a march of five days brought them to the gates of a second Courland city at Apulia which they besieged for eight days, finally forcing from its inhabitants a large payment in silver and a resumption of the former tributary status.

By the early years of the ninth century female graves from the Grobin settlement associated with Gotland become scarce and later graves are those of seafaring Scandinavian males.[8] The change may directly reflect the displacing of the ethnic Scandinavian settler by the transient Viking, whose interest lay in gaining access to the trading markets in the south, at Constantinople, which the Vikings called 'Miklagård' – the great city – and along the Volga. The trade entailed long and hazardous journeys and the best chance of survival lay in travelling in company with other men.

At first glance there would seem to have been little in the region to excite the interest of such a trader and pirate. There were no rich Christian monasteries and churches, no towns to raid. The terrain was marshy and densely wooded. In the north it was occupied as far as Lake Ilmen by Slavs who had been slowly making their way north-east from the Carpathian area. The vast and semi-arid zone of the steppes swarmed with nomadic tribes. But three large rivers, the Western Dvina, the Dneiper, and the Volga, rose in this region of the central Russian plateau, and their relative proximity made it possible to move between river basins. They formed the main arteries of a complex system of tributaries, lakes and smaller rivers connected by portages rarely more than 20 kilometres in length that created two long-distance trade routes connecting the Baltic with the Black and the Caspian Seas, the Baltic–Dneiper and Baltic–Volga routes. Together they gave waterborne access to a new world of markets in the south, among the Christians of Constantinople and the Muslims of the expanding Arab world.

The initial stages of the route led the sailors first into the Gulf of Finland, up the stub of the river Neva and then along the southern shores of Lake Ladoga to the river Volkhov. All of their way thus far was navigable by the ocean-going ships in which they had crossed the Baltic. About 20 kilometres down the Volkhov rapids, in the direction of Lake Ilmen, shallows and sandbanks made it necessary to change to smaller ships for the rest of the journey. Some kind of Swedish settlement seems to have been in existence at this staging-post as early as the seventh century, but its development into the significant Staraja Ladoga settlement began sometime in the middle of the eighth century. It functioned as a port and service centre for ships and crews heading south or returning home to Sweden after trading in Constantinople. In the oldest cultural layer of the settlement, established by dendro-chronology to date from the 760s, the remains of large timbered houses with central fire-pits have been unearthed, along with articles of identifiably Scandinavian origin – such as the ubiquitous combs – that match items found at Birka. The site of a blacksmith and jeweller's workshop has been identified from this same early cultural layer, with forge, furnace, metal workshop and a collection of tools including pincers, jewellery hammers, drills and a tiny anvil.[9] The find of some twenty wooden toy swords from a cultural level identified as Ladoga's oldest, dated to between 750 and 830, may suggest that families had begun to settle in the town by this time.[10] The burial ground at Plakun, on the bank of the river opposite Ladoga, shows characteristically Scandinavian features, with some twenty mounds containing the remnants of cremations in boats, along with a solitary burial chamber.

Two more settlements were established further south along the river, Gorodische and Novgorod. Gorodische seems to have had no specialized trade activity, its primary function being as a military

Trading and colonisation east of the Baltic largely involved Swedish Vikings, known as Rus, who gained access from the Gulf of Finland to the river network that led them down to Constantinople.

outpost guarding the approach to Ladoga.[11] Novgorod means 'new' Gorod, though the settlements appear to have developed simultaneously and were only 2 kilometres apart. It grew up at the northern end of Lake Ilmen and had access by river and portage to the Upper Volga, the Western Dvina and the Dneiper. The neck-rings with pendant hammer that were popular among the devotees of Thor have been found here, as well as amulets with runic inscriptions and a small carved figure identified as a Valkyrie. The Scandinavians called it Holmgård, 'the island city', a name that agrees with the description of the settlement given by the tenth-century Arab historian Ibn Rustah as 'on an island surrounded by a lake. The circumference of this island on which they live equals three days' journey. It is covered with woods and morasses.'[12] He numbered its population in the thousands and summarized their way of life thus:

They have no fields but simply live on what they get from the Slavs' lands. When a son is born, the father will go up to the newborn baby, sword in hand and throw it down. 'I shall not leave you with any property' he says. 'You have only what you can provide for yourself with this weapon.'[13]

Amber, arrows, swords, wax, honey, walrus tusks, fox furs, marten furs, falcons and slaves were what the Vikings brought to these new markets in the south. What they took away from them was silver. A serendipitous result of the Islamic taboo against the reproduction of images is that Arabic coins were stamped not only with epigrams from the Koran but also with the denomination and the year of minting. The find at Ladoga of an Arabic coin dated 786 suggests that the silver trade between the Rus and the Arabs was already under way by this time. In the form of buried hoards some 84,000 silver coins from the Islamic world have been found in what is now Sweden. In addition, 65,000 Arabic dirhams have been found on Gotland alone. The vast size of some of these buried deposits indicates the sheer volume of the trade. The Spillings hoard, discovered in 1999 on a farm in the north-east of the island, weighed 67 kilograms and included over 14,000 coins of Arabic origin, as well as almost 500 silver armbands, some three dozen silver bars and a great many spiral silver rings. Viking Age Scandinavians ignored the face value of silver coins and artefacts and valued them by weight and content alone. The bars and armbands had been fused into equal units of exchangeable weight and about 88 per cent of the coins had been cut, turning them into so-called 'hacksilver'. The hoard was truly enormous. Each Gotland household paid an annual tax to the Swedish king equivalent to 12 grams of silver; if an estimate of the number of farms on Gotland at the time at about 1,500 be correct, then this one hoard alone would have paid the islanders' taxes for six years.[14]

The reluctance of the Rus, who turned up at the court of Louis the Pious in 839 to return northwards by the same route as they had travelled south, indicates that the Baltic–Volga and Baltic–Dneiper river routes to Constantinople were not yet secure. They may have been using the long-distance overland trade route travelled by Jewish merchants between the Near East and France, called *ar-radaniya* in the Arabic sources, that led from the towns of the lower Volga to either Krakow or Prague and then through Germany; but in terms of convenience it could not compare with the potential of the river routes.[15] The securing of these routes became an enterprise intimately associated with the formation of the Kievan or Old Russian State by the leaders of the Rus, and the creation of this Kievan polity was the subject of the earliest written history of Russia, the *Russian Primary Chronicle*, a compilation made in Kiev early in the twelfth century by the monk Nestor, whose own *Lives* of the saints Boris and Gleb was among its sources, along with the Byzantine chronicle of Georgius Hamartolus, a *Life* of Methodius, missionary to the Slavs, and various treaties of the Kievan state with Constantinople, some of which are included in what looks their entirety. Like many of the earliest histories of polities that later turned into nations, the *Russian Primary Chronicle* is a source to approach with caution, but there is general agreement that a basic core of historical fact does underlie the literary improvisations of its compiler(s); the dates given may be inaccurate, but it is accepted that the events to which they refer took place.

After a beginning that locates its cast of tribes in a mythical biblical diaspora, the *Chronicle* approaches historical time with a reference to an attack by the Rus on Constantinople in 852, on which it does not expand. In 859 a tribe referred to as 'the Varangians from beyond the sea' imposed tribute upon a number of other tribes including the

Chuds, the Slavs, the Merians, the Ves and the Krivichians. In a situation that has clear parallels to the one described by Rimbert in the *Vita Anskarii* these tribes rejected the tribute, drove the Varangians back across the sea and set about governing themselves. The task proved beyond them and a period of warfare ensued. In 862 a decision was taken to put an end to the violence by appointing 'a prince who may rule over us, and judge us according to law'. According to the *Chronicle*, tribal representatives then crossed the Baltic to Sweden and approached a group of Scandinavians, known as the Rus, 'just as some of them are called Swedes, and others Normans, Angles, and Goths', and explained the problem to them: 'Our whole land is great and rich, but there is no order in it.' They asked for leaders to be appointed who would emigrate and rule over them. Three brothers named Rurik, Sineus and Truvor, along with their families and retainers, accepted the invitation. Their names have been traced to the original Scandinavian forms 'Hroerekr', 'Signiutr' and 'Thorvadr'.[16] Soon afterwards two of the brothers were dead and Rurik was in sole charge of the territories. Other than that he made his court at Novgorod, nothing is known of him for certain. Some think it possible he may have been the same man as that nephew of Klak-Harald to whom Louis the Pious gave Dorestad in 837, but this has the disadvantage of making him a Dane rather than a Swede.[17] 'On account of these Varangians,' says the chronicler, 'the district of Novgorod became known as the land of Rus. The present inhabitants of Novgorod are descended from the Varangian race.'[18] In all this there are echoes of another story, told by Rimbert, of the siege of Apulia by the Swedes at about the same time. The terms offered by the Apulians included a tribute in silver as well as a promise to the Swedes, 'henceforth to be subject and obedient to your rule, as we were in former times'. We may suspect that Rurik similarly imposed himself further east in the Ladoga area by force rather than invitation.[19]

The similarities between this tale of the 'summoning of the princes' and the story of the Jute brothers Hengist and Horsa, who came to England in the middle of the fifth century to assist King Vortigern of Kent against the Picts, have led to a widespread assumption that it is a historical topos, introduced to fill a blank space. But before consigning the tale entirely to legend we might recall that, as recently as 1905, a newly independent Norway invited a member of the Danish royal family to come to Norway and be their king, and that the invitation was accepted. Over the centuries sporadic objection has been raised to the whole idea of the Scandinavian origins of the Rus, usually on patriotic grounds.[20] Historians of the Soviet era were particularly opposed to it, since it contradicted Marxist theories on the formation of states. But the evidence of Louis' visitors in 839, and of the names of the signatories of successive trade treaties with Constantinople during the formative years of the Old Russian State, seem to leave little room for doubt. An ongoing process of assimilation had still not obscured these origins in 949 when Bishop Liuprand of Cremona visited Constantinople, where he noted that the city was menaced in the north by dangerous neighbours that included the Huns, the Pechenegs, the Khazar and the *Rusii*, 'whom we call Nordmanni'.[21]

The *Chronicle* tells us that two of Rurik's men foraged on down the Dneiper and took control of a small settlement on a hill, known as Kiev, and that on 18 June 860 these two leaders, whose names, Askold and Dir, correspond to Old Norse 'Hoskuld' and 'Dyr', launched an attack with a fleet of 200 ships on Constantinople. There is some doubt that Kiev was settled quite as early as this, and it is possible that Lake Ilmen and the Gorodische settlement were the likelier starting-point of the operation.[22] To a striking degree, the sermons preached by the city's Patriarch Photios in the wake of the raid echo the words in the despairing and apocalyptic letters written by Alcuin after Lindisfarne. There is even the same claim, contradicted by the evidence of familiarity in the 839 entry in the *Annals of St-Bertin*, that the raiders came as a wholly unknown quantity, a 'savage tribe' who had descended on civilization 'out of the farthest north', an obscure and undisciplined rabble, whose journey 'from the ends of the earth' had taken them through countless kingdoms and across 'numberless rivers and harbourless seas'. Their brutality fully matched that of the Lindisfarne raiders. Women, children, oxen and even chickens who got in their way were indiscriminately killed. Like Alcuin, Photios saw the raid as a punishment, inflicted on the

Christians by a god angry with them for their lax morals and depraved ways.[23] The report in the *Russian Primary Chronicle* is less detailed, noting 'a great massacre of Christians' that was interrupted by a storm, 'confusing the boats of the godless Russians' and driving many of the ships ashore, where their crews were killed. The *Chronicle* does not use the terms 'Christians' and 'godless men' with anything like the frequency of the Frankish and Anglo-Saxon annalists, but it is the defining opposition, and as close as it is able to get to giving a reasonable explanation for the terror.

Rurik died in about 879 and the succession passed to his relative Oleg (Old Norse 'Helgi'), who ruled as a regent for Rurik's son Igor ('Ingvar'). Askold and Dir had set up as independent rulers of Kiev and Oleg/Helgi's first priority was to extend the claims of the Rus kingship proper – as he and his family interpreted their position – over the city. Askold and Dir were killed in battle in 882 and Oleg became the first ruler of a united eastern Slavic Rus kingdom. From this point onward the *Russian Primary Chronicle* treats the activities of Oleg/Helgi, and in due course of Igor/Ingvar, as those of the leader of a legitimate polity. He pays particular attention to the securing of the trade route along the Dneiper to Constantinople, a task that was closely bound up with the subjugation of the various Slavic tribes that controlled different stretches of the rivers. In successive years following the occupation of Kiev he launched a series of campaigns against the Drevljane, the Severjane and the Radimichi, which, by 885, had completely secured the Dneiper route for Rus traders. These tribes had all formerly been tributaries of the Khazars, a semi-nomadic Turko-Tartar tribe that was the other great power in the region beside the Byzantine empire, which the Rus had to confront. From about the middle of the eighth century the Khazars had dominated the region between the Black Sea and the Caspian and so controlled trade relations between the Islamic world and northern and western Europe. The transference of these tributary rights was an important first step in the Rus' struggle to wrest regional hegemony of this part of south-eastern Europe away from the Khazars. Around 890 Oleg/Helgi also set about weakening the power in the south-west of the Magyars. Kiev survived an attempted blockade by the Magyars in 898.

The climax of the first years of the Kievan Rus state was an attack on Constantinople in 907. A list of those who manned an invasion fleet said to consist of 2,000 ships included 'Varangians, Slavs, Chuds, Krivichians, Merians, Polyanians, Severians, Derevlians, Radimichians, Croats, Dulebians, and Tivercias', a combination of peoples that might suggest this was already a state enterprise, carried out under the auspices of a de facto Old Russian state.[24] The *Russian Primary Chronicle* tells us that Oleg/Helgi

arrived before Byzantium, but the Greeks fortified the strait and closed up the city. Oleg disembarked upon the shore, and ordered his soldiery to beach the ships. They waged war around the city, and accomplished much slaughter of the Greeks. They also destroyed many palaces and burned the churches. Of the prisoners they captured, some they beheaded, some they tortured, some they shot, and still others they cast into the sea. The Russians inflicted many other woes upon the Greeks after the usual manner of soldiers. Oleg commanded his warriors to make wheels, which they attached to the ships, and when the wind was favourable they spread the sails and bore down upon the city from the open country. When the Greeks beheld this, they were afraid, and sending messengers to Oleg, they implored him not to destroy the city, and offered to submit to such tribute as he should desire.[25]

Oleg/Helgi's nickname in the Russian sources and in Russian oral tradition was 'Veschi', meaning 'the Wise' or 'the Far-sighted', and the improvisational talent that led him to transform a fleet of ships into wheeled wagons shows the nickname was warranted. So, too, does the fact that a major result of the attack was to force a way for the Rus into the great market place of Constantinople.[26]

Byzantine written sources contain no direct reference to this raid of 907, a fact which has led some to doubt that it ever took place at all. But the terms of the peace and trade treaty which followed the attack, and which are given in some detail in the *Russian Primary Chronicle*, show Constantinople, in the persons of the emperors Leo and Alexander, ceding trading terms to the Rus so favourable as to be unthinkable other than as the result of military defeat or the threat of such. Viking enough to know that his first priority must be to reward the loyalty of his men, one of Oleg/Helgi's first demands was for a sum of twelve *grivni* of silver to be paid to each of them. Of particular interest are the names of those who led the Rus delegation in the trade discussions that followed. All are Scandinavian, none are Slavic. It was the ethnically Scandinavian members of Oleg/Helgi's variegated soldiery who retained the highest status: the Karls, Farulfs, Vermunds, Hrollafs and Steinviths. The terms of this agreement of 907, and of what looks like its ratification in an expanded, second treaty of 912, fully endorse the suggestion that the Rus' long-term aim, from the taking of Kiev and its elevation to Oleg/Helgi's capital to the subjugation of the local tribes, had been all along the opening up of Constantinople to Rus traders and travellers.

The Byzantine leaders made an immediate start on the attempt to civilize their new trading partners:

The Emperor Leo honoured the Russian envoys with gifts of gold, palls and robes, and placed his vassals at their disposition to show them the beauties of the churches, the golden palace, and the riches contained therein. They thus showed the Russes much gold and many palls and jewels, together with the relics of our Lord's passion: the crowns, the nails, and the purple robe, as well as the bones of the Saints.[27]

Further west such a display might have invited disaster: here it was a sign of the strength and self-confidence of the Byzantine empire. At the formal ratification of the treaty of 907 they might have realized the process of conversion would have to take its time: while the joint emperors Leo and Alexander kissed the cross, the Rus swore by their weapons and by Perun, a Slavic incarnation of Thor associated with thunder and lightning and generally held to have been the chief god in the old Russian pantheon.[28]

In practical terms the treaty presented elaborate rules for the provisioning, housing and trading practices of Rus merchants visiting the city, and paragraphs dealing with matters such as the return of runaway slaves and the proper treatment of shipwrecked seamen and their property. There were also rules governing the employment of Rus who wanted to work as mercenaries for the emperors, and how the estate of such men should be disposed of in the event of their dying intestate or childless. This is the earliest reference to what later became known as the Varangian Guard, an elite military force that would presently school some of the Viking Age's most ambitious leaders. The treaty of 912 refers to itself as an affirmation of the 'long-standing amity which joins Greeks and Rus', and seventy years prior to this the Rus traders at Louis' court had indeed seemed to be on friendly terms with Constantinople. Yet the scepticism with which Louis the Pious had treated his visitors may indicate that their status remained ambivalent in the main European arenas. It may be that one reason Oleg/Helgi went on the offensive was precisely to insist upon the parity and respect due to a great power that was granted him in the treaties of 907 and 912.

The manner in which Oleg/Helgi allegedly met his death in 913 is about all that belies his reputation as a far-sighted leader. After a seer had prophesied that his favourite horse would be the death of him Oleg/Helgi let the animal live, but never rode it again. Five years after the great attack on Constantinople he was told that it was dead. In delight at having outwitted fate he visited its skeleton and stamped on the skull, disturbing a snake which slithered out of the bones and gave him a fatal bite. The story is echoed in the thirteenth-century Icelandic *Saga of Orvar Odd* in which a hero, confronted by a similar prophesy, attempts to cheat fate by killing and burying the horse. After a long and eventful life he returns home. The earth that covered the horse has all been washed away. Out walking one day he comes across the skull and idly prods it with the point of his spear. A snake emerges, gives him a fatal bite, and the prophesy is fulfilled. Over 300 years old at the time, Orvar Odd had either forgotten about the prophesy or simply didn't care any more.

Oleg/Helgi was succeeded by Igor/Ingvar, Rurik's son according to the *Russian Primary Chronicle*, though the almost forty-year gap between Rurik's death and Igor's succession leaves it open to doubt. The *Chronicle* treats Igor in the same way as Oleg, as the leader of a polity rather than an adventuring Viking. As such, the same three political and military aims were ascribed to both rulers: the building of towns and fortresses; the formulation of laws; and the subjugation of the Slavic tribes and regulation of the tribute system of taxation. As noted before, many of these tributary relations had been wrested from the Khazars. The Khazars practised an advanced taxation system of fixed tribute which both Oleg and Igor seem to have adopted unchanged. The Drevljane, who had never been Khazar tributaries, were among those who paid the Rus in kind, a black marten fur apiece in their case, though others paid in different kinds of furs and some in wax. Tributes were collected annually in the autumn, when the Rus ruler and his retinue left Kiev and journeyed down the western bank of the Dneiper, turning at Smolensk and making their way back up the eastern bank through the lands of the Radimichi and the Severjane. But these remained dangerous and uncertain relationships. A year or so after Igor came to power, the Rus were attacked for the first time by the Pechenegs, a tribe of nomads whose presence made every excursion to the lower reaches of the Dneiper a hazardous undertaking.

In 941 Igor launched an attack on Constantinople, landing with his men on the shores around the city where they tortured, burnt and spread terror in familiar Viking fashion: the chronicler mentions a practice of binding prisoners' hands behind their backs and driving iron nails into their heads. Monasteries and churches were burnt and a large amount of plunder taken. Three Greek armies in action elsewhere were recalled and Igor's men surrounded. Greek fire was used against them and the Rus fled back up the river in disarray.

Three years later they were back. This time the joint emperors, Romanos and Constantine Porphyrogenitos, offered them terms, a tribute in gold and silver equal to that given to Oleg some thirty years earlier. Another trade treaty was negotiated between the two powers, long and detailed in its regulation of the intercourse between Rus and Greek traders. Over three-quarters of a century after Rurik's arrival and the foundation of the Kievan state, almost all the sixty Rus envoys and traders from Kiev who signed the treaty still bore Scandinavian names. Many of the Varangians were Christian by this time and swore their oaths to uphold the treaty before God in a Christian church. Igor himself remained devoted to the thunder god and, on the morning of the oath-taking ceremony, he and the other non-Christian Rus made their way to a hill on which stood a statue of Perun, laid aside their weapons, shields and gold ornaments and took their oath there. A year later he was dead, killed by the Derevlians when he tried to increase their tribute.

For some seventeen years after Igor/Ingvar's death the Rus were led by his widow Olga/Helga, acting as regent for her infant son

Svyatoslov. Little is known about her. She may have been Oleg/Helgi's daughter and the marriage to Igor/Ingvar in 903 Oleg's way of focusing the claims of the ruling family. The fact that her son was the first member of the Kievan ruling family to bear a Slavic name perhaps argues for the possibility that she was a Slavic princess. The chronicler speaks well of her, but the stories told of her years in power are heavily coloured by legendary material. Perhaps as a result of her husband's death on a tax-gathering expedition, she reformed the tax system. The state was divided into districts, each in the charge of a local agent responsible for tax-collection, and the Khazar practice of uniform taxation was adopted. The reform amounted to a centralization of the financial administration of western and northern Russia.[29] Olga/Helga also finds favour with the chronicler as the first member of the Rus ruling house to accept Christianity, which she did at Constantinople in 957. The Byzantine emperor, who was her godfather at the ceremony, apparently offered to marry her afterwards, but was rejected.

By the time of her death in 969 Svyatoslov had been ruler of the Kievan state for about seven years. It was he who finally broke the power of the Khazar Khaganate, invading in 965 and 968 and destroying the fortress at Sarkel on the Don and devastating the Khazar capital Itil, at the mouth of the Volga. In 971 he led another attack on Constantinople. Diplomatic practice in the empire regarded treaties as valid for some thirty years, and this latest in the Rus' thirty-year cycle of campaigns may have been connected with a desire to secure improved terms for themselves as the approaching deadline loomed. This time the imperial forces got the better of him. Svyatoslov and his men took refuge in the garrison town of Dristra, on the south bank of the Danube, and successfully brought matters to an impasse. Svyatoslov ignored a challenge from the emperor to meet him in single combat and offered to strike a deal: in return for grain, a safe-conduct and a confirmation of the right of Rus merchants to trade in the city, he offered to release his prisoners and return to Kiev. The Byzantine historian Leo Diakonus was present at the subsequent meeting on the banks of the Danube and has left us a portrait of Svyatoslov as vivid as any photograph:

The emperor arrived on the banks of the Danube on horseback. He was wearing golden armour and accompanied by a large number of riders. Svyatoslov crossed the river on a kind of small Skyrian boat; he manned the oars just as his followers did. Svyatoslov looked like this: he was of medium height, neither too big nor too small. He had thick eyebrows, blue eyes and a short nose. He was not bearded but wore a long drooping moustache. His head was shaven apart from a single lock of hair on one side of his head, this being a sign of his aristocratic status. His neck was thick, his shoulders broad, and all in all he looked quite magnificent. There was something wild and bleak about him. From one ear hung a large, gold ring with two gems and a ruby in the middle. He wore white, the same as the others, the only difference being that his garment was cleaner.[30]

Svyatoslov conducted his side of the negotiations from his seat in the boat, a firm indication that this was a discussion between equals.[31] Not long afterwards, on the long journey home to Kiev, he lost his magnificent head. Having twice invaded the territories of the Bulgars, he had incurred their hostility and they tipped off the Pechenegs that the Rus leader, with a fairly small band of followers and a large amount of treasure, was moving up the river through their territory. The Pechenegs blocked the falls along the Dneiper and the Rus were compelled to make camp. After a hard winter, with little or no food, they tried to move up the falls again when spring came. Under their leader Kurya the Pechenegs attacked. Svyatoslov was killed and beheaded, his skull hollowed out, bound in gold and turned into a drinking bowl.

Like his name, Svyatoslov's personal style was Slavic. With that single lock of hair he would not have looked out of place among a company of Ukrainian Cossacks 600 years later. Assimilation was the inevitable fate of the Rus warrior elite, stylistically and linguistically. In the *De administrando imperio* ('On the Administration of an Empire'), from the middle of the tenth century and attributed to Constantine Porphyrogenitos, there is a chapter describing the route taken by Rus warrior-traders on their way to Constantinople that includes the Scandinavian names they gave to the falls they came across as they sailed down the Dneiper. None survived into modern Russian. The emperor's account of the journey gives a fascinating picture of the dramatic realities of life for these Rus that puts flesh on the dry bones of their trade treaties with Miklagård.

From Constantine we learn that they would arrive at Kiev in longships and there transfer to boats built locally by Slavs, which they would fit out according to their needs. Often equipment from old ships which had been broken up was used. Leaving Kiev in June, the trade fleet set off on the long journey down the Dneiper. At Vitichev they joined up with more Rus ships. The first of several major hazards encountered was the Essupi rapids. Here some were set ashore and the rest organized into three groups, one at the stem, one amidships, and one at the stern, and the passage of the ship through the rapids directed from the shore by means of long poles. Two more rapids were negotiated in the same way. The fourth rapid was 'the huge one, called in Russian *Aifur*':

All put ashore, stem foremost, and out get all those who are appointed to keep watch. Ashore they go, and unsleeping they keep sentry-go against the Pechenegs. The rest of them, picking up the things they have on board the ships, conduct the wretched slaves in chains six miles by dry land until they are past the barrier. In this way, some dragging their ships, others carrying them on their shoulders, they get them through to the far side of the rapid. So, launching the ships back on to the river and loading their cargo, they get in and again move off.[32]

After passing seven rapids and reaching the ford at Krarios they passed through terrain that made them easy targets for the arrows of Pecheneg warriors. Those who survived landed on the island of St Gregorios, where they would make a sacrifice of thanksgiving to their gods beneath the boughs of a huge oak tree:

They sacrifice live birds. Also they stick arrows in a circle in the ground, and others of them provide bread and meat, bits of anything anyone has, as the practice demands. Also they cast lots about the birds – to sacrifice them, to eat them as well, or to let them live.[33]

Proceeding to the river Selinas, they sailed to its mouth and the island of St Aitherios, where they rested again and carried out repairs to their ships before heading on to the Dniester. At the point where they picked up the Selinas again they were once more liable to be harassed by Pecheneg warriors running alongside on the river banks. When, as sometimes happened, one of the ships was driven ashore and attacked by the Pechenegs the rest of the fleet unhesitatingly went to its aid.

'After the Selinas,' writes Constantine Porphyrogenitos, 'they are afraid of nobody and are able to complete their journey in peace.' He names seven of the rapids that must be forced on the journey down the Dneiper in both Rus and Slavonic, and linguists have identified Scandinavian original forms for all the Rus names given: Essupi, Ulvorsi, Galandri, Aifur, Barufors, Leanti and Strukun. The likely meanings of these are, in modern Swedish: *sov inte* (don't sleep), *holmfors* (island falls), *ringande* (the howling), *alltid farlig* (the always dangerous), *varufors* (steep cliff falls), *leende* (the laughing) and *struken* (the racer). Much later on settlements grew up around these falls and portage points, with pilots and other service industries to assist the traders. The portage officials who collected taxes at these places were known in Russian as *tiun*, from the Old Norse *Pjónn*, meaning 'attendant'. The inscription on the squat, reddish Pilgårds stone that was found at Bogeviken on the east coast of Gotland adds a note of individuality to Constantine's litany of hazardous rapids. Bogeviken was one of Gotland's most important harbours during the Viking Age, and the stone seems to recall a journey undertaken by a band of Gotland brothers that ended in death for one of them at a place called Rustain. It was, the stone tells us, in the vicinity of the fourth of the Dneiper falls, Aifur, 'the always dangerous'.[34]

Because of its position as a large stepping-stone in the middle of the Baltic, Gotland played a central role in Viking Age trade with the east. The islanders presently established a colony of their own in Novgorod, called Gutagård, from where they cultivated the trade route to Hedeby in south-east Jutland, with the island itself an important staging-post along the way. The archaeological remains of some fifty ports or trading places, on both eastern and western sides of the island, have been found and these seem to have been part of a dramatic expansion that started as early as AD 700. Many of them were small settlements at which farmers and fishermen supplemented their income by trading. Others, like Fröjel, Paviken and Bandlundeviken, were large ports where ship-building and repair work were carried out.

The finds indicate that these larger ports had extensive contacts with the outside world. Though it is no proof the Vikings ever traded with merchants from East Africa or the Indian Ocean, a handful of smaller grave-finds on Gotland can actually be traced to these regions, including two rings of ivory, and certain types of sea-shells in female graves dating from the seventh to the tenth centuries that were used as amulets or pendants. Part of a hoard unearthed at Nygårds, in the parish of Väskinde, included a necklace consisting of some 200 beads, of which almost half had been cut from shells originating from the Indian Ocean. It allows for the possibility that Scandinavian traders and warriors, in their search for new markets and novelties with which to enrich their world, may have penetrated as far south as the capital of the Abbasid caliphate in Baghdad.[35]

And if only a few examples of textiles survive, leaving us largely dependent on later, written descriptions for our knowledge of Viking Age clothing styles, the evidence of the Gotland picture-stones is that some horsemen, at least, had been persuaded of the advantages of wearing baggy trousers gathered below the knees, a comfort imported from the east.[36] Another example of the symbiotic nature of the cultural exchange across the Baltic is the stone found at Smiss, in Kräklingbo, with a damaged runic inscription that includes the words '... *eptir Mutifu, son sin* ...'.[37] *Mutifu* has been interpreted by the Icelandic runologist Thorgunn Snædal Brink as a version of the name Mustapha, recalling an Arab settler or perhaps some Gotlander who had converted to Islam.[38]

The unearthing of hoards of buried silver dirham from the Arab world by builders and farmers remains an almost annual event on Gotland. The finds are not confined to one area of the island but dot the map, and the dates cover the island's Viking Age and beyond, from about 800 up to about 1140. Occasionally an individual coin is found that provides dramatic confirmation of a detail previously known only from a written source. About the middle of the eighth century the Khazars are reported to have converted to Judaism. Physical evidence for this tribal initiative was lacking until the discovery, as part of the Spillings hoard mentioned earlier, of a coin inscribed '*Musa rasul Allah*', Arabic for 'Moses is the apostle of God'. This sounds a direct echo of the Islamic 'Mohammed is the apostle of God', with the coin itself being the 'illegal' work of a minter who was hoping to benefit from the high reputation enjoyed by Islamic silver coin. The Spillings hoard is dated to about 870 and its discovery has raised doubts about the widely accepted idea that the production of silver coins in the Caliphate went into decline in the 800s.[39]

During the fratricidal struggle between his three sons that followed Svyatoslov's death, one, Oleg, was defeated and killed. Another, Vladimir, fled to Novgorod and made his way into Scandinavia, leaving Iaropolk as the sole ruler in Kiev. During his brief reign Iaropolk showed a sympathetic tolerance of Christianity.

Vladimir, meanwhile, had gathered an army of Varangian mercenaries. Once he felt strong enough he recrossed the Baltic and declared war on his brother, who was betrayed and killed in 977. Once inside Kiev, Vladimir's Varangian mercenaries conducted themselves as conquerors in a captured city and as soon as possible after assuming control Vladimir got rid of them, retaining only a select few and sending the rest on to Constantinople with a private word of warning to the emperor: 'Do not keep many of them in your city, or else they will cause you such harm as they have done here.'[40] He advised him to scatter the force – 'and do not allow a single one to return this way'.

In his private life, Vladimir lived out the submission to instinct and appetite that marked one of the clearest distinctions between Heathendom and Christianity. He is said to have kept some 800 women for his personal use. We may permit ourselves the conventional raised eyebrow at the figure, but the known fact that he took at least seven wives, including his brother's widow, indicates that self-denial was not natural to him. Perhaps as a way of neutralizing a threatening Christian presence in the city that had developed as a result of Iaropolk's tolerance, he set about an active revival of pagan worship in Kiev. Wooden images of the old gods were set up close to his palace: Perun, with a head of silver and a mouth of gold, Dazhbog, Stribog, Simargl, Mokosh, Khors, guttural names redolent of the harsh period of human sacrifice that followed.[41] The *Russian Primary Chronicle* describes a victory celebration after Vladimir's subjugation of the Iatviagians at which lots were drawn to find a boy and girl to be sacrificed. Ivan, the unlucky youth chosen, turned out to be the son of a former Varangian, Tury, who had returned from Constantinople and converted to Christianity. In his anger and distress Tury is said to have denounced the gods as merely 'wood which is here today and rotten tomorrow. They do not eat or drink or talk but are made by [human] hands', an indiscretion for which he may well have joined his son as a sacrificial offering.[42] In 981 Vladimir waged war on the Vyatichians and imposed a tribute on them based on the number of their ploughs. In 983 he marched against the Yatvingians and seized their territories. In 984 it was the turn of the Radimichians. With the Bulgars, against whom his father had waged sporadic war, he signed a treaty that was to prevail between the parties 'until stone floats and straw sinks'.

The disproportionate number of Scandinavian names appended to the treaty between Igor and Constantinople of 945 confirms that the descendants of Swedish Vikings remained a dominant elite in the Kievan state; the text also makes it clear that a significant number of Kievan Rus – like poor Tury – had already adopted Christianity.[43] As we saw earlier, Vladimir's grandmother Olga is depicted in the *Russian Primary Chronicle* as a saintly figure, ever concerned from the time of her own conversion to persuade her son Svyatoslov to join her. Svyatoslov had resisted, not least because he was afraid that to convert to Christianity would make him an object of ridicule to his retainers.[44] Vladimir, however, realized which way the political wind was blowing. A number of Baltic Slav tribes had been baptized between 942 and 968, Harald Bluetooth in Denmark sometime in the 960s, and at about the same time Mieszko of Poland through the influence of his Christian wife Dobrava. Sometime around 980, not long after abandoning their nomadic way of life, the Magyars, too, under their chieftain Geza, accepted baptism.[45] Once he had made up his mind that the state needed a new religion, Vladimir methodically set about determining which of the major religions to choose: Islam, which had been the religion of the Volga Bulgars since 922; Judaism, to which the Khazars living south of the Bulgars had converted around 865; the Greek Christianity of his grandmother Olga; and the Roman Christianity that prevailed on mainland Europe and in the west. Representatives of each faith were invited to his court to speak in defence and praise of their faith. Vladimir was attracted by the promise of the seventy-two virgins he would enjoy in the next life, but less enthusiastic about the Islamic injunction in this one against eating pork and drinking wine. 'Drinking is the joy of the Rus,' he is said to have objected. 'We cannot exist without that pleasure.' Emissaries of the pope arrived from Germany and found their insistence on the importance of fasting similarly unpopular. The Jewish Khazars' tale of the diaspora seemed to him a poor advertisement for their faith and Judaism too was rejected. By the account given in the *Russian Primary Chronicle*, the apologist for Byzantine Christianity was given a lengthier hearing than the others, and it was he who succeeded in the end.

Vladimir's decision harmonized nicely with certain diplomatic initiatives that were being extended in his direction at about the same time by the Byzantine emperor, Basil II. In 987 two of Basil's generals had revolted. One proclaimed himself emperor. Basil was in real danger of losing control of the region between the Black Sea and the Mediterranean. Early in 988 he swallowed his pride and sent to Kiev, asking for Vladimir's support in retaking the city of Cherson which had fallen into rebel hands.[46] In return he offered him the hand of his sister Anna in marriage. The rider was a familiar one: Vladimir was to agree to be baptized. With little hesitation, it seems, he agreed. Six thousand Rus marched into Byzantine Crimea and put down the revolt, and the rebel stronghold of Cherson was retaken. Given Vladimir's reputation as a barbarian womanizer, Anna was understandably reluctant to fulfil the imperial side of the bargain, but in a heartfelt plea her brother persuaded her of the importance of the alliance:

Through your agency God turns the land of Rus to repentance, and you will relieve Greece from the danger of grievous war. Do you not see how much evil the Rus have already brought upon the Greeks? If you do not set out, they may bring on us the same misfortunes.[47]

She took a tearful farewell of her family and crossed the sea to Cherson with her priests. Vladimir seems to have liked what he saw and in February 988 allowed himself to be baptized in the cathedral of St Basil. Once the marriage had taken place, and he was back in Kiev with his bride, he formally returned Cherson to Basil 'as a wedding gift'.

Vladimir took personal charge of the cultural about-turn that then took place and mounted spectacular displays of the ritual cleansing and humiliation of the old gods. A statue of Perun was tied to a horse's tail and beaten with rods by a dozen riders as it was dragged through the streets to the Dneiper. It was thrown into the river and driven through the waves until its purification was deemed to be complete and it was allowed to drift ashore on to a sandbank. Vladimir then ordered his people to attend on the banks of the Dneiper for a mass baptism in the waters of the river, adding that 'whoever does not turn up at the river tomorrow, be he rich, poor, lowly or slave, he shall be my enemy!'

By all accounts Vladimir's conversion seems to have been more than just an expedient that gave him access to the real political and economic advantages of marrying into the emperor's family. He built churches and supported the work of the Greek missionaries within the Kievan state. He is said to have been reluctant to take human life after his conversion, to have become a generous giver of alms, and to have given up his mistresses. The choice of Slavic and not Old Norse as the language of the Rus Orthodox Church made the process of assimilation irreversible. It also opened up Rus society to the profound and enduring influence of Byzantine culture.

In his later years Vladimir put his sons in charge of the major towns of his kingdom. Tmutorokan on the Taman Peninsula, controlling the passage from the Black Sea to the Sea of Azov, in the region that Snorri believed to be the legendary home of Scandinavian gods and people, was given to Mstislav. The gift marked the furthest reaches south-east of the Baltic Viking expansion, though in truth the degree of assimilation was so complete by this time that it is scarcely accurate to describe them as Vikings, or even Scandinavians, any more.

7

The Danelaw I

Occupation

If, as we have already suggested, the success of the Viking raiders in Ireland is partly to be explained by the fragmentary disposition of power in that country and the way in which this inhibited a coherent military response, then the same might be said of England at the time. From the chaos that followed the Roman withdrawal in the fifth century and the Anglo-Saxon invasions of the sixth century, a number of separate and competing kingdoms had emerged. The largest of these were Northumbria, Mercia, East Anglia, Essex, Wessex, Sussex and Kent. Among the more significant of the smaller territories were the kingdom of the Hwicce, extending over parts of present-day Worcestershire, Warwickshire and Gloucestershire; Lindsey, between East Anglia and the southern parts of Northumbria; and Bernicia and Deira, which appear to have been located within Northumbria itself. By the time the Viking raids began, most of these smaller kingdoms had been absorbed by larger and more powerful neighbours to leave a nucleus of four regional powers: Northumbria in the north-east, stretching from the Tees to the Firth of Forth; East Anglia on the central and south-east coast; Mercia in the central midlands with Wales on its western border; and, in the south-west of the country, Wessex, the territory of the west Saxons. Sussex and Essex, the territory of the south and the east Saxons, were both absorbed in about 825 by Wessex, which emerged as the major power in the land from a long-standing rivalry with Mercia. Yet regional loyalties remained the dominant factor of political life. In 731 Bede had insisted, in the title of his greatest work the *Ecclesiastical History of the English People*, that an entity such as 'the English people' did indeed exist. The reality was, however, that England at the start of the ninth century remained essentially a geographical notion. It was in no sense a 'united kingdom'.

An incident reported in the *Royal Frankish Annals* for 809 illustrates the absence of a centralized political and military power. Driven from the throne by a rival claimant in 808, the Northumbrian king, Eardwulf, had travelled to Rome to enlist papal and imperial support for his efforts to regain power. He returned with envoys from Leo III and Charlemagne. Later, on the party's way back to Rome, it was attacked at sea. A deacon named Aldulf was kidnapped, taken ashore and held until the payment of a ransom by the Mercian king, Cenwulf. The *Annals* call the kidnappers only 'pirates', but the attack has the hallmarks of a Viking enterprise, and the fact that they were able to hold their captive in England while negotiating his ransom is an indication that there must have been numerous fringes of lawlessness between the few and widely separated regions over which the various English kings had control.

This apparently isolated episode is the only bridge between the raids on the north-east of the 790s, and an attack in 835 on the marshy island of Sheppey, off the coast of Kent in the Thames estuary, which marks the opening of a second and very different phase of Viking activity in England. From this point onwards, scarcely a year goes by without a reference in the *Anglo-Saxon Chronicle* to a Viking raid, or of a battle fought between English forces and the 'Heathen men'. In 838 Egbert, king of Wessex, triumphed at Hingston Down over a 'great naval force' that had sailed up the Tamar and made common cause with an army of Cornishmen. In 840 a fleet of thirty-three ships was defeated at Southampton by alderman Wulfheard. Fortunes were reversed in a battle later in the same year at Portland; fifty years earlier, the murder there of the reeve Beaduheard by Norwegians from Hordaland had signalled the start of the violence that was to follow. There was a 'great slaughter' in London and Rochester in the east in 842, presumably by Danish Vikings, and in 843 a fleet of thirty-five Viking ships triumphed again in a battle at Carhampton, near Minehead, in the Bristol Channel. Two years later the men of Somerset and Dorset were victorious in a battle fought at the mouth of the river Parrett.

So far the raiding had been a seasonal activity. The fleets would

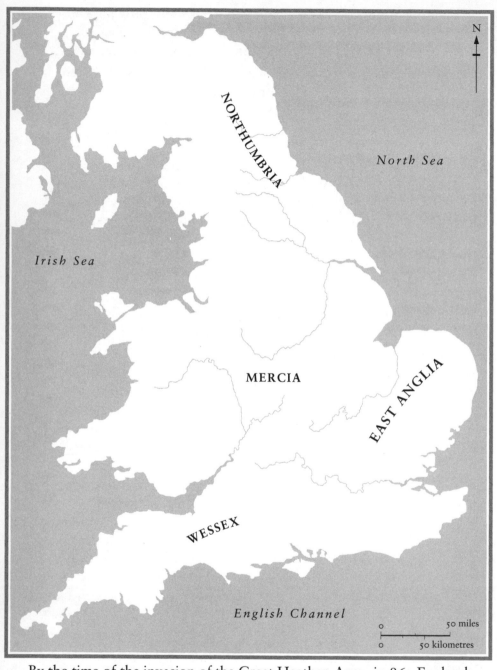

By the time of the invasion of the Great Heathen Army in 865 England consisted of four main kingdoms: Northumbria, Mercia, East Anglia and Wessex.

arrive in the spring, raid throughout the summer and early autumn, and head for a safe base with the approach of winter. For the raiders in the west this would probably be one of the arc of *longphort* bases along the east coast of Ireland: Dublin, Wexford, Waterford and Cork; the home-base of the Vikings who concentrated on the Thames as their point of entry was probably Denmark. All this changed in 851, when a fleet numbered by the *Anglo-Saxon Chronicle* at 350 ships entered the Thames and attacked London and Canterbury and drove King Brihtwulf of the Mercians and his army across the Thames into Surrey. Afterwards they made camp at Thanet and for the first time spent the winter in England. An attempt by a combined force of men from Kent and Surrey to drive them off failed and both of its leaders were killed. In 855 the Vikings moved their winter quarters a step closer to London and made camp on Sheppey. In the south-west of the country, a large Viking force that had been active on the Somme crossed the Channel and penetrated as far inland as Winchester before being halted and driven back over the Channel again.

The desultory violence of the years since 835, and the wolfish escalation of the threat that came with the establishment of winter camps, were all a prelude to the arrival in East Anglia, in 865, of a force that evidently surpassed all previous forces in size and discipline. The *Anglo-Saxon Chronicle* referred to it as 'the Great Heathen Army', and its arrival altered completely the terms of the Viking presence in England, for it came with grand territorial ambitions that it was able to realize in a little over a decade. For most of those years its activities became, understandably, the obsession of the chroniclers. It was under the command of brothers named Halfdan and Ingvar, believed to be the sons of Ragnar Lodbrok. Horses were obtained locally and the army, seemingly following a plan of action, rode north across the Humber estuary and headed for York. Two claimants to the throne of Northumbria, Osbert and Aella, were so preoccupied in fighting each other they failed to recognize the severity of the outside threat until it was too late and the city had fallen. Though they succeeded in breaking back into York both were killed in the subsequent fighting, the Northumbrians were compelled to recognize the invaders as their overlords and the Viking kingdom of York became an established fact. A puppet ruler named Egbert was installed on the throne.

In 868 part of the army marched back into Mercia and the fortress at Nottingham was taken. The rivalries of living memory were irrelevancies by this time and at the request of Burgred, king of the Mercians, the Wessex king, Ethelred, and his brother Alfred both took part in a failed attempt to starve the army out. In 869 the army returned to York and remained there for a year before moving back down the coast to East Anglia. Edmund, the East Anglian king, confronted it on 20 November and his forces were defeated and he himself killed. In 871 the army moved against Wessex. The winter of 870–71 was spent in Reading and in the spring Halfdan and a leader named Bagsecg led their men against Ethelred and Alfred. A series of bloody engagements followed – at Ashdown near Crowborough, at Basing in Hampshire, Englefield near Reading, and *Meretun*. Bagsecg was among the many raiders killed at Ashdown, but the army seemed to have an inexhaustible supply of men and good leaders. The results were indecisive, but this was Wessex heartland, and the willingness of the Viking army to engage so often and so far from its base must have been daunting for Ethelred and Alfred.[1] Ethelred died that year and was succeeded by his brother. Four weeks after his crowning, Alfred faced the army again, its ranks swollen by the arrival of a 'great summer army' that had arrived in the region, and had to concede defeat. At the close of a year which had seen nine full battles south of the Thames, Alfred and the Danes made a peace settlement. The following year the army asserted its superiority over Mercia with the imposition of another peace agreement.

In about 873 King Egbert of York was deposed and fled to Mercia with the archbishop, Wulfhere, and for the next three years King Ricsige ruled, possibly as a Viking puppet, although this is not certain. In 874 the Mercian King Burgred was driven abroad. Here, as they would do on other occasions, the Vikings showed a political shrewdness in their dealings with the conquered. They split the opposition by handing the crown to Ceolwulf, a member of a rival dynasty with a valid claim to the Mercian throne, though the *Anglo-Saxon Chronicle* preferred to dismiss him as 'a foolish king's thegn', who gave his masters hostages and promised them the disposition of the kingdom whenever they should require it and his full military support.[2]

Still a large, disciplined and coherent force, and now under the leadership of Halfdan, Guthrum, Oscytel and Anwend, the army rested for the winter of 873–4 at Repton, on the banks of the Trent, just south of Derby. Repton had been a Christian cult centre and a seat of Mercian royal power from the late seventh century.[3] As such it would have been the focus of a well-organized network of supply and tax-gathering that the invaders could exploit with the minimum of effort. St Wystan's Church itself was incorporated into the D-shaped structure the army dug to defend itself, with its straight side using the cliff that would, in those days, have been the south bank of the river. In what may have been a symbolic display of contempt as much as a practical necessity the church's tower was used as a gate-house.[4]

In the following year the army divided. Possibly in connection with events following the death or the enforced exile of King Egbert, Halfdan marched north to consolidate his hold on Northumbria, staying the winter at a camp on the Tyne and raiding among the Picts and the Strathclyde Britons.[5] His activities in Bernicia, in the north of the kingdom, so disrupted life at Lindisfarne that, like the monks of Noirmoutier before them, the brothers finally abandoned the monastery and set off on the search for a safe haven for the bones of Cuthbert, their patron saint and protector, which lasted for seven years. Following Ricsige's death in 876, Northumbria beyond the Tyne was nominally given to Egbert II. Halfdan shrewdly reinstated Wulfhere as archbishop of York, agitating a rivalry with the see at Canterbury and dabbling in the same tribal waters that had seen Cornishmen align themselves with Vikings against the Anglo-Saxons some thirty years earlier.[6] The final entry for 876 in the *Anglo-Saxon Chronicle* summarizes the events of the year in words of biblical simplicity: 'And that year Healfdene [Halfdan] shared out the land of the Northumbrians, and they proceeded to plough and support themselves.'[7]

Meanwhile Guthrum, Oscytel and Anwend, having taken Mercia, made their way from Repton to Cambridge and stayed there for the next year. Guthrum seems to have had his sights set on the prize of Wessex. Evading Alfred's forces, he and the army slipped out of Cambridge by night and occupied a fortress site at Wareham in Dorset that had, in times of peace, been a nunnery. Alfred was forced to treat with him. Guthrum and his army promised to leave Wessex and handed over hostages as security. It was on this occasion that the *Chronicle*, for the first time close enough to pass on details of the cultural practices of the invaders, noted that Guthrum swore his oath on a holy ring, and that this was 'a thing which they would not do before for any nation'.[8] Guthrum himself must have made the claim. In this he was following the advice of Odin in 'The Sayings of the High One':

> If there's a man whom you don't trust,
> but from whom you want nothing but good,
> speak fairly to him but think falsely.[9]

Instead of leaving the kingdom, he and his men slipped away under cover of night and rode to Exeter. Alfred pursued but was unable to overtake them before they had occupied a fortress. There was another exchange of hostages, more swearing of oaths.

In January 878 the army left Exeter, rode to Chippenham and began driving people from their homes and taking over the land. A brother of Ingvar and Halfdan, whom the Anglo-Norman chronicler Gaimar names as Ubbi, was also in the region at the time, having spent the winter at Dyfed in south Wales with a fleet of twenty-three ships.[10] Alfred's biographer, the Welsh monk Asser, tells us that Ubbi had first 'slaughtered many Christians' before departing for Devon. Ubbi was killed in battle with several hundred of his men. The *Chronicle* adds the detail that 'there was captured the banner which they called "Raven"'. The *Annals of St Neots*, created in about 1105, relate that the original – for each separate army probably had its own flag – had been woven by the three sisters of Ingvar and Ubbi, and that observations of it were used to predict the outcome of battle. The raven was associated with Odin, on whose whim the fortunes of war depended: a lifelike fluttering of the bird in the wind was a sign of impending victory, just as its lifelessness presaged defeat.

If the raven flag failed to flutter for Ubbi and his men it must have blown gloriously for the remainder of the Viking army, for as Guthrum's men drove out some of the West Saxons and received the submission of others who stayed, Alfred was now reduced to the humiliation of flight, heading west to Athelney in north Somerset. For some time, says Asser, his life became one of 'great distress amid the woody and marshy places of Somerset. He had nothing to live on except what he could forage by frequent raids, either secretly or openly, from the Vikings as well as from the Christians who had submitted to the Vikings' authority.'[11] The homely legend of his being scolded by a farmer's wife, ignorant of his true identity, for letting her cakes burn is laid to this difficult time of his life.[12] A more tangible and exalted trace of his presence in the region was the accidental find, in 1693, of the exquisite 'Alfred Jewel' at a site four miles from Athelney. This small, gold-framed image in *cloisonné* enamel shows a seated male figure in a green smock holding what may be a flower and is inscribed, in the Wessex form of Anglo-Saxon, 'Ælfred Mec Heht Gewyran' ('Alfred had me made').[13] Its function is uncertain. It may have been a book-mark or pointer for use with Alfred's own translation of Pope Gregory's *Pastoral Care*, copies of which were sent to each of the Wessex bishoprics.

From his marshy refuge Alfred turned the tables and embarked on a campaign of guerrilla warfare against the invaders, which soon gathered momentum. In May 878, backed by the men of Somerset, Wiltshire and Hampshire, he engaged the Danish forces in a decisive battle at Evington in Wiltshire. Guthrum's men were beaten and driven back to their camp at Chippenham. After a fourteen-day siege they emerged to make peace. Asser describes what happened next:

When he heard their embassy, the king (as is his wont) was moved to compassion and took as many chosen hostages from them as he wanted. When they had been handed over, the Vikings swore in addition that they would leave his kingdom immediately, and Guthrum, their king, promised to accept Christianity and to receive baptism at King Alfred's hand; all of which he and his men fulfilled as they had promised. For three weeks later Guthrum, the king of the Vikings, with thirty of the best men from his army, came to King Alfred at a place called Aller, near Athelney. King Alfred raised him from the holy font of baptism, receiving him as his adoptive son; the unbinding of the chrisom on the eighth day took place at a royal estate called Wedmore. Guthrum remained with the king for twelve nights after he had been baptized, and the king freely bestowed many excellent treasure on him and all his men.[14]

Mixing cultural and conversion diplomacy, Athelstan was the Christian and Anglo-Saxon name given to Guthrum when he was raised from the font, showing that Alfred, like the Carolingians across the Channel, put his faith in a policy of complete assimilation. This time Guthrum/Athelstan kept his word to leave Wessex. In 880 he led his army into East Anglia and shared out the land there. With this, the heart of the area that later came to be known as the Danelaw was complete.

But old habits die hard. Asser complains that, in 885, the East Anglian Vikings 'broke in a most insolent manner the peace they had established with King Alfred'. In the main, however, it seems Guthrum was satisfied to have achieved the respectability of kingship. Alfred could not be as content with his share of the peace. The Viking menace was hydra-headed. In 882 he fought a small naval battle against a Danish fleet, and in 885 engaged with a large force which had crossed from France and besieged Rochester. Alfred's unexpected arrival threw the aggressors into disarray and they fled back across the Channel, leaving behind their prisoners and their horses. He made his way into East Anglia, 'in order to plunder that area' and probably punish Guthrum's men for having supported the attack on Rochester.[15] Initially successful, his ships were finally driven from the mouth of the Stour by a fleet assembled by these same East Anglian Danes. The frequency with which Vikings were making use of the Thames as a port of entry into England clearly demanded Alfred's urgent attention. It was vital to control London and, in 886, he attacked and re-took the city, an act that entrained the submission to him of 'all the English people that were not under subjection to the Danes'.[16]

At some point between this action and Guthrum/Athelstan's death in 890, he and Alfred came to a formal written agreement that marked a watershed in relations between the two sides. Its prologue recognized the reality of the status quo, invoking a peace between 'all the English race and all the people which is in East Anglia'.[17] The boundary between the neighbours was settled as running 'up the Thames, and then up the Lea, and along the Lea to its source, then in a straight line to Bedford, then up the Ouse to the Watling Street'.[18] Legal parity between the two populations was affirmed, with a fine set at eight half-marks of refined gold for the killing of either a Dane or an

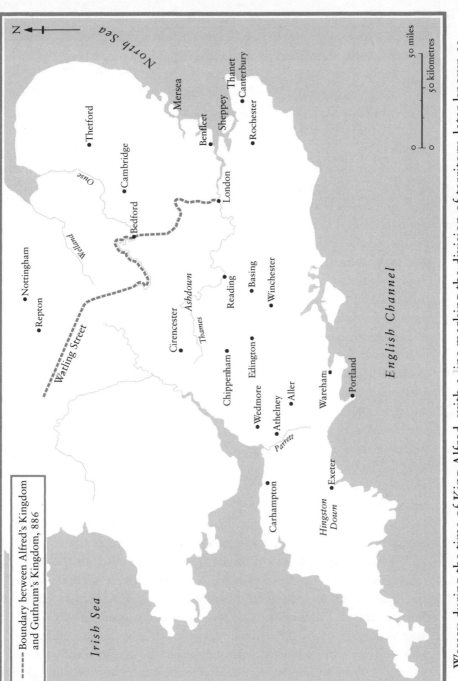

Wessex during the time of King Alfred, with a line marking the division of territory, later known as the Danelaw, that was agreed on by Alfred and the Viking chieftain Guthrum in about 886.

Englishman. The wording of the treaty confirms that trade links already existed between the parties, with terms agreed for the cross-border buying and selling of slaves and other goods.

The sixteen-year period between the invasion of the 'Great Heathen Army' and its subsequent conquest of eastern Britain and the establishment of the Danelaw became a seminal moment in the creation of Scandinavian history, and its events and main characters a radiant for some of the most potent legends and myths that are still associated with the Viking Age. Ragnar Lodbrok's after-name 'Hairy-Breeches' and the equally mysterious after-name of his son, Ivar 'the Boneless'; the alleged Viking practice of a form of torture and execution known as 'the Blood-Eagle'; the death and canonization of Edmund, former king of the East Angles; and the origins of the Viking kingdom of York – all are linked in a tangled web of legend with its origins in this long seminal moment. It is worth stepping aside from the narrative to look briefly at the origins and development of this legendary history, to remind ourselves once again of how close much of Viking Age history is to 'the idiom of legend'.

The earliest reference to a possible historical model for Ragnar Lodbrok is in the 'Ragnarsdrapa' by the Norwegian Bragi the Old, dated to the first half of the ninth century and surviving only in fragments in Snorri Sturluson's *Prose Edda*. It is a 'shield-poem', so called because it appears to describe a number of scenes painted on a shield. The 'Ragnarsdrapa' is the oldest known example of skaldic art, and Bragi himself the earliest skald whom we know by name. We learn from the poem that the shield was a present to Bragi from his lord, a certain Ragnar. As we noted earlier, this may have been the 'Reginfred' who attacked Paris in 845 and who also, according to Saxo Grammaticus, raided in the Baltic in the same decade.

The first references to the name 'Lodbrok' occur almost simultaneously in about 1060. Summarizing the earliest history of the Norman dukes, William of Jumièges writes of a certain 'Lothroc' that he was a king of the Danes who expelled a very large number of people from his territory. Adam of Bremen makes no mention of a 'Ragnar', but in writing of the Viking chieftain Ivar he gives the name of his father as 'Lodparch'.

Ari the Learned was the first to bring the names together in *The Book of the Icelanders*, in which he identifies Ragnar Lodbrok as the father of the Viking leader Ingvar/Ivar, and includes himself among Ragnar's descendants, from which it is clear that Ragnar was already a semi-legendary figure.[19]

The association of the name Ragnar with 'hairy breeches' does not occur until the *Saga of Ragnar Lodbrok and his Sons*, a tale that also offered its thirteenth-century audience an explanation for the invasion of England that cast the Danes as the injured party in search of revenge. Ragnar's heroism is established early on in the saga when he travels to Gotland in response to a challenge to save a princess and win a kingdom by killing an enormous serpent that is threatening both. Protected from its venom by a pair of leather trousers boiled in pitch, he is successful. Saxo tells a similar story but adds the detail that Ragnar used a cushioning of hair beneath his clothes for extra protection, and as a final insurance leapt into the icy seawater so that his breeches would freeze solid before his meeting with the serpent.

Much later on in the saga, during a raid on England, Ragnar is captured and put into a snake-pit by his enemy King Aella, dying only when his tormentors finally realize the secret of his immunity and remove the snake-proof breeches. Ragnar's last words are carried back home to his sons: 'The little pigs would grunt if they knew how the father-pig suffered.'[20] Determined to avenge Ragnar's death, the sons then raise a great army and invade Northumberland. The *Anglo-Saxon Chronicle* refers to the Viking attack on York in 867 and the death of the city's defenders, including its king, Aella; but it does not name any of the Viking leaders, nor does it go into detail concerning the circumstances of Aella's death. The *Saga* is much more forthcoming, describing how the captured king was executed by having 'the blood-eagle' cut on his back. Saxo similarly states that Aella's back was carved 'with the figure of an eagle, exultant because at his overthrow they were imprinting the cruellest of birds on their most ferocious enemy', and gives Ivar as the name of the son responsible for this.[21]

It is possible that these late literary descriptions of 'the blood-eagle' derive from a verse that survives only in fragmentary form, composed in about 1030 by the Icelandic poet Sigvat, in which he exults that

'Ivar, who dwelt at York, carved the eagle on Aella's back.' The *Orkneyinga Saga*, from about 1200, offers a fully detailed account of the practice, describing how Torf Einar avenged his father's murder by applying 'the blood-eagle' to the killer's back, cutting the ribs away at the spine and pulling out the lungs from behind. The victim in this case was dedicated to Odin.[22] Snorri Sturluson tells the same story in *Heimskringla*. But precisely what Sigvat meant by saying that Ivar 'carved the eagle on Aella's back' has been much discussed.[23] Snorri and the author of the *Orkneyinga Saga* took it literally and presumed it to have been a form of execution by torture, in which case the loss of blood involved in the initial stages of such a ritual would have killed the victim well before the fancied resemblance to an eagle was finally achieved. Conceivably, however, Sigvat intended to convey only that Ivar had killed Aella, and to do so poetically by conjuring the image of an eagle, perched on the back of the dead king and working into his flesh with talons and beak, no doubt a common sight in the aftermath of any battle.

Of Ivar's reputation as a cruel man, however, there can be no doubt. Adam of Bremen calls him the most gruesome of all the Danish petty kings who ravaged in Francia.[24] More even than as the torturer of Aella, his notoriety among Christians derived from his role as the murderer of Edmund, king of East Anglia, in 870. The *Anglo-Saxon Chronicle* is again succinct: there was a battle, the Danes 'had the victory, and killed the king and conquered all the land'.[25] Within twenty years a cult of martyrdom had grown up around Edmund's death which acquired a dramatic symbolic power across the mission fields of Europe. The first account that links Edmund with Ivar the Boneless is that of Abbo of Fleury in the *Passio Sancti Eadmundi*, a biography of the saint-king written sometime between 985 and 987. According to Abbo, an army under Hinguar and Hubba (Ivar and Ubbi) invaded England and captured Northumbria. Hinguar/Ivar then made his way south into East Anglia and triumphed over Edmund's army. The king himself was not among those killed or captured, so Ivar mounted a hunt for him and eventually located him in the village of Hellesdon, in Norfolk. He sent a message demanding that Edmund accept Ivar as his lord and share his kingdom with him. Edmund replied that he would do so on condition that Ivar accept baptism from him. The offer was rejected. Ivar had Edmund seized and brought before him, tied to a tree and scourged. Provoked by his insistent calling on Christ, Ivar's men are said to have used him as target practice for their archery. Finally his head was cut off and thrown away in the undergrowth.

The thirteenth-century English chronicler Roger of Wendover used details from Abbo's story for an account of the king's death in which it is, beyond doubt, a martyrdom:

In between the whip lashes, Edmund called out with true belief in the Saviour Christ. Because of his belief, because he called to Christ to aid him, the heathens became furiously angry. They then shot spears at him, as if it was a game, until he was entirely covered with their missiles, like the bristles of a hedgehog (just like St Sebastian was). When Ivar the pirate saw that the noble king would not forsake Christ, but with resolute faith called after Him, he ordered Edmund beheaded, and the heathens did so.[26]

The origin and meaning of Ivar's after-name 'the Boneless' (*Ívarr inn beinlausi*) is as impenetrable as any of the Great Heathen Army myths and legends. The explanation in the *Ragnars Saga* is that he was unable to walk and had to be carried everywhere.[27] 'Boneless' may have been a forbidden or *noa*-name for the wind, reflecting Ivar's prowess as a seaman. The name has been associated with sexual impotence, and with sexual potency. A modern suggestion is that he suffered from the medical condition known as brittle-bone disease.[28] Another theory suggests that the name arose from a confusion between the Latin adjectives *exosus* meaning 'detested', and *exos* meaning 'boneless'.[29] A further possibility is that his after-name should properly be interpreted as Ivar 'the Snake', a metaphorical deduction from the literal meaning of '*inn beinlausi*' as a creature 'without bones' or 'without legs' or 'without feet', and a thoroughly appropriate cognomen for a man of such legendary slyness and cruelty.[30]

Excavations on the site of the Repton camp which was the Great Heathen Army's base in 873 have unearthed finds that, while they hardly confirm any of the theories, have given rise to speculation on the historical person behind the Ivar legends. A number of mounds and burial chambers have been examined within the D-shaped fortress the army built on the Trent. Perhaps the most striking of these, located in what is now the Vicarage Garden, was a chamber containing the carefully stacked remains of some 264 individuals. The majority of these were tall, well-built men.[31] The bones had originally been stacked in charnel fashion against the walls, but had been seriously disturbed by digging done in about 1686. In 1726 an elderly labourer named Thomas Walker, who had been involved in the work, was asked about the discovery:

About Forty Years since cutting Hillocks, near the Surface he met with an old Stone Wall, when clearing farther he found it to be a square Enclosure of Fifteen Foot: It had been covered, but the Top was decayed and fallen in, being only supported by wooden Joyces. In this he found a Stone Coffin, and with Difficulty removing the Cover, saw a Skeleton of a Humane Body Nine Foot long, and round it lay One Hundred Humane Skeletons, with their Feet pointing to the Stone Coffin. They seem'd to be of ordinary Size. The Head of the great Skeleton he gave to Mr Bowers, Master of the Free School. I [i.e. Walker's interlocutor] enquired of his Son, one of the present Masters, concerning it, but it is lost; yet he says that he remembers the Skull in his Father's Closet, and that he had often heard his Father mention this Gigantick Corps, and thinks this Skull was in Proportion to a Body of the Stature.[32]

It is possible that Repton was a Viking war-grave, and the bones those of warriors who had died elsewhere and been taken there for burial.[33] The *Annals of Ulster* for 873 report the death of a Viking chieftain named Imar/Invgar/Ivar, and the *Saga of Ragnar Lodbrok and his Sons* preserves a tradition that Ivar the Boneless was buried in England. Putting together these details, Martin Biddle and Birthe Kjølbye-Biddle, the archaeologists who excavated the site between 1974 and 1993, have cautiously advanced the hypothesis that Ivar the Boneless may indeed have been an exceptionally tall man who, for whatever medical reasons, had to be carried from place to place, and that the remains of the giant at the centre of this grouping might just conceivably be his.[34]

The drama of this rich web of legends about Ragnar Lodbrok, his sons, the invasion of the Great Heathen Army, King Aella and 'the blood-eagle', and the martyrdom of St Edmund cannot, however, obscure the fact that, from the Scandinavian side, we have almost nothing to go on beyond a handful of names in trying to work out the details of the invasion of England by the Great Army in 865. What is abundantly clear – from the *Anglo-Saxon Chronicle*, from other contemporary annals and from Asser's biography of King Alfred – is that this was a well-led, organized, tactically sophisticated and highly mobile military force with very efficient lines of communication. It was perhaps only a lack of manpower that prevented it from making a full take over of England at this point.

Following Alfred's victory at Edington in 878 and the Danish occupation of East Anglia, much of the attention of the keepers of the *Anglo-Saxon Chronicle* was diverted to the activities of Viking forces on the continent. When Viking attacks on Alfred's kingdom resumed in earnest in 892, they encountered resistance of a different order from that of previous raids. Alfred's bonds with the people of Mercia from his marriage, in 868, to the Mercian princess Ealswith, were much strengthened in 889 by the marriage of his daughter Ethelfled to alderman Aethelred, who was the power in that part of the kingdom that remained in Anglo-Saxon hands. The main routes into Wessex were now protected by a network of fortified sites or *burhs*, so disposed as to make any one of them accessible to men living within a twenty-mile radius. Alfred introduced a rota system of conscription that divided the army into two, 'so that always half its men were at home, half on service, apart from the men who guarded the boroughs'.[35] By 885 he had also strengthened his navy sufficiently to defeat the Vikings in a battle in the mouth of the Stour and capture sixteen of their ships. His successes in dealing with the army that came over from the continent in 892 in a fleet of 250 ships under the Viking Hastein/Hasting owed much to the efficiency of these reforms. They finally conveyed the home advantage his forces should always have had, despite the assistance Hasting received from his fellow-Scandinavians settled in East Anglia. Alfred's forces stormed the fortress at Benfleet that Hasting was using as his base and put the garrison to flight, breaking up or burning the ships and capturing all the goods and the women and children sheltering inside and taking them to London. Hasting's wife and two of his children were among them, a hint that the thought of further colonization was on his mind. Though this engagement is the first reference in the *Chronicle* to Hasting, he and Alfred had obviously encountered one another before, perhaps as part of the peace-and-baptism agreement between Alfred and Guthrum/Athelstan in the handing-over of East Anglia:

And Hæsten's wife and two sons were brought to the king; and he gave them back to him, because one of them was his godson, and the other godson of Ealdorman Ethelred. They had stood sponsor to them before Hæsten came to Benfleet, and he had given the king oaths and hostages, and the king had also made him generous gifts of money, and so he did also when he gave back the boy and the woman.[36]

By the summer of 896 it had become clear to Viking leaders that Wessex was never going to become their prize. The army split up, some disappearing into the Danelaw territories of Northumbria and East Anglia. Others, 'those that were moneyless', got themselves ships and crossed the Channel to try their luck on the Seine.[37]

Hasting's story shows that Alfred had evidently not given up on conversion diplomacy and as we noted earlier with certain reservations, it seems the cultural transformation of the Heathen Viking Guthrum into the Christian East Anglian Athelstan had been successful. The restraint in the notice of his death in the *Chronicle* in 890 implies respect: 'And the northern king, Guthrum, whose baptismal name was Athelstan, died. He was King Alfred's godson, and he lived in East Anglia and was the first to settle that land'. As proper kings do, he had issued coins, and the fact that he did so under his baptismal name suggests that the respect was mutual.[38] It was an encouraging sign of the willingness of some Vikings to accept that the religion which they rejected with such ferocious contempt represented a higher form of culture than Heathendom, if only in its aspirations towards a better way of living. For many, though, the religious divide remained a factor in sustaining the sense of 'otherness' necessary to attack, enslave or kill without provocation the innocent and the unarmed. There are even recorded cases of Heathen Vikings turning the tables and encouraging apostasy among their Christian associates or allies. Sometime in the 860s, Pippin II of Aquitaine, a grandson of Louis the Pious who was also a monk, not only went over to the Vikings and fought with them but renounced his vows and became a worshipper of Odin. The *Annals of St-Bertin* mention another monk who joined the Vikings and practised their form of worship, and was executed for apostasy upon capture.[39]

Most of the graves excavated at Repton were those of men who had died violent deaths. One had been killed by spear thrusts to the head including one that passed through the eye. A fierce blow across the top of the thigh may have castrated him and explain the presence between his legs of a jackdaw bone and a boar's tusk, perhaps symbols respectively of Odin and Frey. Marks on the spine suggest that he was disembowelled after death. His sword had been broken and sheathed in a fleece-lined scabbard, and a knife, key and a Thor's hammer amulet completed his grave-goods.[40] Other finds from the same camp indicate that these men also traded as they went, using silver and gold bars for currency as well as coins. There are even signs that metalworking in copper and silver was practised.[41] Viking warriors were known to be willing to trade on their travels, though as the Frankish soldiers lured by a false signal of surrender into the Viking camp at Asselt in 882 discovered to their cost, it could be a risky business. For a dedicated Viking Age trader, however, we must turn to the redoubtable Ottar, who hailed from Hålogoland, high up on the north-west coast of Norway, in his own words 'the furthest north of any who lived in the north'. At some point, probably late on in Alfred's reign, he found himself in Wessex, lecturing King Alfred's courtiers on his life, his home, his travels and his plans.[42] He gave his audience invaluable information on the little-known lands to the north and east of Britain which Alfred added to his translation of Orosius' *History of the World* as a supplement.

Given the state of affairs in Wessex and England during most of Alfred's reign, and bearing in mind the extreme suspicion with which Louis the Pious had greeted his Rus visitors in 839, our inclination is to find Ottar's presence at Alfred's court in every way remarkable. The non-warlike Scandinavian native was not unknown in Wessex. On visiting a newly opened monastery at Athelney, Asser wrote of his surprise at finding among the largely foreign brotherhood a young monk 'of Viking parentage'. He provided his own explanation of the presence of so many foreigners there: Viking terror had been so effective against the Church that few free-born natives could be found

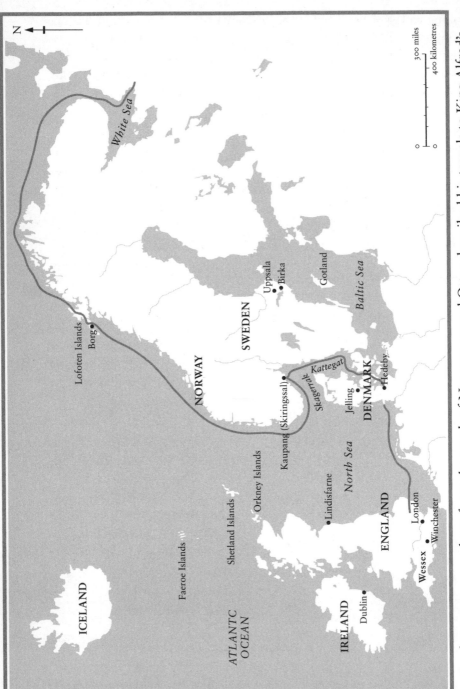

In about 890 a merchant from the north of Norway named Ottar described his travels to King Alfred's courtiers. His route from Hedeby to London is conjectural.

willing to risk their lives by taking holy orders.[43] Even so, and even though a specific goal of his journey seems to have been to see the king, for the report tells us that 'he still had unsold 600 tame deer at the time when he had left to visit the king', and though Alfred is referred to as 'his lord', it seems inconceivable that Ottar should have arrived in England alone and on his own initiative.[44] It is possible, though unlikely, that he was one of the party who spent twelve days with Guthrum at Alfred's court as part of the baptismal agreement after the battle at Edington. More credibly, he may have been one of Guthrum's advisers later, at the negotiations for the treaty of Wedmore.

The homely account Ottar gives of life in the far north of Norway is in striking contrast to the violence otherwise associated with the Scandinavian homelands during the Viking Age, and his talk of his tame reindeer and twenty pigs is a world away from Odin, human sacrifices, blood-eagles and raven banners. The description of his journey down the west coast of Norway to the trading town at Sciringsheal in the south, now identified as Kaupang, just outside present-day Sarpsborg, is uninterrupted by any sudden urge to go ashore and plunder an isolated settlement, and the next leg of the voyage from Sciringsheal to Hedeby, still thriving eighty years after the forcible resettlement of Reric's traders there in 808, is described entirely in terms of the navigational challenges involved.

The form in which the information occurs in the narrative often suggests that Ottar, or Ohthere as the Anglo-Saxons called him, was answering a question. We might see him seated and ringed around by one or more of the curious scribes at Alfred's cosmopolitan Winchester court. A learned courtier leans forward, chin in one hand, quill pen in the other: *Could you make the journey from Hålogoland to Sciringsheal within – say – a month? If you had the wind with you?* And duly makes a note of Ottar's reply: 'He said, that you could not sail there in a month, even if every night you sheltered and every day had a favourable wind.' The question of his economic and social status comes up:

He was a very wealthy man by the standards they use to judge wealth, that is to say, in deer. At the time of his visit to the king he had six hundred unsold tame deer. They call these animals reindeer, and six of them are decoy-deer. These are very valuable among the Sami, for they use them to trap the wild reindeer. He was one of the most powerful men in his country, yet he owned no more than twenty cows, twenty sheep and twenty swine, and the little bit of earth he ploughed, he ploughed with a horse. But their wealth consists mainly in the tax paid to them by the Sami. This tax takes the form of hides, feathers, whalebone, and rope made of whaleskin and sealskin.[45]

The tone implies that Ottar struggled to convince his Anglo-Saxon hosts to share his own idea of himself as a wealthy man. But he freely admitted that the farming land in his country was poor: 'whatever of it can be used for grazing or ploughing all lies along the coast. Even that is very rocky in some places, and wild mountains lie to the east and above, all along the cultivated land.' The land of the Norwegians in the late ninth century was 'very long and very narrow', which is an accurate description of modern Norway, and from Ottar's report it is clear that the main regional identities as 'Norwegians', 'Danes' and 'Swedes' were already in existence at that early date.

One of the many enigmas of the report arises in Ottar's description of his journey south along the coast of Norway to Sciringsheal:

He also said that one had to sail along the coastline. And on his starboard side he had first Ireland, and after that the islands that lie between Ireland and this land. After that it is this land, until he arrives at Skiringssal, and all the way Norway is on the port side.

Ireland, the Orkneys, Hebrides and Britain would not have been visible landmarks for Ottar on his journey south, and this information may have been provided by the scribe for the benefit of native readers of the *Orosius* in which this was to appear. It has also been suggested that, if Ottar himself provided this information, he was in fact referring to embarkation points for journeys to these particular destinations when sailing from the west coast of Norway.[46] This may explain the apparent oddity of his having 'Ireland' and not 'Iceland' on his starboard side. Some assume it to be a scribal error and amend the name. One argument for letting 'Ireland' stand is that, from the perspective of an observer in Wessex, it might have been natural to regard Ireland as an island in the north. Another is that the discovery and settlement of Iceland was so recent that it could not possibly have had time to establish itself as geographical reference point.

8

The settlement of Iceland

Traditions preserved in the *Landnámabók* or *Book of the Settlements* tell us that the first to set foot on Iceland was a Norwegian named Nadodd who set out for the Faroe Islands and was blown off course and ended up off the east coast of the island. Going ashore in the vicinity of what was later named Reydarfjord, he climbed a mountain, but saw neither smoke nor any other sign of human habitation from the top. On his way back out to sea it began to snow heavily, and he decided to call his discovery Snæland, or 'Snowland'. Another story credits the discovery to a Swede named Gardar Svavarsson, who was sailing through the Pentland Firth on his way to the Hebrides to claim property inherited by his wife when he too was blown off course. After a cautious circumnavigation of the island he went ashore at a place he called Husavik ('house point') and spent the winter there before leaving. He gave the island his own name, Gardarholm or 'Gardar's Island'. In another version of the story his mother, a seer, saw the island in a vision and gave Gardar directions on how to get there.[1]

The first attempt to settle was a small venture led by Floki Vilgerdason, a Norwegian from Rogaland. Before setting out on his voyage Floki is said to have sacrificed three ravens. The *Book of the Settlements* explains that this was done because at that time 'sailors in the Northlands had no loadstone' with which to navigate.[2] Floki's techniques of natural navigation were successful and earned him the nickname 'Raven' Floki: 'When he loosed the first, it flew aft astern; the second flew high into the air, then back to the ship; the third flew straight ahead in the direction in which they found land.'[3] Going ashore in Vatnsfjord they found the waters so well stocked with fish and seal that they neglected to make hay in the autumn, an oversight that cost the lives of the sheep and cattle they had taken with them, and put paid to the plan of permanent settlement. At the start of a bitterly cold spring Floki climbed a high mountain and saw in the north a fjord full of drift ice which led him to give the island its third and defining name of *Ísland* or Iceland. The demands of colonization seem to have been beyond this particular little group, for they delayed their departure until too late in the summer and found themselves driven back and had to spend another winter there, sustained this time by a whale they found washed up on the west bank of the fjord. When they eventually did get back to Norway Floki did not speak of the new land with any enthusiasm.

These sightings and landings probably took place sometime in the 860s. The commencement of the settlement proper is dated by Ari Thorgilsson in the *Book of the Icelanders*, the earliest written history of Iceland, to 870, '. . . when Ivar, son of Ragnar Lothbrok, had St Edmund, king of the Angles, killed', striking incidental evidence of the significance Edmund's death had acquired throughout the Christian world by the time of Ari's writing (1122–33). In the topographical description of Iceland given in the *Historia Norwegie*, probably written some time between 1160 and 1175, the author notes its 'innumerable mountains overlaid with unmelting glaciers', and that among these rises Mount Hekla, 'whose whole surface twitches like Etna and when it has shaken with a horrifying earth tremor, it belches up sulphurous fireballs'.[4] Analysis of the tephra layers deposited in the terrain by such eruptions has confirmed, to within a year either way, the accuracy of the date given by Ari. Previous to this there are no signs of human habitation in the soil below the *landnám* or settlement layer.[5] Two other tephra layers, the Katla R layer from about 920 and the Eldgjá from about 935, likewise confirm Ari's statement that within sixty years Iceland was fully settled, and that no significant immigration took place after about 930.

It has been observed that many of the most important actors in Ari's version of events were his own relatives, and that the book is as much a family history as it is an ecclesiastical or national history.[6] Perhaps because his ancestors were not involved he makes no mention of the earlier stories concerning the discovery of the island, and by contrast with other sources he is summary in his account of the arrival of the first permanent settler:

It is said with accuracy that a Norwegian called Ingolf travelled from there [Norway] to Iceland for the first time when Harald Finehair was sixteen years old, and a second time a few years later; he settled in the south in Reykjavik. The place to the east of Minkthakseyr where he first came ashore is called Ingolfshofdi, and the place to the west of Olfossa which he later took possession of is called Ingolfsfell.[7]

The only other items of information Ari adds about the earliest days of the settlement is that the country was at that time richly forested, evidently in contrast to the state of affairs at the time of his own writing, and that there were Christians living on the island, whom the immigrants called *papar*, who left 'because they did not wish to stay here with Heathens'. He writes that they left behind them some of the paraphernalia of Irish Christianity, including the small bells made of iron or bronze that were rung to call monks to prayer, psalters, gospels and other devotional books, and the croziers or staffs that were used as signs of office and as walking sticks.

Dicuil's *Liber de Mensura Orbis Terrae*, written in about 825, adds background to Ari's brief and enigmatic observations. Irish monks of the time practised a peculiar form of devotion known as *peregrinatio* which involved seclusion in remote and wild places, far from the temptations of the world, in search of mystical communion with God. Skellig Michael, off the Kerry coast, where in 824 Viking raiders carried off the hermit Éitgal, was an example of such a retreat. Dicuil relates that some of the most devout of these Irish Christians made their way north in small boats as far as Iceland (which, following Roman usage, he calls *Thule*), to spend the spring and summer months there. Still others made the shorter journey of two summer days and a night's sailing north of Ireland to what were almost certainly the Faroe Islands. Dicuil writes that monks from Ireland had been using these islands as retreats for about 100 years up to the time of his writing, but that now, 'because of Norse pirates, they are empty of anchorites, but full of innumerable sheep and a great many different kinds of seafowl'.[8]

Among the *Immrama*, the collective name given to these tales of intrepid Irish monks, are accounts of the voyages made by St Brendan, which include his description of 'a great hellish mountain which appeared full of clouds and smoke about its summit . . . And the brink of the island was of an appalling height, so that they could scarcely see the top of it, and it appeared full of firebrands and red sparks, and was as steep as a wall.'[9] These vivid images might well describe a volcanic eruption witnessed by Brendan, possibly of Katla, currently shrouded beneath the immense glacier Myrdalsjokull, on the south coast of Iceland.

No archaeological evidence has been found so far to confirm Ari's claim of an early Christian presence in Iceland, and the existence of similar traditions concerning the Faroes has led to suggestions that it is a topos, introduced by medieval Church historians to establish Christ as the spiritual occupant of the islands even before the arrival of the Heathen settlers.[10] Crosses carved on the walls of man-made caves in southern Iceland, like those at Kverkarhellir and Seljaland-shellir, seem to bear a stylistic resemblance to crosses from Argyll, the Hebrides and the Shetlands, leading some archaeologists to suggest a possible link between the stories told by Ari and Dicuil, and monks from the pre-Viking Age Christian settlements associated with Iona engaged in *peregrinatio*, though the link remains speculative.[11]

One redaction of the *Book of the Icelanders* supplements the tale of the finding of the bells, books and staffs with the information that these were found 'in Papey and in Papyli', the former an island off the east coast of Iceland, the latter a region in the south-east of the country. Such place-names are based on the word *papar* and derive from Latin *papa* via the Irish *pabba* or *pobba*. The same *pap-* element occurs in Scotland as Papil in the north of Shetland (Unst), Pabbay in the Outer Hebrides (Barra), and Papadil in the Inner Hebrides (Rum), as well as on the Isle of Man and the Faroes. The *Historia Norwegie* tells us that, as in Iceland, monks were living on the Orkneys before the Vikings came and that they, too, left books behind them when they fled the Vikings, though here the author makes the surreal claim that these identified their former owners as followers of Judaism from Africa.[12] Ari tells us that the monks left Iceland because of an aversion to living among Heathens, but it is inherently unlikely that they would deliberately have left behind their bells and books and staffs. Ari's story is possibly a euphemistic glossing-over of the fact that these too, like so many other members of Christian communities on remote islands around Britain, were simply killed by the first wave of Heathens to arrive.[13]

In the *Saga of Harald Finehair*, Snorri nicely weaves together the three main strands of his story: the tale of how Harald acquired his after-name; an account of the first unification of Norway; and an explanation of when and why the first settlers emigrated to Iceland.[14] The first element is a love-story, for it seems Harald was attracted to the daughter of a local Hordaland king, a girl named Gyda, and sent his men to ask if she would become his mistress. Gyda replied that a petty king like Harald was not good enough for her: why could he not do as Gorm in Denmark or as Erik in Swedish Uppsala had done and raise himself up to be king of a whole country? Only then would she consider his proposal. The returning messengers assumed the king would simply take the girl by force. Instead her spirit and ambition inspired him. Snorri puts the following words into his mouth: 'I make this vow, and the god who made me and rules all things shall be my witness, that never shall my hair be cut or combed till I have possessed myself of all Norway in *scot*, dues and rule – or else die.'[15] Little is known of the details of Harald's subsequent campaign to unify Norway and so make himself worthy of Gyda's love, but the violence involved precipitated a mass emigration to Iceland, led by chieftains who saw no benefit to themselves in the introduction of a monarchy.

Among the scholars who created the idea of the Viking Age towards the end of the nineteenth century, it was natural to relate the high concentration of Viking Age monuments found in Vestfold, on the western side of the Oslo fjord – like the sumptuous Oseberg and Gokstad burials and the stately field of mounds at Borre – to the impression given by Snorri in the saga that Vestfold was the seat of royal power from which Harald's campaign began, and the cradle of modern Norway. However, Harald's only certain connection to Vestfold is a reference, in Torbjorn Hornklovi's contemporary poem 'Haraldskvæthi', or 'the Lay of Harald', to Halvdan the Black, Harald's father, as a king from the east of Norway. In recent years the story has been rewritten by Norwegian historians and archaeologists in a way that reveals much more clearly the logical connection between the first unification and the settlement of Iceland. One of the main sources believed to have been used by Snorri for the genealogies that led him to place Harald in the east of Norway was the 'Ynglinga-tal' or 'Genealogy of the Ynglings', a poem by Tjodolf of Hvin believed to date from about 900. In 1991 the Norwegian historian Claus Krag analysed the 'Ynglingatal' and found that its intellectual world was incompatible with composition by a ninth-century Heathen Scandi-navian, and much more credibly the creation of a Christian Norwegian or Icelandic historian of the twelfth century. He concluded that, rather than being a contemporary Norwegian source from about 900, the poem had evolved over a considerable period of time before reaching the form in which Snorri used it, and that it probably reached this final form in Iceland, perhaps as late as 1200.[16] Krag's arguments are widely, though not universally, accepted.[17] The location of Harald's seat of power in Vestfold had always contained anomalies which the diminished credibility of 'Ynglingatal' as a source went some way towards resolving. Norwegians now generally accept that the heart of Harald's territory and the starting-point of his unification was not Vestfold, but Avaldsnes on the south-western coast of Norway, in Rogaland. Archaeological excavations currently being carried out close to the site of the Olav Church in Avaldsnes, on the island of Karmøy near Haugesund, seem poised to confirm this new scenario. Finds made in three different locations, including a layer of stones that was probably flooring, two spinning weights and a griddle for baking, identify the site as a large, Viking Age estate. A trial shaft dug in the car park by the church revealed a substantial post-hole dated to 900–1030 and so within the period of Harald Finehair's reign. A burnt post to the south of the car park has been dated to 690–840: all the datable finds from the royal palace and its environs have been identified as Viking Age.

It was hardly a country Harald was fighting to gain control over, more a coastal route; the term 'Nordvegr' or 'the north way', used by the trader Ottar for his home-country, implies as much. A decisive battle in the campaign was fought at sea off Hafrsfjord, not far from Stavanger. It is traditionally dated to 879, though many historians prefer a date closer to about 890 as this better accounts for a particularly intense period of emigrations to Iceland between 890 and 910, with refugees that responded to Harald's campaign as to a short-period pressure that, while it lasted, created an emergency.[18] Snorri tells us:

King Harald set the law wherever he won land, that he was possessed fully of all the land by *odal* right and he made all bonders, great and small, pay him a land tax. Over each shire he set a jarl who should administer the law and justice in the land and gather the fines and land dues, and every jarl should have a third of the tribute for living and costs. Every jarl should have under him four or more district chiefs, and each of them should have an income from the land of twenty marks. Each jarl should muster for the king's army sixty warriors and each district chief [*herse*] twenty men. But so much had King Harald increased the tribute and land taxes, that his jarls had greater incomes than the kings had had aforetime, and when that was learned in Trondheim, many great men sought King Harald and became his men.[19]

It may well be imagined that those who found themselves excluded from Harald's new aristocracy of earls, and paying rather than collecting taxes, had little liking for their first taste of the monarchical way and felt the desire to leave and make a fresh start elsewhere. Those in the south-west of the country would have felt the desire most pressingly, and it was from this region that the majority of Iceland's earliest settlers came. As we saw earlier, Harald's determined campaign to make himself monarch of all Norway was the reason given in the *Orkneyinga Saga* for the settlement of the Orkneys and Shetland, from where dispossessed and discontented chieftains harried the coastline of their former home so frequently that Harald moved against them, leading a fleet across the North Sea in about 890 and asserting his dominance over the islands. Snorri writes that Harald's authority at this point even extended to the Isle of Man, and quotes verse by Torbjørn Hornklofi that refers to his fighting in Scotland.

At this point in his narrative Snorri ties up his tale of Harald's after-name. Having met Gyda's challenge and now king of a unified Norway, he sent men to claim his prize. The romance of it all is diluted by the fact that, while waiting for her, he had taken a number of other wives and concubines and Gyda turned out to be only one of at least ten women who bore him sons, sixteen of them in some sources,

twenty in others.[20] She did not even have the honour of finally cutting
and combing his hair. That went to Ragnvald, earl of Møre, whom
Snorri also credits with coining the king's new after-name, turning
Harald Thickhair into Harald Finehair. The gesture of combing is
peculiarly appropriate, for across the geographical and temporal
spread of Viking Age culture the single item most commonly found
in graves remains, as we have sometimes seen earlier, the humble
comb.

Natural factors also played their part in the settlement, in particular
the serendipity of an interlude of climate change, known to climatologists as the Medieval Warm Period or Little Optimum, that lasted
from about 800 to 1200 and made these centuries among the warmest
of the past 8,000 years, opening up previously inaccessible regions of
the northern seas to the intrepid sailor.[21] Ottar made no mention to
Alfred of Harald's campaign, but then Hålogoland may have been
too far north for him to have noticed its effects. As we noted earlier,
he stressed to Alfred the poor quality of the farming land in Norway:
'whatever of it can be used for grazing or ploughing all lies along the
coast. Even that is very rocky in some places, and wild mountains lie
to the east and above, all along the cultivated land.'[22] To those who
struggled to eke a living out of this inhospitable soil, the lure of free
land in an uninhabited country not too far away must have been
strong, and made even stronger by persistent mild and stable weather
all across the region. By the 870s the amount of pack-ice in the
waters of the North Atlantic had fallen dramatically and ice conditions
around Iceland, Greenland and Labrador remained unusually favourable for voyaging throughout the Viking Age.[23] The analysis of ice
samples obtained by boring to great depths, in the extreme case of
north Greenland to a depth of 3,085 metres, and the snow that fell
125,000 years ago, provides an almost year-by-year record of the
degree of severity of successive winters and, on a larger scale, of
the progress of successive ice-ages.[24] The 'ice-thermometer' readings
suggest that Floki Vilgerdason and his would-be settlers were unfortunate enough to reach Iceland at the end of a run of cooler decades in
the middle of the Medieval Warm Period. The tale of his sighting of
an Icelandic fjord 'filled with ice' is about the last time mention is
made of sea-ice around the coast of Iceland for the next 300 years

and we do not get reports of drift ice in the Icelandic annals until the thirteenth century.[25]

In Norway the warmer climate led to the clearance, settlement and cultivation of valleys and hillsides over 100 metres above levels that had not been attempted for over 1,000 years. Even the bizarre, volcanic landscape of Iceland would have looked fertile and inviting. As Ari informed us, at the time of the settlement, Iceland was 'covered with woods between the mountains and the seashore', and the first settlers would have been heartened to find the sedges and grasses and dwarf woodlands of birch and willow familiar to them from Norway. Somewhere between 40 and 75 per cent of the total area seems to have been available as pasture, in stark contrast to today's figure of 20 per cent.[26] Settlers were able to grow barley and oats, although animal husbandry, fishing and bird-trapping remained the main sources of food.

The *Book of the Settlements* is a full and often dramatic account of the colonization of Iceland. Based on a lost original from the early twelfth century it contains the names of over 3,000 people and 1,400 places.[27] After Floki's false start, the first permanent settlers are named as two Norwegian foster-brothers, Ingolf and Leif, Viking adventurers who fell out with some of their associates and killed them. A court awarded their estates to the family of their victims, and the brothers decided to make a fresh start elsewhere. A preliminary reconnaissance trip established that the south of Iceland seemed more inviting than the north, and on a date traditionally given as 874 they set sail.

The author contrasts the approaches of the brothers to the great adventure: Leif was the one who 'would never sacrifice'; Ingolf 'offered up extensive sacrifices and sought auguries of his destiny' before departing.[28] As Floki had done, he made use of natural means to aid his decision-making and on first sighting land threw his high-seat pillars overboard and swore to make his home at the place where they came ashore. They were not found immediately and Ingolf built a temporary home at Ingolfshofdi or 'Ingolf's Head'. Leif settled at Hjorleifshofdi. Each year slaves went out to look for Ingolf's pillars.

In the meantime, Leif's slaves had risen up, killed him and his family and abducted their women. In the spring of the second year Ingolf's men came across the dead bodies and returned with the news to Ingolfshofdi. The author puts a sorrowing response into Ingolf's mouth: 'This was a sorry end for a brave man, that thralls should be the death of him; but so it goes, I see, with such as are not prepared to offer up sacrifice.'[29] It is almost as though this Christian-era writer believed Heathen piety to be better than no piety at all. Ingolf's devout nature was rewarded when, in the third year of searching, his posts were finally washed ashore. He kept his word and moved his farm to the location indicated by his gods.

In the *Book of the Icelanders* Ari gives special prominence to four main settlers as founding fathers and mothers: Rollaug, a son of Ragnvald, that earl of Møre who finally gave Harald his haircut; Ketilbjørn Ketilsson; Aud, the daughter of Ketil Flatnose; and Helgi the Lean, the son of Eyvind the Easterner. Ari stresses the Norwegian origins of each of them, ignoring the fact that Rollaug's family were earls in Shetland and Orkney, that Aud spent much of her adult life in Dublin and Caithness and arrived in Iceland from the Hebrides, and that Helgi's maternal grandfather was an Irish king, Helgi himself having been raised in the Hebrides and Ireland. In this way Ari, and Snorri after him, by explaining the settlement solely as the result of Harald's tyranny, both intend to convey an impression of the aristocratic origins of the new community. Even so, there are hints in the sagas that emigration to Iceland was regarded, by some, as a soft option. When Rollaug asked for the succession to the earldom of the Orkneys, his father Ragnvald was categorical in his rejection: 'You may not be earl, you have no disposition for war. The path that you must follow leads rather to Iceland.'[30] Iceland is surprisingly poor in archaeological remains from the Viking Age, but the chieftains' graves that have been found lack monumentality and are poorly furnished by comparison with those from Norway. Only five boat-graves have been discovered, and in all cases the coffins were small rowing-boats.[31] The likely explanation is that the Icelandic chieftains who cut such proud figures in the later Family Sagas came originally from modest farming backgrounds, and that the literary sources have been prone to glamorize their status prior to emigration.[32] The compendious *Book of the Settlements* gives what is clearly a more accurate picture of the mixed origins of the settlers than Ari, without disturbing the fundamental premise that most of them came originally from western Norway.

At least, most of the male settlers did. A study of the mitochondrial DNA of Icelandic women carried out in 2001 found that it was most closely related to Welsh and British mitochondrial DNA in some 63 per cent of the samples. A parallel study of the Y-chromosomes of a group of Icelandic men showed that about 80 per cent of them were of Norse origin, with the remainder tracing their descent to the British Isles.[33] The likely explanation for the imbalance is that the women came as slaves and concubines of the men, having been taken from their homelands in Viking raids.

King Harald initially tried to extend his authority to Iceland by sponsoring the claim of Uni, son of the Gardar who was one of the first discoverers of Iceland, to be his earl there. When he tried to press this claim Uni was ostracized by the other settlers and presently killed.[34] The rejection of Harald was not universal, however. The first settlers to arrive had taken large, even exorbitant claims, and the *Book of the Settlements* tells us that a second apparent attempt at interference by Harald, when he tried to set limits to the size of claims that could be made, was actually in response to a plea from frustrated late arrivals for the authoritative regulation of such an important matter.[35] It was a potentially dangerous precedent, and must have brought home to the Icelanders the need to take stock of their situation and create effective leadership of their own that would satisfy the majority and reduce the possibility of the aggrieved appealing for help to Norway.

Their solution was to adapt the principle of government by local assembly or *thing*, familiar to them from Norway in the days before Harald Finehair. The island was divided into a number of regional institutions called *goðorð*, each under the control of a chieftain called a *goði* (plural *goðar*). Normally, but not inevitably, a *goði* was the leader of the people living within his *goðorð*, who were known as his *thingmen*; but a farmer was not bound to commit himself to the protection of his local *goði* if he did not choose to do so, and a *goði*'s supporters or *thingmen* could be spread over a wide area. A *goðorð* was the property of the individual *goði*. It could be bought, sold, borrowed and inherited. Initially the number of these institutions was set at thirty-six. Later reforms increased it to thirty-nine and then to forty-eight. This was possible since it seems that, in the early years, there were more chieftains than there were *goðorð*, owing to the flexible nature of the office.[36] In return for a *thingman* manifesting his authority when called upon to do so, the *goði* offered protection and support in disputes in which his *thingman* became involved. The larger the *goðorð*, the larger the force the *goði* could put into the field in any contentious matter requiring that he support a *thingman*.

Legal disputes and matters of common concern were taken up each spring at local meetings of the *thing*. The earliest such assembly to be created was probably that at Kjalarnes, in the south-west of Iceland, where the *goði* was Thorstein Ingolfsson, a son of the first settler, Ingolf. Another was Thorolf Mostrarskegg's assembly at Thorsnes, on Breidaford, which was ringed about with Thorolf's injunctions forbidding men to look on Helgafell, or the 'Holy Mountain', with an unwashed face, and requiring them to leave the assembly grounds for the privacy of a nearby skerry when answering the call of nature.[37] The *Landnámabók* enlarges on the sacral aspect of the *goði*'s obligations at *thing* meetings: he must ensure that

A ring of two ounces or more should be on the stall in each principal *hof* [temple], each *goði* should wear that ring on his arm at all established assemblies in which he himself should participate, and redden it beforehand in gore from the blood of the beast he personally sacrificed there. Everyone who needed to perform legal duties there at court should previously swear an oath on that ring.[38]

By 930, with the available land taken, an awareness of Iceland as a country and of themselves as no longer settlers but Icelanders had arisen among the farmers. This manifested itself in the desire for an assembly that would serve the needs of the entire population. It is thought the decision to establish such an institution may have been taken at the Kjalarnes *thing*.[39] This general assembly, the *althing*, convened annually for two weeks in late June at Thingvellir, or 'the Assembly Plain', a dramatic open-air site on the northern shore of a lake in the south-west of the country. The *althing* and the first Icelandic law code probably came into being at about the same time. Ari tells us that 'when Iceland had been settled widely, an Easterner called

Ulfljot first brought laws out here from Norway (Teit told us) and they were subsequently called Ulfljot's laws'.[40] Ulfljot's laws 'were for the most part modelled on the laws of the Gulathing', says Ari, a natural choice of model, given the west Norwegian origins of the majority of the male settlers. The oldest surviving version of the Gulathing code is the *Codex Rantzovianus*, dated to about 1250, and comparisons of this with the early tenth-century treaties drawn up between the Kievan Rus and Constantinople preserved in the *Russian Primary Chronicle* reveal similarities in the regulation of certain practices, suggesting that parts, at least, of the Gulathing code date from the early 900s.[41]

The *althing*'s presiding officer was the Lawspeaker, a man with an approved reputation for wisdom and a lawyer well versed in the technicalities of the law. He was elected for a period of three years and could be re-elected. It may well be that Ulfljot himself was the first Lawspeaker, since the most important duty of the office was to recite a third part of the law code each year, addressing the assembly from a prominent natural pulpit known as the Law Rock perched on a hillside above the site. Attendance at these annual recitations was mandatory for *goðar*, who also sat on the *althing*'s legislative body, known as the *lögrétta*. Another of the Lawspeaker's duties was to inform the assembly of any new laws passed by the *lögrétta*. He was the assembly's legal oracle and his advice would be sought on problems or disputes over the interpretation of the law as they arose.

We know little of the organization of the *althing* and of the content of the law code prior to the reforms of the 960s, which Ari describes in Chapter 5 of the *Book of the Icelanders*. The first laws were not recorded until 1117–18, and the overriding impression conveyed by the collection of early laws, compiled in the middle of the thirteenth century and known as *Grágás*, or 'Grey Goose', is of a staggering attachment to procedural complexity.[42] The spirit that invests these, and other Viking Age law codes generally, is more readily grasped. As we noted in an earlier chapter, the Viking Age conception of law differed from the Roman conception in the degree to which it was based on a communal rather than an individual response to law-breaking, and the compulsory involvement of members of the community in the processes of confession, arrest and punishment.

The law was so intrinsically a part of communal life in Iceland that a man who was not 'in *thing*' with a *goði* did not even have a legal existence.[43]

The slaves who were bought or captured and taken out to Iceland by the settlers had a legal existence, but only as the property of their owner, on a par with his cattle. Whether slavery was imported as an economic necessity, or was a culturally conditioned import from the old country, remains a matter of debate. The 'Rigsthula', a poem dated as early as the tenth century by some scholars and as late as the thirteenth by others, and thought variously to originate in Ireland, Iceland and Norway, provides a fatalistic anthropology of Viking Age Scandinavian society, though the uncertainty about its provenance means that its source value remains provisional.[44] It describes how Heimdall, the watchman among the Aesir, under the name Ríg, visits three households in turn and in each has sex with the woman of the house. The first is a great-grandmother, named Edda. Nine months later she gives birth to the first slave, a swarthy, rough-skinned child, coarse-fingered and scabby-faced, with a crooked back and big feet. When he grows up he marries a knock-kneed woman with a hooked nose and dirty feet. They give birth to numerous children whose names, such as Stumpy, Smelly, Horse-Fly, Foul, Lump, Coarse, Brawler, reflect their destinies as the slaves of the world. Ríg's remaining unions are with the successively younger Amma (grandmother), on whom he fathers the first of the free yeomen, and Móthir (mother), from whom are descended the race of kings. The point of the divine origin of the three classes is not that all are fundamentally equal but that class divisions are divinely ordained and immutable.[45]

Under Viking Age Scandinavian law, slaves, whether *thræll* (male) or *ambátt* (female), were property before they were people. Early Viking Age societies answered any unease that might have surrounded the institution by the cultivation of a circular logic that showed slaves to be lesser beings, whose inherent contemptibility was demonstrated by the fact that they had failed to prevent themselves from becoming slaves. For Ingolf, the special tragedy of his brother Leif's death was the humiliation of having been killed by slaves. Among the laws of the Swedish Västergötland was a provision that, in the event of such an abomination taking place, no credit at all must be given to the slave as the killer of a free man. The rigidity of the codification was complete: in *Egils Saga* a slave who dares to treat a free man as an equal by challenging him to a fight is killed while bending to tie his shoelaces. Codes of honourable behaviour simply did not apply between the free and the enslaved.[46]

It required a great cultural effort to preserve the lowly status of the slaves, and the echoes of this sounded on into the era of Christianity and the written word in Iceland. The *Book of the Settlements* is careful to tell us that when Ingolf caught up with Leif's killers, hiding out on the Westmann Islands, he surprised them in the ignoble act of eating. Nor did they stay to fight but panicked, scattered and ran, some jumping to their deaths over a cliff. In the Family Sagas, dealing with events between about 930 and 1030, slaves feature only incidentally, and then usually as stock figures of fun or villains. Most are male, reflecting perhaps the fact that the slave population was controlled by the practice of leaving infant females out to die. In the *Saga of Gisli*, Gisli has a slave named Thord whose after-name is 'the Coward'. The author tells us that he had 'as much sense as he had spirit, for he had none of either'.[47] When, in *Egils Saga*, the old Viking decides to spite his family by burying his wealth he gets two slaves to carry the chest for him. Once the digging is done and the treasure is buried he kills them. Egil is old and blind by this time, and it is unnecessary for the sagaman to point out to his listeners that only slaves would be stupid enough to allow themselves to be killed by such a man. In any event, it was not illegal for a man to kill his own slaves – all Egil had to do afterwards was announce the deaths for that to be the end of the matter. Arnkel meets his death in the *Eyrbyggja Saga* because his slave is so preoccupied with the haymaking he forgets the instructions he has been given to send for help.[48]

Perversely, the absence of a fully human status sometimes worked to the benefit of the slave. Under the Gulathing law, a slave who accompanied a free man in a robbery had no guilt in the matter, since 'the man who steals with another man's slave steals by himself'. And a remarkable legal exemption in Icelandic law stated that: 'A thrall has the right to kill on account of his wife, even though she is a bond-maid. But a free man is not allowed to kill on account of a bondmaid, even though she is his woman.'⁴⁹ The children of slaves were also slaves; where only the mother was a slave, the child took the social status of the father. The law also showed occasional glimpses of humanity: a slave who was physically injured was allowed to keep a third of the compensation paid to his owner for the damage to his 'property'.

There were less extreme forms of slavery than outright ownership. Debtors unable to meet their debt could work it off by entering the service of their creditor for an agreed period of time with no other reward than the cancelling of the debt. And for the very poor, an arrangement existed whereby one man could hand over himself and all he owned to another, in return for the promise of being looked after for the rest of his life. Another option was to hand over a child, and in certain circumstances a petty thief could be sentenced to become the slave of his victim.⁵⁰ As we noted earlier, the right of an owner to kill his slave was sometimes used to sacrifice someone to accompany a dead master into the grave. Even this was too much familiarity for some: the ghost of a settler buried with his slave at Asmundarleidi was graceless enough to complain so bitterly about the company that the mound was opened and the slave removed.

> Alone in this berth of stones I lie
> In the sea-king's raven's hold.
> No press of men on the decking.
> On the waves' steed I live.
> Better for the battle-skilled fighter
> Is space than this low companion.⁵¹
> The sea beast is my command.
> Long will that stand in man's memory.

To a modern reader, a striking feature of the Icelandic Family Sagas is the almost complete absence of any expression of wonder or curiosity about the new environment, certain features of which must have struck the settlers as very different from anything familiar to them in the old country: erupting volcanoes; lava fields that glowed in the night; sea-water washing across black sands; hot thermal springs, spouting geysers and steaming solfataras. Perhaps the novelty of it had worn off by the time the sagas were written down. The best-known exception to this apparent indifference to natural beauty is a scene in *Njals Saga* in which Gunnar of Hlidarendi rides down to the ship that will take him away from Iceland after he has been sentenced to three years in exile as an outlaw. He is accompanied by his brother Kolskeggur, who has received the same sentence:

They rode down to Wood River. There Gunnar's horse stumbled and he leaped from the saddle. Glancing up toward the slope and his farm at Hlidarendi he said: 'How beautiful the slope is! It has never seemed so beautiful before, with its ripening grain and new-mown hay. I am going to ride back home and not go abroad.'

Kolskeggur goes on alone to the waiting ship, but Gunnar rides back home. Shortly afterwards, he meets his death. One of many possible interpretations of the scene might be that an aesthetic appreciation of the landscape was not only a luxury but a dangerous luxury. For the first settlers the land was something to be cleared and used. The landscape was a route to be forced and conquered, not a subject for contemplation. The description in *Hrafnkels Saga* of Eyvind's flight across Flotsdal moor, with Hrafnkel in pursuit, vividly conveys its harsh and refractory nature.[52] In a brief section on the topography of Iceland in the *Historia Norwegie*, from the second half of the twelfth century, the author notes how wool or cloth that has been left in the waters of certain springs will turn to 'stone' overnight; and he includes a dramatic account of an underwater volcanic eruption. But it is not until the thirteenth century, and the Norwegian *Konungs skuggsjá* (*King's Mirror*), a didactic work in the form of a dialogue between a father and son, that we get an extended insight into how the medieval mind regarded phenomena such as volcanoes, glaciers, the aurora borealis and the thermal springs. As late as the source is, it comes well before the spread of scientific rationalism and probably sounds an echo of past wonderment more accurately than it predicts future explanations:

Son: What do you think of the extraordinary fire which rages constantly in that country? Does it rise out of some natural peculiarity of the land, or can it be that it has its origin in the spirit world? And what do you think about those terrifying earthquakes that can occur there, or those marvellous lakes, or the ice which covers all the higher levels?

Father: As to the ice that is found in Iceland, I am inclined to believe that it is a penalty which the land suffers for lying so close to Greenland; for it is to be expected that severe cold would come thence, since Greenland is ice-clad beyond all other lands. Now since Iceland gets so much cold from that side and receives but little heat from the sun, it necessarily has an over-abundance of ice on the mountain ridges. But concerning the extraordinary fires which burn there, I scarcely know what to say, for they possess a strange nature.

[...]

I am also disposed to believe that certain bodies of water in Iceland must be of the same dead nature as the fire that we have described. For there are springs which boil furiously all the time both winter and summer. At times the boiling is so violent that the heated water is thrown high into the air. But whatever is laid near the spring at the time of spouting, whether it be cloth or wood or anything else that the water may touch when it falls down again, will turn to stone. This seems to lead to the conclusion that this water must be dead, seeing that it gives a dead character to whatever it sprinkles and moistens; for the nature of stone is dead. But if the fire should not be dead but have its origin in some peculiarity of the country, the most reasonable theory as to the formation of the land seems to be that there must be many veins, empty passages, and wide cavities in its foundations. At times it may happen that these passages and cavities will be so completely packed with air, either by the winds or by the power of the roaring breakers, that the pressure of the blast cannot be confined, and this may be the origin of those great earthquakes that occur in that country. Now if this should seem a reasonable or plausible explanation, it may be that the great and powerful activity of the air within the foundations of the earth also causes those great fires to be lit and to appear, which burst forth in various parts of the land.

[...]

Father: I have no doubt that there are places of torment in Iceland even in places where there is no burning; for in that country the power of frost and ice is as boundless as that of fire. There are those springs of boiling water which we have mentioned earlier. There are also ice-cold streams which flow out of the glaciers with such violence that the earth and the neighbouring mountains tremble; for when water flows with such a swift and furious current, mountains will shake because of its vast mass and overpowering strength. And no men can go out upon those river banks to view them unless they bring long ropes to be tied around those who wish to explore, while farther away others sit holding fast the rope, so that they may be ready and able to pull them back if the turbulence of the current should make them dizzy.

Later the father attempts to satisfy his son's curiosity on the subject of the aurora borealis, another phenomenon of nature we might expect to find referred to frequently in the saga literature but in fact do not find at all:

Father: But these northern lights have this peculiar nature, that the darker the night is, the brighter they seem; and they always appear at night but never by day, most frequently in the densest darkness and rarely by moonlight. In appearance they resemble a vast flame of fire viewed from a great distance. It also looks as if sharp points were shot from this flame up into the sky; these are of uneven height and in constant motion, now one, now another darting highest; and the light appears to blaze like a living flame. While these rays are at their highest and brightest, they give forth so much light that people out of doors can easily find their way about and can even go hunting, if need be. Where people sit in houses that have windows, it is so light inside that all within the room can see each other's faces. The light is very changeable. Sometimes it appears to grow dim, as if a black smoke or a dark fog were blown up among the rays; and then it looks very much as if the light were overcome by this smoke and about to be quenched. But as soon as the smoke begins to grow thinner, the light begins to brighten again; and it happens at times that people think they see large sparks shooting out of it as from glowing iron which has just been taken from the forge. But as night declines and day approaches, the light begins to fade; and when daylight appears, it seems to vanish entirely.

Finally the father describes the mineral-rich 'ale-springs':

Father: . . . There is still another marvel that men wonder at. It is reported that in Iceland there are springs which men call ale-springs. They are so called because the water that runs from them smells more like ale than water; and when one drinks of it, it does not fill as other water does, but is easily digested and goes into the system like ale. There are several springs in that country that are called ale-springs; but one is the best and most famous of all; this one is found in the valley called Hitardal. It is told about this spring, or the water flowing from it, that it tastes exactly like ale and is very abundant. It is also said that if drunk to excess, it goes into one's head. If a house is built over the spring it will turn aside from the building and break forth somewhere outside. It is further held that people may drink as much as they like at the spring; but if they carry the water away, it will soon lose its virtue and is then no better than other water, or not so good. Now we have discussed many and even trifling things, because in that country they are thought marvellous; and I cannot recall anything else in Iceland that is worth mentioning.[53]

The rapidity of the colonization of Iceland owed much to the fact that there were no natives to subdue. Apart from the arctic fox there were no indigenous wild animals for the settlers to compete with either. Everywhere else the Scandinavians of the Viking Age gained a foothold – in Ireland, in England, in the Scottish islands, in Normandy, and later in Greenland and Vinland – they had to fight for it. Their own courage and willingness to adapt played a large part in the success of the venture. So did the elevation of law among them to an almost spiritual prominence, which kept the temptations of indiscipline at bay. The Icelanders were proud of their law. Iceland was as much *vár log* – 'the domain of our law' – as it was a location in the remote North Atlantic.[54] An enduring peculiarity of this pride was that they did not complement the legislative and judiciary powers they had awarded themselves with administrative or executive authority. A verdict handed down in a court of law left the implementation of it to the successful litigant. The practical result was that might rather than right remained the deciding factor. The omission, if such it was, of an executive structure is in contrast to the formalism and sophistication of the legal procedures and has sometimes been seen as containing within itself, even at this early stage in its development, the seeds of the eventual collapse of the Icelandic free state over 300 years later.[55]

9

Rollo and the Norman colony

A glance at the Frankish annals recording events over the years since 820, when the first small fleet of thirteen Viking ships raided around the mouth of the Seine, shows how persistently the raiders used the great river to penetrate the territories of the Frankish empire. In the 840s, fleets under the commands of Asgeir and Ragnar sailed as far as Paris, looting and burning as they went. Rouen was captured and burnt by Asgeir in 841, and when he returned to the Seine in 851 Rouen served as a base from which to raid on foot in the region of Beauvais. A permanent camp was established on the fluvial island of Jeufosse, from which successive generations of Viking leaders were able to exercise control over access to the Seine. The Norwegian Sigtrygg, who spent time in both Ireland and Francia, joined forces with a leader named Bjørn to raid along the Seine as far as Chartres until beaten back in a rare military triumph for Charles the Bald. In 857 the two armies attacked Paris and captured and sacked Chartres. Bjørn was joined by Hasting early in 858 and the attacks from the Seine valley continued. As we saw in an earlier chapter, the power struggle that followed the death of Louis the Pious made things much easier for the Vikings.

Carolingian efforts to preserve order within the divided empire were made more difficult by a development in the system of royal administration whereby those royal officials like the counts, who had formerly been peripatetic and derived their authority from their position within the Carolingian hierarchy, claimed an increasing autonomy that turned them into magnates with local, geographically determined power bases. Dynasties developed, several of which established themselves in the region around what would later become

Normandy, known as the Breton or Neustrian march. In the days of Charlemagne it extended from Calais to the borders of Brittany and its military role within the empire was to prevent the incursions of the notoriously independent Bretons from the west. Fifty troubled years after Charlemagne's death it was clear that the region could not be defended and in 867 the Cotentin and the Avranchin were ceded to the Bretons. Chronic instability in the region persisted as they continued to push eastward without ever establishing themselves as the dominant power in the region.

At the same time the Carolingian churches and monasteries were abusing their privileges of royal immunity to the point at which they more or less rejected any obligations at all to central government. Having neither money, lands nor reliable armies, the Carolingian monarchy was reduced to issuing ineffectual decrees and ordinances. Lawlessness and theft were combated by decrees advising that violators be 'admonished with Christian love to repent'; punishment was to be meted out to the guilty 'as far as the local officials could remember them'. One forlorn decree even required royal officials to swear on oath not to become highway robbers themselves.[1]

To this brew of royal intrigue and looming anarchy Viking raiders added their own particular form of terror. Hasting and Bjørn raided again and again in the Cotentin and Avranchin and turned them into deserted wastelands. In 865 the crews of some fifty ships built a new camp on the Seine at Pîtres, and in 876 another fleet of about 100 ships sailed up the Seine and were bought off in the following year for 5,000 livres by Charles the Bald. Just as it had done in England, Viking terror devastated and demoralized the Christian Church. Bishops were killed at Noyon, Beauvais and Bayeux, and the record of bishops at Avranches ceases after 862, at Bayeux after 876 and at Sées after 910.

The policy of a sometimes well-meaning appeasement had been practised by Frankish rulers for almost a century prior to the agreement made in 912 between Charles the Simple, king of the Western Franks, and a Viking leader named Rollo. Usually these deals involved Frisia, from Rüstringen in the north to Antwerp in the south, and the beneficiaries were Danes. Hemming was given the harbour of Dorestad on the Waal, a tributary of the Rhine, in 807; Louis the

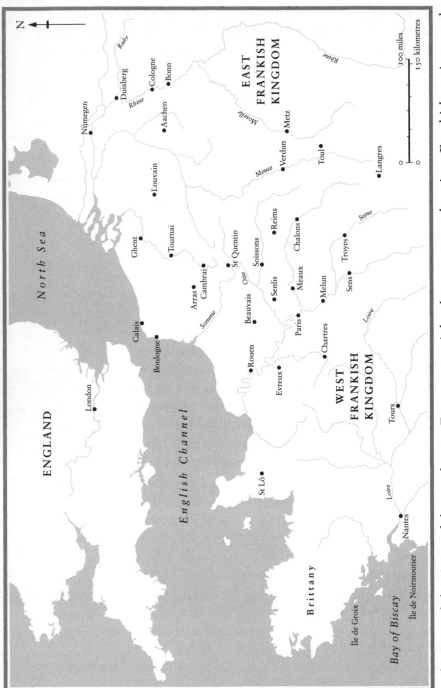

Vikings used the rivers of the north-west European mainland to penetrate deep into Frankish territory and capitalize on the rivalry that broke out between the sons of Louis the Pious after his death.

Pious gave it to Klak-Harald in 829, between 855 and 873 it was in the hands of Rorik, and in 882 Godfrid took it over.[2] None of these episodes turned into a full-scale attempt to settle in Frisia and the archaeological record of the Viking presence there is sparse, but the story of Godfrid's agreement of 882 with Charles the Fat, in which he was given 'land to live on' and a royal bride named Gisla, makes an interesting overture to Rollo's establishment of the colony in Normandy.

Also known to his biographers, chroniclers and poets as Rollo, Rollon, Robert, Rodulf, Ruinus, Rosso, Rotlo and Hrolf, Ganger Rolf or Rolf the Walker, founder in about 911 of what became the duchy of Normandy, is another of those, like Ragnar Hairy-Breeches and Ivar the Boneless, whose prominence among their contemporaries conspired over the years with an almost complete lack of biographical information to transform them from ordinary mortals into dense hybrids of men, myth and legend. As we noted earlier, Dudo of St-Quentin's claim that Rollo was one of the Viking leaders at the long siege of Paris in 885 seems doubtful. A canon of St-Quentin in Picardy, Dudo was commissioned in 994 to write his history of the duchy of Normandy by Rollo's grandson, Duke Richard I. Dudo's account of the creation of the duchy and its subsequent development has suffered more than most from the rigours of source criticism. Much of his information about Rollo's activities prior to the foundation of the duchy is probably the product of a desire to insert retrospectively into significant events someone whose rise to prominence went almost unnoticed in the contemporary record, and thereafter to portray him in as sympathetic a light as possible.[3] Yet Dudo's is the closest we have to a local and contemporary history of the duchy. His successors as historians of the duchy were William of Jumièges, writing some time after 1066, and Orderic Vitalis, who died in about 1142. Both used Dudo as their source, and though they did so with discretion and were able to provide a few extra items of information they did not substantially alter his account of the early days of the duchy. There are only three references to Rollo in independent contemporary sources, each of them brief, none that tell us anything about who he was or where he came from.

His origins, not unsurprisingly, are uncertain. The tradition Dudo records is that he was from Dacia or Denmark, of aristocratic family, and driven out of the country either as a result of what Dudo implies was a form of population control in Denmark that involved the expulsion of whole generations of young men by the drawing of lots, or because the Danish king considered the popular Rollo too great a threat to his power. Rollo made his way to Skåne and from there embarked on a career as a Viking that included making tributaries of the Frisians in Walcheren. In England he struck up an immediate and close rapport with a king whom Dudo calls 'Alstem', and agreed terms of perpetual friendship and support with him. This is regarded as one of Dudo's wilder fictions and a grotesque misjudgement of Alfred of Wessex's character. Yet its oddness is diminished if we take the reference to be not to Alfred, king of Wessex, or even a misdated Athelstan, grandson of Alfred, but to Guthrum, the Danish leader whom Alfred baptized and then recognized as king of the East Angles in 880. 'Alstem' is an acceptably close approximation to Guthrum's baptismal name Athelstan, and we know that Athelstan used the name in minting his coins. Identifying Alstem as Guthrum/Athelstan, king of the East Angles, makes credible the warmth and respect that Dudo tells us sprang up between these two men, apparently spontaneously.[4] When Rollo's emissaries reveal to Alstem that they are Danes, the king's reported reply – 'No region brings forth extraordinary men, and ones actively instructed in arms, more than does Dacia' – has the unique ring of one ex-pat fondly greeting another. Guthrum/Athelstan died in 890 and had been king in East Anglia since 880, dates that easily accommodate these associations. Dudo tells us that Rollo lived to an advanced age and died in about 929 or 930, so if we hazard a guess at a birthdate of about 860 this would make him active by 880 at the latest.

The identification also supplies a logic for this Danish Alstem's recurring problems with a respectless and rebellious native population: 'The English, puffed up and perverse with their audacious insolence, refuse to obey my commands', he complained to Rollo.[5] Placing Rollo at the siege of Paris that took place in 885, Dudo writes as though this were indeed the state of affairs:

And when the English heard that Rollo had laid siege to the city of Paris, and was occupied with Frankish matters, they reckoned that he would not come to the assistance of his friend king Athelstan, and they renounced their fealty. They began to grow insolent and arrogant and fierce, and opposed the king by vexing him with battles.[6]

Dudo goes on to refer to the English as 'perfidious', illogically for a supporter of the house of Wessex, logically for the supporter of a Danish conqueror struggling to assert his authority over the natives. He even tells us that Alstem offered a half share of his kingdom to Rollo, an incredible gesture for Alfred, but for Guthrum/Athelstan only a sensible attempt to solve problems of order in his new kingdom.

The identification of Alstem with the Guthrum/Athelstan known to us from *Anglo-Saxon Chronicle* strengthens Dudo's claim that Rollo was of Danish origins; but in general Dudo's account of Rollo's origins and career has all the vagueness and general applicability of a newspaper horoscope. It suffers by comparison with Snorri Sturluson's more detailed account. In Snorri's *Saga of Harald Fairhair* the future conqueror of Normandy is a Norwegian youth named Hrolf, a son of that Ragnvald, earl of Møre, who was Harald's main ally during the campaign to unify Norway and his ceremonial hairdresser once it was successful. Snorri tells us that Rollo was so big that no horse could bear his weight and he had to walk everywhere, and was for this reason known as Ganger Rolf or Rolf the Walker. It makes him a sort of legendary inversion of Ivar the Boneless who, in one set of stories about him, could walk nowhere at all and had to be carried everywhere. For once it is Dudo who has the more sober explanation for this tale, conceding that in the last year of his life Rollo was 'unable to ride a horse' but adding that this was owing to 'his great age and failing body'. There is no hint of his being an unusually large man.

Like Dudo's Rollo, Ganger Rolf was a successful Viking. He made the mistake of harrying on the shores of the Vik at a time when King Harald himself was in the region. Harald promptly outlawed the young man. Rolf's mother Hild, whose family name was Nevja, tried to persuade him to change his mind, but the king was adamant. Hild then composed this sorrowing verse:

The name of Nevja is torn;
Now driven in flight from the land
Is the warrior's bold kinsman.
Why be so hard, my lord?
Evil it is by such a wolf
Noble prince to be bitten;
He will not spare the flock
If he is driven to the woods.[7]

The lines enjoy the special credibility generally extended to poems embedded in saga texts as more likely to be creations describing contemporary events; yet they have no direct bearing on the identification of Rolf with Rollo of Normandy. This comes unequivocally with Snorri's summation of Rolf's fate after his banishment: 'Rolf the Ganger afterwards crossed the sea to the Hebrides and from there went south-west to France; he harried there and possessed himself of a great earldom; he settled many Norsemen there, and it was afterward called Normandy.'[8] Among Rollo's three half-brothers was Rollaug, a name that transmutes more easily into Latin 'Rollo' than does Rolf. Snorri quotes, moreover, a verse by Einar, earl of Orkney, which shows that Rolf and Rollaug were at some point together in the Orkneys. But arguing against the faint possibility that Snorri somehow got the brothers confused and that it was Rollaug who was actually 'Rollo' of Normandy, is the story mentioned earlier of how Rollaug was told to settle in Iceland by his father, for he had 'no disposition for war'.

Rollo's Hebridean connections are further supported, despite some passing confusion, by the anonymous twelfth-century Welsh history *The Life of Gruffyd ap Cynan*, where the genealogy of Gruffyd's grandfather includes Rollo, here a brother of King Harald Finehair, who subdued 'a large part of France which is now called Normandy, because the men of Norway inhabit it; they are a people from Llychlyn'.[9] 'Llychlyn' looks like a variant spelling of that independent island kingdom, mentioned earlier, comprising the northern and western isles as well as parts of mainland Scotland.

At the close of the nineteenth century, with the Scandinavian nations jostling for position over the emerging reality of a 'Viking Age' and laying claims to its various heroes, the question of Rollo's nationality became for a short time a matter of urgent debate. The Danish historian Johannes Steenstrup used the surviving fragments of a *Planctus for William Longsword*, a grief-poem written by an unknown author shortly after the murder of Rollo's son and successor William Longsword, in 942, to advance arguments for accepting the reliability of Dudo's history that would make Rollo a Dane. The Norwegian Gustav Storm employed the *Planctus* to opposite effect to reinforce Snorri's case for his Norwegian origins, pointing out that the *Planctus*'s description of William as 'Born overseas from a father who stuck to the pagan error/and from a mother who was devoted to the sweet religion' directly contradicts Dudo's claim that William was born in Rouen. Snorri's tale of Rolf's Hebridean interlude, along with the *Planctus*'s reference to his Christian wife, both appear to complement a tradition, recorded in the Icelandic *Book of the Settlements*, and repeated in the so-called *Great Saga of Olaf Tryggvason*,[10] that Rolf had a daughter named Kathlín, or Kathleen, who married the Hebridean King Bjólan.[11] Dudo makes no reference to this daughter, whose name is both Celtic and Christian.[12]

Snorri is very sure of himself in the identification of Rolf with Rollo, and the enigma of Dudo's ignorance of detail concerning his subject's origins that was available to Snorri over 200 years later remains. It may well be that he was trying to rationalize the fact that Rollo was Norwegian but most of his followers Danes. In his *Saga of St Olav*, king of Norway between 1016 and 1028, Snorri revisits Rolf/Rollo's great triumph at the conclusion of a typically brisk genealogical round-up: 'From Rolf the Ganger are the jarls of Ruda (Rouen) descended, and long afterwards they claimed kinship with the chiefs of Norway and set great store by it for many years; they were always the Norsemen's best friends, and all Norsemen, who would have it, had peace land with them.'[13]

Though there are other alternatives – William of Jumièges cautiously gives no pedigree for Rollo and says he was chosen by lot to lead his generation of Seine raiders; and the late tenth-century historian Richer of Reims trenchantly refers to Rollo as a 'pirate' and names his father as a certain Catillus (Ketill)[14] – Snorri's identification remains the most popular, though it is certainly not definitive. Nor is the anonymous thirteenth-century *Saga of Ganger Rolf*, a sublimely wild account of the doings of a man who shares nothing but his name with the hero of Snorri's and Dudo's histories, and the legend of his great size with Snorri's. Contemplating some of his more obvious outrages against both history and common sense, the author admits with a disarming shrug that 'maybe this saga doesn't tally with what other sagas have to say about the same things, not in regard to the various events, or the names of the people, or the brave and bold deeds done by this one or that, or where the various chieftains ruled'. He assures his readers, however, that

those who have assembled these tidings must have based them on something, either ancient verses or else the testimonies of learned men. And in any case, few if any of the stories from the old days are such that people would swear that everything happened just as related therein, since in most cases a word here and there will have been added. And sometimes it's not possible to know every word and every happening, for most things happen long before they're told about.[15]

As we have noted earlier Dudo put the date of Rollo's arrival on the Seine at 876 and placed him at a siege of Paris which, if there be any truth in the story, is more likely to be that of 886. Thereafter he treats him as the only significant Viking leader on the lower Seine. At some point Rollo captured the city of Rouen. Unlike his predecessors, he managed to keep control of it. The *Historia Norwegie* describes in admiring terms the tactics that won the day. The crew of his fleet of fifteen ships dug pits disguised with turfs between the city walls and the river and then lured their mounted opponents into the traps by pretending to run for their ships once the battle was under way. The trick was so successful that they were able to enter Rouen unopposed.[16] Indeed, it seems that Rollo had established himself so firmly there that defeat in a battle against the Neustrian count Robert I in about 911 led not to flight but instead to an invitation from Charles the Simple to join him at the negotiating table, where the king formally recognized Rollo's right to remain in possession of a large part of north-west Francia, pointedly described as already 'too often laid waste by Hasting and by you'.[17] In return Rollo agreed to be baptized and to assist the king in the defence of the realm. The seal of agreement was to be marriage between Rollo and Charles's daughter, Gisla.[18]

The treaty agreed upon in 912, at a meeting between Rollo and Charles the Simple at Saint-Claire-sur-Epte, has not survived and is a historical presumption only; but there is a reference to it in a royal charter of March 918 which deals with the matter of an abbey whose patrimony had been bisected as a result of it:

we give and grant this abbey of which the main part lies in the area of Méresias on the River Eure to Saint-Germain and to his monks for their upkeep, except that part of the abbey ['s lands] which we have granted to the Normans of the Seine, namely to Rollo and his companions, for the defence of the kingdom . . .[19]

Rollo received a further grant of land in central Normandy in 924. The contemporary French analyst Flodoard of Reims tells us:

The Northmen entered upon peace with solemn promises in the presence of Count Hugo, Count Herbert and also Archbishop Seulf. King Ralph was not there, but with his consent, their [the Normans'] land increased with Maine and the Bessin, which in a pact of peace was conceded to them . . .[20]

Rollo died sometime between a final mention of him by Flodoard in 928, and 933, the year in which a third grant of land, usually identified as being the Cotentin and Avranchin areas of Brittany, was made to his son and successor William, known as Longsword. This completed the basic territory of what would become known as the duchy of Normandy. Its boundaries ran roughly from Eu, at the mouth of the river Bresle in the east, across to the river Vire in the west. It was bounded by the English Channel in the north and by the waters of the Avre in the south, an area corresponding to the modern French *départements* of Manche, Calvados, Seine Maritime and Eure. Orne was included, with the exception of Mortagne and Domfront. The validity of Dudo's claim that Brittany was included in the initial grant of land remains uncertain. One small piece of possible evidence in favour is a coin found at Mont-St-Michel bearing the inscription + VVILEIM DUX BRI that is thought to refer to Rollo's son William and to have been issued by him as a duke of Brittany.[21]

Along with the agreement of 878 between Alfred and Guthrum, sometimes known as the Treaty of Wedmore, and the trade agreements

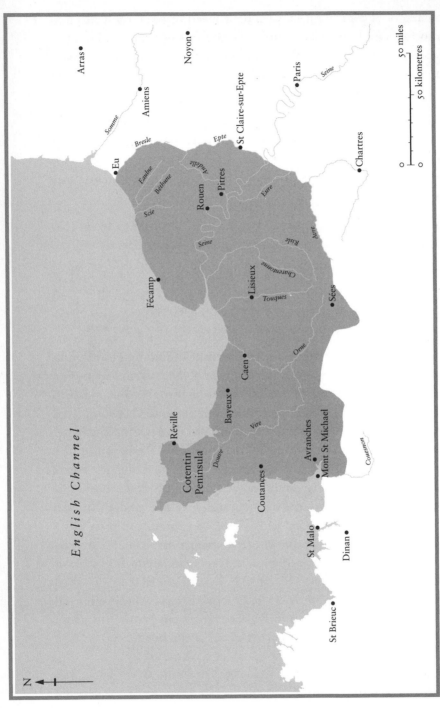

Following the original grant of land to Rollo in 911 the duchy of Normandy had grown to include the Cotentin peninsula by about 933.

negotiated in 907 and 911 between the Kievan Rus and the Byzantine emperor, Saint-Claire appears to be the third example available to us of a negotiated settlement between pagan Vikings and Christian rulers. Each in its own way attempted to invite the raiders into the fold of the nominally civilized world of Christian culture, and each in its own way succeeded. Charles's aims were to put an end to the century-old threat from Viking fleets that used the Seine to attack Paris and to bring stability to a volatile region by sponsoring the authority there of a 'good' Viking leader. From the time Rollo's occupation of its lower regions was legalized he remained loyal to the agreement and Viking attacks on Paris effectively ceased.

The early years of the colony's history are turbulent and hard to follow. In 923 Rollo's forces fought alongside those of Charles around Beauvais, and the grant to him of Bayeux and Maine in the following year may have been an attempt by Charles's enemy, King Ralph of Burgundy, to split the alliance. In 925 the Vikings devastated Amiens and Arras in the east, but were stopped at Eu by a coalition of Ralph's allies in their attempts to expand further east into modern-day Picardy. A further complication was the activities of another band of Viking raiders on the Loire, under the leadership of the otherwise obscure Rognvald. After the death of Duke Alan the Great in 907, the Vikings showed an increasing interest in Brittany, whose Celtic population had maintained a fierce independence of Frankish attempts to incorporate it. By about 919 Rognvald's army had control of all Brittany. In 921 he was formally given Nantes by Count Robert of Neustria, and it seems he may have been expecting the concessions to Rollo in 924 to lead to a Frankish version of the Danelaw which would also involve him, for Flodoard tells us that in anger at not being awarded any land within France at this settlement he led his forces on a series of devastating raids into Frankish crown land, between the Loire and the Seine, until defeated by Hugh the Great, the Robertian count of Paris and duke of the Franks, and compelled to fight his way back to Nantes. He seems to have died shortly after this and with him any prospect of a Viking axis of power connecting Rouen and Nantes and posing the same sort of threat to the whole of France as the York–Dublin axis might have done to the kings of Wessex. His Vikings survived for a few more years, but had been driven out of the area by 939 following a campaign by the Breton leader Alan Barbetorte, or Twisted Beard.

Dudo, in words similar to those in the *Anglo-Saxon Chronicle* that announced the Danish takeover in Northumbria and East Anglia, says that Rollo 'divided that land among his followers by measure, and rebuilt everything that had long been deserted, and restored it by restocking it with his own warriors and with peoples from abroad'.[22] What flimsy documentary evidence there is suggests that he took seriously his new role as the representative of the king's authority in Normandy, and for his own sake and the sake of his sponsor attempted to restore order and respect for the law to the region. The government of the Norman rulers was illiterate for most of the first century of its existence and as Dudo tells us so little about the specific nature of Rollo's administration we do not even know whether he continued to surround himself as a Frankish count with the *hird* of a typical Viking chieftain, nor whether he imported from Scandinavia the system of naval levy known as the *leithanger*. There is, however, nothing to suggest that he introduced government by *thing* meeting, and plenty of hints that it was autocratic in the Frankish tradition. Dudo claims that Rollo passed laws against robbery and violence that made them punishable by death, a novelty by comparison with Carolingian law, which exacted only a fine.[23] Two of his anecdotes show that, from the very start, Rollo responded to slights or challenges to his authority with the same implacable faith in the efficacy of terror he had shown as a Viking.

Rollo had introduced a decree ordering that farm implements be left out in the field and not taken into the house at the end of the day. To make it appear as though they had done so and been robbed, it seems that a farmer's wife hid her husband's ploughing implements. Rollo reimbursed the man for his loss and ordered the trials by ordeal of the potential suspects. When all survived the ordeals he had the wife beaten until she confessed. And when the husband admitted that he had known it was her all along, Rollo handed down a finding of guilty on two counts: 'The one, that you are the head of the woman and ought to have chastised her. The other, that you were an accessory to the theft and were unwilling to disclose it.' He had them both hung 'and finished off by a cruel death', an action which Dudo credibly claims so terrified the local inhabitants that the territory became and remained free of petty criminality for a century afterwards.

The second tale also shows how central was the Viking idea of personal honour, and how fatal to it the taint of unmanliness. Shortly after Rollo's marriage to Charles's daughter Gisla, two of Charles's warriors paid her a visit. Gisla entertained them in private. Presently rumours began circulating, to the effect that Rollo had failed to consummate the marriage. Any suggestion of sexual impotence, casting doubt on the legitimacy of his heirs, would have seemed particularly dangerous to Rollo. Suspecting that Gisla's visitors were the probable authors of the rumours, he had them arrested and summarily executed in the public market place in Rouen. The story, with its possible hint at Rolf's homosexuality, provides another glancing point of contact with the *Saga of Ganger Rolf*, whose 'Rolf' is said to have been uninterested in women. As an illustration of Rollo's decisive ways, the tale has a certain symbolic value; but as history it is compromised. Gisla was one of the king's six daughters by his first wife, Frédérune, and as the couple did not marry until 907 Gisla would have been, at most, five years old at the time of the Saint-Claire treaty.[24] That the child-marriage took place as a diplomatic seal on the agreement that gave Rollo a foothold in the Frankish aristocracy need not be doubted.

Dudo is more interested in persuading his readers of the genuine nature of Rollo's conversion than in providing details of the legislative and executive structures of the new regime. He solves the delicate problem of how to deal with Rollo's Heathendom in the years before baptism and the respectability of legitimate rule by a literary trick involving Hasting, or Anstign, as he calls him, amplifying whatever natural qualities of cruelty Hasting may have possessed to turn him into a Heathen archetype of purest evil:

> Death-dealing, uncouth, fertile in ruses, warmonger-general,
> Traitor, fomenter of evil, and double-dyed dissumulator,
> Conscienceless, proudly puffed up; seducer, deceiver, and hot-head.
> Gallows-meat, lewd and unbridled one, quarrel maintainer,
> Adder of evil to pestilent evil, increaser of bad faith,
> Fit to be censured not in black ink, but in charcoal graffiti.[25]

He lists the holy places burnt by Hasting during his ravages in Western Francia, including his own monastery at St-Quentin, the churches of St-Médard and St-Éloiat Noyon, and St-Denis and Ste-Geneviève. Rollo, by easy contrast, becomes the 'good' Heathen, the Viking whose natural instincts always inclined him towards the Christianity he eventually espoused. Dudo credits him with the restoration of churches he and his men had been responsible for ravaging, the reopening of monasteries they had made uninhabitable, and the rebuilding of the walls and defences of cities and towns torn down by them. He even makes Rollo's piety retrospective and tells an incredible tale of how he brought over with him from England the relics of a holy virgin, Hameltrude, carried them up the Seine on board his longship and deposited them in the church of St-Vaast. In further proof of Rollo's piety, while still wearing the white baptismal robes and under his baptismal name 'Robert', he spent, we learn, the first seven days of his expiation at St-Claire in handing out gifts of land to various churches in the diocese of Rouen, having first ascertained which of them were considered most venerable and which were protected by the most powerful saints. Not until the eighth day did he finally turn his attention to the allocation of land to his own men.

Many of these, it seems, were not willing to join their leader in abandoning their Heathen beliefs. In a letter written before 928 Guy, the archbishop of Rouen, approached his colleague Hervé at Reims for advice on the best way to deal with apostate Heathen converts. In language that recalls the exasperation of Louis the Pious' bishops at the behaviour of Klak-Harald's following, who practised their own form of serial baptism in the 820s, Hervé passed the question to Pope John X, asking what was to be done with Heathens, 'when they have been baptized and rebaptized, and after their baptism carry on living as Heathens, killing Christians as the Heathens do, slaughtering priests and eating animals that have been sacrificed to their idols'.[26] In reply, the pope counselled patience and persistence, urging them to regard Rollo and his colonists as merely inexperienced in the ways of the new faith, and their conversion as not an event but a process which would inevitably take time to complete. He also reminded Hervé that 'the calamities, the oppression, the dangers which have threatened our regions have come not only from the Heathens but from Christians too'.[27] Flodoard tells us that in 943 there was an engagement between the Frankish Duke Hugo and a group of Normans 'who had arrived as Heathens or who were returning to Heathendom: a large number of his own Christian soldiers were killed by them'. Later in the entry for the same year we hear of an otherwise unknown Viking Norman leader named Turmod, 'who had reverted to idolatry and to the gentile religion' and was apparently also trying to 'turn' the Norman ruler Richard (Rollo's grandson) and involve him in a plot against the Frankish King Louis. In 1906 a tenth-century longship burial on a commanding headland on the Île de Groix, some 6 kilometres off the coast of southern Brittany, was excavated and found to contain two bodies as well as the remains of dogs and birds. Among the wealth of finds recovered were swords, arrowheads, lance-heads, rings, tools, gaming pieces and dice. Like the Oseberg ship, it had been dragged overland to a previously prepared site. Unlike the Oseberg ship it had then been burnt, the spectacle being framed by twenty-four shields.[28] This is the only known archaeological evidence of a ship being burnt as part of a Viking burial ritual, and Ibn Fadlan's literary description of the Rus funeral ceremony for their dead chieftain on the banks of the Volga gives us some idea of what the ritual may have involved.[29] One of the two bodies was that of an adolescent and the archaeologist Julian D. Richards has suggested that here, too, may be the signs of a human sacrifice. The Île de Groix funeral probably took place after the official conversion to Christianity of most of the Vikings in the region, and the sumptuous nature of the ceremony may hint at a conscious act of apostasy.[30]

In his detailed study of the Norman conversion, the French scholar Olivier Guillot noted that Flodoard seems to have regarded the conversion of Rollo and his settlers as a process that was demonstrably under way as early as 923, and there is evidence that Rollo was sincere in his desire to embrace certain aspects of Christian culture. As we saw earlier, tradition tells us that his Scottish-born daughter bore the Christian name Kathleen, and both the children of his later association with a woman named Poppa were given Christian names. If his son Guillaume (William Longsword) also had a Scandinavian name then this has not come down to us. Rollo's daughter had both a Norwegian name, Gerloc, and a baptismal name, Adèle. The reference in the

Planctus for William Longsword to William as 'born overseas from a father who stuck to the pagan error/and from a mother who was devoted to the sweet religion' might be no more than a factual comment on Rollo's early life. Adémar of Chabannes, however, writing about 100 years after Rollo's death, described his last days as a time of religious madness, in which the Heathen 'Rollo' rose up against the Christian 'Robert' and in a desperate attempt to atone for the betrayal of Odin and Thor ordered the beheading of 100 Christians as sacrifices to them.[31] This was followed by a frenzied attempt to balance the books yet again when he distributed 'one hundred pounds of gold round the churches in honour of the true god in whose name he had accepted baptism'.[32] Adémar is the only ancient historian to doubt the truth of Rollo's conversion. His story provides a rare and persuasive insight into the violent tensions that could arise when devout men change the object of their devotion as a matter of political convenience. In Rollo's case they were seemingly mind-wrenching.

The large and consistent Viking military presence throughout the ninth and tenth centuries in the western Frankish kingdom has left little material archaeological trace. In 1927 the Norwegian archaeologist Haakon Shetelig visited museums along the Loire and the Seine and compiled a list of holdings that included an axe, seven spears and twenty-one swords, most of them dredged from the rivers or constituting stray finds. The Swedish archaeologists Arbmann and Nilsson complemented Shetelig's list in 1968 with another two axe-heads from Rouen, and in 1987 a Viking Age sword was unearthed in the basement of the museum at Denain. A lance ferrule and a helmet fragment, possibly of Nordic origin, were excavated in Brittany, at the Camp de Péran (Côtes d'Armor).[33] The discovery in the burnt ramparts of Camp de Péran, originally a Celtic fortified settlement, of a coin from York minted between 905 and 925 dates its restoration by Vikings to the early years of the tenth century. Alain Barbetorte is known to have landed at Dol in 936 and fought with the Vikings, an event that has been associated with the evidence of the destruction of the camp.[34] Another earthwork, at Trans, Ille-et-Vilaine, may have been built or renovated by the Loire Vikings as they retreated from Nantes in 939.

In 1870 a navvy working on a road near Pîtres on the Seine came across two characteristically Viking Age brooches known as 'fibulas', which archaeologists have related to the presence of a Viking fleet at Pîtres in 865. Dated to the second half of the ninth century and of probable Norwegian origin, they come from the grave of a female and provide further evidence that Viking bands travelled with women who were either camp-followers or, as in the case of Hasting in the 890s in Wessex, wives. During a particularly low tide at Reville, in the Bay of Seine, a Frankish necropolis that included possible Viking Age graves was uncovered in 1964. Two ship-settings were seen, of a type familiar from Gotland and parts of Denmark and Sweden, and a third with an unusual arrangement of stones with four right-angled slabs ringed by three stone circles.[35] A vase resembling vases found at Birka is the only artefact to have been found, and the cemetery is once again under water. A recent excavation of the area around Rouen Cathedral shows that the layout of streets appears to have been redesigned in the early tenth century and that the modifications gave the ancient town a layout reminiscent of Anglo-Saxon towns.[36]

The linguistic traces of the Scandinavian roots of the Norman colonists are slightly more extensive. Dudo's silence on the subject of how the Viking colonists administered Normandy is only partially broken by the survival of a small number of words of Scandinavian origin into the duchy's thirteenth-century law codes.[37] The word *ullac*, meaning a sentence of outlawry, derived from Old Norse *útlagr*, and *hamfara*, or the crime of assault inside a house, from *heimsókn*. A number of words to do with fishing, whaling, boat-building and the laws covering the status of wrecks were also of Scandinavian origin.[38] The settlement of the land by Rollo's captains produced over the years a small crop of place-names of Scandinavian origin. Compounds first recorded between 1025 and 1200 include Bramatot, Coletot, Esculetot, Gonnetot, Herguetot and Ketetot. These were formed by combining the personal name of the Viking landowner with a genitive 's' – respectively Bramis, Kolis, Skúlis, Gunnis, Helgis and Ketils – and -*tot*, deriving from the Old Norse word *tomt* or *toft* (cf. 'Lowestoft' in the English Danelaw), meaning 'plot' or 'piece of land'. Other typical Scandinavian elements compounded in place-names include *bec, dalle, hom, hogue, londe* and *torp* (cf. English 'Scunthorpe'). A number of personal and family names found in present-day Normandy can also be traced back to the Viking settlement via intermediary Latinized forms known from the eleventh century. These include Ásbjørn – Osbernus – Auber; Ásfridr – Ansfridus – Anfray; Ásketill – Anschetillus – Anquetil; Thorvaldr – Turoldus – Thouroude.[39] Names like Murdac and Donecan may indicate that some of the colonists were Norwegians who arrived via Ireland and Scotland, just as certain personal names and examples of agrarian terminology that occur in the region between Bayeux and the river Orne indicate that others came via England.

For all that Dudo is now regarded with some scepticism as a reliable source for the settlement of Normandy, his history remains a vivid and interesting document. Two of his anecdotes have played a major role in creating the image of the Viking as an independent, heroic, proud and manly ideal. It seems that once the details of the meeting at Saint-Claire had been agreed upon, Rollo was advised that, as Charles's vassal, it would now be fit and proper for him to kiss the king's foot. Rollo declined: 'I will never bow my knees at the knees of any man, and no man's foot will I kiss.' He ordered one of his men to do so instead. The man stepped forward, took hold of the king's foot and lifted it to his lips without bending himself. The king fell over backwards, provoking 'a great laugh, and a great outcry among the people'.[40] The laughter was presumably from the Vikings and the outcry from the Franks; but the story is a good illustration of the reality behind the agreement, that Charles's grant to Rollo was a concession to reality.

When William of Jumièges tells us that Rollo was chosen as a leader by the drawing of lots we add the tacit presumption that he was also known by his peers to be the best leader; and yet an insistent streak of egalitarianism attaches to the Viking war band. As part of his claim that Rollo was present at the 886 siege of Paris, Dudo describes an encounter at Damps between the Vikings and Charles's go-between. The emissary asked by what title their leader was known, and was told 'By none, because we [are] equal in power.'[41] They were then asked if they would be willing to bow to Charles the Simple and devote themselves to his service and accept grants of land from him, to which the reply was: 'We will never subjugate ourselves to anyone nor cling to anyone's service nor take favours from anyone. The favour that would please us best is the one that we will claim for ourselves by force of arms and in the hardship of battle.' The sentiments recall Ibn Rustah's story of the Rus father throwing down a sword in front of his infant son and convey a specifically Viking ethic of self-reliance and self-assertion through violence. Despite the rapid cultural and linguistic assimilation to Frankish ways that took place, this code survived the transition from Viking to Norman. In his *Deeds of Count Roger and his brother Duke Robert*, written about 1090, Geoffrey Malaterra, a Norman writer living in southern Italy, formulated a set of general characteristics of the Normans which seem to reflect this continuity of values.[42] He writes of an astute people, eager to avenge injuries and looking to enrich themselves from others rather than from work at home. Much interested in profit and power, they are hypercritical and deceitful in all matters, 'but between generosity and avarice they take a middle course'. Mindful of their reputations, the leaders are notably generous. They are skilled in flattery and cultivate eloquence 'to such an extent that one listens to their young boys as though they were trained speakers'. They work hard when necessary and can endure hunger and cold. When times are good they indulge their love of hunting and hawking, and they cultivate a sizeable streak of dandyism in their clothing. The aesthetic care that was formerly lavished on the longship was transferred to the horses' livery as Viking pirates became Norman cavalry, and the practice of decorating and personalizing one's weapons continued. It is another reminder that Viking culture was not so much primitive, as contemporary Christian scribes so determinedly described it, but essentially different.

Richer of Reims tells a story that epitomizes the determination of the first generations of Viking leaders in Normandy not to be deprived of their newly won land and their status as Frankish aristocrats. In 941, as a vassal of the Frankish King Louis IV, William Longsword made his way to Attigny, where the most powerful leaders in Francia were gathered to confer. Finding the doors barred against him on his arrival, he simply broke them down and voiced his rightful claim to a place at the table. The sight of the Emperor Otto and not his patron in the seat of honour affronted him, however, and before allowing the meeting to proceed he obliged Otto to yield his seat to Louis. A year later and, according to Richer, as a direct result of the insult to Otto, William was murdered.[43] The succession passed to his ten-year-old son Richard and precipitated the most serious crisis the colony had faced so far in its short life. In 944 Louis IV and Hugh the Great mounted a joint attack on Normandy, with Hugh attacking Bayeux and Louis occupying Rouen. It seems that Louis could not countenance the thought of Hugh's occupation of Bayeux and, as so often before, dissension among the Frankish allies worked to the advantage of the Vikings. Hugh took the king into captivity and ended his hostility to the Normans. His troops helped Richard's men regain possession of Rouen, and in the wake of their victory Hugh gave his daughter Emma in marriage to the young count. The family ties thus established with the Capetians further increased the status of Normandy's ruling family, and with surprising speed the threat to the survival of the duchy had vanished.[44] Hugh continued to offer military support to Richard I and in 954 defeated a certain Harold in what may have been another attempt to retake the duchy. Richard's marriage to Emma was childless, and after her death he married Gunnor, the mother of his two children and a member of a powerful family of Viking settlers from the west of Normandy. This second marriage strengthened his position in the Cotentin region.[45]

When a large group of people settles in a foreign country it tends initially to accentuate its roots in an attempt to stave off cultural entropy. Smaller groups, like the Vikings who settled in Normandy, let go more quickly. Dudo tells us that William Longsword had to send his son Richard to Bayeux to learn the Danish tongue, since the language was no longer spoken in the area around Rouen; although this is generally regarded as, at best, an exaggeration, the linguistic position of those in Normandy was unlike that of their fellow-Scandinavians in the colonies of the Danelaw across the Channel, where the native and immigrant languages resembled one another closely enough for a fusion of the two to evolve. Mutual incomprehensibility must have hastened the demise of the spoken Scandinavian languages in Normandy, much as it did among the Kievan Rus, another warrior aristocracy who settled in a minority in a linguistically remote community. But even though they had traded in their longships for horses, the Normandy Vikings retained a number of their cultural traditions. While slavery was being replaced in other parts of the Carolingian empire by serfdom, the colonists in Normandy developed Rouen as an important centre for the trading of slaves. The trade brought such prosperity to the region that it was still thriving at the end of the eleventh century, occasioning a rebuke from the Lombard cleric Lanfranc to his master, William the Conqueror, and a request that he forbid slavery throughout his territories.

There are many possible suggestions for a date at which the assimilation process could be said to have advanced so far that it is no longer meaningful to refer to the Normans as Vikings and to look for Scandinavian elements in their cultural manifestations. Olav Haraldson, the future saint-king of Norway, was baptized at Rouen in 1013, the last Norwegian king to visit the duchy; and those soldiers from Normandy who fought beside the Dublin king Sihtric Silkbeard at the Battle of Clontarf in 1014 were the last to do so in a Scandinavian cause. As late as 1025, the court of Richard II at Rouen received a visit from Olav Haraldson's court poet, Sigvat, who may have done what skalds do and composed praise poetry for his host in return for honour and gifts. Richard II, known as 'the Good', was the first of the Norman rulers to use the title 'duke', which he did from 1006. Perhaps the clearest sign of the irrevocable transition from Viking to Norman is the history his father asked Dudo of St Quentin to write in 994. It must have been among the last acts of Richard I, and there is profound significance in the fact that he chose to have his family remembered in prose, on parchment and in Latin and not, as his forefathers would have done, in verse, on stone and in Old Norse.

10

The master-builder

Harald Bluetooth and the Jelling stone

By the early tenth century the effective independence of Brittany, Flanders and Aquitaine and the gift of Normandy to Rollo had further fragmented what remained of the legacy of Charlemagne and Louis the Pious. Its decline was paralleled by other disruptions. Following the death of Horik the Young in 870, central authority among the Danes went into eclipse for some sixty years. Chieftains named Sigfred and Halfdan did not share their predecessors' cautious interest in Christianity and are known only as leaders of Viking raiders. Sometime around 900 the brothers Gorm and Hardeknud returned from England to emerge as leaders of the Danes. Hardeknud's return to England left Gorm as the most prominent Jutland chieftain and under him a gradual revival of Danish regional power began.

Among the eastern Franks, the death in 911 of the German King Louis the Child brought the Carolingian dynasty there to an end. Power in the region passed into the hands of a small number of dukes, and with the emergence of the threat from the Magyars these men sought leadership to organize resistance. Their choice eventually fell on the Saxon duke, Henry, called the Fowler, and in 919 he assumed the title of king. Henry won back Lotharingia from the western Franks and established new marches along the Elbe after a series of victorious campaigns against the Wends. In 934 he campaigned against Slesvig and compelled the baptism of the chieftain Gnupa. By 934 he was able to claim overlordship over Denmark. As a result, Bishop Unni of Hamburg-Bremen and a group of monks from the abbey at Corvey resumed the missionary activity of the Christian Church in Denmark.

Henry's successor Otto, known as the Great, restored the Church to crown control and sought a return to the order and authority once associated with Charlemagne. There was a symbolic aspect to his crowning at Charlemagne's old capital Aachen in 936. At his coronation banquet the nobles were required to serve him as vassals, as in the days of the emperor. Otto formally accepted the Christian connections between secular and religious power. Later he invaded Italy and claimed the imperial throne for himself. The pope initially declined to crown him as emperor; in 962, however, after he had responded to pleas for help from Rome against the threats of Berengar of Ivrea, a self-styled king of Italy who had occupied the northern Papal States, the coronation duly took place. Otto styled himself *augustus* and gave the name of Sacrum Romanum Imperium, or Holy Roman Empire, to his collected territories. The king of the eastern Franks was now ruler over a coherent swathe of territory that extended from Germany in the north to Italy in the south. It was not as large as Charlemagne's empire, but after a century of chaos its creation symbolized the return of order to central Europe. For another 1,000 years it would remain a part of the political map of the continent.[1]

A consequence of the return of a superpower to the region was a revival of the border tensions that existed between Danes and eastern Franks, and of the efforts Christian rulers had been making since the days of Charlemagne to bring the Danes into the fold. Ferociously and cruelly, according to Adam of Bremen, King Gorm resisted the mission of Bishop Unni.[2] His son, and for the last fifteen years of his reign his co-ruler, Harald, known as Bluetooth, was more receptive to the new faith.[3] In 948 a papal letter addressed to Archbishop Adaldag of Hamburg reasserted Hamburg-Bremen's position as head of the Church in all Scandinavia, and gave the archbishop the rights of investiture across the territories. Three bishops were appointed that same year to the sees of Århus, Ribe and Hedeby in Jutland, that part of Danish territory over which Harald's writ ran.[4] Horit, Liafdag and Reginbrond were their names, suggesting German or Frisian origins rather than Danish. The appointments would seem to confirm both Harald's early interest in and tolerance for Christianity, as well as Otto the Great's use of the Church as a political institution.

Though his enthusiasm initially stopped short of baptism, it seems religious discussions remained a part of the conversation among Harald's *hird*, for it was as a result of one of them that his conversion presently came about. The circumstances are described in some detail in an almost contemporary source, the *Res gestæ saxonicæ*, a history of the Saxons written by the monk Widukind of Corvey in about 970. Widukind asserts that the Church had long considered the Danes to have accepted Christianity, while recognizing that Christ had, in fact, only been admitted to a pantheon. Christianity's crucial insistence on exclusivity remained unacceptable. At table at Harald's court one evening a discussion arose on the relative merits of the gods. The Heathens agreed that Christ was a divinity but only a minor one, and less able than either Odin or Thor to enact miracles and give proofs of his power. Poppo, a missionary bishop at the court, rejected this and went on to claim that these others were not gods at all but demons. Harald challenged him to demonstrate the truth of what he was saying by submission to ordeal. In everyday life the ordeal was a last resort in legal or disputed matters where the process of compurgation had failed.[5] In the bishop's case, it seems, the last resort was also the first. Poppo is reported to have accepted the challenge without hesitation.

The ordeal was a trial of physical endurance carried out under controlled conditions that was designed to solicit the judgement of supernatural powers on the matter at issue. It could take a number of different forms. One obliged the plaintiff to walk through fire. Another required him to stretch his bared arm into a cauldron of boiling water to retrieve a ring, stone or other small object from the bottom. In an ordeal by cold water the accused was bound and thrown into a pond or stream, to sink if innocent or float if guilty. The logic held that in the latter case the pure nature of the water would reject the impure nature of the accused. In another variant, the accused was compelled to eat crumbs of dry bread and cheese. Choking on these was a sign of guilt. The particular ordeal Poppo volunteered to undergo required him to carry a lump of hot iron in his hand for a set number of paces before throwing it. Its use was rare and restricted to matters involving religion.[6]

Harald had Poppo kept under observation until the time appointed for the ordeal. A passage in Gregory of Tours' *Books of Miracles* explains the necessity for this.[7] Gregory describes an earlier ordeal, arranged to show which of two rival claimants held the favour of Christ, that required each man in turn to reach into a cauldron of boiling water and retrieve a ring from it. One lost his nerve overnight and, rising early the next day, tried to fix the outcome by smearing his arm with a protective ointment. Clearly people would not have used a test that always provided the same answer, and one has to assume that a number of such protective measures were known about, and that steps were taken to prevent them being used. There were variables too: in the case reported by Gregory, the temperature of the water may have varied considerably as the successful ordealist took an hour to locate the small ring as it swirled about in the cauldron. Even here there were nuances of divine judgement at work that discouraged cheating: when he afterwards observed that the water at the bottom of the cauldron was almost cold and that at the top only pleasantly warm the other responded by plunging his arm in up to the elbow. Instantly, says Gregory, the flesh was seared to the bone.

A passage in the laws of the Skåne district, known in their earliest written form from the early thirteenth century, may give some idea of the conduct of the ritual that Poppo faced. The hand that he had chosen to use would have been washed and he would have been instructed afterwards to touch nothing until the moment arrived to take up the iron. If the ordeal involved 'throw-iron' he would have had to walk nine paces before throwing it. Widukind says only that Poppo carried it long enough to satisfy Harald. Afterwards a mitten was placed over the ordealist's hand and the wound kept sealed for four days. The mitten was then removed and the wound examined: a clean wound was an affirmation of protection, truth, power or whatever was the appropriate response to the type of question being asked. A dirty wound was interpreted as rejection or failure.

These various steps in the process of Poppo's ordeal are clearly identifiable in a series of seven gilded bronzes from the early thirteenth century, discovered in 1870 affixed to the pulpit and covered in a thick layer of oil paint, in the church at Tamdrup, in Horsens. A first image shows Poppo and Harald together, the former urging conversion on the king, the latter rejecting it. The second image shows the iron heating above the flames. In the third picture the bishop shows the king his hand after the removal of the mitten, and in the fourth we see the momentous result of the ordeal: Poppo baptizes the naked king, who is standing in a barrel of water. The next image shows the Danish king genuflecting in front of an altar. A sixth image is damaged but has been interpreted as showing the king and his queen together making the gift of an altar decoration to the church.[8] Widukind tells us that Poppo's hand was unblemished by the ordeal. However, one must suppose that here, as in many such cases, the demeanour and courage of the ordealist during the appalling few seconds of the trial must also have had some bearing on how the result was judged. Poppo's bearing and his willingness to suffer for his beliefs perhaps impressed King Harald every bit as much as the state of the bishop's hand following the ordeal.

In this way Poppo brought to fruition the work of a long line of Christian missionaries sponsored by Christian kings, from the Anglo-Saxon Willibrord, who had attempted to convert the Danish King Angantyr in about 720, to Ebbo of Reims, and Anskar and Autbert, who had tried to help Klak-Harald introduce the faith to Denmark with the assistance of Louis the Pious in the first half of the ninth century. Harald recorded his conversion in a most dramatic way, commissioning the erection of a great, pyramidal rune-stone in Jelling, in central southern Jutland. Saxo Grammaticus tells us that, on a Jutland beach, Harald came upon the massive red and black granite stone, nearly 2.5 metres high and weighing almost ten tons, and had it dragged to Jelling by men yoked to it like oxen.

The Jelling stone is among the most remarkable and instructive of all Viking Age documents. Normalized, the runic inscription that dominates one of the three sides, referred to as the A side, reads: *Haraldr konungr bað gera kuml þessi ept Gorm, fôður sinn, ok ept Þyrvé, móður sína, sá Haraldr er sér vann Danmôrk alla ok Norveg ok dani gerði kristna* ('King Harald had this monument made in memory of Gorm, his father, and in memory of Thyrwi, his mother; that Harald who won for himself all of Denmark and Norway and made the Danes Christian').[9] The hands of two men have been identified in the carvings that cover its two other sides and it has been estimated that the complete set of decorations took them about a year to finish. The B side depicts a struggle between two animals that have been identified as a lion, though its mane and head more closely resemble those of a horse, and a serpent with its tail in its mouth.

On the C side of the stone is the first significant native representation of Christ to have survived in Scandinavia. The suffering Christ had no immediate appeal to a warlike people whose gods included masters of violence like Odin and Thor, and from the beginning the missionaries' focus in the Scandinavian fields was on Christ's power and his warrior-like attributes. This, after all, was the power Poppo was defending when Harald challenged him to carry the iron, and this was the power that persuaded Harald to convert. So the Christ of the Jelling stone is the Christ triumphant, fierce-eyed and ready to do battle with the demons of Heathendom. This may explain why the figure on the stone is depicted with arms extended but no visible cross to support him. Indeed the whole looks more like an exultant stretching than a scene of execution. Instead of a cross his arms and body are looped around by stylized branches, as though he were hanging from a tree. An interpretation that relates the stylization to mainstream Christian and European iconography suggests that these might be vine scrolls, familiar in Christian iconography from as early as the fifth century as symbols of both Christ himself and the Church.[10] Another possibility is that the carvers regarded the cross as an optional background framing device for the image of the man. It is also possible that the design reflected the persistent syncretism that transformed the Christian lion into a Scandinavian horse and the Christian snake into the world-encircling Midgard serpent, and that to a contemporary Danish spectator the figure on the stone would seem to be hanging in the branches of a tree, perhaps recalling to him or her Odin's nine days and nights hanging in Yggdrasil as he waited for the chance to swoop down and steal the runes. Whether by design or not, the iconography of the stone thus encouraged an acceptance of the new god by portraying Christ as a shamanic god, engaged in a ritual with which the spectator or 'reader' was already familiar. In contemplating the resonance the great stone must have had for contemporaries, it is useful to recall that, like other rune-stones, it was brightly coloured in red, blue, yellow and grey.

As we noted earlier, Dudo's history of Normandy was an advertisement for the cultural assimilation of the duchy's Viking founders and a statement by Rollo's grandson, Richard I, of his self-identification as both Christian and European. The crucial distinction between the

Norman document and the Danish document was that, while the latter too advertised the ruler's Christian modernity, it did so in a form that was ancient and resolutely Scandinavian. The first known runic alphabet consists of twenty-four letters; from the first six of these it derives its name, the *futhark*, the term being modern. By Harald's time it had been known in Denmark, Norway and Sweden for several centuries. Snorri Sturluson gave us the mythological explanation of its origins. Rational explanations include the suggestion that the letters derived from the Latin and Etruscan alphabets, adapted to avoid curves and horizontals so that they could more easily be inscribed in stone, wood, metal and bone. It is believed that knowledge of them was taken into the north by the Rhineland Heruli, along with the worship of Woden.[11] A spear found in a warrior's grave on a farm at Øvre Stabu in Toten, in Norway, with a word made up of eight runes etched on the blade and meaning something like 'the tester', is the earliest known example of the use of runes in Scandinavia.[12] The written word was held to possess an innate magical power and many of the numerous surviving *bracteates* – coin-like objects of gold with images punched on one side only and worn as necklaces or amulets – were stamped with runes that were believed to carry a protective medicinal power.[13] 'Beer', rich in vitamins from the malted barley from which it was made, is found frequently. So is 'onion'.

The use of metal and stone as a medium gave runic messages a greater durability than vellum or parchment, but limited the length of message it was possible to write. If this was regarded as a problem, then it was partially solved by a rationalization among Scandinavian runemasters in about the middle of the eighth century that reduced the original twenty-four letters to the sixteen of the so-called 'younger *futhark*', in which a single rune represented several of the more common sound values. As with homonyms, the sense emerged from the context. In a later development, diacritics were added to change the sound values of certain runes.

Runes could be used to identify the possessor of an object, or sometimes its maker, and finds from the quayside in Bergen include wooden pins that had either been stuck into or tied on to piles of goods as markers by merchants. Some used them to claim the simple immortality of graffiti: 'Halfdan was here', carved a wandering tenth-century Scandinavian on the balustrade in the gallery of the Hagia Sophia cathedral in what is now Istanbul. As the runes from the Oseberg find appear to show, graffiti could also take the form of a moment's existential meditation. Some runic inscriptions are more enigmatic than others. The Rök stone in Östergötland, carved in the ninth century by Varin in memory of his dead son Vämod, has 760 well-preserved runes covering its five sides; after the father's simple tribute comes a long passage which includes a poem with apparent allusions to long-lost heroic lays and legends, and passages using displacement and clandestine runes to further obscure the meaning of the message and, perhaps, intensify its occult power. Poems are also found on the Turinge[14] and Gripsholm stones,[15] and the Karlevi stone dated to about 1000, from the island of Öland in Sweden, which preserves a complete stanza of skaldic verse.[16]

The north had a long tradition of raising unmarked stones or *bautas* as a way of memorializing the dead. In Denmark in the tenth century this practice developed to include the inscribing of such stones. The Jelling stone is a rare example of the rune-stone as record of a specific and momentous affair of state. More frequently, runic inscriptions followed a simple, conventional formula: X *put up this stone in memory of Y, his brother/father/son/mother/comrade-at-arms/travelling companion.* This might be supplemented with a short comment praising the bravery of the dead man. The Tirsted stone, from the Danish island of Lolland, exemplifies this tradition. A suggested interpretation of the script is: 'Ástráðor and Hildungr raised this stone in memory of Fraði, their kinsman. And he was then the terror of men. And he died in Sweden and was first in Friggir's retinue of all vikings.'[17] For its time it is remarkable only in a rare contemporary use of the word 'viking'.

The magical power that was believed to reside in the runes was sometimes used by a runemaster to try to protect a grave from the attentions of robbers with the threat of a curse: the inscription on the Stentoft stone in Blekinge warned any potential robber that his reward would be a state of ceaseless wandering and an ostracism which even the dead would observe after his or her death. Besides protecting the dead, curse-runes were also carved to bind the occupant to the grave and prevent him or her from wandering and causing trouble among the living.[18] Memorial stones raised by Heathens might occasionally include an allusion to religious beliefs. One such is the Læborgsstenen in North Jutland, from the later years of the tenth century, which tells us that 'Ravnunge-Tove carved these runes for Torvi her queen.'[19] The inscription is decorated above and below with Thor's symbol, the hammer, to much the same protective end as Christians would decorate gravestones with a cross. The names indicate that both the carver and the memorialized woman were devotees of Thor.[20]

In recent years runic scholars have also recognized that another function of the commemorative rune-stone may have been as a 'declaration of inheritance'.[21] Incidentally a potted biography of a woman named Gerlög who survived the deaths of her two husbands and numerous children, the 300 runes on the Hillersjöhällen stone in Uppland in Sweden are also a thorough documentation of the legitimacy of her claim to be the inheritor of their properties.[22]

The story behind the inscription on the stone raised by Harald's father Gorm to honour Thyrwi, his wife and Harald's mother, remains enigmatic: *Gormr konungr gerði kuml þessi ept Þyrvé, konu sína, tanmarkar bót* (King Gorm made this monument in memory of Þyrvé, his wife, Denmark's salvation). Sven Aggesen says that she foiled an attempt by Otto the Great to compel her to marry him so that he might incorporate Denmark into his empire,[23] while the *Saga of the Jomsvikings* records a tradition that it was Thyrwi's foresight that saved the Danes from famine.[24] She had the rare distinction of being honoured twice on separate rune-stones, and it is a pity we do not know more about her. Respect for the past is a fluctuating phenomenon and her stone had been moved several times before 1590 when it was found, half-buried in the ground south of the church at Jelling. It was rescued and placed beside Harald's larger stone. Coming several decades after Ottar used the name in the account of Scandinavian territories he gave to Alfred the Great, the occurrence of *tanmarkar* on her stone is the first known use on native soil of the name Denmark.

Following a general runic convention, the lettering on Thyrwi's stone reads vertically, from the bottom upwards, though there was no real consistency in the layout and direction of inscriptions. Often the shape and size of the stone would dictate whether they be written left to right or right to left, with the orientation of the runes making it clear which way to read. For lengthier inscriptions, alternating lines might be written in opposite directions, going left and then snaking to the right for the next line. Sometimes the lines bent around at the end, so that one line reads left to right and the next right to left and upside down. By contrast, the inscription on Harald's stone adds to its syncretic intensity by following strictly the conventions of Christian Latin tradition to read from left to right. The peculiarity suggests that the designs may have been copied and adapted from a Latin manuscript.

But perhaps the most vivid expression of Harald's determination to marry the new Christian teachings to familiar and traditional Scandinavian forms lies in the work he did to transform the complex of monuments at Jelling into one single great monument. Now only a small tourist and farming community, in Harald's time and for centuries before that Jelling was a power centre for Danish chieftains, and the site of an enormous ship-setting that may have been Gorm's monument to Thyrwi. Measuring 170 metres from stem to stern it is the largest such monument known in the world. Examples from other, smaller settings in Denmark suggest that Thyrwi's stone may originally have stood at the prow of the setting. Harald set about the task of obscuring the imagery of this Heathen monument in the spirit of his new faith. He raised large mounds about 70 metres in diameter and some 11 metres high at each end of the ship, obliterating without entirely dismantling it. A number of the *bautas* were uncovered during excavations of the south mound in 1941–2.[25]

During a drought in the summer of 1820, the well at the top of the older, north mound ran dry. Attempting to dig deeper, the Jelling villagers were astounded to discover that the mound was hollow. The sheriff was summoned and a descent made into what turned out to be an oak-lined burial chamber. A half-metre-high deposit of earth, disturbed by the digging, covered the floor. A small silver cup was found, along with sundry metal fittings and the carved wooden figure of a man, about 15 cm high. Traces of paint show that his coat had been coloured blue and his hair and beard red. Of the original occupant of the chamber there was no sign.

Viking Age literature is rich in descriptions of *haugbrott*, the act of breaking open and entering a mound containing the remains of the dead. Very often the grave was entered as an act of exceptional daring with the aim of retrieving some object, often a sword, of symbolic military and political power. Perhaps the most compelling example in saga literature describes the descent of Grettir the Strong into the mound of Kar the Old, a site of hauntings and mysterious night-time fires. After a desperate struggle with Kar, Grettir succeeds in cutting off his head and putting an end to his revenancing. Among the wealth of grave-goods he then hoists up to the waiting Thorfin is a sword of outstanding beauty. Grettir covets it but Kar's son Thorfin recognizes it as a family heirloom and will not let Grettir have it.[26]

Sven Aggesen and Saxo in their 'Histories' both describe how King Uffi's father led his son to the hiding place of a sword of special powers that he had buried in a mound. The *Book of the Settlements* relates how the Icelandic pioneer Leif went raiding in Ireland just prior to the first great voyage of emigration with Ingolf. In his travels there he came across 'a big underground house, which he entered. All was dark till light shone from a sword which a man was holding. Leif killed this man, and took the sword from him and great riches too, and from there on was known as Hjorleif, Sword-Leif.'[27]

Literature was here reflecting a familiar aspect of Viking Age life. The nineteenth-century excavators of the Gokstad ship-mound found evidence that they were not the first to have disturbed the grave. Nikolay Nikolaysen shared an assumption, common at the time, that the motive for such an act can have been nothing more profound than robbery, and in his published account of the excavation he paid little attention to it. The Oseberg mound likewise had been entered, although here aspects of the break-in gave Gabriel Gustafson food for thought. With a precision that suggested forehand knowledge, the shaft had been dug directly into the burial chamber where the bodies of the dead women lay, and their remains dragged out into the shaft and left there in a disordered state. The beds in which the bodies had reposed had been not merely broken but comprehensively destroyed. It looked as though ritual disordering, rather than the search for treasure, had been the purpose of the entry, and the urgent need to make the grave uninhabitable for the dead.

From the size of the shafts it was obvious they could not have been the work of a couple of local thieves emboldened by an evening's drinking. Entry must have been a prominent and public act that took many days and many hands to complete.[28] Most of the mounds in the burial grounds at Borre, not far from the Oseberg site, show identical signs of having been broken open at some point. It is possible that Viking Age grave-mounds were raised as symbols of political power in the landscape, and that a ritual attack on them was also an attack on a specific political power. As we noted earlier, this may account for the partial destruction of the Borre mounds of the Danish kings Klak-Harald and Hemming on their trip across the waters of the Vik back in 813 to reassert their authority over rebellious Norwegian tributaries.[29]

Another suggested motive for *haugbrott* is that it may have been done to retrieve the bones of especially brave or powerful men that could then be used in the forging of a weapon which would, in a literal sense, partake of the dead hero's courage and power. To the same end of enhancing the spirit of the sword or the spear, the bones of bears or wolves were used in the firing process.[30] The blacksmith's is one of the very few trades explicitly mentioned on a rune-stone and beliefs like these might go some way towards explaining his high and sometimes almost mystical status in the Viking Age.[31]

And yet none of these possibilities seems applicable to the empty north mound at Jelling, which bore no signs of disturbance from the outside. The excavation of the south mound carried out in 1941 revealed that it had never been used as a grave at all, and its purpose remains obscure. Perhaps Harald intended it for himself, but the circumstances of his death made burial there impractical or impossible. It may be that Poppo or some other Christian advised him against it, on the grounds that the Heathen symbolism of a mound burial would be inappropriate for a Christian king. A large post, standing at its centre and positioned on the central axis of the outlined ship-setting, shows how carefully Harald's engineers worked to incorporate the original shape into their design. Harald positioned his great stone where it still stands today, exactly midway between the centres of the two mounds, and on the central axis of the ship-setting, and another possibility is that the south mound was raised simply to complete a symmetry and focus the whole monumental complex on the stone.

In the space between the Jelling stone and the north mound Harald built a church. It burnt down, as did the two oak churches that followed it. A stone church built around 1100 has survived to the present day. A serendipitous result of the installation of a heating system in 1976–9 provided what is in all likelihood a solution to the mystery of the body missing from the burial chamber beneath the north mound. A grave-chamber discovered below the floor of the first church contained the bones of a middle-aged man about 5 feet 8 inches (173 cm) tall, haphazardly spread about the chamber.[32] Among the material finds were several hundred fragments of gold thread, probably the remains of a costly garment, and two strap decorations, with beautifully ornamented animal heads, in conception and execution identical to the heads depicted on the silver cup found in the north mound. These decorations were in a style so distinct from other examples of Viking Age art that art historians of the Viking Age have given it its own name, the *Jelling style*. Its significance for this story is the high degree of circumstantial evidence the cup and the strap decorations provide that the north mound was the original resting place of the bones discovered beneath the church, and the further likelihood that they were those of Harald's father, King Gorm the Old.

We may reasonably doubt the sincerity of Rollo's conversion to Christianity as part of the price paid for his land in Normandy, and we may point to political reasons why Harald Bluetooth may have found it advisable to embrace Christianity, not least Otto and the revived presence of a superpower on his southern borders. But this act of *translation*, if such it was, in all its filial piety, seems to show a genuine commitment to a new and Christian set of beliefs on the nature of the afterlife.[33] Gorm the Old had the possibly unique distinction of being buried for a third time on 30 August 2000, beneath the latest version of the Jelling church. Among those present at the re-interment of his remains was the Danish queen, Margrethe II, herself a member of the Jelling dynasty, honouring the memory of the founder of the line twenty-nine generations earlier.[34]

If the complex of monuments at Jelling tell us something of Harald Bluetooth's inner life, then other monuments that survive from his reign reveal more of his political concerns. The series of five ring-forts known as *trelleborgs*, from the first of them to be identified, and the wooden bridge at Ravning Enge appear to be intimately connected with the claim Harald made on the Jelling stone, that he had 'won for himself all of Denmark and Norway'. They may also shed light on the obscure nature of the relationship between Denmark and Germany during the rule of Otto the Great, and on the tensions focused on the borders in southern Jutland.

In the *Short History of the Kings of Denmark* Sven Aggesen tells us that Harald inherited the kingdom from his father Gorm the Old.[35] Under the circumstances it might make the claim on the Jelling stone that Harald 'won for himself all of Denmark' redundant or even hollow. Denmark was favoured among the Scandinavian countries on a number of counts. The land was more fertile than land in either Norway or Sweden, and the cluster of islands to the east of the Jutland peninsula gave it control over trade relations between the Baltic countries in the east and mainland Europe. Naval power enabled it to maintain control over this trade route, and through naval power it was able to maintain its hegemony over the west coast of Sweden and the province of Skåne as well as the region around the Oslo fjord.[36] This regional prominence was a fact of Scandinavian political life by the beginning of the ninth century, and probably for some time before that. Harald Finehair's primitive unification of Norway was achieved during the final decades of the ninth century, and it was undoubtedly facilitated by the dynastic instability among the Danes that lasted from the death of Horik the Younger until the advent of Gorm the Old, whose rule ended in about 935. We shall shortly examine in more detail developments in this newly unified Norway following the death of Harald Finehair in about 940. Here it is enough to say that, as was the case with Charlemagne and the Carolingian inheritance, Harald's many sons turned out to be a curse rather than a blessing. As Norway's fortunes declined so did Denmark's ascend. We have no record of any military activity launched by Harald Bluetooth across the waters of the Vik; yet some such activity seems a logical explanation for the claim on the Jelling stone that he had 'won Norway', if we interpret this to mean that he won back the tributary status of the people living in the south and east of Norway that had been lost under Harald Finehair. Significantly the stone stops short of claiming that Harald also made the Norwegians Christian.

The unification or reunification of Denmark, and the restoration of Denmark's regional power around the waters of the Vik and the Kattegat, were probably both served by the creation of the *trelleborgs*. In 1934 a motor-cycle sports club in Slagelse, in Zealand, were looking for a new arena in which to practise. They applied for permission to use the interior of a nearby large, circular earthen structure, to which no one had previously paid any particular attention. The National Museum of Denmark withheld permission until they had satisfied themselves that it was of no great antiquity, and the finds from the preliminary excavations turned out to be so unexpected and extraordinary that the club never did receive permission. For the next fifty years the site became the focus of intense archaeological activity.[37] The Trelleborg was the first of several similarly enigmatic structures to be identified as Viking Age forts in subsequent years, and its name was used as a generic for these at Fyrkat in Hobro; Nonnebakken in Odense; and at Aggersborg on the northern side of the Limfjord in northern Jutland.[38] The Slagelse Trelleborg was 136 metres in diameter, the fort at Aggersborg even larger at 240 metres. Two other forts, at Borgeby and at a second site, also known as Trelleborg, have been found in Skåne. Each of these earthen forts, moated around the sloping outside walls, was built to a pattern, perfectly circular and with gates at each of the cardinal points of the compass connected by two perfectly intersecting roads. Inside the Slagelse fort each of the four quarter-circles formed by the bisecting roads contained four identical square buildings, 30 metres long and with the bowed walls characteristic of the long-house of the period. In a perimeter beyond the walls that was protected by a second earthen wall and a moat, the remains of another fifteen similar buildings were found. A cemetery was located here. Though they varied in size and in individual points of detail, each of the other *trelleborgs* conformed to this basic pattern and there can be little doubt that they were the product of the same engineering vision. The Slagelse fort was built in the winter of 980–81. Tree-ring dating of the other forts confirms that they were built at about the same time, in the later years of the reign of Harald Bluetooth.

The name *trelleborg* may derive from *trel* (pl. *trelle*), meaning the wooden staves that lined the earthen walls of the fort both inside and out. Or it may indicate that they were built by slave-labour. A treaty of 1269 between Novgorod and the Hanseatic towns referred to a settlement of pilots on the Volkhov as *Kholopij gorodok*, a name that translates literally as *the town of slaves*. In the Latin version of the treaty of 1270 the name was rendered as *Drelleborch*.[39]

A greater mystery concerns their purpose. Recent excavations in the extended vicinity of the fort at Slagelse have shown that some kind of service community grew up around it. Weights, silver coins from the east and pieces of hack silver and jewellery are all evidence of trading activities, and the find of a so-called casting-cone of bronze shows that handicrafts were practised on the site.[40] The remains of nails at the fort and between the fort and the nearby river might indicate that ships were repaired there. And yet, by contrast with buildings in other Viking Age settlements that have been excavated in recent years, the *trelleborg* forts and their houses show no signs of having been either repaired or maintained. The finding has proved difficult to reconcile with what was, for a long time, a popular theory that the forts were built as training camps and garrisons for Viking youths involved in raiding in the west and in the Baltic.[41]

The same enigmas attach to another of Harald's extraordinary feats of engineering, the bridge at Ravning Enge that crossed the swampy valley of the river Vejle, 10 kilometres south of Jelling. It was built at the same time as the *trelleborgs* and its construction showed the same mastery of precision and symmetry. Five and a half metres wide and capable of bearing loads up to five tons, Ravning Enge remained, at 760 metres, the longest bridge ever constructed in Denmark until the erection of the Lillebæltsbro about 1,000 years later in 1935. Ropes stretched between hazelwood poles guided the builders in their work with such accuracy that across the full length of the bridge the deviation from a perfect straight line was never greater than 5 cm. In all, 1,120 piles were lowered into the water until they hit solid ground or a load-bearing obstruction and then levelled off to the same height to take the transverse planking. Yet for all the obsessive care lavished on this magnificent construction it too, like the *trelleborgs*, shows no signs of ever having been repaired. Archaeologists have estimated its functional life as at most five years.[42]

As extraordinary as it might appear, the *trelleborgs* and the Ravning Enge bridge seem to have been nonce constructions. The pious inscriptions on a number of rune-stones in Sweden make it clear that in post-conversion Scandinavia the building of a bridge was considered a peculiarly Christian sort of good deed. Ravning Enge, however, was almost certainly not for the benefit of the local community. As an essential element of Harald's unification strategies it made it possible for his soldiers to cross the Vejle marshes in all seasons and to connect with the Army or Ox Road. For the duration of the Viking Age and after, this was the overland 'motorway' between the north and continental Europe, stretching from Viborg in the north of Denmark to the trading centre of Hedeby in the south. Along with the L-shaped disposition of the *trelleborgs* across Danish territory, from Jutland in the north to Skåne in the east via Nonnebakken, it may bear physical witness to Harald's claims on the Jelling stone to have won for himself all of Denmark, with the enormous and overawing Aggersborg in the north facing directly across Skaggerak and the Vik to Norway.

Only a year or two after his conversion, political anxieties aroused by threats from Otto in the south in 968 led Harald to develop the venerable Danevirke in the area around Hedeby into a single, coherent fortress settlement. These precautions were seemingly enough to forestall any intended attack, and with Otto's death in 973 it was Harald who attempted to exploit the situation by invading the land south of the Eider. The Germans repelled his attack to such good effect that by the following year they were in possession of all of southern Jutland, including Hedeby and the Danevirke. By the end of the decade, with the *trelleborgs* and the Ravning Enge bridge in place and assuring his rapid logistical access to the south, Harald was able in 983 to launch a successful counter-attack and recover the lost territory. Border tensions evaporated, and with them the need to maintain the great garrison forts and the Ravning Edge bridge.

Harald was a remarkable king indeed, industrial, restless and forward-thinking. Inevitably, his decision to embrace and promote Christianity proved controversial and his unification campaign unpopular with the powerful. It is possible that, in the last years of his life, disaffected conservative forces looked to his son Sven to depose him, in the hope that Sven would revoke Harald's reforms. Sven is said to have risen against his father and driven him out of the country. Weakened by an arrow-wound Harald made his way with his *hird* to Jumne, at the mouth of the river Oder, and died there in 987. In the *Short History of the Kings of Denmark* Sven Aggesen mentions, almost in passing, that Harald renounced his faith at the end of his life.[43] The fact that he was not canonized despite his work for the Christian Church might indicate the truth in the claim. For Adam of Bremen, however, Harald remained a model Christian king until the day of his death. He hailed him as 'the first to order the Danes to become Christians, the one who filled all of the north with priests and churches, innocently wounded as he was, exiled from his own land for the sake of Christ, and it is my certain hope that he will one day bear the triumphant crown of martyrdom'.[44]

Jumne is believed to have been on the site of Wolin in present-day Poland, and has been identified as the location of the fortress Jomsborg, home to the Jomsvikings, heroes of the thirteenth-century *Saga of the Jomsvkinga* and among the most potent literary legends of the Viking Age. If the story of Harald's being driven into exile is true, then the origins of the tales concerning this dedicated band of warrior-heroes may lie in the further fate of the now leaderless remnants of the *hird* who survived him, and for whom return to Danish soil was not a practical alternative. If the *trelleborgs* did, indeed, house garrison communities of some sort, the codes of conduct operating within them may have provided a historical basis for the laws of membership and conduct that are noted in the saga as being those of the Jomsvikings:[45] that membership of such military brotherhoods was restricted to men between the ages of eighteen and fifty; that family connection were to count for nothing in deciding whether or not to admit new members; that a member might not flee from an opponent as brave and as well-armed as himself; that the expression of fear was forbidden no matter how hopeless the predicament; that members were to avenge each other as they would their own brothers; that all booty taken on an expedition, regardless of value, was to be put into the common store; that it was forbidden to start a quarrel inside the fort; that women were forbidden to enter the fort; and that absence from the fort for more than three days was not permitted.[46]

Dudo gave us the story of Rollo's man who stood up to kiss the foot of King Charles the Simple and sent him tumbling on to his back. The *Saga of the Jomsvikings* gives us another emblematic tale of Viking fearlessness. Following their defeat at Hjórungarág by a fleet under the command of Norwegian earls, the Jomsvikings are captured and called to their execution, one after another. Some go haughtily, some insolently. All go bravely. One is a seventeen-year-old 'whose hair was long and golden-yellow like silk'. Asked how he views the prospect of death the youth replies, with a splendid mixture of stoicism and vanity, that he has lived the best part of his life and has no desire to survive his companions. Pride and reputation, however, continue to concern him and he makes a special request of his executioner:

I want to be led to slaughter not by slaves but rather by a man not lower than you; nor will such a one be hard to find – and let him hold my hair away from my head so that my hair will not become bloodstained.[47]

A man steps forward and twines the long fair hair around his hands. As the executioner Thorkel brings down the sword the youth jerks away and the sword slices off the assistant's arms below the elbow. The young man coolly inquires whose hands these are in his hair. Youth, sharpness of wit, bravery and vanity are the essential qualities of the heroic Viking and the young man has shown all four in abundance. He is reprieved and invited to become a member of Earl Erik's *hird*. And yet the realities of Viking Age war are hardly glamorized by scenes in the saga of men interrupting battle to remove items of clothing because the heat of the day has made them uncomfortable; nor of ships that return to shore to pick up fresh supplies of stones, the stone for throwing being the weapon of choice for the average foot-soldier or sailor throughout most of the Viking Age.

Such details remind us of how differently things were done in the past. The distinction is emphasized by a naming culture that has handed down to us Ragnar Hairy-Breeches, Erik Bloodaxe, Halfdan the Black and Ivar the Boneless, and scores of other personal names that dramatize the cultural gap between the Viking Age and our own times. For reasons best known to marketing people, 'Bluetooth' has recently been resurrected as the name of a form of wireless communication (never *blåtann*, always English 'Bluetooth', even in Scandinavia). If King Harald did indeed have a prominent blue or black tooth at the front of his mouth this may have been a simple case of dental decay. There is, however, a slight possibility the name might be related to the recent discoveries of twenty-four skeletons of young Viking Age males, in locations spread across Denmark and Sweden, whose teeth have horizontally filed furrows on the frontal upper part of the tooth crown. The work appears to have been done by people skilled in the practice. The furrows are usually several, though single furrows occur, and the modified teeth are at the front of the mouth. Their significance is obscure, but a suggestion put forward by the researchers is that the furrows may have been coloured to make them visible from a distance, perhaps in an erotic or a warlike signalling, in which case Harald's would have been blue.[48]

Harald Bluetooth's son, successor and probable usurper, Sven, bore the less enigmatic after-name Tveskegg or Forked-Beard. Within thirty years of Harald's death Sven would become the most powerful Scandinavian king we have so far met, and we might cautiously suppose that his dream of empire derived in part at least from close observation of his own father's manifest ability to build on the grandest scale.

The Danelaw II

Assimilation

The treaty between Alfred and Guthrum, with its reference to the distinct parties to the agreement as 'all the English race and all the people which is in East Anglia', starkly recognized that the invasion of the Great Heathen Army in 865 had brought about a far-reaching change in England's demographic make-up.[1] As we saw earlier, the boundary between the new neighbours was settled as running 'up the Thames, and then up the Lea, and along the Lea to its source, then in a straight line to Bedford, then up the Ouse to the Watling Street'.[2] The first use of the term 'Danelaw' to define the regions where Scandinavian influence was most intense does not occur until 130 years after the share-out of land, in two legal compilations made by Wulfstan, Archbishop of York, which use the Anglo-Saxon terms 'on Deone lage' and 'on Dena lage'.[3] No surviving documents relate to the separate acts of settlement of the eastern part of Mercia and of Northumbria, but a document dated to the second half of the eleventh century lists the shires comprising the Danelaw as Buckinghamshire, Middlesex, Suffolk, Norfolk, Essex, Hertfordshire, Cambridgeshire, Huntingdonshire, Bedfordshire, Northamptonshire, Lincolnshire, Derbyshire, Leicestershire, Nottinghamshire and Yorkshire.[4] For the familiar reason that the Vikings practised little self-documentation not much is known for certain of how things developed in these areas during the intervening years. The raiding and the hostile settlement had far-reaching consequences for Anglo-Saxon England. The seven kingdoms, which had been reduced to four by the time of the Lindisfarne raid and to two by the time of Alfred the Great, underwent a final rationalization under Alfred's successors into one kingdom under the rule of one king. The creation of an English monarchy laid the foundations for a model of kingship so efficient that later Scandinavian kings and conquerors were able to take over England and run it in their own interests with a minimum of administrative adaptation. The sixty or seventy years that the process took culminated in the expulsion from York, in 954, of the city's last Scandinavian ruler, the Norwegian Erik Bloodaxe. His eviction and subsequent death signalled the end of independent Scandinavian power in England.

It is tempting to describe this process as the re-taking of the Dane-law, as though it involved a single and coherent campaign aimed at wresting back territories wrongly taken from 'us' by 'them'. The moral basis for such an attitude is what Norwegians call *hevd*, a right established not in law but in possession and usage over time. This is the right Alcuin was unconsciously invoking in his letter to Ethelred, king of Northumbria, after the Lindisfarne attack, that it was 'nearly three hundred and fifty years that we and our fathers have inhabited this most lovely land, and never before has such a terror appeared in Britain as we have suffered from a pagan race'. In this he was over-looking the fact that the Vikings were simply doing to him what 'we and our fathers' had done to the Britons 350 years earlier. *Hevd* led Alcuin to consider the Angles and the Saxons the rightful owners of England, but *hevd* is a relative concept. The irony of Alcuin's position is that the genetic survey carried out for the BBC by the team from UCL in 2000 found it impossible to distinguish between the DNA of the fifth-century Saxon invaders and ninth-century Vikings. The notion of a persisting racial identity is one of history's most obstinate and mischievous myths. It was natural, however, that the English should have seen the Scandinavian settlers in the east of the country as usurpers and thieves from whom it was right and proper to attempt to recover stolen property. It was just as natural for the Scandinavian settlers to nourish dreams of appropriating an even larger share of the new country, and to collude with and harbour those of their own cultures and countries when one or another leader arrived with an army that seemed capable of realizing these dreams. Call it what we will, tribal, racial or cultural solidarity set the political agenda for the unfolding of events over the next 100 years.

The campaign to repossess the occupied lands got off to an inaus-picious start. Ethelred I, the last of Alfred's three brothers to hold the throne of Wessex before him, left an infant son Aethelwold at his death. Grown to manhood, Aethelwold rose and contested the succession of Alfred's son Edward in 899. Driven out by Edward, he persuaded the Viking Northumbrians of York to accept him as their leader. Shortly afterwards, with the help of East Anglian Danes, he mounted a military challenge to Edward. It failed, and he met his death on the battlefield at Holme. The last East Anglian king whose name we know, Eohric, fell with him. That the direct threat to Wessex from Danish East Anglia should have been so rapidly neutralized lends credibility to Dudo's account in his Norman history of the trouble Guthrum had with his disobedient and rebellious English subjects, whom he was able to subdue only with the help of Rollo. East Anglia was, in any case, always going to be the most difficult part of Danish-occupied territory for the invaders to hold on to. Alfred's treaty with Guthrum was a personal agreement between two leaders that established the dividing line between their territories. It made no claim to regulate the terms of the Scandinavian settlements in Northumbria and Mercia. That Mercia in the midlands should have been the next to fall, after a longer resistance, and York in the far north after one even longer, is a direct reflection of the relative distances of the Danish kingdoms from Wessex.

We saw earlier how the old rivalry between Wessex and Mercia had fallen away as their leaders made common cause against the invaders, and how Alfred's marriage to a Mercian princess, and the marriage of his daughter Ethelfled to Ethelred, the leader of English-occupied Mercia, strengthened the dynastic bonds between the two kingdoms. Throughout the early years of his campaigning, Edward continued to enjoy the support of Ethelred and his Mercians. The inspiration to continue Alfred's policy of creating fortified *burhs* at strategically important points across the territory under English control came from that quarter. In the west, Mercia's vulnerability to raiders using the Bristol Channel, and the open invitation to Irish-based Viking fleets in the north-west of the British isles to penetrate inland via the Dee and the Mersey, had to be urgently addressed. Struggles for power among the invaders themselves remained concentrated on Dublin. The brief respite that followed the intervention of the king of Lochlain in 853 ended with the death of his successor in

873. Three turbulent decades followed, at the end of which the Vikings were driven out of Dublin by Caerball, leader of the Leinster Irish. This expulsion has been associated with the Cuerdale hoard, found in May 1840 by workmen repairing the embankment on the south side of the river Ribble at Cuerdale, near Preston. Until dwarfed by the discovery of the Spillings hoard on Gotland in 1999, it remained the largest trove of Viking silver ever unearthed. Among the numerous items in the hoard were bossed penanular brooches and thistle brooches, stamped arm-rings and neck-rings, rings from east of the Baltic, Slavic beads, Carolingian and Pictish items, a coin from Constantinople, a handful of Kufic dirhams, a large number of coins from Anglo-Saxon mints and some 5,000 coins minted within the Danelaw.[5] The dates on the coins give a *terminus ante quem* of around 905, which accords nicely with the expulsion from Dublin. After a failed attempt to settle in Anglesey, an army of expelled Norwegians under Ingamund landed in the Wirral peninsula, between the Dee and the Mersey, and demanded to be allowed to stay. Ethelred's health had failed by this time and his role in the negotiations was taken by Ethelfled. She gave her permission. Aware, however, of the attractions of wealthy Chester, she had the city walls repaired in 907, and established a garrison there that could control the peninsula. The Wirral, and those other parts of north-west England later occupied by Norwegians, never formed part of the physical entity of 'the Danelaw'; and perhaps it was for this very reason they thrived in their historically rather neglected colony. Over 600 place-names of Scandinavian origin on the Ordinance Survey maps of the Wirral area amply demonstrate the size and permanence of their settlement.[6] The DNA traces tell the same story: in a study of the Y-chromosome of 150 Liverpool men carried out by a team from the University of Nottingham in 2007, findings showed that 50 per cent were likely to have been of Norwegian descent.[7]

In 906 the *Anglo-Saxon Chronicle* records a peace agreement entered into 'from necessity' between Edward and the East Angles and Northumbrians, but it was a routinely uneasy peace, and following a number of skirmishes the Northumbrian Danes swarmed into English Mercia in 910. The combined levies of Wessex and Mercia under Edward caught up with them as they were making their way back to their own territory and inflicted a heavy defeat on them at Tettenhall in Staffordshire. The *Chronicle* proudly records the names of twelve Viking leaders who fell in the battle, a setback which greatly reduced Northumbria's power to challenge Wessex for the dominance of England, and led to a concentration of the kingdom within the city of York.

Following her husband Ethelred's death in 911, Ethelfled raised no protest when Edward annexed Oxford and London, which were clearly easier for Wessex to defend than Mercia; and her action in fostering Edward's son Athelstan further strengthened the regional and dynastic ties. She continued the remarkably successful policy of creating *burhs* along the strategic routes that led into Mercia from the west, fortifying Bridgnorth in 912 to control the middle reaches of the Severn; Stafford and Tamworth along Watling Street the following year; Warwick, to guard the use of the Fosse Way, possibly in response to a raid in 914 by Vikings based in Brittany who landed in South Wales; and Runcorn in the Mersey estuary.[8] In the east she drove the Danes from Derby in 917, after fierce fighting in which four of her personal favourites were killed inside the walls of the town.

Edward, meanwhile, battled his way up the east coast against Danish armies whose forces were at times supported by visiting Viking fleets. The fortification and colonization of Hertford in 911 protected London from hostile approaches along the River Lea, and control of Essex came with the building of garrisons at Maldon, Witham and Colchester. Buckingham and Bedford were strengthened to protect the Lower Ouse and, in connecting the defences of the Ouse with those of the Dee and the Mersey, *burhs* created at Towcester, Nottingham and Bakewell brought to completion what was clearly a logically formulated plan to make the hostile penetration of the interior of England by river a fraught and dangerous enterprise for any ambitious Viking. In all, twenty-eight of these fortifications were built in the years between 910 and 921.

The *Chronicle* gives vivid detail of the fighting in the crucial year of 917, with Viking armies from Northampton being frustrated in their attempts to take Towcester and an East Anglian army being repelled with heavy loss of life by the men of Bedford.[9] The English were greatly encouraged by their successes, and a large army of men from Kent, Surrey and Essex seized Colchester after another fierce battle. By the close of the year Cambridgeshire, Huntingdonshire and Northamptonshire were under Edward's control, as well as the whole of East Anglia. Ethelfled's forces took Leicester in 918, and in June of that year she received the submission of the Danes of York.[10] The Viking kingship there was as little settled as East Anglia. By the following year the leadership had changed again, reverting to another reputed grandson of Ivar the Boneless, Ragnald, who seems to have held it once before, in 911, briefly but long enough to strike his own coins. This was probably the same chieftain who fought a sea-battle off the Isle of Man in 914 and, as a king of the *Dubhgall* or 'black foreigners', fought the Irish in the area around Waterford in 917. After ravaging in Ireland and Scotland he faced an alliance of English and Scots forces at Corbridge, and in 919 threatened and then took York. His second, brief reign ended with his death in 921, at which he was succeeded by Sihtric, another of Ivar's grandsons.

By 920 Edward was king of all England south of the Mersey and Humber. The entry in the *Anglo-Saxon Chronicle* for that year sums up the result of ten years of ceaseless campaigning by Edward and Ethelfled:

In this year, before midsummer, King Edward went with the army to Notting-ham, and ordered to be built the borough on the south side of the river, opposite the other, and the bridge over the river Trent between the two boroughs. Then he went from there into the Peak district to Bakewell, and ordered a borough to be built in the neighbourhood and manned. And then the king of the Scots, and Ragnald, and the sons of Eadwulf and all who live in Northumbria, both English and Danish, Norsemen and others, and also the king of the Strathclyde Welsh and all the Strathclyde Welsh, chose him as father and lord.[11]

When Ethelfled, known to admiring chroniclers as 'the Lady of the Mercians', died on 12 June 918, she left a daughter, Elfwynn. Now fully convinced of the possibility of a unified England under Wessex kingship, Edward received the submission of the Mercians and briefly allowed Elfwynn to continue in her mother's role. The experiment lasted less than a year. In 919, three weeks before Christmas, she was removed from office and taken to Wessex. Her further fate is unknown, but it seems likely she entered a convent. The king's action marked the definitive end of Mercia as an independent kingdom.

Edward was a talented maker of diplomatically rewarding matches and established good contact with the rulers of Flanders, as well as marrying his daughter, Eadgifu, to Charles the Simple. In other ways he showed himself a man of vision and foresight. The 'Burghal Hidage', a listing of the *burhs* dated to some time after 914, contains a conscription formula that reflects the military purpose behind these creations. But in time these *burhs* transcended their military origins and, with their garrisons, mints and trading populations, came to play a major role in the development of cities and townships in England, so that they can properly be entered on the long list of negative credits attributable to Viking violence. Edward brought new thinking to his enlarged kingdom. The new Mercian shires he created along with *burhs* took their names from towns, with the area administered from Gloucester being known as Gloucestershire, from Hereford as Herefordshire and so on.[12] The boundaries of these new shires cut across the traditional boundaries of the old kingdoms. In so doing they added impetus to the breakdown of familiar geographical regions and political institutions which Viking raiding and settlement had begun, accelerating and simplifying the way to the eventual creation of a single English kingdom.

Edward died at Farndon, on the Dee, on 17 July 924. In his translation of Augustine's *Soliloquies* his father Alfred had noted the existence of men living pleasant lives, at ease in winter as in summer, adding ruefully 'as I have not yet done'.[13] Edward might have echoed him. Yet Alfred had Asser to fill out and colour with personality the stark spaces between the terse reportings of his campaigns in the annals. With no biographer to give life and colour to it, the only impression we have of Edward's life is that conveyed to us by the annalists, of a bleak and endless succession of days given over to fighting Vikings.

He was succeeded by his brother, Athelstan, who shared his skills as a maker of diplomatic marriages, and added his own remarkable ability to adopt talented children. Three future rulers of foreign countries were brought up at his court, including Håkon, known as Athelstansfostri, a son of the Norwegian king, Harald Finehair. One of his sisters was married to the future Otto I, another to Hugh, duke of the Franks, a third to a king of Burgundy.[14] Significantly excluded from his shield of protective alliances were the Danes and the Viking colonists in Normandy.[15]

Early in 926 he gave his sister Eadgyth in marriage to Sihtric of York, having first issued the traditional demand that Sihtric convert to Christianity. According to Roger of Wendover, Sihtric soon followed the equally traditional Viking response of abandoning the new religion at the first opportunity, along with his new wife, and returning to his old gods. When Sihtric died in 927, his son by an earlier marriage, Olaf, attempted to succeed him with the support of a leader of the Dublin Vikings. Athelstan, wearied as so many Anglo-Saxon and Frankish Christian rulers had been before him by the casual attitude of Vikings towards conversion, drove him out and for the first time a Wessex king ruled directly over York. A small coin hoard unearthed on a farm in Harrogate has been associated with this particular period of unrest in the north-east.[16] One of the coins bears the Latin inscription *Rex totius Britannia* (King of all Britain), a claim Athelstan repeated in the charters of his reign, where he also styled himself 'Emperor [using the Byzantine word *basilius*] of the English and of all the nations round about'. As the first Anglo-Saxon king to make such claims, Athelstan's gestures show that his goal was indeed the unification of England under one king.

Yet his kingdom remained far from secure. Constantine, king of the Scots, challenged him in 934, and when that challenge failed Constantine allied himself with that Olaf whom Athelstan had driven out of York. They were joined by Owen, king in the Welsh-speaking kingdom of Strathclyde in the south-west of Scotland, and while Athelstan and his men were campaigning in the south of England, Olaf's army of Irish-Norse Vikings and Northumbrian Norwegians raided and caused havoc in Mercia. In 937 Athelstan with his brother Edmund at the head of a large army marched north and confronted them in a great battle at Brunanburh, now identified with some certainty as Bromborough in the Wirral peninsula.[17] The battle lasted all day, and by the end of it the alliance was destroyed and the northern threat to the kingdom removed. Olaf made his way back over the sea to Dublin and Constantine returned to Scotland, abdicating in 943 after a reign of forty years to spend the last ten years of his life as a monk at St Andrews. Brunanburh was the outstanding event of Athelstan's reign[18] and, as such, the stuff of literature. The battle was immortalized in a Latin poem from which William of Malmesbury quotes, and it was noted in a number of histories and annals, including the *Annals of Ulster*. Its most famous memorial is the Anglo-Saxon poem that is in its entirety the entry for that year in the *Anglo-Saxon Chronicle*:

In this year King Athelstan, lord of nobles, dispenser of treasure to men, and his brother also, Edmund atheling, won by the sword's edge undying glory in battle round Brunanburh. Edward's sons clove the shield-wall, hewed the linden-wood shields with hammered swords, for it was natural to men of their lineage to defend their land, their treasure and their homes, in frequent battle against every foe. Their enemies perished; the people of the Scots and the pirates fell doomed. The field grew dark with the blood of men, from the time when the sun, that glorious luminary, the bright candle of God, of the Lord Eternal, moved over the earth in the hours of the morning, until that noble creation sank at its setting. There lay many a man destroyed by the spears, many a northern warrior shot over his shield; and likewise many a Scot lay weary, sated with battle.

The whole long day the West Saxons with mounted companies kept in pursuit of the hostile peoples, grievously they cut down the fugitives from behind with their whetted swords. The Mercians refused not hard conflict to any men who with Olaf had sought this land in the bosom of a ship over the tumult of waters, coming doomed to the fight. Five young kings lay on that field of battle, slain by the swords, and also seven of Olaf's earls, and a countless host of seamen and Scots. There the prince of the Norsemen was put to flight, driven perforce to the prow of his ship with a small company; the vessel pressed on in the water, the king set out over the fallow flood and saved his life.

There also the aged Constantine, the hoary-haired warrior, came north to his own land by flight. He had no cause to exult in that crossing of swords. He was shorn of his kinsmen and deprived of his friends at that meeting place, bereaved in the battle, and he left his young son on the field of slaughter, brought low by wounds in the battle. The grey-haired warrior, the old and wily one, had no cause to vaunt of that sword-clash; no more had Olaf. They had no need to gloat with the remnants of their armies, that they were superior in warlike deeds on the field of battle, in the clash of standards, the meeting of spears, the encounter of men, and the crossing of weapons, after they had contended on the field of slaughter with the sons of Edward.

Then the Norsemen, the sorry survivors from the spears, put out in their studded ships on to Ding's mere, to make for Dublin across the deep water, back to Ireland humbled at heart. Also the two brothers, king and atheling, returned together to their own country, the land of the West Saxons, exulting in the battle. They left behind them the dusky-coated one, the black raven with its horned beak, to share the corpses, and the dun-coated, white-tailed eagle, the greedy war-hawk, to enjoy the carrion, and that grey beast, the wolf of the forest.

Never yet in this island before this by what books tell us and our ancient sages, was a greater slaughter of a host made by the edge of the sword, since the Angles and the Saxons came hither from the east, invading Britain over the broad seas, and the proud assailants, warriors eager for glory, overcame the Britons and won a country.[19]

Two years after the battle at Brunanburh Athelstan died, and Olaf returned from Ireland to press his claim to York once more. As coins from the mint at Derby show, this time he succeeded. Again Wessex found itself faced with a Viking kingdom spanning the north of England, with potential allies in the north-west and along the east coast, and with Dublin and the Isle of Man in the Irish Sea as strategically vital components. The union of Dublin and York under one ruler might have proved an irresistible military force had Olaf not died in 941. His cousin, Olaf Sihtricsson, inherited that same potential; but after a campaign by Athelstan's successor Edmund he was compelled to accept Christianity and relinquish the territory gained by Olaf south of the Humber. The following year, in 944, the Danes of York rejected him, and the disintegration of the kingdom continued apace. After a short and provocative reign, Erik Bloodaxe, the oldest of Harald Finehair's sons, had been driven from the throne of Norway by his brother, Håkon Athelstansfostri. According to his saga in *Heimskringla*, Håkon was helped in his campaign by ships and men provided by Athelstan, just as Athelstan had provided military and naval support for another of his foster-sons, Alan Barbetorte, in the campaign to reclaim Brittany that began in 936.[20] The account given by Snorri of Håkon's adoption by Athelstan[21] is obviously legendary and nothing is known of how the friendship between the English and Norwegian kings came about; by himself as by others, however, Athelstan was regarded as a very important king indeed in Europe at the time. William of Malmesbury, in the *De Gestis Regum Anglorum*, says that 'foreign kings rightly considered themselves fortunate if they could buy his friendship either by marriage alliance or gifts',[22] and goes on to describe a visit paid to Athelstan after his recapture of York by two Norwegian emissaries, Helgrim and Osfrid, who brought with them a king's gift of a ship from Harald Finehair to Athelstan, 'which had a gold beak and purple sail, surrounded inside with a dense rank of gilded shields'. A passage in *Egil's Saga* may provide evidence of a tradition of further ties between the Norwegian and English royal houses at this time, when a young Norwegian named Thorstein, involved in a property dispute back home in Norway, visits Athelstan's court with a plea to the English king to ask his foster-son Håkon to intercede on his behalf in the dispute.[23] The claim in the *Historia Norwegie*, that Erik Bloodaxe made his way to England after being driven out by Håkon, and was warmly received by the king, baptized and 'appointed earl, commanding the whole of Northumbria', likewise suggests continuing good relations between the royal families of England and Norway.[24] The English king involved may have been Athelstan, but more likely it was later, during the reign of King Edred. Snorri Sturluson tells a similar story of Erik's being baptized and given York to rule by an English king. Erik appears to have been an acceptable choice to the Northumbrians until the arrival of his wife, Gunnhild. The pair were driven out and Gunnhild returned to Denmark with her sons. Roger of Wendover says that Erik was betrayed, ambushed and killed as he made his way across remote Stainmore in Westmorland in 954. Two twelfth-century Norwegian sources, the *Historia Norwegie* and the *Ágrip*, tell a different story and make the intriguing claim that, after being driven from York, Erik set out on a Viking expedition to Spain and was killed there. Whichever story is correct, both describe the ignominious and lonely death of a nearly-man. Erik was known as 'Bloodaxe' during his own lifetime, after killing two of his own brothers who may have become a focus of discontent with his rule. Unfortunately for him, brother Håkon was out of his reach and had a powerful protector. The image of a short, broad sword on a silver penny struck during one of his brief reigns at York serves as a fitting epitaph to his violent and uncompromising character. Erik was the last independent king of York. With his death, the territories that had constituted the Danelaw were, after almost 100 years, in English hands once again.

Though the English repossession of York has the neatness and drama of concluding a 'campaign' to re-take lands lost to the invaders, the battle at Brunanburh in 937 seemed to contemporaries and near-contemporaries of greater significance. Another presence at Brunanburh on the English side was that of Oda, bishop of Ramsbury in Wiltshire. The poet does not mention him, but later stories place him there and credit him with miraculously restoring Athelstan's sword.[25] The legend adds interest to the otherwise bald account of the battle in the 'F' annals of the *Anglo-Saxon Chronicle*, which note only that Athelstan and Edmund triumphed 'with the help of Christ'. That Christian legend should place this particular man on this particular field of battle has a cultural significance that probably equals the military significance of Athelstan's victory, for Oda's father was, in the whispered tones of one source, 'said by certain people to have come to England with Ubba and Ivar'. He was, in other words, the son of a Heathen Viking.

Visiting the newly reopened monastery at Athelney, Alfred's biographer, Asser, had been surprised to find so many foreign monks there and attributed it to the fact that Viking violence had frightened the native English away from the monastic life. Among the foreign novices he was surprised to note 'someone of Viking parentage who had been brought up there'; how much more would the elevation, within a half-century, of a first-generation Danish immigrant to the highest church office in the land have surprised him. Oda was the kind of immigrant the royal house of Wessex must have dreamt of, and it is hardly a slur on his character and on the many talents he showed as bureaucrat, diplomat and Christian leader to wonder if his appointment, four years after Brunanburh, to the archbishopric of

Canterbury might reflect an early grasp, among the English intelligent-sia, of the benefits of 'positive discrimination' towards the right kinds of Danish settlers. As the proud boast sounded in the last few lines of the poem on Brunanburh shows, tribal and cultural self-awareness were an essential part of social identity in early medieval times. Oda's antecedents as the child of a Viking father were no secret, and the authorities will have hoped that his success might encourage other settlers to follow him.

Most of what we know of Oda's life and career comes from Byrhtferth of Ramsey's late tenth-century *Life* of his nephew, St Oswald. As a young man, Oda left his parents' home and attached himself to a Christian, Athelhelm, probably identical to a man of that name who was successively bishop of Wells and archbishop of Canterbury, where his religious education began.[26] Oda became Athelhelm's protégé. After travelling to Rome with him in 923 he was appointed by Athelstan to the bishopric of Ramsbury, a position he held for the next fifteen years.

Oda became a close and trusted royal adviser. When, in 936, Hugh the Great of the Franks summoned Athelstan's nephew Louis d'Outremer ('from beyond the seas'), to cross the Channel and claim the Frankish throne, Athelstan sent Oda over first to conduct the negotiations and obtain the proper safeguards for Louis.[27] It was apparently on this trip that Oda, impressed by the devotion and discipline practised at the famous monastery of Fleury, adopted monastic habit as an expression of personal piety.

As archbishop of Canterbury under Athelstan's successor, Edmund, Oda continued to enjoy royal favour. In 940 he negotiated on behalf of Edmund with the kingdom of York, still then in Danish hands and represented on the Danish or northern side by Wulfstan, archbishop of York. With Wulfstan and a number of other bishops, Oda was responsible for the series of injunctions that made up Edmund's first law code and covered issues such as the celibacy of the clergy, the penance for killing, sexual offences, the payment of tithes and other church dues, the maintenance of churches and the excommunication of perjurers.[28] As a scholar he took it upon himself to make a compi-lation of early English canonical materials, for the enlightenment 'of King Edmund and of the whole people subjected to his excellent rule'.

Tentatively dated to the first years of his pontificate, this document has been interpreted as a clear indication of Oda's intention to reaffirm the Church's most basic principles, values and moral obligations, as well as to restate the moral and political obligations of the king and his court to the Church.

Perhaps the most pregnant of his reforms concerned East Anglia, which was probably Oda's birthplace and his earliest childhood home. The bishopric there had been a casualty of the Vikings in the 860s, since which time it had been supervised from London. Some time in the mid-950s Oda re-established it at Elmham. He also made improvements to the cathedral church at Canterbury, and added to Canterbury's collection of relics, importing the bones of St Ouen from Rouen in Normandy, another part of the world in which the descendants of Vikings were trying hard to make the transition to Christian values. We know too little of Oda's life to compare his influence on Athelstan, and on Edmund later, with the sort of influence Alcuin had on Charlemagne; but Edmund's appointment of Dunstan as abbot of Glastonbury, which heralded the monastic revival of the second half of the tenth century, may well have owed something to Oda's influence and to his enthusiasm for the cause of reform, as might the appointment of Ethelwold to the abbey at Abingdon, by Edmund's successor, Edred. In 957 Oda was given the estate of Ely. Once, before the arrival of the Danish armies, Ely had been the most important of the East Anglian religious houses, and it may well have been his intention to restore it to its former glory. If this were so, it was thwarted by his death in 958. In the years following, the programme of rebuilding and revitalizing a monastic life that had been so thoroughly demoralized by Viking hostility is known, after its leading light, as the Age of Dunstan. Archbishop Dunstan and his supporters enjoyed the great benefit of building on work that had been started before their time by others, including, perhaps pre-eminently, Oda – acting from Christian conviction, certainly, but perhaps fired as much by a personal desire to make some reparation for the role played in its demoralization in the first place by his own people.

If literary legend only enhanced Oda's role on the English side at Brunanburh in 937, it was probably entirely responsible for the presence there of Egil Skallagrimsson, the poet, warrior, drunkard, killer and eponymous hero of the saga. Along with Oda and the seafaring trader Ottar from Hålogoland, he completes a fascinating trio of non-royal Scandinavians whose fates brought them into contact with the kings of Wessex as they struggled to come to terms with the Viking menace. Strict chronology was not a concern of the author of *Egil's Saga*, but the internal evidence of the story is that his life and adventures spanned the period from 910 to about 990.[29] Like the skilled storyteller that he was, the author was careful to involve his main character in a crucial role in some of the most important historical events of his time, and in Egil's case this included the battle at Brunanburh.[30] Certain details in *Egil's Saga* indicate that the author knew a great deal of the history relating to the engagement. When he calls the field of battle 'Vinheith' he sounds a close echo of the name 'Wendune' given as the site by Simeon of Durham; he also offers a plausible explanation for the long delay between the announcement of the battle, and Athelstan's eventual arrival at the site, telling us that Athelstan was so shocked at the size of the force ranged against him that at first he gave way before it and made his way south, in order to build up an army as he travelled northwards through the country, 'for people thought it would be a slow mustering, in view of the numbers needed'.[31]

The descriptions of the tactical manoeuvring which precede the battle extend over several chapters of the saga and give a vivid idea of the conventions and logistics of a full-scale man-to-man encounter in Viking Age England. Playing for time as he raises an army, Athelstan

sent a man with a message to King Olaf saying this, that King Athelstan wished to appoint a battle-field and meet him in fight at Vinheid by Vinuskog wood. He asked that they should not raid in his land, but whichever of them had victory in battle was to rule the kingdom of England. He appointed their encounter for a week ahead, but the one who arrived first should wait for a second week. It was the custom then that when a king had been challenged to battle he could not raid without dishonour before the battle was ended. King Olaf complied, and halted his army, did not raid, and waited for the fixed day. Then he moved his army to Vinheid.

. . .

[Olaf] sent men of his up on the moor to the place appointed for battle. They were to find tent sites, and make ready before the army came. When the men reached the place agreed on, hazel stakes were put up indicating the site where the battle was to be. The place needed to be chosen carefully so that it should be on level ground where a great host was to be drawn up. As it was, the moor where the battle would be was level, but on one side a river flowed down, and on the other there was a big wood. King Athelstan's men had pitched their tents where there was the shortest distance between the wood and the river, and even so that was a long stretch. Their tents went the whole length between wood and river. They had organized their tents so that there was no one in every third tent, and few people in any. When King Olaf's men came up it was crowded in front of all the tents and they could not go into them. King Athelstan's men said that all the tents were full of men, so that there was barely room for their army.[32]

The day appointed for the battle passes, and still Athelstan himself has not arrived from the south. His men send a message to King Olaf, offering him a silver shilling for every plough in the kingdom if he will forgo the hostilities and lead his forces back over the border into Scotland. Olaf's men advise him to reject the offer, certain that the English will improve upon it, and this is done. Athelstan's messengers request a truce lasting three days, one in which to ride back with the offer, a second for them to discuss it with their king, and a third for the return journey. The request is granted. Three days later they are back with the improved offer. Once again the invaders' greed gets the better of them. Olaf says he will accept, on condition that Athelstan throw in the whole of Northumbria, along with all its tributes and dues. The messengers negotiate another three-day truce in which to deal with this new demand. But by this time Athelstan has arrived with his army. His men explain their delaying tactics to him, and now at last he gives his true response:

'Take these words of mine to King Olaf. I will grant him permission to go home to Scotland with his army, and he may pay back all that money which he has unlawfully seized in the realm. Then we will establish peace between our countries, and neither shall make raids on the other. In addition King Olaf shall become my vassal, and hold Scotland from me, and be king under me. Go back now, and tell him how things are.'

The counter-offer is duly refused, and battle is joined. Egil's involvement is explained as the result of an incident described earlier in the saga, after a character called Eyvind the *Braggart* has been employed by Harald Bluetooth to take charge of Danish defences 'against the Vikings'.[33] One of Eyvind's first actions in this capacity is an attempted ambush of Egil and his crew that goes badly wrong for him and in which Egil kills most of his men. It is in flight from the repercussions of these killings that Egil makes his way to England, where he learns that King Athelstan is advertising for mercenaries and that the rewards are likely to be high. During the battle he acquits himself with great distinction. Afterwards he terrifies friend and foe alike with his demeanour as he sits at Athelstan's celebratory table, still fully armed, glowering, his shaggy eyebrows riding up and down his forehead, alternately tightening and relaxing his grip on the hilt of his sword, neither drinking nor socializing until the wise Athelstan, discerning a need for appreciation, takes his own sword from its scabbard, removes a ring from his own arm and slipping it over the point of the sword offers it to Egil, who duly raises his own sword in acknowledgement and takes the king's gift on its point.

Egil was not a settler. Excepting only his willingness to submit to *prima signatio* (or 'prime-signing') so that he could fight alongside Athelstan's Christian forces at Brunanburh, he remains, throughout his saga, an aggressively unreconstructed Viking. One of the motifs of the tale is his enduring conflict with Erik Bloodaxe and Erik's queen Gunnhild. He kills one of their sons in Norway and is forced to flee to Iceland. Just before he leaves, an idea occurs to him:

Egil went ashore on to the island, picked up a branch of hazel and went to a certain cliff that faced the mainland. Then he took a horse's head, set it up on a pole and spoke these formal words: 'Here I set up a pole of insult against King Erik and Queen Gunnhild' – then, turning the horse's head towards the mainland – 'and I direct this insult against the guardian spirits of this land, so that every one of them shall go astray, neither to figure nor find their dwelling places until they have driven King Erik and Queen Gunnhild from this country.' Next he jammed the pole into a cleft in the rock and left it standing there with the horse's head facing towards the mainland, and cut runes on the pole declaiming the words of his formal speech.[34]

Gaunt monuments like this one, known as *niðstöng* or shame-poles, are found scattered across saga literature. Egil's variant is grotesque enough in its own right, but it has been slightly censored by the author and in the context of the saga the force of it remains obscure. In its unadulterated form it contained an accusation of homosexuality that emerges more clearly in a passage in the *Vatnsdaela Saga*, in which the brothers Thorstein and Jokul challenge two other men, Finnbogi the Mighty and Berg the Bold, to a duel. Bad weather prevents Finnbogi and Berg from reaching the duelling site, though not the brothers. When it becomes clear that their opponents are not going to show, Thorstein and Jokul take a pole from a sheep-fold and carve a man's head at one end of it. An insult is then carved in runes along the pole, a mare is killed, its breast opened and the pole stuck inside the opening. The gruesome apparition is then turned to face in the direction of Finnbogi's farm.[35] Jokul has already warned Berg that 'you must now turn up to the duel if you have a man's heart rather than a mare's', and the symbolic force of his construction when his opponents fail to show lies in the open identification of Finnbogi as a female of the species.

A still more complex version of the insult is found in the *Saga of Bjorn, Champion of the Hitardal People*. The friendship between two men who both love the same woman ends when one of them tricks her into marrying him by falsely reporting the death of the other. The bad feeling between the former friends simmers for years. It reaches its bizarre climax one day when a carved wooden statue appears on the boundary of the liar's property. The carving shows two men standing close together, one behind the other, one with a black hat on his head. Both are bent forward. 'People thought ill of the encounter,' the author tells us, 'and said that it was not good for either of them who stood there; but it was worse for the one who stood in front.' Specific prohibitions in the laws of the Norwegian Gulathing and in the Icelandic *Grágás* reflect the seriousness of the homosexual insult:

If a man composes *ýki* about another man, the penalty is lesser outlawry.[36] It is *ýki* if a man says about another man or any one of his possessions that which cannot be, and does so to dishonour him. If a man makes *nið* about another, the penalty is lesser outlawry and is to be prosecuted with a jury of twelve. It is *nið* if one man cuts a wooden *nið* against another, or carves or raises a *nið* pole against another.[37]

According to *Grágás*, the use of any one of the words *ragr, strodinn* or *sordinn*, all three of which carried the connotation of homosexuality, justified the killing of the man who used them, by the wounded party. A revealing curiosity in the sexual sociology of the time is that only statements implying that a man took the passive part in the homosexual act were classified as criminal; the law did not concern itself with accusations involving the active partner.[38]

This homosexual insult seems to have had a particular currency during the difficult period of transition from Heathendom to Christianity, reflecting the moral and psychological tensions that arose from the inversion of established values promoted by Christianity. The late eddic poem known as the 'First Lay of Helgi Hundingsbani' includes an episode of *flyting*, or ritual exchange of insults, between two heroes, Sinfjötli and Gudmund, in which Sinfjötli 'reminds' Gudmund of the number of times he has had him:

> On Sága's Ness full nine wolves we
> had together – I gat them all.[39]

A variation on this couplet played a central part in events surrounding the conversion of the Icelanders to Christianity in the year 999, which we shall look at in detail later. One of several missions preceding the conversion failed after Thorvald, an Icelandic Christian working with a Saxon bishop, had been made the subject of a verse which improvised on the concept of the godfather in the Christian baptismal ceremony to accuse the pair of homosexuality:

> The bishop gave birth to nine children,
> Thorvald was father to them all.

Though Thorvald was allocated the less shameful 'active' role in the poem, the offence remained great enough for him to slough off his Christianity and kill his tormentor. In sorrow at his companion's failure to observe the Christian injunction against killing, the bishop is said to have abandoned the mission. *Njal's Saga* also offers examples of how the sexual insult was used by Heathens intent on resisting what were perceived as the feminine values of Christianity. In a dramatic scene at an *althing* meeting, the Christian Njal leads his party in assembling a pile of goods as compensation to Flosi's party for the murder of Flosi's kinsman, Hoskuld. Njal tops off the pile with a silk scarf and a pair of boots. Flosi does not want reconciliation, and no one will answer him when he picks up the scarf and mockingly demands to know whose contribution this might be. Njal's son, Skarphedin, then asks who he thinks it might be and Flosi replies, as offensively as possible, that he suspects it might be Njal, 'that beardless man, because a lot of people, when they look at him, are unsure whether he's a man or a woman'. The reference is to the practice, introduced by Christian missionaries and followed by the convert Njal, of going clean-shaven. Skarphedin counters the offence to his father by reclaiming the silk scarf and tossing a pair of dark blue breeches to Flosi, assuring him that he will have more use of those. Flosi asks why, and Skarphedin tells him: 'People say that every ninth night you're the bride of the Swine Mountain troll, and that he turns you into a woman.' Njal's brave attempt to solve the conflict in the spirit of Christianity drowns as the primitive emotions aroused by these exchanges flare up into full-scale violence.

The *Saga of Gudmund Dyri* provides another example of the enduring association in the Viking homelands of the Christian with the unmanly. For having backed the wrong side in a local conflict, an Icelandic chieftain, Gudmund, tells a local priest, Bjørn, that his wife will be made available to any tramp who wants her, and that 'something' will be done to him, Bjørn, that will not be less of a humiliation. What the 'something' is, beyond the humiliation of not being able to protect his woman, is not specified. Bjørn seems to assume that he is being threatened with homosexual rape.[40] Unable to sleep, he gets up in the night and visits Gudmund. He offers him everything he owns, if only Gudmund will withdraw the threat. As things turn out, the threat is not prosecuted.

Responses such as Gudmund's were not, to the Viking mind, a subject for disapproval. If Heathendom involved an uncompromising acceptance of human nature as found, then the Christianity into which Christian kings persistently tried to draw Viking leaders represented, even if only in its most exalted manifestations, the best model of a civilized future available to contemporary thinkers. With dramatic cultural tensions between Scandinavians and Christians present at the start of the insular Viking Age in 793 and still active in 954, the appearance of men such as Oda, in whom an attachment to the new religion overrode any former cultural and tribal loyalties, was vital if the new and fragile unity of England were to survive.

Oda might serve as the extreme and accelerated personification of a general process of assimilation and integration that followed the Viking occupation of territories in the Danelaw and in other parts of England and the British Isles. This process of assimilation is difficult to trace or characterize, not least because the size of the Scandinavian settlement remains uncertain. Between the setting-up of the Danish kingdoms which was complete by about 880 and the Norman conquest of England in 1066, there must have been a continuous flow of Danish and Norwegian immigrants into the occupied areas, though there is no documentary evidence of it. Documentary evidence does not become available until the creation of Domesday Book in the eleventh century. With the help of various charters of the twelfth century, attempts have been made to estimate the size of the settlements based on the evidence of personal names. About 60 per cent of Lincolnshire farmers, 40 per cent of East Anglian farmers, and roughly 50 per cent of the northern Danelaw had names of Scandinavian origin.[41] Even here we are on uncertain ground, for the vagaries of fashion might be leading us into the false assumption that everyone with a Scandinavian name was, in fact, of Scandinavian descent.

Place-names might seem to offer a reliable guide to the extent of the settlements, but this is another complex matter with many variables and imponderables, and without the work of specialists such as Eilert Ekwall, Margaret Gelling, W. H. F. Nicolaisen and Gillian Fellows-Jensen to guide us we should be able to make very little sense of it as evidence. There are major concentrations of Scandinavian places-names in Yorkshire and Lincolnshire, and relatively few in East Anglia, which survived as a fully independent Danish kingdom only until 902 and after that as some kind of compromised unit until the death of a last and unnamed Scandinavian king in battle in 917. They are almost entirely absent from the southern parts of the Danelaw that included Buckinghamshire, Hertfordshire and Middlesex. Though never formally part of the Danelaw, the areas of north-west England, from Cheshire through Lancashire and Cumbria up to the lower fringes of Galloway, are also rich in Scandinavian place-names.

Assessments of the quality of the land settled have been attempted on the basis of place-names. It seems that the first settlers from the disbanded Great Heathen Army did not change the names of the places in which they chose to settle. Not until the increased levels of settlement and cultivation after 900 did the Danes give new names to the parcelled-out areas of the old English estates and to the new settlements created by draining or clearing tougher terrain. Settlement names that used a number of Old Norse words for 'marsh' probably reflect new reclamations of marshy land in the area in this early period of Scandinavian settlement in the Danelaw. Redcar in North Yorkshire and Broadcarr in Norfolk both contain the element *kjarr*, meaning 'brushwood' and indicating an area of marsh overgrown with brushwood.[42] *Mosi* meaning 'moss' is found in the Lancashire Chat Moss and Rathmoss, and in Cumberland in the names Mosser and Mosedale. River names are the most resilient of all classes of toponyms,[43] and here the Scandinavians followed in the footsteps of the Anglo-Saxons who had, in their time as colonists and settlers, adopted a high percentage of native British names for rivers. Though there are few rivers with entirely Old Norse names, a number in the northern Danelaw like the Beela, the Greta and the Liza use the Old Norse suffix *á*, meaning 'river'.[44] Water was a major factor in the choice of settlement site, as names of fords, bridges and connecting causeways indicate. Both Ferrybridge in the West Riding of Yorkshire and Ferriby in Lincolnshire, meaning 'ferry settlement', are built on the Old Norse *ferja*, meaning 'ferry'.

Gil, denoting a 'ravine or a deep narrow valley with a stream', as compounded in Lowgill and Long Gill in the Forest of Bowland, is found across those areas of north-west England such as Cumbria and the Lake District, which bear such a striking resemblance to the homeland of the Norwegians who settled there. The establishment of settlements after the land had been cleared of trees is suggested by the presence in their names of such Old Norse elements as *lundr, skógr, vithr*, with -*thveit*, meaning a 'clearing', the most common among these. Like the names reflecting farms and settlements established after the draining and clearing of marshy land, they suggest many of the later settlers created new farms rather than simply taking over existing ones. These terms seem generally to be used for the secondary development of places with less good potential, very often on higher ground, which may indicate that not all the new settlers had the pick of the land.[45] The numerous town and topographical names with -*thveit* in and around the Lake District, such as Bassenthwaite, are often found on valley slopes which would have required a considerable amount of clearing before they could be used for farming.[46] Place-names with -*thorp*, of which almost 600 examples have been recorded,[47] seem likewise to have been used for land that was at least initially not promising, not the pick of the settlements and required a lot of clearing. The most common Scandinavian place-name element found in the Danelaw is -*by*, which occurs in nearly 900 place-names in England (and Scotland). In Scandinavia, names ending in -*by* would most often be compounded with a topographical feature; in England almost two-thirds of the recorded instances involve a personal name, probably that of the first Scandinavian settler:[48] Rollesby in Norfolk was probably settled by Rolf, Ormesby in South Lincolnshire by Ormar, and Scratby in Norfolk by Skrauti.[49] Occasionally, where an older English name caused problems of pronunciation for the settlers, it would survive in an adapted form. Thus Shipton became Skipton, Cheswick became Keswick and Charlton became Carlton.[50] A rare example of an English place-name being replaced was Anglo-Saxon *Norðworðig*, meaning 'northern enclosure', which the invader-settlers renamed 'Derby', denoting 'a place with deer'.[51]

A wealth of words passed into the English language as a result of the Scandinavian settlements. Among the most striking adoptions were the Old Norse personal pronouns 'they', 'them' and 'their', replacing Old English 'hie', 'him' and 'hiera'. Many words with an initial *sk* sound, such as sky, skill and skin, derive from Old Norse, as do everyday words like anger, husband, wing, thrive, egg, bread and die. The history of the word 'egg' highlights some of the difficulties in interpreting the evidence of common borrowings. In competition with Old Norse *egg*, Anglo-Saxon *æg* survived into the sixteenth century as *eye* (pl. *eyren*), and as late as the end of the fifteenth century was still causing confusion. William Caxton complained of the difficulties in the *Eneydos* in 1490: 'What sholde a man in thyse dayes now wryte, egges or eyren, certaynly it is harde to playse every man.'

Opinions differ over the implications of borrowings at such a fundamental level; it may indicate that a minority of Scandinavian settlers enjoyed, from the start, a high social status which encouraged a local desire to copy their language; or the fact that borrowing took place at this mundane level, rather than at the higher levels at which Norman French later influenced the vocabulary of government and culture, might suggest that Danish influence on Anglo-Saxon English came about through the sheer numbers of those speaking it, rather than from their elevated social status.[52] Again, fashion is notoriously hard to plot into such analyses, since it moves as readily up as down the social scale. Despite the apparent brevity of the period of Scandinavian dominance in East Anglia, Scandinavian names remained common there into the twelfth century, and while the persistence for centuries of feminine names such as Thora and Gunnhild might indicate that settlers imported their wives from home rather than marrying local women, it might equally reflect an enduring fashion for these names. Alcuin, we recall, rebuked the king of Northumbria and his courtiers for copying the hair-styles of the Heathens, and the monks in the monasteries for preferring to listen to *Beowulf* while they dined rather than Christian texts. One of the most common male names used in the Danelaw was 'Halfdan', meaning 'half-Dane'. 'Thor' was another.

Opinion varies as to how long Norse survived as a spoken language in those areas of the British Isles in which Scandinavian speakers settled. In Normandy, as in Kiev, the native tongues were linguistically so remote from Old Norse that a quick adoption of the native languages was a necessity of life. It seems, however, that there were sufficient similarities between North Germanic Old Norse and West Germanic Anglo-Saxon for them to be mutually comprehensible with a little effort and good-will, facilitating the import and export of words as convenience, density of linguistic population, and fashion dictated, and encouraging a much longer survival of Old Norse in the

Danelaw than in Kiev or Normandy. The inscription on a stone, found in 1902 at a farmhouse in Pennington in Cumbria, mixes Old Norse and English runes. The presence of Norman decorative features on the base of the stone dates it to the twelfth century and shows that Norse was, if not still spoken, at least not forgotten in the area. Owing to the thoroughgoing nature of the Norwegian colonization of Shetland and the Orkneys a local form of Old Norse known as Norn may have been spoken into the eighteenth century, before finally giving way to Scots.

Some of the monumental art associated with the Scandinavian invaders and settlers of England and the islands of Britain shows a similar combination of Irish or Anglo-Saxon sources with imported Scandinavian styles. A well-known example is the stone cross found at Middleton, in Yorkshire, which depicts in its lower panel a warrior in a peaked helmet with his spear, axe, sword, shield and knife. Above the panel is the cross, and on the other side a Scandinavian creature in the Jelling style, which we have encountered before on Harald Bluetooth's great stone. The sculptor of the great stone cross found at Gosforth in Cumbria used Christian elements inspired by the high crosses of the Irish monasteries, in combination with Scandinavian mythological scenes and ornamentations in the ring-chain Borre style, so named after a characteristic example of the style on a metal fitting found at Borre, in the Norwegian Vestfold. On its eastern face is a representation of Christ bleeding on the cross; close by is a woman holding out a drinking horn, a representation of a Valkyrie, familiar from Gotland picture-stones that depict the welcoming of the dead hero into Odin's Valhalla; a scene on the south face appears to show Odin and Mimir; another showing two figures fishing from a boat may illustrate the story of Thor's encounter with the Midgard serpent. The 4.5-metre-high monument is evidently a reproduction in stone of a cross made in wood. In another of its many syncretic moments it symbolizes both Yggdrasil, the tree of life of northern Heathendom, and the cross of Christianity. Some scholars now believe that, far from being a spontaneous effect, this mingling of styles in monumental form was a technique deliberately employed by Scandinavian chieftains, in particular those from Norway, as a way of re-creating in the minds of followers in the new country visible and traditionally accepted symbols of power familiar to them from 'the old country', in circumstances where, by the very fact of recent settlement, no such physical manifestations of past landed power existed.[53] The incorporation of Heathen imagery into the monuments was, in this perspective, both a reassurance and an affirmation of continuity within change.

Although the areas of England occupied by the Great Army and its descendants never formed a coherent political unit corresponding to Wessex and Mercia, for the medieval annalists and historians who coined the term 'Danelaw' it was the insistence of the invader-settlers on importing their own law and administration into the areas in which they settled that became the defining characteristic of the new model of England that arose as a result of the Viking invasions.[54] One of the more striking results of this insistence was that Old Norse *lagu-* was presently adopted into English as 'law', replacing Anglo-Saxon *æ*. The 'by-' element in modern English compounds relating to local government, such as 'by(e)-laws' and 'by(e)-elections', derives similarly from the Old Norse word meaning 'town' or 'settlement'. The invader-settlers brought the tradition of the *thing* meeting with them, familiar to Norwegians from the Eyrathing in Trondheim, the Gulathing in western Norway, and the Borgarthing from the Sarpsborg region to the south of Oslo, and to Danes from the *thing* held at Viborg. The Tynwald on the Isle of Man, which still meets annually on 5 July, is etymologically the same word as *thingvellir*, where the Icelandic *althing* met from the earliest days of the Free State until 1798. Ingimund and his group of exiled Norwegians established a *thing* at what is now Thingwall in the centre of their settlement on the Wirral peninsula.[55] Thingwall is very likely the place where Ingimund, dissatisfied with the offer of land made to them by Ethelfled, stood and exhorted his men to join him in an attack on Chester – 'Let us beseech and implore them first. And if we do not get them willingly in this way, let us contest them by force.'[56] The settlers divided Yorkshire into separate administrative units which became known as Ridings, a noun derived from Old Norse *thriðjungr*, meaning 'the third part'. These Yorkshire Ridings were later divided into areas called *wapentakes*, derived from the word *vápnatak*, meaning 'weapon-taking'. In the Scandinavian homelands the word referred to the raising of weapons as a gesture of assent to a decision or verdict reached at a *thing* meeting; in England the meaning was extended to cover both the actual assembly itself, and the area represented by the assembly.[57] From King Ethelred's laws (III), issued at Wantage in 997, it is apparent that the *wapentake* was the basic unit of local administration for the areas that fell under the group of districts known as the Five Boroughs, namely Derby, Stamford, Lincoln, Nottingham and Leicester, corresponding to the *hundred* in the rest of England.[58] Domesday Book of 1086 used the terms indiscriminately, suggesting that by that time there was no real difference, and that the form chosen was largely a matter of the majority voice of the local population.[59] The North, West and East Ridings of Yorkshire survived as local government districts of the county until well into the twentieth century.

There is not enough surviving evidence to enable us to judge whether parallel law codes were necessary because the societies involved cultivated fundamentally different ethical systems, or whether they were largely a symbolic statement of separate cultural identity by the Scandinavians. There is no doubt that certain legal matters and crimes were treated differently under the distinct law codes. A legal stipulation from the time of Edward the Elder on the subject of fugitives allowed for their separate treatment in Wessex, and in 'the eastern or northern kingdoms'. In Wessex, the laws of Wessex were to apply; in the Danelaw areas, the issue was to be settled 'in accordance with the provisions of the treaties'.[60] Evidence of a separate legal culture is still found in the law code issued at Wihtbordesstan by King Edgar in 963. Clause 2.1 strikes a note of ambiguity as the king stipulates that: 'It is my will that secular rights be in force among the Danes according to as good laws as they can best decide on. Among the English, however, that is to be in force which I and my councillors have added to the decrees of my ancestors, for the benefit of all the nation':[61] his 'will' in the matter appears only to affirm that, as far as the Danes are concerned, it is an irrelevance. Other clauses in the same law code hint at a change in attitude in which the distinct nature of the Danelaw as an area is still recognized, but only up to a point. Edgar presents himself as showing largesse towards the settlers, allowing them to live by laws familiar to them from their homelands, as a reward for their loyalty, 'which you have always shown me'. Yet he also announces a measure concerning stolen property which is to be 'common to all the nation, whether Englishmen, Danes or Britons, in every province of my dominion'.[62] By the end of the tenth century and the reign of Ethelred, the position seems to have been that, while differences of procedure were acceptable, different standards of justice were not.[63]

As we saw earlier, the Wessex dynasty's policy of building fortified *burhs* across the length and breadth of England as landmarks in the gradual repossession of formerly Viking territories led to the growth of towns and cities in England during the Viking Age. The Vikings' fortification and expansion of the five midland towns of Derby, Leicester, Nottingham, Lincoln and Stamford in the attempt to counter the Anglo-Saxon retaliation was likewise a contributory factor in the growth of these towns. But it was the rapid expansion of the city of York, essentially the capital of Viking-occupied territories in the east of England, that was the major contribution of the Vikings to the development of urban life in England. Originally fortified by the Romans to control the Celtic tribes in the region, the settlement was abandoned after almost four centuries of occupation. Following a period of neglect, it was taken over by the Anglo-Saxons. As Eoferwic, it became the capital of the northern kingdom of Deira. The pattern of streets laid down by the Romans was restored and the walls fortified. With the coming of Christianity to the region the town enjoyed a widespread prestige and prosperity which survived its incorporation in the seventh century into the kingdom of Northumbria. It was this prosperity that attracted Viking raiders to York in the first place. From the time of the arrival on the east coast of the Great Heathen Army in 865, Eoferwic was the scene of almost constant fighting between invaders and natives. Once they had triumphed, the Vikings showed an accommodation to the Church that allowed the archbishopric of York to carry on as usual. Indeed, Wulfstan of York was said to have preferred Scandinavian to West Saxon masters and the rule of Eric Bloodaxe, after his acceptance as king of York in 948, to the rule of Edred.[64]

With settlement came the freedom to indulge commercial instincts. The act of capture and the subsequent infighting had wiped out most traces of previous settlements. If they wished to go on living there, the

Vikings had no choice but to reconstruct what they had destroyed. Streets and houses were rebuilt, workshops opened. Through a century of uncertainty and fighting the city prospered and grew. Pressure of space within the narrow streets led, in time, to the replacement of the earlier wattle-and-daub buildings with two-storey structures in timber. According to Byrhtferth of Ramsey, by the year 1000 it had a population of 30,000. Even the more sober modern estimates of 8,000 to 10,000 based on Domesday Book still suggest a city that was large by contemporary European standards.[65] This rapidly swelling population left behind plentiful archaeological documentation of its thriving social and commercial life, and of the activities of craftsmen and women working there in textiles, metal, leather, wood, glass and bone. Byrhtferth tells us that merchants came to York 'from all over the place'. A coin minted in Samarkand in the early tenth century has been found there, as has a cowrie shell stemming from either the Red Sea or the Gulf of Aden. The city's bread was made from flour ground by lava millstones imported from the Rhineland, its wine traded from Germany, its silk from Constantinople. Such remarkable social and commercial enterprise has even led to an identification of Viking and late Anglo-Saxon York as the site of the first true manifestation in England of an urban middle class that is more conventionally located to the London of some six or seven hundred years later.[66] Here the transition from raiders to traders ran its full course.

. Buried in 834, the Oseberg ship was excavated in 1904 by a team under the leadership of Professor Gabriel Gustafson (*centre*).

.. In 1926 the reconstructed ship was transported on rails through the streets of Oslo to be ferried over to a purpose-built museum at Bygdøy.

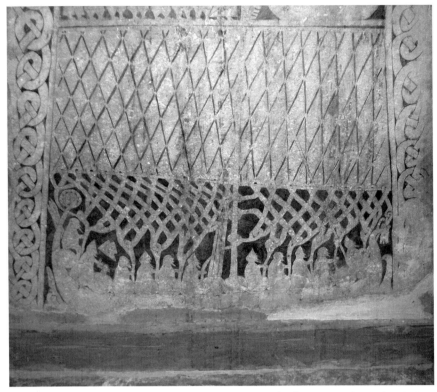

3. The Gotland picture stones are our only source of information about the rigging on Viking longships. On Smiss (I) from Stenkyrka the sail is controlled by the man on the left. Just below him a man holds the steering oar.

4. The Oseberg ship on display in the Bygdøy museum.

5. A wooden bearing dial used for navigation, found at Wolin in 2000. This complemented the earlier find of a similar incomplete dial near Uunartaq Fjord in southern Greenland in 1948.

6. Lindisfarne, site of the attack of 793, in which the raiders 'trampled the holy places with polluted steps, dug up the altars and seized all the treasures of the holy church' (Simeon of Durham).

7. The Lindisfarne Stone, believed to be a near-contemporary depiction of the raid. The monks probably had less than an hour in which to prepare themselves for the attack.

8. Odin had only one eye. According to the myth the other was given in exchange for a drink from the giant Mimir's well of wisdom.

9. This one-eyed 7 cm high bronze figurin from Svenstorp in Skåne, southern Swede has also been identified as Odin.

10. The so-called Eyrarland Thor, from tenth-century Iceland or earlier. Thor was especially popular among Icelanders and regarded as the foremost defender of the old faith against Christianity. Often supposed to be holding a stylized version of his hammer, a recent suggestion is that he is blowing through his beard to raise the wind. See page 298.

11. Thor stylized in the form of a hammer-shape amulet in gold and silver.

12. A 7 cm high bronze statue of Frey, the god of fertility, discovered in 1904 in Rällinge in Sweden. A similarly priapic but very much larger statue was worshipped in the temple at Uppsala.

13. Freya was the goddess of fertility. The identification is suggested by the prominent necklace she wears, which may be the 'Brisingamen' associated with her name by Snorri Sturluson and by the fact that she also appears to be pregnant.

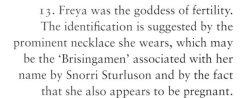

14. Loki represented the elements of chaos, creativity and unreliability in the gods' enterprises. Snorri refers to a tale in which dwarves sewed his mouth shut, as it appears to be on this stone (c. 1000), found on the beach near Snaptun, Denmark, in 1950.

15. According to Adam of Bremen, Uppsala on the west coast of Sweden was the centre of the cult of Heathendom and the site of a major sacrificial festival held every ninth year. See page 29.

16. Human sacrifice was not common but did occur. The third panel down on the 3 metre high Hammars (I) stone, now in Bunge museum, may depict the ritual sacrifice of a child or dwarf, with the three triangles hovering over the scene indicating a dedication to Odin. See page 30.

17. The Inchmarnock hostage stone, found in 2001 and 2002. See page 70.

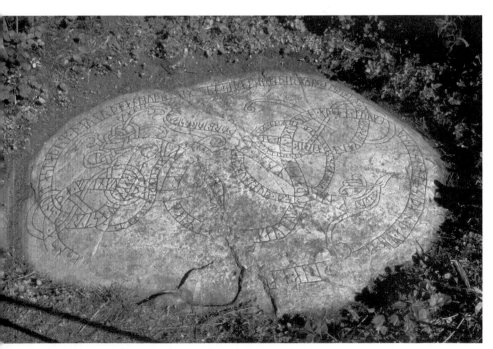

18. The Swedish Hillersjö stone is from the second half of the tenth century. The *c.* 300 runes are both the briefest of sagas relating the life of a woman named Geirlaug, and a statement of her property rights.

19. Gilded altar piece from Tamdrup Church, *c.* 1200. *Top left*, the Danish King Harald Bluetooth rejects Poppo's attempt to convert him. *Top right*, the bishop endures the ordeal of carrying hot iron. The iron, in the shape of a mitten, is held over the flames. *Bottom left*, Poppo shows the king his hand, unharmed by the ordeal. *Bottom right*, Poppo baptizes Harald. See pages 199–200.

20. As part of a campaign to make his authority visible throughout his kingdom, Harald Bluetooth built a number of the large, ring-shaped forts known, from the first of them to be identified, as *trelleborgs*. This one is at Slagelse. See page 210.

21. Harald Bluetooth was the great monumentalist of Viking Age Scandinavia. The so-called A side of the Jelling Stone (c. 965) carries the text of his claim to have converted the Danes to Christianity. See page 200.

22. The B side of the Jelling Stone depicts a struggle between a horse-like animal and a serpent. See pages 200–201.

23. The C side of the Jelling Stone carries the earliest known significant representation of Christ in Scandinavian art.

24. Ingolfshofdi, on the south-east coast of Iceland, the dramatic headland where Ingolf, the first settler, made a temporary home while waiting for his high-seat pillars to be washed ashore.

25. The Icelandic settler and chieftain Thorolf Mostrarskegg named this mountain Helgafell (Holy Mountain). He decreed that all life on it was sacrosanct, and that no man might look at it with an unwashed face.

26. Thingvellir, where the Icelandic Althing met. The flagpole faintly visible in the centre marks the site of the Lawrock from which the Lawspeaker, Thorgeir Ljosvetningagodi, addressed the crowd at the dramatic assembly of 999.

27. The Spillings hoard, dated to about 870 and discovered in 1999 on a farm in the north east of Gotland, included over 14,000 coins of Arabic origin. According to Snorri, Odin promised his followers that each man who came to him in Valhalla should have the use of 'what he himself had buried in the earth'.

28. The harsh Greenland landscape dwarfs the ruins of the monastery at Ketilsfjord. Settlement in Greenland and Iceland was considered by some the easy option for a young, male Norwegian, but life in the new colonies was a constant struggle against the elements.

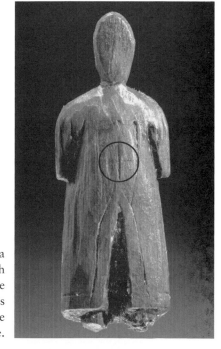

29. This small carving in walrus ivory is from a thirteenth-century Thule Eskimo site on the south coast of Baffin Island and is thought to be a native representation of a European. The cross that appears to be incised on the chest may suggest a cleric, or the figure might be female.

30. About twenty-six stones were raised in memory of those who died on a journey east with Ingvar the Far-Travelled in about 1036. This one commemorates Gunnleif, who 'could steer a ship well'. The cross and inscription both indicate that Gunnleif was a Christian. See page 365 ff.

31. The Sandnes Christ, probably early fourteenth century, found on a farm in the Western Settlement of Greenland, is in dramatic contrast to the much earlier representation on Harald Bluetooth's Jelling Stone.

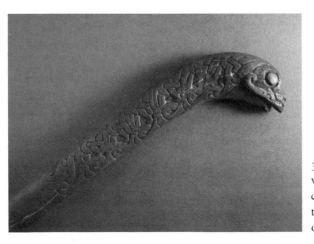

32. Ulfkils käpp (walking-stick) was a product of the cosmopolitan court created at Lund in Sweden by the Danish King Cnut at the height of his power. See page 380.

12

When Allah met Odin

At about the same time as Harald Bluetooth was erecting his great monument to Viking Christianity at Jelling, and the Wessex dynasty was completing the first unification of England with the expulsion of Harald's brother-in-law Erik Bloodaxe from York, seafaring Vikings of the old-fashioned sort (Erik perhaps among them) were making, after an interval of almost a century, a second series of violent investigations of the territory and peoples of al-Andalus (Muslim Spain and Portugal), and the northern and western shores of Africa.

Muslim civilization had grown dramatically since the founding of the religion in Mecca in about 610 and Mohammed's emigration to Medina in 622. The territorial and cultural expansion eastward and westward during the period of the Umayyad caliphs in the eighth century created an empire that extended from the borders of China to the Atlantic Ocean, from the Sahara to the Caspian Sea, from India to al-Andalus. With the rise to power of the Abbasid caliphs in the middle of the eighth century, the capital of the Islamic empire moved east, from Damascus to Baghdad. A dramatic rise in interest in Hellenistic and Persian culture followed, and the writing of local, Arab-nationalist literature that had characterized the Umayyad period was replaced by a universal literature. Much of it was scientific. As well as mathematics and cosmography, it reflected a vivid interest in the history and geography of the many peoples with whom the expansion of the seventh and eighth centuries had brought the Arabs into contact. The postal service of the Islamic empire assumed an important role in this trend, facilitating communication and knowledge of the routes and roads that bound the far-flung and disparate parts of the vast empire together; its head of staff was a leading political figure who was also chief of the security service.[1] Books written initially for the purpose of describing the routes connecting the empire presently evolved into textbooks that nurtured an abstract interest in the history and geography of the peoples of the world, and most of what we know of the encounters between Vikings and Arabs in the territories bordering on the east and west of the Muslim empire is derived from books written in this spirit of enlightenment.

In the east, the Arab geographers and historians used the term *ar-Rus* for the Scandinavians they met in Russia and the surrounding regions; those in Spain and western Europe used the term *al-madjus*. The term *al-madjus* was not coined for the Vikings but was applied to them by Arab scholars in the belief that they were fire-worshippers, like the Persian Zoroastrians, whom they erroneously believed to practise cremation of the dead. 'Their religion is that of the Magi,' wrote the late thirteenth-century historian Al-Watwat, 'and they burn their dead with fire.'[2] Ibn Said, a thirteenth-century geographer and traveller, offered a persuasive logic when he explained the worship of fire among northern peoples by the fact that 'nothing seems more important to them than fire, for the cold in their lands is severe'.[3] *Al-madjus* derives from Old Persian *magush*, which is also the etymological root of the Spanish word *mago* meaning 'wizard' or 'astrologer', and of the English word 'magician'. It is familiar in Christian culture from the story of the three wise men, or *magi*, who travelled to Bethlehem to hail the birth of the infant Christ.[4] The Vikings were also known as *Lordomani* and *Lormanes* in western Latin and Spanish sources.[5] From the earliest times, Arab scholars were aware of the fact that they were dealing with the same people, whether they encountered them east of the Baltic, on Spain's Atlantic coast, or in the Mediterranean: a geographical study written in 889 by al-Yaqubi refers to the Viking attack on Seville in 844 as 'by the Magus, who are called the Rus'.[6]

This raid on Seville is generally regarded as announcing the start of the Iberian Viking Age, although the Scandinavian arabist Arne Melvinger noted that Ibn al-Atir, the thirteenth-century historian, used the term *al-madjus* to identify a force that came to the aid of Alphonse II, king of Galicia, during his campaign against the Arabs in 795. Based on this, Melvinger went on to contemplate the possibility of a Viking presence on the peninsula a full half-century prior to this.[7] He accordingly found it less easy than other commentators have done to dismiss, as poetic licence or simple factual error, Notker the Stammerer's description of Charlemagne's distress as the emperor sat at supper in an unnamed coastal town in Narbonensian Gaul and watched a small fleet of longships carrying out a raid on the harbour, for he was able to suggest a possible connection between Notker's Vikings and the *al-madjus* who fought for Alphonse II in 795.[8] The Arab military actions against Bayonne in 814, and in 823 and 825 in the Mundaka–Guernica fjord area of what is now Biscay, have all been related to the possible presence of *al-madjus* bases in these areas. These *al-madjus* can hardly have been Persian Zoroastrians, but the persistent use by Arab writers of the same term to denote both groups makes certain identification impossible.[9] An objection to the argument for a Viking presence on the peninsula at such an early date is that they had almost certainly not yet established themselves sufficiently in either Ireland or western Francia, the natural staging-posts such bases would seem to require for the undertaking to be logistically credible. There is also the view of a school of Basque historians who posit a late conversion to Christianity in the Vascony area, and take all references to *al-madjus* in the Arab histories of raids and battles of the ninth and tenth centuries to be to Heathen Basques rather than Vikings.[10]

As a development of the large-scale penetration by river of the northern territories of the Frankish empire, the first serious Viking attack on the Iberian peninsula in 844 came from a fleet that had navigated its way up the Garonne as far as Toulouse before retracing its route and heading south into the Bay of Biscay, following the coastline west past the tiny kingdoms of Asturia, Cantabria and Galicia that divided Christian Europe from Muslim Spain, raiding in Gijon and La Coruña on the way before being met and heavily defeated by Asturian forces under King Ramiro I. Many longships were lost in the attack and the fleet retreated to Aquitaine (or, if we allow the possibility, to a base in Bayonne).

A few months later a fleet of eighty longships, with square brown sails that 'covered the sea like dark birds', appeared off Lisbon, in the

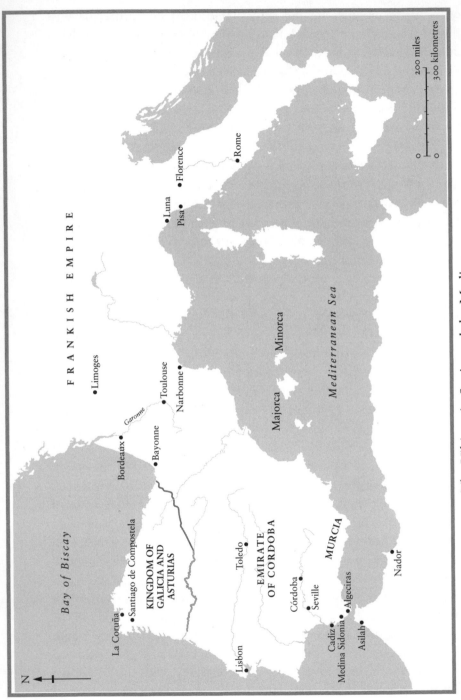

The Vikings in Spain and the Mediterranean

Bay of Biscay

La Coruña
Santiago de Compostela
KINGDOM OF GALICIA AND ASTURIAS

Bordeaux
Bayonne
Garonne
Toulouse
Narbonne

FRANKISH EMPIRE

Limoges

Pisa
Luna
Florence
Rome

Lisbon
Toledo
EMIRATE OF CORDOBA
Córdoba
Seville
MURCIA
Medina Sidonia
Cadiz
Algeciras
Asilah
Nador

Majorca
Minorca

Mediterranean Sea

N

200 miles
300 kilometres

estuary of the Tagus, and over a thirteen-day period engaged in three sea-battles with local ships before heading further south. The harbour at Cadiz was occupied, and while one group made its way inland to Medina-Sidonia, the main body of the fleet sailed up the Guadalquivir into the very heartland of al-Andalus and established a base on an island not far from Seville. The city was taken, seemingly without resistance, for most of the inhabitants had fled to Carmona or up into the mountains north of Seville, and for some two weeks the city was in Viking hands. With the banks of the great river a noted centre for the breeding of horses they were able to range far and wide across the region in their plundering. As other ships arrived to join the occupying force, those occupants who had not managed to flee were massacred. Others – women and children – were taken captive. It seems the sheer unexpectedness of the raid on Seville astounded the authorities in the capital of Cordova, for it was some time before the emir Abd al-Rahman II thought to order the army out against them. With the help of catapult-machines the army drove the Vikings out of the city and some 500 of them were killed. Four Viking ships were captured intact.

In the middle of November the Vikings were again defeated, again with heavy loss of life. Thirty longships were burnt, and the corpses of Viking captives hung from the palm trees of Seville and Talyata. In symbolic triumph, the heads of the expedition leader and 200 of his men were sent to the Berber emir in Tangier. What remained of the fleet made its way back north up the coast. Abd al-Rahman II's response to the dreadful novelty of these raids from the sea was to build a number of warships of his own and to establish a chain of lookout posts along the Atlantic coast. Seville was restored, its defences strengthened and an arsenal established.

There is no record of any further Viking activity in the region until the arrival in 859 of a second fleet of sixty Viking ships. Two that were sailing in advance were spotted and captured off the coast of the Algarve, complete with their cargo of booty and slaves. The rest sailed on, passing the Guadalquivir, which was now too well guarded to force, and making land at Algeciras, where they burnt down the mosque. Resuming their voyage, probably with the intention of entering the Straits of Gibraltar, they were driven by bad weather down the Atlantic coast of Morocco as far as Asilah. Making their way back to the Straits they entered the Mediterranean and followed the coast of North Africa as far as Nakur, a town identified as modern Nador, near what is now the small Spanish enclave of Melilla. Over the course of the next eight days they raided the beaches for slaves. This fleet was probably the same one that then went on to raid in the Balearic Islands of Formentera, Majorca and Minorca, landed at Rosellon near present-day Perpignan, plundered and burnt the monastery on the banks of the river Ter and even reached the north Italian city of Luna (now Lucca). Returning along the coast of al-Andalus, they attacked Pamplona and captured García, king of Navarra, whom they ransomed for 70,000 gold coins. A long and well-established Viking Age tradition holds that the leaders of this expedition were Hasting (aka Anstign, aka Hastein, aka Astignus) and Bjørn Ironside.

The attack on Luna was made, according to Dudo, because Hasting erroneously believed it to be Rome and was unable to resist the lure of an assault on the very heart of institutionalized Christianity. Feigning contrition for his evil ways, Hasting contacted local Christian leaders and allowed himself to be baptized. Returning to his men he outlined the plan: they were to pretend he had died and request permission for his body to receive a Christian burial within the city. Once inside the walls, it was a simple matter for him to leap from the coffin and lead his men in a massacre of the innocents of the city. Luna was certainly plundered; but the tactics used to gain entry to the city are less certain, and the ruse of 'playing dead' was a familiar example of Viking and Norman cunning that was also attributed to other heroes of the age, including the legendary Danish King Frodo, Robert Guiscard, the eleventh-century Norman duke of Apulia, and the eleventh-century king of Norway, Harald Hardrada.

As a postscript to this first round of ninth-century Viking raids on the Iberian peninsula and beyond, the *Fragmentary Annals of Ireland* for 867 offer a dramatized account of the background to the Africa campaign which ingeniously relates it to the arrival of the Great Heathen Army in England, and again emphasizes the role of slave-taking and slave-trading in such enterprises:

At this time came the Aunites (that is, the Danes) with innumerable armies to York, and they sacked the city, and they overcame it; and that was the beginning of harassment and misfortunes for the Britons; for it was not long before this that there had been every war and every trouble in Norway, and this was the source of that war in Norway: two younger sons of Albdan (Halfdan), king of Norway, drove out the eldest son, i.e. Ragnall son of Albdan, for fear that he would seize the kingship of Norway after their father. So Ragnall came with his three sons to the Orkneys. Ragnall stayed there then, with his youngest son. The older sons, however, filled with arrogance and rashness, proceeded with a large army, having mustered that army from all quarters, to march against the Franks and Saxons. They thought that their father would return to Norway immediately after their departure.

Then their arrogance and their youthfulness incited them to voyage across the Cantabrian Ocean and they reached Spain, and they did many evil things in Spain, both destroying and plundering. After that they proceeded across the Gaditanean Straits, so that they reached Africa, and they waged war against the Mauritanians, and made a great slaughter of the Mauritanians.[11] However, as they were going to this battle, one of the sons said to the other, 'Brother,' he said, 'we are very foolish and mad to be killing ourselves going from country to country throughout the world, and not to be defending our own patrimony, and doing the will of our father, for he is alone now, sad and discouraged in a land not his own, since the other son whom we left along with him has been slain, as has been revealed to me.' It would seem that that was revealed to him in a dream vision; and his other son was slain in battle; and moreover, the father himself barely escaped from that battle— which dream proved to be true.

While he was saying that, they saw the Mauritanian forces coming towards them, and when the son who spoke the above words saw that, he leaped suddenly into the battle, and attacked the king of the Mauritanians, and gave him a blow with a great sword and cut off his hand. There was hard fighting on both sides in this battle, and neither of them won the victory from the other in that battle. But all returned to camp, after many among them had been slain. However, they challenged each other to come to battle the next day. The king of the Mauritanians escaped from the camp and fled in the night after his hand had been cut off. When the morning came, the Norwegians seized their weapons and readied themselves firmly and bravely for the battle. The Mauritanians, however, when they noticed that their king had departed, fled after they had been terribly slain.

Thereupon the Norwegians swept across the country, and they devastated and burned the whole land. Then they brought a great host of them captive with them to Ireland. For Mauri is the same as nigri; 'Mauritania' is the same as nigritudo. Now those black men remained in Ireland for a long time.[12]

The Arabic records that tell of the third series of Viking raids on the peninsula that began in June 966 sound a weary and frightened echo of the responses of Anglo-Saxon and Frankish chroniclers at their reappearance, and at the predictably violent nature of their errand. The experiences of previous encounters over 100 years earlier had etched itself on the communal memory. The thirteenth-century Moroccan scholar Ibn al-Idari wrote of the response to the sighting of a fleet of twenty-eight ships off the coast of what is now Alcacer do Sal, in the province of Alentejo, just south of Lisbon, 'that the people of the region were very alarmed, because in former times al-magus had been in the habit of attacking al-Andalus'.[13] Descriptions of the size of the fleets, their movements and doings have the same fearful precision of the western chroniclers, and their sentences are punctuated in the same way by outbursts of pious despair: 'May Allah destroy them!' Ibn al-Idari cries out, in the middle of a tale of how the caliph, al-Hakam, hit upon a plan of disguising some ships in his own fleet as longships, in the hope that they would function as decoys and lure the Vikings into the Guadalquivir harbour.

The nucleus of this Viking fleet was the large remainder of an army of Danish Vikings which had arrived in the duchy of Normandy early in the 960s at the request of Duke Richard I to give him military assistance in a regional conflict. Some returned home once the business was settled; some accepted Richard's offer of land in return for baptism; the remainder set off raiding in Galicia and Leon in the north-west of Spain, even-handedly attacking both Christian and Muslim targets along the way. After encountering some resistance, they were joined in 968 by a fleet of 100 ships under a leader known to the Muslims as Gunderedo and threatened the Galician town of Santiago de Compostela, by this time a place of pilgrimage to the shrine of Saint Joseph (Jakob) and, as a result, a very wealthy town. They landed at the head of the Arousa inlet and, while the bishop of Compostela tried to organize resistance, spread terror through the region, burning down buildings, killing and thieving. When at length the bishop arrived at the head of an armed force they withdrew to a place called Fornelos. In a later engagement, the bishop was killed by an arrow and the demoralized Galician troops fled the field of battle and left the people to the mercies of the Vikings. For the next three years they remained a dominant and terrifying presence in the area. Why this dominance in Galicia did not translate into formal possession is not clear; but the last recorded raid in this particular series was an overland advance in June 972 to the Algarve by a Viking army.

A fourth and final wave of Viking attacks that lasted from 1008 to 1038 was notable for the involvement of Olav Haraldson, a future king of Norway, whose redemptive career as a crusader among his own people we shall consider later. The raids were concentrated in the south-west of Galicia. In the most notorious of them, the Vikings sailed up the Miño river to the town of Tui, which they burnt and destroyed. Bishop Don Alfonso was captured, along with a great number of other Christian officials, presumably for ransom, though the records do not say so. Olav's court poets, Sigvat and Ottar the Black, both refer to their master's adventures in Spain. The fact that Snorri does not do so in his *Saga of St Olav* may be a discretionary omission by a Christian author who was self-consciously writing a hagiography in which such details had no place. Twenty years later the Vikings were back in Galicia, briefly this time but apparently again successfully, for their commander made himself a name there and was remembered as 'the Galician Wolf'.

Other records exist, left by Arab travellers who encountered the Vikings under less fraught circumstances than these and who were able to indulge their anthropological curiosity to leave us an elliptical view of Viking culture that is largely missing from the wounded accounts of Christian scribes in the British Isles and in mainland Europe. We have already met Ibn Fadlan, who closely observed, among other things, the funerary rituals of the travelling band of Rus traders he met on the Volga in 921, and the geographer Ibn Rustah, who travelled to Novgorod with the Rus at a slightly later date than his fellow Muslim and noted down his impressions of the people and their home. Ibn Fadlan's descriptions veer dramatically from admiration at the physique of the Rus – 'I have seen the Rus as they came on their merchant journeys and encamped by the Volga. I have never seen more perfect physical specimens, tall as date-palms and ruddy-complexioned' – to disgust at their failure to wash themselves after defecating, urinating and having sexual intercourse.[14] The day began with a slave-girl who passed among the members of the group carrying a pitcher of water in which each washed his hands, face and hair and then cleared his nose and spat. The process was repeated until all had used the same water in the same fashion. With the Volga flowing by outside, the economy would seem unnecessary. Perhaps some bonding ritual was involved that reinforced the group identity and strengthened its internal loyalty. Constantine Porphyrogenitos, in his description of Rus traders making their way down the Dneiper to trade in Constantinople, drew particular attention to the 'one for all and all for one mentality' that guided their behaviour. Ibn Rustah observed the same thing: 'If one group of them is challenged to war, they all join forces. They stand firm as one man against their enemies until they have won the victory over them.' His account is generally more sympathetic than Ibn Fadlan's and is free from the latter's occasional flourishes of disgust:

They keep their clothes clean and the men adorn themselves with armbands of gold. They treat their servants well and dress exquisitely because they are such keen traders. (. . .) They are generous to each other, honour their guests and treat well those who seek refuge with them, and all who come to visit them. They do not allow anyone to annoy or harm these. And whenever anyone dares to treat them unfairly they help and defend them.[15]

Walrus tusks and furs were no doubt valuable and rare commodities to take to market in the Arab world, but Ibn Fadlan and Ibn Rustah both noted the importance of slave-trading:

They terrorize the Slavs, whom they reach by ship. They take prisoners there and transport them to Hazaran and Bulgar and sell them there. They do not own fields, but live entirely off what they bring from the land of the Slavs.[16]

Ibn Fadlan observed that each Rus woman wore pinned to her breast a band of silver, copper or gold, its size determined by the wealth of her man, from which a knife hung. Around their necks the women wore gold and silver rings, each ring representing 10,000 dirham or Arabic coins. For much of the early Viking Age the status of the dirham was such that it was a universally accepted currency, in much the same way as the American dollar is today,[17] and was widely copied or counterfeited. Some of the dirham from the Vårby hoard found near Stockholm have small Christian crosses added above the Islamic inscription, suggesting they may have been struck in a Christian area. Dirham make up a regular feature of the coin hoards unearthed across the Viking world, from Cuerdale in the north-west of England to Spilling's Farm in the north-east of Gotland. The sheer volume of them is testimony to the extent of the trade relations that existed between Arabs and Vikings in the east, with Gotland and Birka as the main channels for conveying the coins westward; but as we noted earlier, for a Viking the value of the dirham remained its silver content, not its monetary value. Dirham were for daily use, and the fact that so many of them were buried underground by Vikings in their own territories suggests that they were so plentiful as to have attained the status of a surplus material.[18]

It was inevitable that misunderstandings should arise as these Arab travellers tried to make sense of the ritual and mores of this alien culture. Ibn Rustah wrote that the friends of a dead warrior dig him a grave resembling a large house and place him in it, along with his clothes, his gold arm-bands, food, drink and coins, and that his favourite wife is buried alive with him before the grave is closed. There are no indications from any native Scandinavian source that the Vikings practised suttee. What is likely is that such travelling bands, be they Vikings, Rus or *al-madjus*, developed, as self-contained groups far from home do, their own set of rules and rituals that were unique to them. The degree to which the group observed by Ibn Fadlan was a self-sufficient unit is suggested by the presence among them of their very own priestess, the 'Angel of Death', whose functions included the ritual stabbing of the slave-girl who had 'volunteered' to accompany her dead master into the next world. Ibn Rustah likewise noted the terrifying power of the Rus priests:

They have their wizards, who decide on what they own as though they were their masters, and tell them to sacrifice to their creator whatever they decide of women, men and cattle. And once the wizards have made the decision, they are compelled to carry out their instructions. The wizard then takes the person or the animal from them, puts a rope around the neck and hangs them from a gallows until dead.[19]

Ibn Fadlan's group was rich enough to sacrifice an entire ship as a crematorium for its dead chieftain and his slave, but his informant told him that only the greatest chieftains warranted such ceremony. Rank-and-file members of the band were buried alone in small boats, while dead slaves were simply left to rot where they died. The cultural similarities between the Volga and Oseberg funerals include the use of ships as coffins and the provision of food, or perhaps companionship, for the dead in the form of freshly killed horses and dogs. The Volga funeral involved the sacrifice of a slave, and, as we noted earlier, one of the women in the Oseberg ship may have been sacrificed to accompany her mistress. But in terms of the imagined afterlife the differences are striking: the climax of the funeral on the Volga came with the burning of the ship, in which it resembles the ceremony carried out on the Île de Groix off the north-west coast of France, but is distinct from both the Oseberg and the Gokstad ship-funerals, where neither ships nor bodies were cremated.

Ibn Fadlan is the more sensationally inclined of these two great Arab observers and rounds off the *Risala*, or 'little book', as his account of his meetings with the Rus is known, by asserting that their king spent most of his time on an enormous throne studded with precious stones. Forty sexual slaves sat beside him, and whenever it pleased him to he would take one in full view of his men. When he wished to mount his horse the animal was led to his throne, when he dismounted he did so directly on to his throne. Most striking of all, Ibn Fadlan claims that he did not even leave the throne to answer the call of nature but used a salver. This has the ring of a traveller's tale to it, and lacks the obvious credibility of the account of the funeral and the events leading up to it. The main purpose of the embassy of which Ibn Fadlan was a part was to instruct the Bulgar *kagan* in the Islamic faith. Bearing in mind this religious goal, there is perhaps a point of contact between his reactions to the Rus and those of Alcuin, who was so clearly uneasy at the lack of physical modesty on the part of Heathens he had come across before Lindisfarne. There is an almost homoerotic quality to Ibn Fadlan's description of the magnificence of the Rus as physical specimens, which he struggles to quell with disgusted descriptions of their lack of hygiene. Like the Christian Alcuin, Ibn was effortlessly convinced that, as a Muslim, he represented the higher culture. One exchange makes it clear that the Rus did not agree. Ibn Fadlan noticed his interpreter in conversation with one of the Rus and asked him what they had been talking about. The interpreter told him:

'He said, "You Arabs are stupid!" So I said, "Why?" and he replied, "Because you take those who are dearest to you and whom you hold in highest esteem and you bury them under the earth, where they are eaten by the earth, by vermin and by worms. We burn them in the fire, straightaway, and they enter paradise immediately." Then he laughed loud and long. I asked him why and he said, "Because of the love which my god feels for him. He has sent the wind to take him away within an hour."' Actually, it took scarcely an hour for the ship, the firewood, the slave-girl and her master to be burnt to a fine ash.

Among the Vikings, uniformity of procedure on socially significant occasions like births, marriages and deaths waited on the introduction of Christianity and the spread of the written word for its imposition. But in his cheerful arrogance, this particular Rus seems to have known that, in one respect at least, they had the future on their side.

Ibn Rustah also tells us that the Rus were covered to their fingertips in tattoos depicting trees, figures and other designs. This is of a piece with what Alcuin and that other, anonymous, Anglo-Saxon commentator noted concerning the personal vanity of the Heathens, especially their fashion for 'blinded eyes', which may have been a form of eye-shadow. An Arab source leaves no doubt that eye make-up was common among the Rus: 'once applied it never fades, and the beauty of both men and women is increased'.[20] Tattooing was banned in 787 by Pope Hadrian because of its association with Heathendom and superstition, and Christian disapproval may account for the absence of any reference to tattoos in the descriptions of men and women in the sagas written down in the Christian era.[21] Only a clutch of stray references, literary and archaeological, have survived to confirm that it was indeed practised. In the 'Sigrdrífumál', a gnomic poem on the deeds of Sigurd the Dragon Slayer collected in the *Codex Regius*, the hero wakes a Valkyrie named Sigrdrífa whom Odin has condemned to perpetual sleep for her disobedience, and compels her to reveal secrets to him. One verse ascribes a magical power to tattooing:

> Ale-runes you will want   if another man's wife
> tries to betray your trust;
> scratch them on your drinking horn,   the back of your hand
> and the need-rune on your nail.[22]

Another indicates that tattoos could have a medicinal function:

> I'll teach you lore for helping   women in labour,
> runes to release the child;
> write them on your palms   and clasp her wrists
> invoking the disir's aid.[23]

Özti, the 5,000-year-old hunter whose body emerged from the melting permafrost in the Öztal Alps in 1991, had at least fifty-seven tattoos on various parts of his body. Many were concentrated in areas where the joints bore signs of being worn and painful, and researchers have speculated that they might have combined magic with a form of acupuncture.[24] Tattooing may also have had a ritual significance. An unusual comb, with runic inscriptions dated to about 550–600, was found at Bømlo, in South Hordaland, in Norway, along with a number of bone pins, including one with an iron tip and a small, iron-dressed, hammer-like head. It is possible that in its entirety the find might have been equipment associated with a rite of passage initiating young girls into womanhood that involved tattooing and ritual decoration of the hair.[25]

These encounters between Allah and Odin on the Iberian peninsula and along the coast of the Mediterranean left few lasting traces. Slavers routinely took the precaution of transporting their captives overseas to discourage escape attempts and slaves taken by *al-madjus* in the region were not offered for sale locally and did not lead to the development of local trade relations. The only known diplomatic contact to have arisen out of the raids is a mission, said to have taken

place in about 845, to the court of the *al-madjus* king who had led
the attack on Seville the year before, with the aim of establishing
friendly ties with him. The Arab emissary was a renowned poet and
ladies' man known as al-Ghazal, or the Gazelle, a name given to him
in his youth in tribute to his good looks. The wealth of detail in the
account by the twelfth-century Spanish scholar Ibn Dihya includes a
description of the land of this king of the *al-madjus*:

They came next to the royal residence. It was a large island in the ocean, with
running water and gardens. Between it and the mainland is a journey of three
days. Innumerable of the al-Magus live on this island. Close to it are many
other islands, large and small. All the inhabitants are Magus. And the closest
mainland also belongs to them, several days' journey away. They were
formerly Magus, but now follow the Christian religion, since they have
abandoned the worship of fire and the religion they followed previously, and
converted to Christianity, excepting the inhabitants of some of the islands
belonging to them which are further out at sea. These continue to observe
the old religion with the worship of fire, marriage with mother and sister and
other abominations.[26]

This sounds like Denmark, with the king's hegemony over 'the closest
mainland' a reference to Vik in south-eastern Norway and Skåne in
southern Sweden, in which case al-Ghazal's host would have been
King Horik, who was baptized by Anskar and encouraged Christianity
in Denmark, though without making it compulsory.[27] Most of Ibn
Dihya's account is a literary entertainment describing the king's
wife's infatuation for her Arabic visitor. Al-Ghazal visited her frequently and she showered him with gifts. He became her lover, and
satisfied her curiosity about his people and their customs. He made
verse in praise of her: 'I am enchanted by a Magus woman, who will
not let the sunlight of beauty dim, who lives in the most remote of
Allah's lands, where the traveller finds no tracks.'[28] His companions
warned him to stop seeing her and accepting the gifts and al-Ghazal
cut his visits down to one every second day. When the queen, who in
al-Ghazal's verse bears the non-Scandinavian name 'Nud', was told
the reason for the change in his routine she laughingly reassured
him that

Our ways are not like that, and there is no jealousy among us. Our women stay with their men of their own free will; a woman stays with her man as long as it pleases her, and leaves him when she wearies of their life together.[29]

The independence of women from the Heathen north generally was a source of great surprise to Arab travellers. One noted that 'among them women have the right to divorce. A woman can herself initiate divorce whenever she pleases.'[30] Ibn Dihya adds that, until the coming of Christianity, no woman was forbidden to any man, the exception being when a high-born woman chose a man of lower standing. This was held to shame her, and her family kept the lover away from her. Al-Ghazal, reassured by Queen Nud's words, resumed his daily visits until his departure. The impression of a Danish society free from sexual jealousy is countered by Adam of Bremen, who states plainly that women who were unfaithful to their men were immediately sold.[31]

No authoritative Arab historian of the time mentions this mission, nor do any of the biographers of al-Ghazal, and the great French arabist, Évariste Lévi-Provencal, judged the whole story to be a fictional improvisation based on a journey to Constantinople known to have been made by al-Ghazal in the winter of 839/840.[32] This was the year in which the Rus turned up at the court of Louis the Pious in Ingelheim on their way back from Constantinople. Lévi-Provencal speculates that al-Ghazal may have met these Rus or heard talk of their land and their customs, with his report from this encounter forming the basis of Ibn Dihya's later improvisation.

The sole Viking Age artefact to have emerged in Spain is a small cylindrical vessel made of deer horn, with a pattern of holes around it and a handle at one end. It is a rarity among such artefacts in that it was not found accidentally by the digging of archaeologists but had been in use in the Church of San Isidoro, in León, for several centuries until it was finally identified and installed as an exhibit in the town museum. All three of the dominant Borre, Jelling and Mammen styles of the second half of the tenth century have left identifiable traces on the design on the vessel, a gripping beast motif made up of as many as eight smaller beasts. The mingling of styles suggests a transitional phase between the Jelling and Mammen eras, and a tentative dating to the end of the tenth or beginnning of the eleventh century. The provenance of the vessel is obscure, but it may have been part of a large donation made to the church in León by King Fernando I (1037–1065) and his Queen Doña Sancha in 1063. How it came to be in their possession and what its original function may have been are unknown.[33] Other traces of the Viking presence are slight. Generally speaking, it was too sporadic to leave a significant impact on the local language and place-names. In the province of León there is a village called Lordemanos, which may indicate a local settlement of Vikings, and near Coimbra, in Portugal, a village named Lordemão invites similar speculation, as do villages named Nordoman and Nortman. In Vascony, Vikings who settled in Bayonne may have taught the Basques how to hunt the whales that arrived in the Bay of Biscay every autumn. Predictably, the handful of loan-words from Old Norse into Basque, Spanish and French are connected with maritime and fishing activity. The fishermen of Bermeo, the most important fishing-port in the Basque country, use 'estribor', compounded of 'styr' and 'bord', to designate 'starboard', and 'babor', from 'bak' and 'bord', to mean 'port'.[34] Among place-names in the region with otherwise unknown origins, Mundaka, on the mouth of the river Oka, may derive from Old Norse 'munnr', meaning 'mouth'.[35]

The wave of raids between 966 and 971 marked the climax of the Viking Age in Galicia. Briefly, there was a danger that the province might turn into a Spanish Normandy.[36] But it did not, and the raids on the Iberian peninsula and beyond had no lasting political or cultural significance. They were episodic and piratical, long and daring journeys undertaken in search of riches and adventure, and as such perhaps more authentically 'Viking' in spirit than the colonizations. There are no conversion stories here, no discourse with local aristocrats, no attempts on the part of the adventurers to establish large-scale settlements and farm the land. Yet we know enough by now to realize that there is no such thing as a typical Viking, and an enigmatic and unusually charming recollection of their presence is a tale told by one Arab chronicler of a certain group of al-madjus who got lost or separated from their companions in al-Andalus, somehow evaded execution, converted to Islam, and married local girls. They started a farm at Isla Menor, on the Mediterranean coast between

Alicante and Cartagena, where they presently established a reputation as producers of what was reputed to be the best cheese in the region.[37]

13

A piece of horse's liver

The pragmatic Christianity of Håkon the Good

The great leaders of the Viking Age were wary of making claims that could not be substantiated. As we saw in Chapter 10, Harald Bluetooth's boast on the Jelling stone, that he had 'won for himself all of Denmark and Norway and made the Danes Christian', meticulously avoids any suggestion that he had also made the Norwegians Christian. In *Heimskringla*, Snorri says that Harald did indeed send two of his earls to Norway to try to impose Christianity, and that the mission was successful in the Vik, 'where King Harald's might prevailed'.[1] By Harald's standards it was obviously not successful enough. As had been the case in Denmark, and as would later be the case in Sweden, the conversion of Norway came about largely through the efforts of native kings.

At about the time of the Jelling boast, the ruler in Norway was Håkon, later known as 'the Good' that son whom Harald Finehair had sent to England to be fostered by King Athelstan at the court of Wessex. Harald would have known that his son would be raised in the Christian faith and must have been content at the prospect. With Athelstan's assistance, in about 936 Håkon had driven out his brother Erik Bloodaxe and taken over the throne of Norway. On the assumption that where kings led, their subjects would follow, the English may have hoped that his accession would signal an end to any further west Scandinavian threats against them.

From the *Ágrip*, however, we learn of the great difficulties Athelstan's foster-son faced in trying to introduce Christianity to the Norwegian earls during the early years of his rule:

In his time many people were converted through his popularity, and some gave up Heathen worship though they did not take baptism. He built some churches in Norway and appointed men of learning to them. But the people burned the churches and killed the priests, so that he could not continue because of their depredations.[2]

It may have been an incomplete report of Håkon's missionary efforts that led Harald Bluetooth to presume that the formal conversion of the Norwegians had already taken place. There is potential support for this theory in one interpretation of the inscription on the Kuli stone, found under the floor of a barn in 1913 on the island of Kuløy in Nordmøre, just north of Romsdal. In a reversal of the more familiar scenario in which a scholar sees runes where there are only glacial striations, this stone, with a cross inscribed on one side, spent fifty years in the museum at Trondheim before the Norwegian historian Aslak Liestøl noticed that it had two lines of runic script cut along one of its edges. The interpretation of the inscription is still debated by runologists, but the majority settle for something like this: *Tore and Hallvard raised this stone after Ulvljot, Christendom had been twelve winters in the realm.* This is significant for a number of reasons, not least because it is the first known use of the word 'Christendom' in Norway. It has not, however, acquired a status, comparable to the Danish Jelling stone, as Norway's 'birth certificate'. Harald Bluetooth's importance as a Danish king makes it possible to give a fairly accurate estimate of the date at which the Jelling stone was raised; but of Tore, Hallvard and Ulvljot we know nothing. The dating of Ulvljot's death is pre-Christian in its relativity. It is not plotted along an unbroken time-line that begins with the birth of Christ and moves forward to the present moment, but instead relates to the adoption of Christianity as a significant but local event. The result is that the Kuli stone cannot be dated with any certainty at all.[3] The 'twelve winters' may be counting back to the *thing* meeting at Moster in 1024, at which Christian thinking began to influence the law in Norway. Or it may relate to the conversion campaigns of Olaf Tryggvason and the Drageid *thing* meeting of 996. A third possibility is that the twelve years referred to on the stone may have been counted from Håkon the Good's first serious attempt to introduce Christianity to Norway, which would date the inscription to some time in the late 940s, not long before the erection of the Jelling stone. If Håkon's efforts were initially successful, as the *Ágrip* suggests they were, this may have inclined Harald to instruct his rune-master to omit any claim to have converted an already converted people.

Even if there is substance to this latter hypothesis, the inscription on the Kuli stone would hardly have met with general assent in Norway, for the essence of Håkon's story as told by Snorri in the *Saga of Håkon the Good* is the same as that sketched in the *Ágrip*, of the resistance he met from powerful local chieftains to his attempted innovations. The poignancy of it lies in his attempts to compromise with these powerful, conservative forces. To the *Ágrip*'s description of what happened when he tried to introduce the Church as an institution, Snorri adds details of Håkon's personal faith, telling us that the king observed Sundays and the Friday fasts, and that he tried to introduce a Christian version of the midwinter festival. In doing this he was striking at the heart of institutionalized Heathen culture in Norway. Little is known of how time was measured before the introduction of the Christian calendar, but it is believed that the Heathens observed a so-called 'bound' lunar year, which followed a lunisolar calendar of the type described by the Venerable Bede in the *De temporum ratione*.[4] The twelve months of this year, each lasting from one full moon to the next, had no connection with the twelve, thirty-day months of the Christian calendar. Linguists believe that two of the names of the months used in Iceland after the introduction of the Christian calendar, *thorri* and *gói*, are probably survivals from the Heathen lunisolar calendar.[5] The year was divided into winter and summer half-years of six months each, and into quarters by four great communal feasts. An autumn sacrifice started the year, and this was followed by the midwinter feast of *Jól*. *Jul* remains the standard term for Christmas in all three Scandinavian languages, and *yule* enjoys a perilous survival in modern English. The etymology of the word is unknown, but the feast's connection with Odin is apparent in that one of his names was Jólnir; and its antiquity is attested by its occurrence in the 'Haraldskvæthi', composed for Harald Finehair by Torbjørn Hornklovi in about 900, where the poet says that the king '*Úti vill jól drekka*' ('will drink in Yule'), and adds the obscure reference '*ok Freys leik heyja*' ('and play Frey's game').[6] Snorri says that the ritual brewing and drinking of ale took place, and that horses and cattle were sacrificed and the blood collected in what he calls *hlaut*-vessels, from which toasts were drunk.[7] Odin, Frey, the obscure Njord and possibly Thor were hailed in this fashion.[8] The mixture of blood and alcohol may explain the name Jólnir, denoting Odin's manifestation of himself as god of the intoxication that encourages fellowship, and of the ecstasy that facilitates supernatural communication between men and gods. The toast was drunk '*til árs oc til frithar*'. The first element was a prayer for good catches at sea and good harvests on land; the second prayed for peace, and for good luck in breeding, for livestock and people alike. It may suggest that 'Frey's game' in Torbjørn's poem was a euphemism for the sexual act.

All of these traditions were challenged by Håkon at the *jól* feast that was held in the sixteenth year of his reign at Mære, near Trondheim,[9] when he addressed the assembly and proposed the end of the sacrificing, and the conversion of all to Christianity. His proposals caused outrage. The king's role in these quarterly feasts was central and crucial. Kingship in the Heathen north was a sacral office. Kings were of divine descent and traced their ancestry back through the Swedish Yngling dynasty to the gods Frey and Njord. As such, they stood in a privileged relationship to the gods. The privilege was a two-edged sword, for a king remained accountable to his people through the qualities of the time in which he ruled. We noted earlier the extreme example of the pre-historical King Domaldi, sacrificed by his people at Uppsala in a last plea to the gods to end a period of famine and need. Håkon may not have liked it, but he belonged to this line of sacral kings and was duty-bound to lead his people in festive observations. Sacrificing and the law were inextricably intertwined, and a king who declined to lead his people in the rituals was no longer a king. Worse, there was no longer a valid law.

The conservatives in the Trøndelag were aware of Håkon's reforming tendencies and were ready for him. Eight of the most important regional chieftains had divided the duty of resistance between them, says Snorri: 'the four of the outer Tronds should destroy Christianity and the four of the inner Tronds should require the king to come to the offering'.[10] At the feast Håkon was given a straight choice, either to 'ratify the ancient laws' or be driven from office. Earl Sigurd was the leading chieftain in the region and Håkon's kingship, proclaimed in the Trøndelag in about 936, had been with his support. He conveyed to the people that Håkon had agreed to their demands and was prepared to drop his insistence on conversion to Christianity. This proved not enough. To remain as king he must play to the full the king's part in the hallowing of the law. Snorri's superbly dramatized account describes the king's response, how he withdrew from the company and took his meals in the company only of a few of his closest Christian associates, until Sigurd persuaded him that he must take the high-seat and play his full part in the ceremonies. The unhappy king then enacted a fateful series of gestures, each more compromising of his Christian faith than the one before. He took the drinking horn, which Sigurd had already blessed in the name of Odin, and made the sign of the cross above it. People demanded to know what he was doing. Sigurd reassured them that their king was merely blessing the goblet in the name of Thor. Snorri's literary embroidery played on the physical similarity, widely noted at the time, between the hammer of Thor and the cross of Christ, one which enterprising silversmiths of those syncretic times exploited in the creation of small 'double' symbols which could represent both gods simultaneously, depending on which way up it was held. Håkon was then driven to a second act of betrayal of his faith. When the flesh of the sacrificed horse was offered to him he rejected it. He likewise refused to drink the sacrificial stew. The people now turned against him and were ready to seize him, when Earl Sigurd came to his rescue:

Sigurd calmed things down, suggesting that the king hold his mouth over the handle of the kettle, on which the fat smoke of the boiled horse-flesh had settled; first the king wrapped a linen cloth over the handle, then he opened his mouth and inhaled over it before returning to the high-seat.

But, as Snorri concludes, this satisfied neither party. As the likelihood of violence increased, Håkon finally made his choice and without first making the sign of the cross above them ate the slice of horse's liver and drank from the sacrificial broth.[11]

These pragmatic gestures marked the turning-point in his relationship with his people. While the author of the *Historia Norwegie* censored him for apostasy and for preferring mammon to god, Snorri eulogized him as a king who brought prosperity and good harvests to the land and called him 'the most beloved of kings'.[12] The length of Håkon's reign is uncertain, with estimates ranging from fifteen years to twenty-seven.[13] From about 955 onwards he was increasingly plagued by the harrying of Erik Bloodaxe's sons in Norway, fighting with the support of men supplied by Harald Bluetooth. In about 960 at a battle at Fitjar, on the island of Stord, he was mortally wounded by an arrow, allegedly shot by a child. Some medieval historians attributed his death to the sorcery of his brother Erik's wife, Gunnhild, always a baleful presence in the sources, whether plotting Egil Skallag-rimsson's downfall or urging her sons on against Håkon. To the author of *Historia Norwegie*, the shame of being killed by a low-born child made it 'as clear as daylight to every bleary-eyed man and barber' that this was Håkon's divine punishment for having 'dared to renounce the Christ-child'.[14] Inverting the thrust of a number of Viking Age stories of inter-faith marriages, in which the wife is usually Christian and the husband Heathen, the *Ágrip*, dated to about 1190,[15] says that Håkon's wife was a Heathen, and that it was for her sake that he abandoned Christianity. The author goes on to describe the contrition of the king's final hours:

And when the king saw that he was near death, he deeply repented of his offences against God. His friends offered to carry his body west to England and give it church burial. 'I am not worthy of that,' said he. 'In many ways I have lived like the Heathens, therefore I should be buried like the Heathens. In this way I could hope for greater mercy than I deserve at God's hands.[16]

His friends removed his body to Saeheim, in North Hordaland, and he was interred with conspicuously Heathen honours beneath a great mound. In what may have been a gesture of respect for his compromised Christianity, no grave-goods were buried with him.

Eyvind Skaldaspiller's great poem in praise of him, 'Håkonarmál', was perhaps what gave the author of the *Ágrip* his cue in the prose account of Håkon's death. Though steeped in the Heathen lore that was the staple and foundation of skaldic art, it manages to convey vividly the densely mixed nature of spiritual life in Norway at this time. After describing Håkon's death in battle, Eyvind imagines the king's unease at the prospect of meeting Odin in Valhalla, understandable in one who had been so reluctant in his Heathen devotions. Valkyries bring news of Håkon's imminent arrival to Odin, and Odin sends two favoured sons to greet him:

> Said the rich Skogul,
> 'Gondul and I shall ride
> To the gods' green home
> To tell Odin
> That quickly the prince
> Comes to see him.'

> 'Hermod and Bragi',
> Said the war father Odin,
> 'Go forth to meet Håkon,
> For that warrior king
> Is called hither to the hall.'

> The king said this –
> He came from the fight,
> And stood bloody and pale –
> 'Fierce in mind
> Odin seems to me,
> Ill is his look.'[17]

Eyvind bestows a posthumous reassurance on Håkon, telling him that Odin would welcome him gratefully, for in having 'spared the holy places' he showed a tolerance that Heathens had learnt not to expect from kings who were Christians.

> Now it is known
> That the king had guarded
> Well the temples,
> So Håkon the Good
> Was welcomed with gladness
> By the kind gods.

> That warrior king is born
> On a lucky day
> Who has such a lofty mind.

His time here
Shall always be
Full of praise and glory.

For Eyvind, it was this tolerance of the old ways, rather than any perceived Christian quality, that was the essence of Håkon's 'goodness'. The salutation in the final verse of the poem borrows from 'The Sayings of the High One', to which Eyvind adds his own comment on the bad 'king's luck' that was to follow shortly with the rule of Håkon the Bad:

Cattle die, kinsmen die,
the land is laid waste;
since Håkon left for
the Heathen gods,
need rules and bellies are empty.[18]

The Kuli stone gave us the first use of 'Christendom' in a native Norwegian source; Eyvind's poem marked the first occurrence of the word 'Heathen' in Old Norse literature.[19] *Heithin god* ('Heathen gods') was a Christian description of the Old Norse pantheon, derogatory in the same way as the Latin *pagani*, both implying that their worshippers were country bumpkins. A century earlier Eyvind would simply have said 'the gods', and his perhaps unthinking use of the term is a hint that the days of the old gods were fewer in number than he cared openly to admit.[20]

In Denmark Harald Bluetooth was keen to restore to the full Danish hegemony over Norway which had fallen into abeyance during the century of decline that lasted from the death of Horik in 854 until the revitalization process started by Harald's father Gorm. After Håkon's death he visited Norway and reintroduced the direct rule of a Danish king in the Vik and Østfold regions of the Oslo fjord. With his blessing, the sons of Erik, under the leadership of Harald *gráfeldr*, or 'Greycloak', ruled in the west of the country from Lindesnes and northward. They had been baptized in England with their parents, probably as part of the deal with Athelstan or one of his successors whereby Erik was recognized as ruler of York. But though they tried to introduce Christianity, 'they could do nothing to make the men of the land Christians; but wherever they came they broke down temples and destroyed the sacrifice, and from that they got many foes,' Snorri says.[21]

Politically if not spiritually Erik's sons built on the legacy of Harald Finehair and Håkon the Good and consolidated Norwegian power in Norway. With the defeat in battle of the earl of Lade, the Trøndelag region came under their control. Their authority seems to have been recognized in northern Norway as well, increasing until Harald found it inappropriately great. At some point he changed his allegiance and offered his support to their most bitter rival, the exiled Lade earl, Håkon, son of that Sigurd who had guided Håkon the Good through the earlier crisis. Harald Greycloak was killed in battle at Hals on Limfjord, Jylland, probably about 974. With his death the last, direct descendant of Harald Finehair to occupy the throne of Norway was gone, to make way for the last Heathen king to rule Norway. That Harald should have supported a Heathen claimant to the throne against its legitimate Christian rulers shows the significance in the 'conversion moment' of the act of baptismal sponsorship: Erik's sons might have been Christians, but they were not 'his' Christians.

'Vellekla', a praise poem for Earl Håkon Sigurdsson by the Icelandic skald Einar Helgason, hailed him as lord over sixteen Norwegian earls. But he was himself subject to a Danish overlord, and during much of his reign Harald Bluetooth, too, had to acknowledge the overlordship of the German king and Holy Roman Emperor, Otto the Great, and of his son and successor Otto II. The emperor posed the same kind of threat in the name of expansionist Christianity as Charlemagne had done to Godfrid's Denmark at the turn of the eighth century, and, as we noted earlier, this threat may have been a factor in Harald's eventual acceptance of Christianity. But the privileges of membership of the club of Christian peoples remained obscure, and in 974, at least ten years after Harald had joined it, Otto II invaded Denmark in reprisal for Danish raids on Holstein.[22]

Håkon Sigurdsson paid Harald an annual tribute of twenty falcons. More importantly, he was bound to provide military assistance should Harald ever call upon him.[23] 'Vellekla' includes references to Håkon's answering the summons from Harald to help him defend his territory against Otto, and of Håkon's fighting Otto by the Danevirke.[24] Before he returned to Norway, Harald sponsored his baptism and sent him back home with a number of missionary priests.[25] As soon as he was able, Håkon compelled them ashore and renounced his conversion. With his intervention against Otto he seems to have regarded his debt to Harald as paid and to have conducted himself thereafter as sole ruler of Norway in the west.

Harald was as little pleased by this as he had been by the independent ways of the sons of Erik Bloodaxe, and in 986 he despatched a fleet up the west coast of Norway to bring Håkon to heel. The Danes were joined by over 100 ships of the Jomsvikings; but it was Håkon who triumphed on the day at the battle at Hjörungavåg. Though none of the shorter historical works from the end of the twelfth century that deal with events in Norway mention Hjörungavåg at all, the creative imagination of later skalds and sagamen turned the battle into a source of some of the most powerful myths associated with the Viking Age.[26] The *Saga of the Jomsvikings* and Snorri's *Saga of Olaf Tryggvason* both tell the tale of the line of Jomsviking prisoners being beheaded one by one, each man boldly disdaining to show fear as he is called forward. The *Saga of the Jomsvikings* contains a fuller account than does Snorri of the tradition referred to earlier concerning Håkon's sacrifice of his seven-year-old son Erling for success in battle:

Now the earl goes ashore on the island called Prime Signed and into the trees. He faces north, goes down on his knees and prays. In his prayer he calls on his protector, Thorgerd Holgabrudr. But she is angry and will not hear his prayer. He offers her great sacrifices, but she remains unmoved. The situation begins to seem hopeless to him. Next he offers her a human sacrifice, but she will not accept it. Finally he offers her his son, whose name was Erling and who was seven years old. She agrees to accept the boy. The earl gives the boy to his slave Skofte, and he takes the boy away and kills him.[27]

Håkon's victory at Hjörungavåg saw off the Danes' attempt to extend their control over Norway to the south-west and west of the country. Temporarily at least, it strengthened his cause among the conservative forces in the land that appreciated his uncompromising adherence to Heathendom, and to the responsibilities imposed on a leader by Heathen practice and tradition. For all this, 'Vellekla' praised

Håkon. And yet Einar's verse would turn out to be the last time a skaldic poet could avail himself, unfettered, of the full range of images, *kennings* and metaphoric allusions to Heathen mythology upon which skaldic verse depended for its composition, before the encroaching tide of Christianity finally reached Norway and made the practice of the art dangerous, and then undesirable, and finally redundant.

Following the expulsion of Erik Bloodaxe from York in 954, England had enjoyed a quarter-century of respite from Viking attacks. One of the two men responsible for their resumption was Olaf Tryggvason. Olaf's is one of the emblematic careers of the Viking Age, describing in clear trajectory his graduation from marauding sea-king to missionary land-king. His life and career are the subject of one of Snorri Sturluson's longer sagas, of another even longer, by a different author, called *The Greater Saga of Olaf Tryggvason*, and of a lost saga written in Latin by Odd Monk, which nevertheless survives in a free translation. The *Greater Saga* in particular is infused with a legendary hindsight born of Olaf's achievements as a grown man, and of the role he played as trail-blazer to Olav Haraldson in finally bringing the Norwegians to Christianity.

Snorri's saga of Olaf Tryggvason has been described as 'particularly unreliable'.[28] In the light of his posthumous status among Christian writers, the story of Olaf's childhood reads almost like a Scandinavian version of the infancy of Jesus. Born in 968, he was the son of Trygve Olavsson, a petty king in the Vik area.[29] According to saga tradition he was a distant relative of Harald Finehair, which made the family from the start a threat to the dynastic ambitions of the sons of Erik Bloodaxe and their mother Gunnhild.[30] In Snorri's narrative Harald Greycloak has Trygve killed but is unaware that Trygve's wife Astrid is pregnant when she escapes. When her time comes she is rowed out to an island on a lake and gives birth there to Olaf.

The following year the wicked Gunnhild gets wind of the birth and organizes a hunt for the child. Astrid and her tiny band of protectors have to flee eastwards into Sweden and the territory of the Svear. Even among the Svear they are pursued, and when Olaf is three years old his mother crosses the Baltic to join her brother Sigurd in Kiev where, as a member of Vladimir's *hird*, he enjoys a high status. En route the group is attacked. Mother and child are separated, Olaf is captured and presently sold to a peasant for the price of a goat. Shortly afterwards he is traded on to an Estonian farmer, this time in exchange for a coat. Some six years later, his uncle Sigurd chanced by the farm of his owner one day. Realizing who the boy was he took him back to Kiev and to Vladimir, who became his foster-father.

Snorri tells us that Olaf's career as a Viking began as early as 980, when he was no more than twelve years of age, and volunteered to recover for his foster-father certain territories that Vladimir had lost. The *Historia Norwegie* prefers a less biblical version of the story, which has Olaf fostered in Sweden by a man named Torolv Luseskjegg. Slavers attacked their party as it made its way to Russia, Torolv was killed and Olaf sold into slavery. Rescued by chance by a relative, he was taken to Novgorod and grew up in hiding there. At the age of twelve he made his name by avenging the killing of his foster-father, a feat that brought him to the attention of Vladimir, who in due course adopted the boy.[31]

Whatever the truth of his early years, we need not doubt that by the time of his first appearance in the *Anglo-Saxon Chronicle* in the year 991, where Anglo-Saxon nasalization renders the name as 'Anlaf', Olaf had become a seasoned Viking raider. In command of a fleet of ninety-three ships, he ravaged in Folkestone and Sandwich before sailing up the coast to threaten Ipswich. From here his army came ashore at Maldon in Essex.

Though not in itself a decisive event, the battle that then took place against an English army under Byrhtnoth became the subject of the *Battle of Maldon*, a poem regarded as one of the finest achievements of Anglo-Saxon literature.[32] The battle is thought to have taken place on or about 10 August, on the banks of the Pante, now the Blackwater, with the Vikings marshalled on the offshore island of Northey, and the English awaiting them on the mainland.[33] As the unknown poet describes it, in a prelude to the engagement a warrior advances and calls over the water to the English:

> A viking messenger stood on the bank,
> Called clearly forth and made his declaration,
> Proudly proclaimed the message of the seamen

> To Byrhtnoth as he stood upon the shore.
> 'Bold seamen send me to you, order me
> To tell you that you speedily must send
> Rings for defence; it would be better for you
> To buy off this armed onslaught with your tribute
> Than that our hardy men should deal out war.
> We need not fight if you can come to terms.
> We will establish with that gold a truce.
> If you who are in charge here will agree
> That you are willing to protect your people,
> And pay the seamen at their own demand
> Money for peace, and take a truce from us,
> We with that treasure will embark again,
> Go back to sea, and keep the peace with you.'

Byrhtnoth will have none of it:

> Angry and resolute he answered him:
> 'Do you hear, seaman, what this people says?
> They plan to give you nought but spears for tribute,
> Poisonous point and edge of tried old sword,
> War-tax that will not help you in the fight.
> Go, viking herald, answer back again,
> Tell to your men a much more hostile tale:
> Here stands an earl undaunted with his troop,
> One who intends to save this fatherland,
> Ethelred's kingdom, and my liege lord's land
> And people. It shall be the heathen host
> That falls in fight. It seems to me too shameful
> That you should take our tribute to your ships
> Without a fight, now that you have advanced
> So far on to our soil. You shall not win
> treasure so easily; but spear and sword
> Must first decide between us, the grim sport
> Of war, before we pay our tribute to you.'[34]

Northey is joined to the mainland by a narrow causeway which is passable at low tide and the first Viking to set foot on it was easily shot down. The Vikings then requested permission to cross the causeway unimpeded so that battle might commence. For reasons best known to himself, Byrhtnoth granted the request. The fatal result of this act of decency or over-confidence is that the English were soundly beaten on the day. The futility of opposing any further what was clearly a particularly strong and well-disciplined army was evident, and on the advice of Sigeric, archbishop of Canterbury, the English King Ethelred, known as 'the Unready', agreed to pay a tribute of 10,000 pounds to the Vikings, 'because of the great terror they were causing along the coast'.[35] A treaty drawn up between the two sides is eloquent of the plight of the English at this time, helplessly agreeing both to employ their attackers to defend them against future fleets and to supply them with food for as long as they wished to remain.[36]

The reign of Ethelred has been characterized as a period in which treachery was ubiquitous, and the entry in the *Anglo-Saxon Chronicle* for 992 reinforces the impression of a wealthy society on the verge of moral disintegration. In that year Ethelred secretly ordered all serviceable ships to assemble in London to prepare for a surprise attack on the Viking fleet at sea. This English superfleet was to be under the command of two bishops and two earls. One of the earls, Ælfric, betrayed his king:

The Ealdorman Ælfric sent someone to warn the enemy, and then in the night on the day before which they were to have joined battle, he absconded by night from the army, to his own great disgrace, and then the enemy escaped, except that the crew of one ship was slain.[37]

The Viking fleet headed north, sacking and looting Bamburgh and around the mouth of the Humber. In 994 it returned south, and on 8 September Olaf attacked London with a fleet of ninety-four ships, accompanied this time by the Danish king, Svein Forkbeard. They tried and failed to burn the city down before embarking on a campaign along the coast and on land through Essex, Kent, Sussex and Hampshire. Ethelred offered them tribute and provisions in return for peace. His offer was accepted, and the army settled for the winter at Southampton, the richer by 16,000 pounds.

A delegation of leading churchmen visited Olaf and invited him to accompany them to Andover. Already baptized, he now submitted to confirmation, with Ethelred as his sponsor. The terms of the earlier treaty were restated, the English once again agreeing that 'if any fleet harry in England, we are to have the help of them all; and we are to supply them with food as long as they are with us'.[38] In exchange, Olaf gave his word that he would never return to England with warlike intent. The *Anglo-Saxon Chronicle* notes that he kept his promise. Along with Alfred's treaty with Guthrum in about 878 and the St Cloud agreement between Rollo and Charles the Simple in about 911, it stands as a rare example of the success of this policy of spiritual incorporation that had been tried so many times before by exasperated and exhausted Christian rulers.[39] Unfortunately for Ethelred, it would avail him little.

Olaf had already, it seems, decided that his army was now large enough, loyal enough, and he himself rich enough from his piracy to be able to sustain their loyalty, to pursue what must always have been his ultimate goal, the crown of Norway. His new, monotheistic religion gave him the moral, military and intellectual justification he needed to set about imposing himself as the sole ruler of the Norwegians in the name of Christianity.

Rather like Hastıng in the saga of Rollo of Normandy, it was Earl Håkon's fate to be cast in the Christian-era sagas as the 'bad' Heathen, the better to illuminate the brightness of the Håkon who preceded him, and the near-saintliness of his successor Olaf Tryggvason. Snorri tells us that he had squandered the good-will he earned at Hjörunga-våg by a habit of borrowing other men's wives for his use, and that when Olaf appeared with his army Håkon found few friends ready to back him. Theodoricus Monachus records that, on his way to Norway, Olaf called in at the Orkney Islands and gave firm indication of his resolve by threatening to take the life of Earl Sigurd's three-year-old son before his father's eyes should Sigurd refuse to accept baptism. Theodoricus seemed to approve: 'Just as it is written: "Fill their faces with shame, and they will seek thy name, O Lord", so the earl feared both the righteous wrath of Óláfr and that his son would die.' Yet he also recognized the realities of the Orkney earl's situation: 'So by believing or, rather, by consenting, he was baptized along with all the people who were subject to him.'[40]

In Norway Olaf met and defeated Håkon and his son Erlend in a naval battle in the fjord at Agdenes. Håkon fled and suffered, according to legend, an ignominious death, killed by a slave in the pig-sty in which he had taken refuge. 'As often happens to one sad at heart', writes Theodoricus, 'sleep had stolen upon him.' The victorious Olaf decapitated the dead Håkon, as well as his killer, and a rejoicing crowd threw stones at the heads as they were displayed. Later they set fire to Håkon's body. It was only now, says Snorri, as part of this outpouring of hatred, that people began to call their late ruler 'the Bad' or 'the Evil'.[41]

According to the accepted chronology, Olaf was twenty-seven years old when he was hailed as the new king in Trøndelag.[42] At once he set about the task that had defeated Håkon the Good, and Harald Greycloak and his brothers after him, of converting the country to Christianity. Not for him the subtle and disappointed compromise between cross and hammer: at an early stage of the campaign he herded eighty priests of the old faith, men and women now regarded as sorcerers, into a temple and burnt them along with the images of the gods. Report of the sheer terror inspired by his methods preceded him as he travelled the country. The Trøndelag, a bastion of Norwegian Heathendom, was cowed into acceptance of the new faith. Even those converted by Harald's missionary earls in the Vik had reverted to the old faith and Olaf struggled hard to force them back. The degree of his success in the regions of Nordmøre and Sunnmøre is uncertain, but with the help of his brother-in-law, Erling Skjalgsson, the people of the Gulathing region, from Hordaland down to Sogn, were persuaded to accept Christianity.[43] The men of Hålogoland, the region of Alfred the Great's visitor Ottar, proved particularly recalcitrant and some of Snorri's most extreme tales in the *Heimskringla* of Olaf's determination to succeed centre on events that took place in the far north of the country. Raud, a chieftain from Salten, who has been among the fiercest opponents of Christianity, is finally captured by Olaf's men:

The king had Raud brought before him and told him he should submit to baptism: 'I don't want your property', he told him. 'I would rather be your friend, if you can show yourself worthy of my friendship.' Raud raged against him and said he would never believe in Christ, and he blasphemed wildly.

The king was furious and told Raud he was going to give him the worst death imaginable. He had him tied with his back to a pole, then put a piece of wood between his teeth to wedge his mouth open. He took a snake and tried to force it into Raud's mouth, but Raud blew at it and the snake wouldn't go in. Then the king took a hollow stalk of angelica and put it in Raud's mouth and put the snake into the angelica (some people say he used his horn). He drove it through the angelica with a red-hot iron, and the snake passed into Raud's mouth, down his neck, and bored its way out through his side: Raud lost his life. King Olaf then helped himself to all kinds of gold and silver goods and other costly items, like weapons. He forced all Raud's followers to allow themselves to be baptised. Those who refused he killed or tortured.[44]

Snorri's story might well contain concessions to the idiom of folklore, but it conveys a compelling sense of Olaf's fanatical devotion to his self-appointed task of unifying the country in the name of one religion. The obsession occupied the brief span of his reign so completely that Norway and its people must always have remained a foreign land to him, a man who had spent almost his entire life outside its boundaries.

Olaf seems to have shared Harald Finehair's clear sense that a country settled by so many Norwegians must also logically belong to him, and one of the enterprises of his short reign was the attempt to convert the Icelanders, now over 100 years into their settlement and still to all intents and purposes a Heathen people. The matter struck him as so urgent that after just one year on the throne he had dispatched a missionary bishop named Thangbrand to remedy the state of affairs.[45] This marked the first step in what is probably the most striking and well-documented account of the conversion to Christianity of any of the Viking Age peoples. We shall look at its continuation in a later chapter.

14

Greenland and North America

Although Icelandic society had no executive force to implement the sentences arrived at by the courts, the strong were not always exempt from punishment. Ari the Learned assures readers of the *Book of the Icelanders* that 'many chieftains were convicted or exiled for manslaughter or assault' during the later years of the Saga Age.[1] The fate of Erik the Red, leader of the Viking Age colonists who settled Greenland, is proof that there was substance to Ari's claim.

Erik's father Thorvald had emigrated to Iceland after being outlawed from Norway for some killings. In the early 980s, as a grown man, Erik himself became involved in a feud over the death of some slaves, in the course of which he killed a neighbour, Eyjolf Sauer, and a man known as Hrafn the Dueller.[2] Relatives of Eyjolf took the case to court and Erik was found guilty and sentenced to outlawry. *Grágás* distinguished between three degrees of severity for such a sentence. For the most serious crimes a man might be declared a *skógarmaðr*, literally a 'man of the forest', compelled to live apart in forests and other deserted places. His property was confiscated, none was allowed to shelter him and it was a crime to help him leave the country. Should he manage to do so he was forbidden ever to return. In Iceland he might be killed by anyone without retribution, abroad he might be killed with impunity by any Icelander.[3] For the least of crimes a sentence of *heraðssekt* was passed which entrained exile from a particular district for a period of time. On the presumption that the author of the saga was referring to these laws, it would seem that the court decided Erik's punishment should fall between these two degrees of severity and sentenced him to the Lesser Outlawry, in contrast to the Full Outlawry of the *skógarmaðr*. The conditions of the Lesser

Outlawry were that he pay a fine, leave Iceland within three summers and remain away for another three.[4] Three places where he might live in sanctuary while waiting to leave were indicated to him by the court, each no more than a day's journey from the other. The roads between these places were also his sanctuary, to a distance of a bow-shot from the main track, provided that he did not use them more often than once a month, and on his way to take ship out of the country. Erik left his home at Haukadale in the south of the country and presently settled on the island of Eyxney. Here he became involved in an obscure dispute over personal property which a neighbour had borrowed and failed to return. In the ensuing fight Erik and his party again came out on top. Again the relatives of the men who were killed took them to court and at the assembly at Thorsness Erik and his men were sentenced to the Full Outlawry. Erik at once set about planning to leave the country. As he was getting his ship ready to leave, the relatives of his victims scoured the countryside for him in a bid to kill him before he could get away.

Some seventy years prior to this train of events, a man named Gunnbjørn Ulfsson who had set sail for Iceland from Norway had been driven off course and sighted unknown land in the south-west, to which he gave the name Gunnbjørn's Skerries. These are believed to have been islands off Tasiilaq, on the east coast of Greenland.[5] Other Icelanders before Erik had been tempted to follow up these sightings; some are even said to have made landings on the north-east coast of Greenland, though their names are not recorded and they are not regarded as the European discoverers of the island. Erik sailed from Iceland with the intention of locating this land and possibly settling it, and *Erik's Saga* describes his explorations of its south and south-west coasts over the next three years. Erik's power, or perhaps the status that came with this voyage, seems to have earned him special treatment, for the saga tells us that he then returned to Iceland.[6] He named the island Greenland, according to the saga because 'people would be much more tempted to go there if it had an attractive name'.[7] This was about midway through the Medieval Warm Period, and the relatively mild temperatures in the region and ice-free approaches from the sea will have made the name seem less fanciful than we might now be inclined to suppose.

The Book of the Settlements names ten chieftains whom Erik persuaded of the attractions of the new land, and when the fleet set sail it comprised twenty-five ships. These would in the main have been not longships but *knarrs*, like the Skuldelev 1 ship found in Roskilde fjord, more sturdily built than the warship, with decking fore and aft and around the sides, broad in the beam, high at the stem and stern and with a prow that bent inward. The *knarr* had a large, square sail, but when necessary it could be rowed by oarsmen seated on the fore and after decks. The families, their livestock and possessions would have travelled in the open, central cargo hold which in harsh weather would have been covered in hides for protection. The ships that were used in the colonization of Iceland are known to have lasted well into the tenth century. The timber native to Iceland was not tall enough for the construction of new, large ships, and at least some of the vessels used for the Greenland crossing were probably the patched-up remnants of the fleet that had transported the settlers to Iceland 100 years previously.[8] In good weather the voyage might have taken four days; for a heavily laden armada like this it must have taken considerably longer. Fourteen of the original twenty-five ships completed the journey.

The colonists established themselves in two settlements. The Eastern Settlement, on the southern tip of the island, was the larger of the two, extending from the area around Cape Farewell to Tigssalukfjorden, north of Ivigtut. Erik built himself a farm near the top of what became known as Eiriksfjord (now Tunugdliarfik), to which he gave the name Brattahlid. The name means 'steep slope', though the slope is not notably steep. The smaller Western Settlement was 400 miles further up the west coast, in the Nuuk area around Godthaab (Good Hope) and Lysufjord, where Erik's youngest son Thorstein owned a half-share in a farm. There can have been no shortage of good-quality farming land for such a small group of settlers, so Erik must have had other reasons for encouraging some families to start a second settlement, among them possibly the fact that the more northerly settlement cut the distance to the rich fishing whale- and seal-hunting grounds around Diskos Island by half, providing an obvious benefit for the export trade in walrus ivory, a commodity that became much prized in Europe.[9]

Early written sources put the number of farms in the Eastern Settlement at 190 and in the Western at 90;[10] but by the late twentieth century, the archaeological traces of about 220 farms had been discovered in the larger settlement and about 80 in the smaller.[11] Estimates of the total population during the colony's best years put it at somewhere between 2,000 and 4,000. Government apparatus appears to have been minimal, with local power residing in the chieftains as family heads. The idea of an *althing* or General Assembly was imported from Iceland, and in all likelihood it met at Erik's farm at Brattahlid. While he lived, Erik was the undisputed leader of the colony, and after his death Brattahlid continued to be a site of special authority.

It was at Brattahlid that the first church was built, although not on Erik's initiative. The story told in *Erik's Saga* of Christianity being brought to the island by his son Leif on the instructions of Olaf Tryggvason is probably only a part of the hagiography that grew up around Olaf after his death,[12] but there is otherwise a good correspondence between the information in the saga about this church and the discovery of an ancient cemetery made in 1961 by workmen digging the foundations for a school dormitory on the site who came upon a large number of skulls. Archaeologists took over the site for the next few summers and excavated, in all, the remains of 144 men, women and children from the cemetery. The outlines of a tiny, U-shaped church were also discovered at the centre of the graveyard, 2 metres wide on the inside and 3.5 metres long, with turf-and-timber walls that were over a metre thick. At most there would have been room for a congregation of between twenty and thirty people inside. The saga attributes the building of this church to Erik's wife, Thjodhild, and says that her Christianity was a source of dissension between the couple. Erik was reluctant to abandon his Heathendom, and Thjodhild refused to live with him after she was converted. Her piety, says the saga, 'annoyed him greatly'.[13] The statement that the church at K'agssiarssuk, as Brattahlid is now known, was built 'not too close to the farmstead', was a metaphorical illustration of the split between them which the archaeological evidence reinforces: the remains of Thjodhild's church were found about 200 metres south of the main building on the site that is presumed to have been Erik's farmhouse.

Identifying the sex of the dead and estimating their ages at death posed formidable practical problems, but researchers concluded that a majority of the sixty-nine men were between the ages of thirty and fifty, and that ten of the thirty-nine women were between twenty and thirty and another ten between thirty and fifty. The average height of the men was 171 cm, with several individuals as tall as 185 cm, about the same height as the average Danish male at the time the excavations were undertaken. The average height of the women was 156 cm. Particular interest attached to three bodies found buried close to the church wall. By the tenets of medieval theology these would have been first in line for resurrection when Judgement Day came, and the obvious privilege of their situation has led archaeologists to speculate that they may be the remains of Thjodhild, Erik – a reluctant Christian perhaps, but the founder of the colony – and their son Leif. Only a few of the others had been buried in coffins, perhaps reflecting the scarcity of native timber. The remainder were probably buried in shrouds, in accordance with the basic church requirement that a corpse be not buried naked, though no traces of shrouds were found. By contrast, the clothes of those buried in the cemetery of a later church at Herjolfsnæs that marked the southern limit of the Eastern Settlement, excavated by Poul Nørlund in 1921, had been remarkably well preserved in the frozen earth and provided a unique insight into the daily wear of the Greenland colonists.[14] The find included some thirty gowns, seventeen hoods, five hats and six stockings, woven and not knitted, for the art of knitting had not then been invented.[15]

To the degree to which it was practicable, daily life for the ordinary settler reflected the patterns familiar from Iceland and Norway. Families minded small fields in the vicinity of their homes. Cows, horses, pigs and goats were farmed, and sheep kept for their wool and milk rather than meat. Bear, reindeer, hares and birds were hunted and trapped and whale, walrus and seal hunted at sea. The fjords were fished for cod and salmon. A farm discovered by two hunters in 1990, at the head of a branch of the Ameralik fjord, east of Nuuk and at the heart of the Western Settlement, became the subject of an extensive archaeological excavation that has provided us with a vivid narrative of the everyday life of the tenants. The farm was occupied for some 300 years, from about the middle of the eleventh into the fourteenth century.[16] At a distance of roughly 60 miles from the outer coastline, it was located on the eastern side of a plateau, about 60 metres above sea-level, on a rim of thinly vegetated land some 3 metres above the level of the plateau. A thousand years ago this was wetland and meadow, very amenable to the kind of animal husbandry with which these settlers were familiar. The site was not isolated, with neighbours less than a mile away at Nipaitsoq, a settlement at Sandnes, which could easily be reached by water.[17] This latter was possibly the farm mentioned in the early thirteenth-century *Saga of the Greenlanders* as being part-owned by Erik's youngest son, Thorstein.

Climate variations over the year could range from 25° centigrade in the summer to −50° in the winter, so that maintaining heat was a primary concern of the successive families who lived there. Stone and turf were the materials used for the first house built on the site, with walls that were in places 2 metres thick. Wood was used for interior partitioning, ceiling posts and panelling. Benches ran along the walls on both sides of the main room. The remains of what may have been a cooking pit were found at one gable-end, where the house faced out towards the meadows. It seems this first house was later turned into stabling for animals and that it burnt down not long afterwards.

The buildings that were raised on the site from this time onwards were unique to Greenland, with all the household functions gathered under the one roof. It seems to have sprouted rooms, with new ones being added on as required over the course of time, at right-angles to the main orientation of the house. A total of sixty-three separate rooms have been identified, the results of eight distinct phases of building activity, though only a fraction of them would have existed at any one time. One that contained a fireplace or oven, with three openings to regulate the draught, was identified by the archaeologists as a kitchen. In another, numerous textile fragments, spindle whorls and warp weights, and part of an upright loom suggested that weaving was done there, and a living room was identified from finds associated with eating and housework. Rooms that were abandoned were turned into stabling for the livestock. Roofing was a patchwork of branches, turfs and loose joists held up by wooden posts standing on flat stones, with each room having its own individual covering.

Turf, or a combination of turf and stone, was used for the walls, sometimes with an insulating fill of rubble. Fireplaces were found in many of the rooms, box-shaped structures of flat stone usually built up against a wall next to a door-opening, their bases lined with smaller stones for ease of cleaning. The number of these, by contrast with the single, rectangular, centrally positioned long-fire familiar from excavated Icelandic houses, reflects the continuing battle against the cold. Wood and scrub from the surrounding countryside were important sources of fuel. As these ran low, dried dung was probably used, as well as turf and the blubber of whales, seals and walruses. Rooms were kept small and the ceilings just a fraction above head-height. The warmth from the animals stabled in the surrounding rooms would have been a valuable and much-appreciated source of heat. At some points boards were laid down to make it easier to get about the house, and as leftover food was simply thrown on to the floor archaeologists found plentiful evidence of a thriving world of mice and microfauna below the ripe macroworld of the humans. From personal experience, too, they learnt of the eye-watering smell of ammonia that must have greeted the inhabitants each morning as the sun thawed the upper layer of the permafrost. Some 80 per cent of the heat from an open fireplace literally goes up in smoke, and at times of extreme cold the families must have conditioned themselves to make do with minimal smoke-hole ventilation. Living with these smells and the other discomforts on a daily basis, they would soon have ceased to notice them. Although other farms excavated in the vicinity had bath-houses, no trace of one was found here. One of the earliest of the Eastern Settlement houses, excavated near the modern town of Narsaq, in southern Greenland, actually had its own indoor water-supply and stone-covered sewage system that worked by channelling water seeping down from fields above the house into specially constructed ditches.[18]

The walls of these dwellings have long since vanished, and for all we know there may have been many openings in them to admit light and let out smoke in the winter. But under any circumstances, in the dead of winter, with only about five hours of daylight, houses must have been dark inside. Fireplaces would have been an important light-source, and small carved soapstone lamps that consumed blubber appear to have been used. But the puzzle of how work was done indoors in such conditions, including intricate handiwork like weaving, remains. Poor and failing eyesight must have been at least as common in Viking times as it is today, and it is possible that in former times the dexterity and sensitivity of the hand were greater than the eye and compensated adequately for the disadvantages of darkness or impaired sight.

Despite living lives that seem hardly to distinguish them from animals, the generations who farmed at Ameralik were distinctly and even heroically human. Locks and keys were found, implying a structure of authority in which certain people controlled access to certain things. They also suggest chests that may have been used for seating. No purpose-built chairs were found, but the vertebrae of whale were, and these may well have been used as stools. The most common solution to tired legs, for most people, however, was not chairs but the squatting position. Trousers preserved in Danish and German bogs at Thorsbjerg, Damendorf, Marx-Etzel and Daetgen show a distinctive pattern of strengthened seat construction which supports the idea that squatting was the position of choice, not only for professional craftsmen but for most everyday household and farm work. Narrow-legged and wide across the buttocks, they were without the central seam of modern trousers which would have split under the strain of prolonged squatting, and are a fine example of the way in which Viking Age clothing was purpose-made rather than merely primitive.[19]

Soapstone, horn, reindeer antler, bone and wood were carved to make household items, like the shaped wooden case for sheep-shears found at neighbouring Sandnes,[20] and the high-quality woollen clothing spun by the settlers for their own use also found an export market,[21] as did the spiral tusks of the narwhal, which were traded in the south as the horns of unicorns. Finds of dice and gaming pieces show that in their spare time the home entertainments of these Greenlanders linked them culturally with fellow-Scandinavians as far away as the island of Gotland. There are rare signs of childhood as a separate state too, in the form of tiny, scaled-down copies of soapstone vessels, wooden knives, ships and shoe-lasts, and perhaps it was a child who cut the crude image of a four-legged creature found on a piece of wood. Pieces of wood with names incised in runes tell us that Thor was the name of one member of the community, Bardr of another. A girl called

Björk is immortalized in rare knot-runes carved on the lid of a wooden box, along with a dragon's head and a symmetrically curling plant. Björk may have lived on a neighbouring farm at Austmannadal, where other finds carry her mark. Joel Berglund, one of the archaeologists in charge of the excavation, tells us the box was never finished and wonders whether the lid may be all that remains of a failed love-affair.

Life ceased to be sustainable on 'the farm beneath the sand' sometime in the fourteenth century. The Medieval Warm Period was coming to an end, to be succeeded by a period of sharply falling temperatures that climatologists refer to as the 'Little Ice Age'. As the temperatures fell, the ice sheet advanced and the meadows and wetland around the farm flooded, becoming a heavily sedimented lake that could be used by neither man nor beast. With grazing no longer possible and ready access to fresh water gone, a day came when the last occupants of the farm had to face the inevitable and pack up and leave. The skeleton of a goat found beneath a collapsed wall suggests that the animals were abandoned. Ice presently made access to the south and south-west coast of Greenland difficult for ships from Iceland and Norway, and as these vital lines of contact began to fracture the colonies suffered. The Western Settlement was the more exposed of the two in regard to the climate change; it was also the first natural target for the nomadic Thule-culture Eskimos of the north as the cold drove them southward down the coastline. Rumour reached the inhabitants of the Eastern Settlement that the sister colony had been attacked and that it was occupied by Eskimos, and in about 1350 a small force under a Norwegian named Ivar Bardarson sailed up the coast to investigate the situation. When he reached the Western Settlement he found no sign of either colonists or invaders, and the cattle, goats, sheep and horses living wild. Thirty years later, in 1379, the *Icelandic Annals* noted an attack on the Eastern Settlement by Eskimos, whom the Scandinavians called 'Skrellings': 'The Skrellings attacked the Greenlanders, killed eighteen of them, and carried off two boys, whom they made slaves.'[22] This notice may have been the inspiration for a papal letter of 1448, attributed to Nicholas V but of questionable authenticity, which refers to incidents 'about thirty years ago when, God permitting it, a barbarous and pagan fleet from neighbouring shores invaded the island'. Having destroyed the settlement, they 'led captive to their shores the unfortunate inhabitants of both sexes, and more particularly those who seemed best able to bear the hardships of servitude and tyranny'. According to the letter, many of these managed to escape and make their way back to the colony, which they tried to rebuild. The papal letter, addressed to two Icelandic bishops, requested that the bishops ascertain whether the stories were true and, if so, to provide pastoral care for them. A second papal letter, written by Alexander VI in about 1495, also expressed concern about the spiritual life of the Greenlanders and noted in passing that 'no vessel has touched there during the past eighty years'. The pope referred to the rumours that, during that time, 'many who were formerly Catholics have forgotten the faith of their baptism, and that no memory of the Christian religion is found, except a corporal, which is shown to the people once a year'.[23] There is no record of either letter resulting in a journey to Greenland. In 1585 an Englishman, John Davis, reached the west coast of Greenland but found no Europeans there. The *Gottskalk's Annals*, Icelandic annals kept by the priest Gottskalk Jónsson in the sixteenth century, are believed to have been based on a now lost set of annals up to the year 1394, after which its entries became Gottskalk's own formulations based on diplomas and oral memories.[24] To these later years of the annals belongs an entry recording that the colonists '*ad Americae populos se converterunt*'. Over the years this statement has excited dramatic speculations and theories involving a full-scale emigration of the remaining colonists to North America where, willingly or otherwise, they became absorbed by North American Indian tribes. But *Americae* is an obvious anachronism, and Gottskalk more likely intended to convey only that, under pressure, the settlers finally abandoned their religion and their pretensions to European civilization and reverted to Heathendom, becoming like the peoples of America, by which term he meant the Inuit. In the early years of the last century Vilhjalmur Stefansson, the Icelandic explorer and anthropologist, advanced a theory, on the basis of personal observation of the Cooper Inuit of Cambridge Bay in Nunavut, that interbreeding had taken place between the Inuit and the Norse. However, DNA testing on saliva samples from 350 Inuit from Greenland and the Cambridge Bay area, carried out in 2002 by Gisli Palsson and Agnar Helgason of the University of Iceland, failed to reveal anything which might have supported the theory.[25]

The archaeological evidence bearing on contacts of any kind between the Norse settlers and the Eskimos is sparse and hard to interpret. Norse materials have been found at Inuit sites throughout Greenland, but whether the material arrived there as a result of wars, plundering, trading or even looting from a Greenland ship crushed in the ice is impossible to say. In the far north-west of the island, sites that were occupied in the twelfth or thirteenth centuries have turned up a gaming piece, a fragment of chain mail, a piece of woollen cloth and the leg of a metal cooking pot, as well as the inevitable comb. Another site on the east side of Ellesmere Island yielded a similar clutch of material finds, while the recent discovery of a hinged bronze bar from a folding balance, at a site on the island's western side, is similar to finds made in the footsteps of traders across the Viking Age world, and a hint that relations between the two cultures were not necessarily always fraught.[26] In its way, the discovery of this sophisticated piece of technology is as evocative and thought-provoking as that of the wooden bearing-dial, found in 1948 at Uunartoq fjord, near the Eastern Settlement, during the excavation of a Benedictine convent which turned out to have been built on the site of a house from the settlement period.[27] Another enigmatic find is that of a small figure, carved in walrus ivory in a style typical of Thule Inuit art of the time and found at a thirteenth-century site on southern Baffin Island, on the North American side of the Davis Strait. The figure wears a tunic of unmistakably European design, and the incision of what looks like a cross on the chest suggests an attempt to depict a priest or bishop. Another possibility is that it represents a woman in her work-clothes; European men and women of the period wore very similar clothing, making any more definite identification of the figure problematic.[28]

In 1858 the Danish geographer Hinrich Rink collected a number of Inuit folk-tales and beliefs concerning the Norse colonists from Danish missionaries who had been to Greenland and found Inuit living among the abandoned farmsteads. One of the most substantial describes the motiveless killing of two Greenlanders by an Eskimo at Kakortok, or

Julianehåb, in the south-west of the island. The murders ignite the chain of revenge and counter-revenge familiar from saga literature, and the story ends with the killing of Ungortok, the chief of the *kavdlunakker*, as the Eskimos called the settlers.[29] Ungortok may be an Inuit approximation of the Norse name 'Ingvar'. Another of the tales collected by Rink reads like a version of the slaving raid, referred to in Pope Nicholas V's letter. It describes how large ships of unknown provenance appeared suddenly in the Greenland fjords. The nomadic Inuit were able to hide from them, not so the Norse in their fjordside farmsteads. The raids may be associated with the explorations of the Greenland coast known to have been carried out by a Portuguese explorer and slaver named Joao Fernandes in about 1500. Fernandes had business connections with Bristol, and Bristol had respectable trading links with Iceland in the early and middle years of the fifteenth century. However, English pirates and slavers from Hull and Bristol are known to have raided in Iceland in the first half of the fifteenth century, and some unrecorded pirate fleet may well have been active in Greenland and made its contribution in this way to the disappearance of this Scandinavian foothold in the Arctic.

The King's Mirror, that handbook of advice and knowledge which we consulted earlier for its descriptions of some of the natural phenomena of the populated Arctic north, puts in the mouth of the omniscient Father a neat summary of the immense difficulties faced by the Greenland settlers:

But in Greenland it is this way, as you probably know, that whatever comes from other lands is high in price, for this land lies so distant from other countries that men seldom visit it. And everything that is needed to improve the land must be purchased abroad, both iron and all the timber used in building houses.[30]

The reference in this thirteenth-century source to their having to buy even the timber with which to build their houses sounds an oblique epitaph for the demise of what was, along with the adventures among the tribes of the Volga and the Arabs of the Iberian peninsula, among the most surprising of Viking Age adventures: the apparent attempt to extend the Greenland colony across the Davis Strait and into North America. It may have been the activities of hunters working far to the north of the Western Settlement, north of Disko Island in the area they called Nordsetre, that first excited the notion of crossing the waters of the Davis Strait to see what lay on the other side. That hunters did penetrate this far north would seem to be indicated by the find of a rune-stone on the island of Kingigtorssuaq, at Upernavik, 200 miles north of Disko. The inscription is little more than the familiar announcement of a presence, and six enigmatic runes that have never satisfactorily been interpreted and may only be a recording of the date.[31] Hunters following the summer ice drifting from the north and the walrus that used it would presently reach a point at which the narrow Davis Strait was further narrowed by the accumulation of drift-ice. Following the walrus through open water along the curve of this ice would have driven the hunters west, to a point at which Baffin Island on the other side of the water was visible.

From excavations carried out recently under Patricia Sutherland of the Canadian Museum of Civilization at a site near the present-day trading post of Kimmikut in southern Baffin Island, evidence has emerged to suggest that Europeans – perhaps hunters like these – may have crossed these waters many years prior to the date of about 1000 traditionally given for the first such crossing to North America. The finds include a small carved wooden mask with a long and possibly bearded face, yarn spun from the fur of the arctic hare, and notched tally-sticks. As neither yarn nor wood was part of Inuit culture at the time, these have been identified as of Scandinavian origin. Though the rat was not native to the Arctic, microscopic amounts of rat droppings found at the Kimmikut site may also attest to the presence there of Scandinavians, with the first results of radio-carbon analysis of samples of rat-hairs indicating that this was some 75 to 100 years before 1000.[32]

The dating and interpretation of these finds remains provisional, however, and the established history of the North American adventure is based on literary sources in the form of two sagas, the *Saga of the Greenlanders* and the *Saga of Erik the Red*, known together as 'the Vinland sagas' and both written over 200 years after the events they describe. The story begins with an account of a voyage from Iceland

made in about 985 by a man named Bjarni Herjolfsson to see his
father in Greenland. Bjarni drifted off course in thick fog and found
himself well to the south of his intended goal. Tacking back northward, he sailed past what had seemed to him three new and unknown
lands, upon each of which he single-mindedly refused to land on the
grounds that they were not Greenland.[33] The *Saga of the Greenland-*
ers, believed to be the older of the two, describes five expeditions to
the new lands in the west, one of which failed to arrive. In this account,
the first person to see the new lands after Bjarni Herjolfsson was Erik
the Red's son, Leif, who carried out the first dedicated journey of
discovery some fifteen years after Bjarni's sighting, with further explorations being carried out by other members of Leif's family.

The *Saga of Erik the Red* conflates all the journeys into a single,
full-scale adventure, under the leadership of Thorfinn Karlsefni and
his wife Gudrid, with Leif's role reduced to that of the initial and
accidental discoverer. The Icelander Ólafur Halldórsson is one of a
number of modern scholars who find in the *Saga of Erik the Red* clear
traces of the genealogical obsession of the era, which led the author
to promote Thorfinn as the discoverer of Vinland in order to enhance
the prestige of his descendants, and in particular to strengthen the
campaign for the canonization in the thirteenth century of a direct
descendant of the couple, Bishop Björn Gilsson.[34] Other differences
of detail and focus between the two sagas seem to have been made on
literary grounds, or possibly as a result of new sources of information
coming to light.[35] Hauk Erlendsson, in his fourteenth-century redaction of the *Saga of Erik the Red*, is known to have altered a number
of details in his version, including the sailing directions given in
Chapter 8 of the saga, and it is hardly possible to know whether his
reasons were political, literary or even practical.

Three distinct regions of the journey southwards after the crossing
of the Davis Strait were named by the explorers, each reflecting the
topography and to some extent also the economic value to them of
the region. The first was Helluland, which translates as something like
'land of rocky slabs', and was clearly the large and barren Baffin
Island. Sailing past the southern tip of the island, the first site of
practical interest to the explorers in their search for timber and iron
would be Ungava Bay, in the north-east corner of Labrador, a densely

forested region of black spruce and larch that marked the beginning of the vast Markland. Following the coastline brought the explorers to the Strait of Belle Isle, with land visible on both sides for the first time as they slipped through the 18-km-wide channel between Labrador and Newfoundland that brought them into the Gulf of St Lawrence. Where the idea of Markland ended and Vinland began is unclear, but the Gulf forms an almost self-enclosed sea and following its coastline would have brought the explorers back to their starting point, in the Strait of Belle Isle.[36] It was here, on the north-eastern tip of Newfoundland, that they established the settlement at L'Anse aux Meadows, which remains the only authenticated Viking Age settlement site discovered in North America.[37]

The suggestion that the Vinland of the sagas was L'Anse aux Meadows was made as early as 1914 by a Newfoundlander, W. A. Munn; but it was not until 1960 that the Norwegians Helge and Stine Ingstad located a likely site and began the excavations that presently unearthed what were indisputably the remains of a Norse settlement. Scholars were long of the opinion that the site could not be the Vinland of the sagas; but with the gradual revelation of its full extent and of the resources that would have been required to construct it, this has changed and the identification is now widely, though not universally, accepted.[38] Among the more persuasive factors are modern estimates that the three residential halls unearthed could have provided living accommodation for between seventy and ninety people. With a population at this early stage of no more than about 500, this represented a sizeable proportion of the colony's human resources. Estimates based on the modern reconstruction of the site indicate that a workforce of about sixty men would have needed about two months to build the three houses, and it seems unlikely that a fledgling settlement like Greenland could have afforded the manpower and the time necessary to build and maintain more than one such site.

About a third of the 150 radio-carbon dates for the L'Anse aux Meadows site are connected to the period of Norse settlement there, dating it between 980 and 1020. Three houses, two of which were on the scale of the largest halls of Icelandic *goði*, were built on a terrace about 100 metres up from the shoreline and looking eastward across Epaves Bay. A stream now named Black Duck Brook meandered

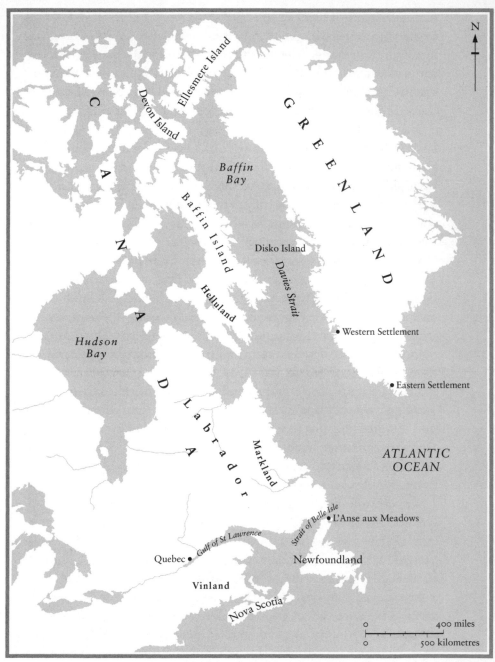

N

The Greenland colonists in North America, with the site of the excavated settlement at L'Anse Aux Meadows.

across in front of them on its way to the sea. On the far side of the brook the remains of a charcoal pit kiln identifies the location of the community's smithy, which seems largely to have been employed in the manufacture of iron nails: eighty-one fragments were found in the vicinity of a small building on the eastern side of the northernmost house of the settlement, where repairs to the boats were carried out.

The houses were built of turf, with timber roofs which could not have been expected to last more than twenty or at the most thirty years in the wet coastal climate, and they show no signs of having been repaired.[39] The explorers brought cattle with them, but neither barns nor stabling were found, perhaps another indication that this was not intended as a permanent settlement but rather as a base for the preparation and forwarding of timber for the homeland.

The *Saga of the Greenlanders* refers to just one Vinland camp, Leifsbudir, or Leif's camp. The *Saga of Erik the Red* names two, Straumfjord, or Fjord of currents, and Hóp, or small and land-locked bay. Birgitta Wallace, an archaeologist who worked on the site for many years, identifies Straumfjord as the L'Anse aux Meadows site, with Hóp as the summer camp well to the south, too small and too infrequently occupied to leave any significant archaeological trace. On the strength of the find of white walnuts within Norse wood-working waste at the main site, she locates Hóp somewhere below the northern limit for this tree, specifically in north-east New Brunswick, which also defines the northern limit of the grape-vines for which the explorers named the region. Wallace is able to explain the name by pointing to the high status of wine in the north in the Viking Age. For Leif and his family to have access to their own supply of grapes was a development that must have been as surprising as it was welcome.

But they were not left in peace to enjoy these luxuries. The sagas describe the souring of relationships between the Norsemen and the local inhabitants, a tribe of native Americans encountered at Hóp, whom they also referred to as 'Skrellings'. Modern research identifies them as the ancestors of the Beothuk and the Mi'kmaq, tribes whose fascination with the colour red the Greenlanders were able to exploit in trading furs for red woollen cloth. Mutual suspicion and cultural misunderstandings were rife, however, and fighting broke out. Men were killed on both sides. For the colonists, life itself was the most dangerously scarce of all their resources and, rather than risk significant and irreplaceable losses, they withdrew and made their way back to the base at Straumfjord. It was probably the realization of how thickly ringed around with hostile neighbours these as well as any future settlements were going to be that put an end to the Greenlanders' attempts to establish themselves on the new continent. The possibility of making their own wine may have been attractive, but only timber was a necessity of life.

Markland had it in plentiful supply. It was closer and without the disadvantage of a population of hostile natives, and there can be little doubt that the trip across the Davis Strait to Ungava Bay to cut timber and gather bog-iron for use in the Greenland smithies was made with such regularity that it was no longer considered worthy of further note by those keepers of the Icelandic record who made occasional notes of events concerning their neighbours. Recent finds at the late culture layer of the 'farm beneath the sand' of the hair of bison and brown or black bears, neither of which is indigenous to Greenland, suggest the colonists may also have hunted across the water.[40] The Icelanders, it seems, were interested in Greenlandic affairs primarily where these directly involved themselves. The only further references in their annals to crossings of the Davis Strait are the report that an Icelandic-born bishop of Greenland set off to look for Vinland in 1121, with what result we are not told; and the entry for 1347 regarding a small ship with a crew of seventeen or eighteen Greenlanders carrying timber from Markland back to Greenland which had been driven off course and landed in Iceland. The narrowed focus seems to show that a sense of something akin to national identity had arisen among the Icelanders. We have no way of knowing whether their neighbours in the west ever had time to cultivate such a luxury, before the extinction of the colony. Probably not. Probably life was simply too hard, too desperate to allow of it. A wooden crucifix, found beneath a bench during excavations on a farm at the head of Austmannadalen in the Western Settlement, depicts not the strutting and muscular Christ Triumphant characteristic of much early Viking Age Christianity, but a mournful, emaciated, suffering Christ, slumped on the cross. In conception and execution it is as far removed from the Jelling stone as could be imagined, and it makes apt symbolic comment on the harsh fate endured by these Norse Greenlanders.

15

Ragnarök in Iceland

The *Book of Settlements* names several baptized Norwegians among the first settlers in Iceland: Helgi the Lean, Orlyg the Old, Helgi Bjola, Jorund the Christian (a woman), Aud the Deep-minded (also a woman), and Ketil the Fool. These remained Christians for the rest of their lives. Once they were gone, it seems that their children reverted to the old beliefs and resumed the practices of sacrificing to Odin and Thor. There were Christian Icelanders, not least among the wives and slaves, many of whom were from Christian communities in the British isles, but for a long time Christianity remained a minority culture. The religion began making dramatic inroads into Denmark and the Scandinavian peninsula during the second half of the tenth century, and in the final two decades its austere demands began to sound with some urgency in Iceland.

Among ordinary Icelanders, Thor was probably the most popular of the gods, and it was to Thor that Heathens looked as their champion in the hardening struggle to resist Christianity. In many ways this was a war of words, with poetry playing a prominent part in the campaigns. Heathen poets impugned the manhood of the Christians, and Christian poets mocked the Heathens for their superstition and stupidity. The first missionaries to preach the gospel in Iceland were a Saxon bishop named Fredrik and a native convert and former Viking known as Thorvald the Far-Traveller. On an occasion when Thorvald and Fredrik were preaching in the west of the country, a priestess named Fridgerd enacted a sacrificial ceremony within hearing distance of the two. Thorvald captured his disappointment in verse:

I preached the precious faith,
no man paid heed to me;
we got scorn from the sprinkler
– priest's son – of blood-dipped branch.
And without any sense,
old troll-wife against poet
– may God crush the priestess –
shrilled at the heathen altar.[1]

Though they allocated Thorvald the active and less shameful position in putative acts of male sexual intercourse involving Bishop Fredrik, the *nid* verses composed about him had so provoked Thorvald that he killed two of his tormentors, for which he was outlawed and driven from Iceland. We should not, however, rule out the possibility that this proof of a vigorous sense of personal honour in a convert made men more respectful of Christianity, lessening the view of it as an alien, perverse and remote faith.

Kristni Saga, a history of the introduction to Iceland of Christianity, written by an unknown author and dated by most scholars to the mid-thirteenth century, identifies Thorvald as a companion of Olaf Tryggvason, and says that Olaf dispatched him on the mission, at about the same time as he claimed the throne of Norway and began his attempts to impose Christianity on the people. The *Ágrip* credits Olaf with the conversion of Norway, Iceland, Shetland, Orkney and the Faroes. Later and unreliable sources imply his involvement in the conversions of Denmark, Greenland and the Kievan state.[2] As a Christian and a monarch, Olaf could consider himself a modern man twice over. A country without a king, a Heathen commonwealth, Iceland was, by contrast, an anomaly twice over, and Olaf saw himself as its natural corrective. There is a literary demonstration that this was a modern way of thinking in a *tháttr* called *The Tale of Thorvald Chatterbox*, in which Olaf Tryggvason entrusts the eponymous hero with the task of converting an obstinate Heathen chieftain named Bård the Stout to Christianity. When Bård has finally accepted the king's faith he sums up what has happened to him: 'I don't trust any idol or devil. I've gone from one country to another and met both giants and black men, and they none of them got the better of me; so I have long trusted in my own strength and ability (*trúa á matt ok megin*).' 'I've thought myself very self-sufficient up to now,' he adds. 'I've served neither kings nor other noblemen. But now I want to become your man, king, and follow you as long as I live.'[3] This was the model of kingship created 200 years earlier by Charlemagne, and it had become the standard model. Harald Finehair had hoped to make Iceland into an earldom under the Norwegian crown and, as his candidate for the title, backed Uni, son of the Gardar who was one of the first discoverers of Iceland. Olaf's interest in Iceland was essentially an updating of this political ambition in the name of Christianity.

Olaf next sent an Icelander named Stefnir to preach the gospel in Iceland. Stefnir's was a muscular brand of Christianity. Once he realized that persuasion was not working he turned to violence, riding about the countryside with his band of men and destroying temples and places of worship and idols. The Heathens gathered against him and he took refuge with his family at Kjalarness. During the winter his ship was badly damaged in a storm. The delighted followers of the old gods interpreted this as a sign that the Aesir did not wish Christ and his followers well:

> Now Stefnir's prow-falcon (sea
> streams through the hollow ship)
> is by fierce mountain flurry –
> fell weather – entirely destroyed.
> But we must believe that – bonds
> must be in our land – such roaring
> (the river rages with ice)
> is ruled by the Aesir's power.[4]

A scholarium in Adam of Bremen's *Gesta Hammaburgensis* notes that '*Apud illos non est rex, nisi tantum lex*' ('Among them there is no king, there is only the law'), and it is some indication of their alarm at Christianity's intolerant nature that, in a direct response to Stefnir's activities, the Icelanders now turned to the law to discourage the fanaticism of the followers of the religion.[5] The new legislation was known as *frændaskömm*, meaning something like 'relation-shame', and it required a legal response to blasphemy that covered the damaging and dishonouring of sacred sites and images. Prosecution was mandatory. First refusal fell to those relatives of the accused who were closer than fourth cousins but more distant than second cousins, a condition that reinforced the principal responsibility of the family for the conduct of its individual members. At a practical level the stipulation ensured that, in the event of a conviction, the property of the blasphemer would remain within the family. The legislation thus underlined the role of the private and the familial in preserving the structure of Heathen society, in contrast to a centralizing and anti-individualizing tendency in Christianity that was well illustrated by the Church's insistence that the dead be buried in public, church ground and not in private, family ground. Stefnir was prosecuted by members of his own family under the new legislation and sentenced to leave the country.[6] Although there is no record of his having converted or even prime-signed anyone, his activities had inflicted further damage to the status of the religious traditions in Iceland.

Olaf sponsored a third mission, under a turbulent and self-willed Saxon named Thangbrand. Thangbrand was temperamentally similar to Thorvald, and allowed himself to be similarly provoked by verbal attacks. *Kristni Saga* tells us that numerous poets composed and broadcast offensive verse about him.[7] Thangbrand killed one of them, Vetrlidi, as he was out cutting turf with his servants. Another, named Thorvald the Weak, was killed at Grimnes, in the south-west of the country. Thangbrand was outlawed that summer at the *Althing*. The weather prevented his first attempt to leave and he had to spend the winter in the west. He and his men were ostracized. The Heathens refused to trade with them, and they were driven to taking food by force and leaving behind payment for it. This was reported as theft, and a fight followed in which eight Heathens and two of Thangbrand's men were killed. Another attempt to leave was thwarted when Thangbrand's ship was carried out to sea and badly damaged, occasioning a second verse in which the weather was seen as an agent of the Aesir's displeasure at the Christian presence. Thor was specifically credited with raising the storm in a verse by a woman poet named Steinun:

Thor drew Thvinnill's animal,
Thangbrand's long ship, from land,
shook the prow's horse and hit it,
and hurled it against the sand.
On sea the ski of Atall's land
Will not swim henceforth,
For a harsh tempest sent by him
Has hewn it into splinters.

Before the bell's keeper (bonds
Destroyed the beach's falcon)
The slayer of giantess-son
Broke the ox of seagull's place.
Christ was not watching, when
The wave-raven drank at the prows.
Small guard I think God held
– if any – over Gylfi's reindeer.[8]

Ari tells us that when Thangbrand at last got away and returned to Trondheim, he told king Olaf that it was 'beyond all expectation that Christianity might yet be accepted here'.[9] Due to what Theodoricus Monachus calls 'the innate obduracy and savage nature of the inhabitants', he had made only a small number of converts during the two years of his mission.[10] Among them, however, were four very influential chieftains: Hall of Sida; Gizur the White; Gizur's son-in-law, Hjalti Skjeggjason; and Thorgils of Ölfus.[11] The furious king ordered the detention of all Icelanders in Trondheim, confiscating their property and issuing threats to have them killed or disfigured. It seems that Gizur and Hjalti somehow got wind of what was happening and made the journey over from Iceland. They urged the king to stay his hand and to let them make a fresh attempt to convert their people. They pointed out that Thangbrand had killed men, and that his behaviour and demeanour were hard to accept from a foreigner. Being natives, they assured the king, they would have a better chance of success. Gizur was Olaf's second cousin, and the family connection no doubt added weight to his plea that his fellow-countrymen in Norway be not held to account for the conservatism of Icelanders in Iceland. Olaf agreed to let them lead another attempt, but as insurance he held on to four hostages, one from each of the Icelandic Quarter districts. All four were related to leading chieftains.

Accompanied by a priest named Thormod, Gizurr and his party set off for Iceland the following summer, in June 999, in time to attend the *althing* meeting at Thingvellir at the end of the month.[12] They landed first on the Westmann Islands off the south-west coast of Iceland before proceeding to Landeyjar on the mainland. They had a journey of about 100 kilometres in front of them. At first they had to make their way along the coast on foot, for this was the territory of the *goði* Runolf, a chieftain whose name occurs in several sources as among those most passionately opposed to the introduction of Christianity, and none of his *thingmen* would sell them horses. Not until they reached Háfr, in the area around Holt, where Hjalti's brother-in-law lived, were they able to ride. Travelling on from there, they joined a number of other Christians heading for the annual assembly.

At the *althing* the previous year, Hjalti had been convicted of blasphemy and outlawed for declaiming a verse about Freyja from the Lawrock:

> I don't mean to mock the gods,
> but Freyja seems to me a bitch.

There was no point in the party advertising its contempt for the legislations of a lawful assembly, and Hjalti was persuaded to stay behind with a small group of men at a place called Laugardal. Gizur and the others continued their journey. At their overnight lakeside camp they received word that their opponents would prevent them, by force if necessary, from entering the assembly grounds, and so sent a message to their supporters at Thingvellir asking them to ride out to meet them. The headstrong Hjalti decided that the issue was so momentous it justified breaking the law anyway, and he and his men rejoined Gizur.

The Christians reached the assembly site at Thingvellir. With a convicted outlaw among them, the provocation could hardly have been greater. The tension was so great, says Ari, that 'it came so close to a fight that no one could tell how things would work out'.[13] It was perhaps at this point that the Heathen leaders learnt that King Olaf was holding hostages, for, as the complexity of the situation became apparent, the tension lessened sufficiently overnight for Gizur and Hjalti to make their way to the Lawrock the following day and deliver speeches to the crowd gathered on the grassy slope below.

It was the prelude to a day of extraordinary and intricate drama. After Gizur and Hjalti had finished saying what they had to say a procession of men, Christian and Heathen, approached the Lawrock, named witnesses, and declared that they would not live under the same set of laws as each other. Political and social chaos beckoned. Some of the Christians asked Hall of Sida to be their Lawspeaker, and to devise a separate law code for them. Hall declined and passed the request on to the assembly's elected Lawspeaker, Thorgeir Ljosvetnin-gagodi. Hall offered him a sum of money as a fee, presumably the funds provided for the party by its sponsor, King Olaf. In effect, Thorgeir was being asked to set up a separate law code that would have required a separate assembly with its own, Christian, hallowing rituals, so that two communities of faith could carry on separate but parallel lives. Presumably some kind of physical division of the land into separate administrative communities was also envisaged.[14]

Thorgeir was the grandson of a settler from Rogaland, in the west of Norway.[15] He had three wives, by whom he had fathered nine sons and one daughter. He also had two sons outside marriage, one of whom was known as Finni the Dreamwise, well known for his gift of second sight.[16] Thorgeir had been the Icelanders' Lawspeaker for some fifteen years, since 985, and was almost certainly the finest legal mind in the country. He agreed to give the matter his full consideration and made his way back to his booth, as the summer shelters that housed those in attendance at the *althing* were known. Inside, he lay down. Both Ari and the author of *Kristni Saga* tell us, with peculiar precision, that he spread his cloak over his head, and remained in this position for the next twenty-four hours. While he lay thus, tensions flared again. Thorgeir was not a Christian, but to the Heathens this was not in itself enough to ensure a decision in their favour, and they determined to make a major sacrifice to the gods, offering two people from each of the Quarters. The Christians, with Hjalti taking the lead, took the moral high ground by offering to improve on the gesture. In a passage sometimes used to suggest that human sacrifice was in fact a disguised form of capital punishment, *Kristni Saga* reports Hjalti's words to his fellow believers:

Heathens sacrifice the worst people, and push them over cliffs and crags; but we shall make our selection on the basis of people's virtues and call it a victory offering to our Lord Jesus Christ. We must therefore lead better lives and be more careful to avoid sin than before, and Gizur and I will come forward as the victory offering for our Quarter.[17]

It may have been only an exchange of words, for as the story proceeds we hear no more of sacrificing. In the morning, Thorgeir emerged from his booth and sent word that people should gather below the Lawrock to hear what he had to say. There is a temptation to regard the reproduction of direct speech in an early medieval history as a sign of literary invention. What Thorgeir had to say, however, was so momentous that parts of his speech may well have been memorized by some who heard it, and passed on to succeeding generations. In this case anyway it seems churlish to suspect the authenticity of Ari's account:

He began his speech, and said that he thought people's affairs had come to a bad pass, if they were not all to have the same law in this country, and tried to persuade them in many ways that they should not let this happen, and said it would give rise to such discord that it was certainly to be expected that fights would take place between people by which the land would be laid waste. [. . .] 'And it now seems advisable to me,' he said, 'that we too do not let those who most wish to oppose each other prevail, and let us arbitrate between them, so that each side has its own way in something, and let us all have the same law and the same religion. It will prove true that if we tear apart the law, we will also tear apart the peace.' And he brought his speech to a close in such a way that both sides agreed that everyone should have the same law, the one he decided to proclaim. It was then proclaimed in the laws that all people should be Christian, and that those in this country who had not yet been baptised should receive baptism; but the old laws should stand as regards the exposure of children and the eating of horse-flesh. People had the right to sacrifice in secret, if they wished, but it would be punishable by the lesser outlawry if witnesses were produced.[18]

Thorgeir was a Heathen, and Heathens were in a majority in the land, and we can only suppose that his words were greeted with a stunned silence by most of those present. Yet his decision was accepted, and a mass baptism took place before the assembly broke up. Most are said to have submitted to the ceremony in the cold waters of the Öxará river that traverses the assembly site, but in what may have been a show of displeasure the people of the Northern and Southern Quarters postponed their immersion until they reached the hot springs at Reykjalaug, in Laugardalr. The author of *Kristni Saga* duly records the baptism of the Heathen diehard Runolf, whose son was among the hostages being held by King Olaf. Runolf was probably the moving spirit behind the *frændaskömm* legislation, and is named in some sources as the man who prosecuted the case against Hjalti Skjeggjason for the blasphemy against Freyja.[19] Hjalti's pleasure at his discomfiture is evident in the words attributed to him when Runolf's turn came: 'Now we're teaching the old *goði* to nibble on the salt,' he reportedly said, referring to the practice of placing salt on the tongue as part of the ceremony.

Northern Heathendom had an end-time which was called Ragnarök, or 'the fate of the gods'. Snorri describes it in some detail in the *Glyfaginning* section of *The Prose Edda*. Synthesizing detail from 'The Seeress's Prophecy', 'The Sayings of the High One', 'Vafthrudnir's Sayings' and 'Grimnir's Sayings' from *The Poetic Edda*, he tells us of the belief that it would be announced by the Fimbulvinter or 'terrible winter', three years of catastrophic snowfall, wind and frost separated from each other by summers of black sunlight that brought no respite. Abandoning all hope, the inhabitants of Midgard would surrender to greed, incest and civil war. At the climax of this long and dreadful night the enemies of the Aesir, the forces of chaos which they had for so long succeeded in containing, would finally burst from their restraints: Midgardsormen, the great world-encircling serpent, would come lunging out of the ocean, dragging the tides in over the land behind it and flooding the world. The giant wolf Fenrir, one of Loki's monstrous offspring with the giantess Angerboda, whose destiny is connected with the idea of swallowing the sun, and who has been captured and bound by a chain forged by dwarves from the incorporeal things of the world, like the breath of the fish, the sound made by a cat in motion and the roots of a mountain, will break free and fulfil his destiny. The frost-giants will arrive on board a ship made from the uncut fingernails of the dead. In a last act of betrayal, Loki will be at the helm. The skies will open, and the fire-giant Surt and his hordes come flaming forth across the heavenly bridge called Bifrost. These furious and violent forces will seek together and head for the plain called Vigrid with the single and consuming aim of wiping out the gods. Heimdall, the watchman of the Aesir, will sound a great warning blast on his horn, at which the gods and every fallen warrior whom Odin ever called to join him in Valhalla will ride to Vigrid to face them in a last great battle to preserve the world, even knowing they are predestined to fail. Odin, wearing a golden helmet and carrying his spear Gungnir, takes on the wolf Fenrir. Close beside him Thor with his hammer fights against the world-serpent that he once so nearly caught in an earlier adventure, when he cast his fishing-line into the ocean using a bull's head as bait, and the serpent took the bait. Frey confronts Surt, Heimdall faces Loki. Thor kills the serpent but is himself mortally wounded by its venom. He staggers away nine paces, collapses and dies. Heimdall and Loki kill each other. The wolf swallows Odin, the fire-giant Surt disposes of Frey and then spreads fire across the earth until everything is consumed and the light vanishes. But in an elegiac coda Snorri describes how the sun returns, and reveals that not all the gods were killed, nor every human being either. Life and worship start up again, but this time the world is repopulated by a just and happy generation whose goodness is to be rewarded by the coming of 'the mighty god from on high, who is ruler of all'.[20] This coda, with its prediction of the advent of a single and omnipotent god, is one of several places at which the story is coloured by ideas of the imminence of Judgement Day, an apocalyptic mood that was especially prevalent in Christian culture in the years 1000 and 1033. The prophecy also shows the influence of Christian thought in recognizing the link between cause and effect, and an ethical acceptance of the relationship between guilt and punishment.

A recent theory suggests that the myths of the Fimbulvinter and Ragnarök may have historical origins in a huge volcanic eruption, at an unknown location but recorded in ice-core analysis from the

Antarctic in the form of a distinct layer of sulphate dated to 533–534 plus/minus two years. Though the Byzantine historian Procopius does not mention the eruption itself, there may be a literary echo of it in his *De Bello Vandalico* or the *Vandal War*, where he relates that in 536 'a remarkable wonder was observed, for throughout this whole year the sun shone like the moon, with no radiance, as though in perpetual eclipse, its light feeble and not at all as normal. With this phenomenon came war, hunger and other mortal threats.' Tree-ring analysis from the Scandinavian countries reflects the onset of a dramatic short-term change in the climate at about this time. The long near-eclipse, which was also recorded in China, lasted until the autumn of 537, and it has been related to the striking increase in the number of gold hoards buried across the Scandinavian north in the middle of the sixth century, with the suggestion that these were offerings made to placate the gods and bring release from the frightening and unnatural absence of a summer. The Fimbulvinter of 536–537 was followed by a decade of relatively cold summers and the pandemic of the Justinian plague of 541–542, which is estimated to have wiped out half the population of Europe. It is not hard to see how memories of this dreadful time, and the fear of its return, might have been passed down through the generations and evolved in folk-memory into the potent myth of Ragnarök, in which the decimation of the population of Europe was recast as the death of all but two of the inhabitants of Midgard, a woman named Life and a man named Leifthrasir ('tenacious of life'), in an apocalyptic war that pitted the gods of Asgard against the forces of hostile natural chaos, symbolized in the myth by the sun-eating wolf Fenrir and the fire-hurling giant Surt, along with their company of giants, monsters and serpents, in which the gods were almost – but not quite – wiped out.[21]

When it did arrive, the 'doom of the gods' bore little resemblance to the dramatic scenarios and heroic deaths of 'The Seeress's Prophecy', 'Vafthrudnir's Sayings' and *Gylfaginning*. Instead it turned out to be a low-key affair, a sober speech delivered by a middle-aged legal expert standing beside a rock, which probably took not much more than an hour or so to deliver. Even wearing his euhemeristic hat in the *Ynglingasaga*, Snorri had given Odin a more heroic death than this: 'Odin died in his bed in Swithiod; and when he was near his death he made himself be marked with the point of a spear, and said he was going to Godheim, and would give a welcome there to all his friends, and all brave warriors should be dedicated to him.'[22] This was a unique day in the bloody and violent history of those times – a set of gods was abandoned and an entire cultural heritage condemned to obsolescence at the insistence of a handful of fanatics. And yet beyond some light skirmishing, no violence occurred at all. It is reasonable to ask why.

To the cynic or realist it seems obvious that the money handed by the Christian Hall of Sida to Thorgeir was a bribe, or at the very least an inducement, intended to influence the decision. Another realist explanation points to the fact that relatives of four of the most powerful men in Iceland were being held as hostages by the Christians pending the mission of 999, among them a son of the leader of the Heathens. Much the most widely accepted explanation, one that was accepted even by the author of the *Kristni Saga*, is that the decision reflected the political and cultural good sense of the Lawspeaker. In a word, Thorgeir's was a *rational* solution to a difficult and dangerous problem. From the Birka heathens who rebuked Herigar for choosing to go it alone in becoming a Christian and accused him of cultural treason, to the thought attributed to Louis the Pious by Saxo Grammaticus, 'that there could be no agreement between minds which embraced opposing forms of faith', the highest demand of reason was that a society be united and integrated.[23] This was recognized to be the overriding condition for the achievement of the most desirable of all goals, peace. In his speech from the Lawrock, Thorgeir provided what was probably a literary or legendary example of the futile warring between neighbouring kings in Scandinavia, Dagr and Tryggvi, and the contentment that came when peace was agreed between them.[24] It is possible that his understanding of the dangers faced by a community divided by religion and law owed something to his knowledge of events in England following the invasion of the Great Heathen Army and the share-out of land around 880. No formal integration of the revised population had taken place between English and Danes since the 865 divisions of the land. We noted earlier certain paragraphs of King Edgar's 'Wihtbordesstan' law code of 962 that acknowledged this lack of integration: 'It is my will that secular rights be in force among the Danes according to as good laws as they can best decide on. Among the English, however, that is to be in force which I and my councillors have added to the decrees of my ancestors, for the benefit of all the nation.'[25] As we shall shortly see, the continuing existence of separate Anglo-Saxon and Scandinavian cultural identities on the same island had momentous consequences for the stability of English society.

Another possible explanation for the passive acceptance of Thorgeir's decision is that northern Heathendom in general, and Icelandic Heathendom in particular, was in a moribund state by the year 999, and that a passionate minority was able to roll over with relative ease a majority grown at first insecure and finally indifferent in its religious faith. We noted earlier the possibility that 'The Seeress's Prophecy' was composed as an act of liturgical defiance, an Old Norse parallel to the Jewish–Christian sibyl–oracle tradition, with Heimdall as a Heathen prototype of Christ as Saviour.[26] Hjalti Skjeggjason's disrespectful verse about Freyja may have been only a prominent example of a tendency in the times, perhaps affecting the young in particular, to regard the Aesir not as awe-inspiring beings but rather, as Snorri Sturluson learnt to know them, the harmless and even half-comic heroes of an obsolete folk-tale. The eddic poem 'Trymskvadet', describing how the red-bearded giant-killer Thor was obliged to dress up as a very unconvincing bride in order to recover his hammer, and the tale of how Odin stole the mead of poetry in a raid on the mountain home of its owner, the giant Suttung, and of his flight home as an overweight eagle whose emergency defecation of his surplus burden brought bad poetry into the world, entirely lack the sense of the numinous that we associate with gods and are closer to the harmless fun of Rudyard Kipling's *Just So Stories*. There is an air of almost affectionate contempt to such stories that is not far removed from the mood of Hjalti's ditty at the Lawrock in 998.

A grave excavated at Skriddalur, on the banks of the Thórisár river in eastern Iceland, in 1995 and dated to a period shortly after 955–957 by the find of a single English coin minted by King Eadwig, has been described as one of the wealthiest ever found in the country. The occupant, a man of between thirty and forty years of age, had been buried with his horse, his sword, shield, axe, spear and arrow points, whetstones for sharpening his sword, as well as weights for trading purposes and a flint for making fire, and it has been suggested that this comparative wealth may reflect a deliberate attempt to revive the status of Heathen practices and customs in the northern world in the face of Christianity's advances, much as the elaborately Heathen Île de Groix ship-burial off the coast of southern Brittany may record a reaction against the Christianization of Rollo and his forces in nearby Normandy after 912.[27]

The expression of Heathen spirituality could take different forms. We have seen how Ingolf, the first settler, threw his high-seat pillars into the sea on sighting the coast of Iceland, vowed to build his home at the place where they came ashore, and kept his vow. Thorolf Mostrarskegg sanctified a mountain on his land and forbade anyone even to look it at with an unwashed face. In *Hrafnkels Saga* we met a chieftain so devout that he killed the boy who blasphemed against Frey by riding the horse as though it were just any stallion. Literary creations or historical beings, it is hard to imagine men of the stripe of Ingolf, Thorolf and Hrafnkel wandering away from the Lawrock after Thorgeir's speech and calmly taking their place in a queue to be baptized in the Öxará river. By the summer of 999, Heathendom may have declined into something men were less willing to kill for, and not at all willing to die for.

These are all modern attempts at understanding that offer rational explanations of why Thorgeir's decision was accepted. As such they have a natural attraction: when Thorgeir lay down in his booth and covered his head with his cloak, he was 'thinking through' the pros and cons of the decisions he had to take. With a little more concern for their personal comfort, this is the approach modern politicians might take when faced with an important decision. Rational theories to account for the enigma of Thorgeir's decision have at times been supplemented by explanations that invoke the irrational. The Christian author of the *History of the Ancient Kings of Norway*, Theodoricus Monachus, believed that divine intervention had taken place at the *Althing* meeting and that god had touched Thorgeir's mind.[28] In more recent times the theory of divine intervention has been revived, though the divinity in question is not the god of the Christians.

Scholars have noted the precision with which Ari tells us that the Lawspeaker lay down and covered his head with his cloak, though he does not explain why this was important. Taken with the clear implication that he then lay undisturbed, and presumably fasting, for the following twenty-four hours, the suggestion has been made that he was engaged in a religious act, that Thorgeir sent his spirit on a journey to discover the will of the gods in the matter. The great Icelandic scholar, Sigurdur Nordal, was among the first to raise the possibility, suggesting that Thorgeir's deliberation was an exercise to gain divine strength.[29] Comparisons have been drawn with scenes in saga literature which appear to describe the behaviour of poets engaged in the mystical act of seeking inspiration for a composition. The most familiar is from *Egil's Saga*: 'And as the autumn passed, Egil became very depressed, and often sat with his head down in his cloak. Arinbjørn spoke to him and asked among other things: ". . . What are you composing now? Let me hear it".' For the author of the saga the state of inspiration, whether in the mystical art of composing poetry or in divination, was associated with this covering of the head with the cloak.[30] In the *Geirmundar tháttr*, the poet Bragi appears to use mystical techniques associated with composing poetry to acquire supernatural information concerning three children who are playing on the floor in front of him, at the conclusion of a scene in which he is described as sitting in a high-seat, playing with a stick in his hand and 'mumbling into his cloak'. Ari does not tell us that Thorgeir mumbled or muttered, but the use of a cloak around the head or face to withdraw from the visible into the interior and invisible world seems to have been a part of the practices of both composition and divination. The shaman described in the *Historia Norwegie* seance covered himself with a cloth or cloak for the duration of his spirit journey to ensure that no living being, such as a fly, could disturb the trance with its presence.[31]

The suggestion that Thorgeir engaged in an oracular consultation of a shamanic nature provides a credible explanation of why the Heathen majority accepted his decision. It was because they knew how it had been taken. It was the way things were done, and they accepted the result of the process, whether they liked it or not. Odin was well known for his enigmatic and inscrutable ways and, while it may have disappointed them that the king of the gods should have solicited his own demise in this way, it may not entirely have surprised them. Indulging the further implications of this for a moment, it affords us the rare spectacle of an old god finally wearying of the demands of his position and with a sigh of relief handing over to a younger god with fresh ideas. Unlike the god of the Christian, Odin felt that he understood little of the world he had created, and an insatiable curiosity to know more about it was his outstanding characteristic. His resignation would leave him free to wander the world with his staff and his long coat, broad-brimmed hat pulled down over his one good eye, in pursuit of more knowledge and more understanding.

The perversity of fate was something with which Heathens were quite familiar. In his *Vita Anskarii*, Rimbert describes an episode that took place during the apostle's early attempts to convert the Birka Swedes. Upon arriving in the town, Anskar discovered that King Bjørn had no personal objection to Anskar's mission. However, the king continued:

> on this account I have not the power, nor do I dare, to approve the objects of your mission until I can consult our gods by the casting of lots and until I can inquire the will of the people in regard to this matter. (. . .) It is our custom that the control of public business of every kind should rest with the whole people and not with the king.

Rimbert writes that, as soon as the chieftains were assembled, 'the king began to discuss with them the mission on which our father had come. They determined that inquiry should be made by the casting of lots in order to discover what was the will of the gods.'[32] The procedure followed was probably similar to that observed by Tacitus among the Danes.[33] This involved cutting a branch from a fruit-bearing tree and dividing it up into a number of smaller sections on which markings were made. These were then tossed on to a cloth spread on the ground. Three were picked up, studied, and their oracle interpreted by the priest or soothsayer, who was then able to give a categorical answer to the question asked. Continuing his narrative, Rimbert writes that 'the lot decided that it was the will of God that the Christian religion should be established there'. It did not surprise Anskar, who had been assured in a vision that the outcome would be favourable, but it did surprise almost everyone else. An elderly chieftain rose to address the 'noise and confusion' in the crowd. He referred to personal experience of the benefits of Christianity in peril on the sea and at times of crisis, and stressed that the power of Christ lay in his being above fate, in his being always reliable, always trustworthy, always helpful to his worshippers. 'Consider carefully,' he said in conclusion, 'and do not cast away that which will be to your advantage. For, inasmuch as we cannot be sure that our gods will be favourably disposed, it is good for us to have the help of this God who is always and under all circumstances able and willing to succour those who cry to Him.' Despite support like this, King Bjørn was unable to give Anskar permission to preach at Birka until he had put the matter to a second assembly, in the southern part of his territory. Those in attendance were told what had happened at Birka, and 'by divine providence the hearts of all became as one, so that they adopted the resolution passed by the former assembly and declared that they too would give their entire and complete assent'.[34] As we have seen, it proved a temporary triumph only for the Christian mission to the Swedes.

In both these cases, the decisive factor was unity. Whether the words he spoke were his own, or were dictated to him by Odin, there is no mistaking that this is what Thorgeir saw as the heart of what he had to say about the prospect of Iceland being divided along religious and legal lines: 'let us all have one law and one religion. For this will turn out to be true, that if we rend asunder the laws we shall also rend the peace.' From its beginnings in the 870s, Icelandic society, with its Heathens, its handful of Christians, its smattering of godless men who trusted only in their own might and main, and its syncretic gamblers who were happy enough to take out extra insurance against a bad harvest by adding Christ to their personal pantheon, had been what we would today call a pluralistic and multi-faith society. But when crisis threatened in 999 there was no doubt at all in the Lawspeaker's mind: everyone should believe in the same god, or at least pretend to do so.

'It was then proclaimed in the laws that all people should be Christian, and that those in this country who had not yet been baptised should receive baptism; but the old laws should stand as regards the exposure of children and the eating of horseflesh. People had the right to sacrifice in secret, if they wished, but it would be punishable by the lesser outlawry if witnesses were produced':[35] Ari reports the three exemptions almost as though they were afterthoughts rather than crucial concessions that removed what must have seemed, to the rank-and-file population, among the main objections to the adoption of Christianity.

Abortion as a method of birth-control enjoys the advantage that the unborn child remains unseen during the process. Viking Age societies faced a harsher reality where newly born children, in certain circumstances, could be left outside to die of exposure. The practice seems always to have been regarded as shameful. 'In those days poor people were permitted to carry their children out to die. But it was always considered bad,' says the author of the *Saga of Thorstein Oxfoot*. The same point is made in the *Saga of Gunnlaug Snake-tongue*,[36] though the example given there is not caused by poverty. An Icelander named Thorstein, a son of Egil Skallagrimsson, describes to a Norwegian friend skilled in the interpretation of dreams one in which two eagles on the roof of his house began a fight to the death for a lovely swan that belonged to him. The Norwegian told him it meant that his wife was pregnant with a daughter, and that the swan on the roof symbolized the child grown to a marriageable age. The eagles were two suitors who would both die in the fight for her hand. Like the Kievan prince Oleg, Thorstein attempted to outwit fate and told his wife that if she gave birth to a girl she must leave it outside to die. The author of the saga explains: 'For when the land was still entirely Heathen, it was by way of being a custom that those men who had few means and many dependants would have their children left to die of exposure, though it was always considered a bad thing to do.' His wife Jofrid rebuked him:

'Your words are unworthy of a man of your standing. No one in your easy circumstances can see fit to let such a thing happen.'

'You know my temper,' Thorstein warned her. 'There will be trouble if you disobey me.'

Jofrid disobeyed him and had the infant taken in secret to be brought up by her sister-in-law. Six years later, Thorstein learnt the truth.

Understanding that fate cannot be avoided he tells Jofrid that he will not reproach her, because 'for the most part, things turn out as they will'. The saga which then unfolds is a realization of the dream he had before his daughter was born.

Jofrid's attempt to dissuade her husband from his decision is echoed by the wife of another affluent man in the *Finnboga Saga*. Here a husband who wished to punish his wife for having unwittingly married off an older daughter without his knowledge forces her to expose her newborn daughter. She protests in vain that only the very poor had the right to do such a thing, yet she agrees and asks only that the child be left out with a piece of meat in its mouth. The minimal chance of survival offered by this pays off, and the child is found by a couple who raise her as their own.[37]

Both stories indicate that the children left out to die in this way were normally females. Women, as the bearers of children, were regarded as a biological liability in times of famine; and in times of war, the numbers of men killed set a greater premium on replacing lost males. Another factor in the economic equation that sustained the practice may have been the financial burden among poor farmers of the bridal dowry. There were exceptions to the general rule, though we need to reach ahead into the Christian era to find them. In the Swedish *Dalalagen* law code, preserved in a manuscript from the middle of the fourteenth century, with its content dated to about a century earlier, a passage on the punishment for killing a bride set the compensation due to her husband for his unborn daughters at double the rate for his unborn sons. But that Viking society was male-oriented is beyond all doubt: on memorial rune-stones in the east-coast Swedish province of Södermanland the number of sons commemorated could be as many as five and was often more, while the number of daughters referred to never exceeded two.

Below infant girls on the scale of human values were children born with severe physical deformities. Even when we have nominally come to terms with the fact that different periods of time use the mind in very different ways, the credence of the most learned men of the early medieval period such as scholars Alcuin, Rimbert and Adam of Bremen, to whom cynicism, suspicion, doubt or downright disbelief of some fantastical story or claim seemed utterly foreign, is still remarkable to us. In Adam we may read of the dog-headed offspring of the inhabitants of the Baltic *terra feminarum*, whose heads are down in their chests and who communicate by barking; or of the Alaner or Albanere, men born with grey hair; or of an unusually long-lived race of pale green people – and presume these to be essentially confessions of ignorance, a literary version of 'here be dragons'. But deformities suggestive of some of these descriptions are mentioned in Viking Age law codes: children with their faces twisted down on to their chests; or with toes where their heels should be; or having skin like a dog. On, into the age of the written law code, it remained the law that such children could not be baptized but must be left outside to die of hunger or cold.[38]

Among the many grave-mounds and fields excavated in Viking Age Scandinavia, only a handful of children's graves have been identified. In the ten, large-scale Viking Age graveyards that have been completely excavated on Gotland, only three children had their own graves. Two small graves from the Mulde parish of Fröjel, dated to the eighth century, contained the remains of infants who had been cremated and laid to rest with beads, bracelets and animal-shaped bronze brooches. The grave-goods were proportionately smaller than normal size. Another grave at Vallstena, dated to the middle of the tenth century, was that of a girl of about five or six years of age. Her assortment of grave-goods included, among the beads and brooches, a brooch with a key, a pair of tweezers, a comb, and a knife on a chain. Unlike the Fröjel grave-goods, these were full-size. In Viking Age societies the key that was worn pinned at the breast was the symbol of a woman's authority in the family, and the presence and significance of such a key-brooch in this particular little girl's grave remains an enigma.

At the Ire grave-field in the parish of Hellvi, on the north of the island, the body of a boy aged about twelve was found, buried with a horse and a dog. Weapons, including a large sword, two spearheads, a penanular ring pin, a knife, and items pertaining to horses including a horse-comb, bridle and rings were found with him. A second boy of about the same age was also buried with horse and dog and a selection of grave-goods associated with the grave of an adult. The boys may have been from families of high standing; or the burial may only confirm the theory that, in a society in which infant mortality was common, perhaps as high as 50 per cent, children became adults and were treated as such beyond the age of twelve.[39]

Thorgeir's second important exemption was that old laws should stand as regards the eating of horse-flesh. We noted in earlier chapters the central importance of the preparation and consumption of horse-meat in the rituals of Heathen culture. Christians saw this as a blasphemous equivalent of the bread and wine taken at Holy Communion, and in the long and slow process of the conversion of the north generated a taboo against it that grew so powerful that even today horse is hardly eaten in the Scandinavian countries. Under the circumstances, this was a remarkable concession Thorgeir was offering. Even so, according to Ari, the dispensation was withdrawn a few years after the adoption of Christianity. This must have occasioned at the very least a change of diet, for at the time of the conversion the main form of subsistence in Iceland was livestock farming that included the management of herds of half-wild horses for food.[40] Once the critical early decades of cultural transition had been successfully negotiated, however, the use of horses as food seems to have resumed.[41]

The third of Thorgeir's dispensations was that men might continue to sacrifice if they wished, but only in private; if witnesses to the act could be brought it was punishable by the Lesser Outlawry, entailing a fine and banishment for three years. Literary use of the dangers of secret sacrifice is made in a passing reference in the early thirteenth-century *Saga of Hallfred the Troublesome Skald*, probably the work of a monk at the Thingeyrar monastery in Iceland, in which a mischief-making Norwegian enemy of the Icelandic skald tries to make trouble for him with their leader, Olaf Tryggvason:

Once the king asked where Hallfred was, and Kalf replied, 'Likely he is up to his old habit of offering sacrifice in secret. He carries about with him an image of Thor made of tusk. He's deceiving you, king, and you have not tested him.'

The king sent for Hallfred so that he could speak for himself.

'Is it true,' said the king, 'that you carry an image of Thor about with you and offer sacrifice to it, as is said of you?'

'It is not true, king,' said Hallfred. 'Search me. Even if I wanted to, I couldn't hide anything now.'[42]

Nothing to support Kalf's accusation was found on Hallfred, but the poet's record of resistance to the new religion was well known to the king and Kalf's accusation was a gamble that might have paid off. Hallfred Ottarson was a historical person. Some time in the middle of the tenth century his father emigrated from Norway and settled at Vatnsdal, in the north of Iceland. The short saga about him is one of a handful set in the tenth century that tell the stories of young Icelandic poets who fall in love and whose love is either unrequited or in some other way troubled. They compose erotic poetry about the objects of their desire that brings them into conflict with rivals, or with the law. Some of them, like the rivals symbolized by the two eagles in the *Saga of Gunnlaug Snaketongue*, die as a direct result of their love. The sagas are improvisations woven around the contents of the poetry these young men left behind them. Unlike the sagas themselves, their verses are probably contemporary survivals and what can be gleaned from them has a high degree of historical credibility.[43] Poetry had a status close to divine in northern Heathendom. If the *goði* were responsible for maintaining the practical relationship that existed between men and gods, the skalds were the curators of the metaphysical superstructure of lore that lay behind the rituals. In both of Snorri's variant accounts of his origins, Odin is equally the inventor of poetry. A special relationship existed between him and his poets and they will have felt the cultural threat that lay behind Christianity more keenly than most. What makes Hallfred Ottarson so fascinating as a poet is that his verses, and the short saga in which they are embedded, afford us a rare insight into a mind tormented at the personal level by the enforced change of faiths.

In Snorri's view Hallfred was one of the greatest skalds and he uses many examples of his work to illustrate and explain the poetic art in the textbook *skáldskaparmál* section of the *Prose Edda*. Hallfred had the unique distinction of being a court-poet to the Heathen earl Håkon the Bad, for whom he composed the *Hákonardrápa* in about 990; and to Håkon's Christian successor as ruler of Norway, Olaf Tryggvason. According to his saga, Hallfred and Olaf met for the first time shortly after Olaf came to power. Hallfred and his crew were trying to leave Norway to avoid being forced to become Christians, but were prevented from sailing by bad weather. *Kristni Saga* suggests that they were among those detained by Olaf in Trondheim after the outlawing from Iceland of Thangbrand the missionary.[44] The king preached to them at his court in Lade. Despite Olaf's proven record of force against those who opposed him, Hallfred dared to set conditions for his baptism: the king must grant him a permanent attachment as his court poet, and he must be his godfather at the baptismal ceremony. Olaf agreed, Hallfred was baptized and his religious instruction began. The saga relates that one day not long afterwards he approached the king and asked him to listen to some verses he had composed in his honour. When the king replied that he was too busy Hallfred said that was his prerogative, but that if he refused to listen, then he would abandon the new faith. He went on to express his disappointment at the quality of the lore associated with the new faith which the king had forced upon him. The king complained that he was a *vandrædaskáld*, a troublesome poet, but agreed to listen, and the nickname stuck. Hallfred's guarded hostility towards the new faith, and the fact that it had been forced on him, came close to getting him in very serious trouble with the king. In a remarkable scene involving the two and played out before an audience of Olaf's retainers, Hallfred composes a short series of verses that flirts perilously with his love of the old gods, driving the king to growing anger and frustration as he uses all his art to delay the revelation of the real subjects of his *kennings* or metaphorical disguises until the very end of his verses.[45] It is almost as though, in this virtuoso display of his art, Hallfred is bidding a last farewell to the religious culture that had so enriched his poetry and brought him so much pleasure. Although the love-story then takes over for much of the rest of the saga, the theme of Hallfred's troubled relationship with Christianity returns at the end. The poet, now about forty years old, is sailing back to Iceland with the intention of settling down at last. He falls ill on the voyage, and in his dying moments sees his female guardian-spirit, dressed in a coat of chain mail, striding across the waves behind the ship. He rejects her, but in his last verse remains uncertain of his fate after death.[46]

Now this day would I die
– young, I was hard of tongue –
greeting without regret
my grave, if surely saved.
Naught I repent, though not
– knowing that all must go –
fearless of hell-fire; God
defend me from that end.[47]

The Christian scribe who wrote down the story took pity on Hallfred and spared him the torments of hell: after his death the poet's body was placed in a coffin, along with his arm-ring, his cloak and helmet and cast into the sea. It drifted ashore on Iona. Viking raiders had long since ceased to visit the island, but it seems their spirit lived on among some of the abbot's servants, who broke open the coffin, stole the treasures and sank the body in a bog with a stone around its neck. The culprits were caught, Hallfred's body recovered and given a proper Christian burial. A chalice was made from his arm-ring, his cloak turned into an altar cloth, and his helmet melted down to make candlesticks.

Olaf, tormentor, mentor and finally gift-giver, was by this time long dead. He survived the conversion of the Icelanders by no more than two or three months. The *Ágrip* relates that he had married a sister of his former Viking raiding partner Svein Forkbeard, now securely in possession of the throne of Denmark. The marriage was the subject of obscure complications involving a ruler of Poland to whom she had already been married against her will. In Olaf's view, though seemingly not in Svein's, this invalidated the marriage. The old rivalry for power in south and eastern coastal Norway between Danes and Norwegians revived, with Svein withholding his sister's dowry, and Olaf gathering an army with which he intended to confront him in Denmark. Unfortunately for him, his violent imposition of the new religion had left him with few friends in his hour of need. He sailed to Wendland with eleven ships, but the army that he was expecting to follow him simply turned back once he was out of sight. Olaf sailed on, hoping to link up with friends across the Baltic who had formed part of his *hird* in his days as a Viking leader. Svein was much the more powerful and influential leader of the two, however. He persuaded the Swedish King Olaf and the Norwegian Earl Erik, a son of Håkon the Great, to join forces with him, and their vast fleet encountered Olaf Tryggvason's flotilla in a battle at Svolder. Despite the overwhelming odds against them, Olaf's forces are said to have acquitted themselves bravely, but in the end they were defeated. As the battle neared its close he was seen alive astern on the high-deck of his enormous longship, the *Long Serpent*. Earl Erik moved aft to confront him, 'a light flashed before him, as though it were lightning, and when the light disappeared, the king himself was gone'.[48] Olaf's body was never found. Remarkable rumours attended upon his disappearance, including one that he had escaped with his life and wandered to the Holy Land and entered a monastery. To others it seemed obvious that he had fallen or jumped overboard. With obvious admiration for his missionary work, the *Ágrip* concludes that, however Olaf died, 'it is likely that God has his soul'. Had Olaf Tryggvason's body been found at the time then perhaps he, and not the next Olav to rule the Norwegians, would have become the patron saint of Norway.

If, in the longer perspective, the enrolment of the Icelanders in the gradual unification of European peoples within a single religious faith was both unavoidable and desirable, in the shorter run the benefits were perhaps harder to identify. At the individual level, as travellers and traders, the conversion may have spared them the simple embarrassment of being old-fashioned in a modern world, country bumpkins clinging to outmoded ideas at the rim of the known world. Politically it may have preserved their proud independence by averting the immediate threat of an invasion from Norway, though Olaf Tryggvason's death preserved that even more surely. And yet one cause of the decline and eventual fall of the commonwealth was that it never managed to harmonize the two social realities that were present at its birth, the democratic and the aristocratic. To the medieval mind, the idea of a society with no formal leadership, or at best an ad hoc leadership, was astonishing to the point of being unnatural. Something of the same surprise in Adam of Bremen's observation *Apud illos non est rex, nisi tantum lex* ('Among them there is no king, there is only the law') lies behind Dudo of St-Quentin's recording of Rollo's response to the Frankish emissary who had asked for the name of their leader. 'We have no leader. We are equal. You will have to negotiate with all of us.' But even Rollo, once he had become a respectable, landowning Christian leader, saw the necessity of abandoning the egalitarian model of leadership if his duchy were to survive and prosper.

From his episcopal see hundreds of miles across the sea, Adam of Bremen described the state of affairs in Iceland after the conversion:

The island is very large, and its inhabitants are many; they live entirely from cattle-farming, and wear hides. Nothing can grow there, and there is very little timber. They live in holes below the ground and are content to share what they have with their cattle. They live in a holy simplicity, desiring no more than what nature offers them, and echoing happily the apostle's words: *And having food and raiment let us be therewith content.* Their mountains are their towns, the bubbling springs their delight. Happy, I tell you, are such people, who envy no one in their poverty.[49]

Adam died in 1060, well within living memory of the Saga Age, but in its own way his description of life among the Icelandic settlers is as much an idealization as the dramatizations of the Family Sagas in the thirteenth century. A harsher and more disturbed picture of life in post-conversion Icelandic society emerges from the pages of the sagas collectively known as the *Sturlunga Saga*, after a leading family whose fortunes are among those described in them. After 100 years or so of relative stability, in about the middle of the twelfth century Icelandic society entered a period of violent chaos. The Sturlung Age, as it was known, was characterized by a power struggle of a particularly vicious kind. In the *Sturlunga Saga* we meet chieftains who have their enemies tortured, maimed, castrated and blinded; who kill the old as readily as the able-bodied; and priests who abuse their calling and openly take mistresses. This helpless spiral into barbarism may have been encouraged by the half-hearted abandonment of one set of cultural mores and values, and the imperfect and unconvinced adoption of another and very different set that led, over time, to a state of confused moral disorientation from which it proved too hard to recover.[50] In

1263 the exhausted combatants handed over control of the country to the crown of Norway. Almost seven centuries would pass before Iceland regained its independence.

16

St Brice, St Alphege and the wolf

The fall of Anglo-Saxon England

Despite the propensity of Athelstan of Wessex to describe himself as 'king of all Britain' from about 930 onwards, it was not until his brother Edred succeeded in driving Erik Bloodaxe from York and ending the Viking kingdom there in 954 that there was real substance to the Wessex claim. Edred died the following year and was succeeded by his nephew Eadwig, crowned at the age of fourteen in a ceremony at Kingston-upon-Thames at which Dunstan, abbot of Glastonbury, had to rebuke the boy for drunken and lascivious behaviour. Two years later, in 957, his fourteen-year-old brother Edgar, possibly encouraged by Archbishop Oda of Canterbury, rose against him. A brief period of power-sharing ensued, but with Eadwig's death in 959 England once again had a king recognized throughout the country. Following a coronation delayed until 973, Edgar travelled to Chester to receive the submission of six kings, including leaders of the Scots and the Welsh. His reign coincided with a lull in Viking raids that permitted him to attend to various reforms that earned him the approval of the *Rule of St Benedict*, which said that 'he ruled every-thing so prosperously that those who had lived in former times . . . wondered very greatly'.[1] As we have noted earlier, the evidence of his law codes is that he accepted the existence of separate legal communi-ties within the kingdom and made no attempt to impose his authority 'among the Danes'. The Icelandic Lawspeaker Thorgeir had been adamant that a community divided by law could not survive. Time would tell whose political instincts were right, his or those of King Edgar and his advisers.

Edgar died two years after his coronation and was succeeded by his son Edward. The House of Wessex remained plagued by succession problems, however, and Edward reigned for only three years before he was murdered at Corfe in 978, allegedly on the instructions of his stepmother Aelfthryth, Edgar's third wife and widow, to clear the way for the succession of her ten-year-old son Ethelred. This clutch of short reigns by short-lived kings had been favoured, since the time of Edgar, by a diminution of Viking activity in England that owed much to Harald Bluetooth's domestic preoccupations with the unification and Christianization of Denmark. Sporadic raiding on England resumed in the 980s. England was known to be a wealthy country, and once the defeat of Byrhtnoth at Maldon in 991 had persuaded the Danish royal house that the English were too weak to defend themselves or their wealth the raids increased in frequency, with ever-larger forces demanding ever-larger sums of money in return for what turned out to be ever-shorter respites from attack.

We have already met Ethelred in Chapter 13 as he struggled to deal with the armies that Olaf Tryggvason and Sven Forkbeard brought to England in the 990s, including the agreement with Olaf never again to return with hostile intent. Olaf may have been neutralized by baptism and his ambitions in Norway, but for the next three years the *Anglo-Saxon Chronicle* continues to record the doings of a Viking army that killed and burnt in Cornwall and Devon, razing Ordwulf's abbey church at Tavistock, and in Wales killing the bishop of St David's. Sven's name was known to the English chroniclers of these atrocities and the fact that he is not mentioned suggests that he was not involved in the raiding. In 998 the army was in Dorset and carried on more or less as it pleased. It spent the winter on the Isle of Wight and in 999 sailed east again, into the Thames and up the Medway to Rochester. Most of west Kent was laid waste and everywhere, in that bleak refrain that echoes wearily through the Viking years of the *Chronicle*, 'the Danes had possession of the place of slaughter'.

It was on the basis of his activities and decisions during these years that a thirteenth-century reader of the *Chronicle*, punning on the literal meaning of his name, 'Noble counsel', dubbed King Ethelred 'Unraed', or 'No counsel', later corrupted to 'Unready'. His loyalty to alderman Ælfric of Hampshire shows that he was indeed a poor judge of character. Earlier we saw how, in 991, the year of Maldon and the first danegeld of 10,000 pounds, Ælfric, by warning the enemy, had sabotaged a plan to muster a fleet in London strong enough to trap the Viking army at sea, and for good measure fled the night before battle was to be joined, with the result that a planned annihilation of the Viking fleet resulted in the destruction of a single ship and the slaughter of its crew.[2] If this betrayal was common knowledge we can only wonder at the fact that he was not severely dealt with by Ethelred. And yet he was not.

Amid all this wretchedness, the revival of monastic life in England that had started with Oda and continued under Dunstan at Glastonbury went on, but even here Ælfric was part of the problem and not the solution. At one point in his career he received a letter from Pope John censuring him for his theft of property and estates from the abbey at Glastonbury, and warning him that if he persisted he would be 'delivered for ever with Judas the betrayer to the eternal flame'.[3] In 1003 the *Chronicle* sighs that Ælfric was 'up to his old tricks' again: rather than face a Viking force fresh from the destruction of Exeter the alderman claimed to be ill, pretended to vomit and left his men in the lurch.[4] Yet we have the *Chronicle*'s word for it that Ælfric was one of those 'in whom the king had most trust'.

Ethelred's fears and frustrations mounted. Levies that were mustered to resist the Vikings mysteriously evaporated just as battle was about to begin:

Then the king with his councillors decided to advance against them with both naval and land levies; but when the ships were ready there was delay from day to day, which was very galling for the unhappy sailors manning the vessels. Time after time the more urgent a thing was, the greater was the delay from one hour to the next, and all the while they were allowing the strength of their enemies to increase; and as they kept retreating from the sea, so the enemy followed close on their heels.[5]

In 1000 Ethelred marched north to Cumberland 'and laid waste very nearly the whole of it'. The *Chronicle* offers no reason for this. Given the record of his armies against the Vikings, it is tempting to suggest that Ethelred went there largely in order to vent his frustration on the hapless landscape. Presumably he wanted to prevent the Vikings using the region as a base for any attempt to revive the kingdom of York. The anxiety and sense of impending hopelessness at the divided and warring realm must have been symbolized for Ethelred and the English with the news that, in the year 1000, 'the enemy fleet had sailed away to Richard's realm in the summer', this despite the fact that Ethelred had a peace treaty with the Norman duke, brokered for him in 991 by Pope John XV, which especially enjoined Richard to receive 'none of the king's men, or of his enemies'.[6]

The following year they were back again, penetrating England through the Exe, killing and burning as before. Pallig, a Danish earl who had entered into an agreement with Ethelred, offering support in exchange for gifts of 'manors, gold and silver', simply reneged on the agreement when the time came and joined forces with his fellow-countrymen. Again the English levies were mustered, 'but as soon as they met, the English levies gave ground and the enemy inflicted great slaughter on them'.[7]

There is a reference in the poem the *Battle of Maldon* to someone referred to only as the 'hostage' from Northumbria fighting on the English side, and the presence of a man from the northern Danelaw in an army led by an Essex alderman may perhaps have been an attempt to insure against betrayal by holding an important hostage from an area thought to be sympathetically inclined towards the invaders.[8] The English, 130 years after the partitions enforced by the Great Heathen Army, remained deeply unsure where the loyalties of the Scandinavian settlers in the east and north of the country lay: over the generations, had they become acculturized to an English way of being and seeing? Or had they retained a strong 'tribal' sense of Scandinavia as their homeland that was leading them instinctively to support each fresh band of invaders that arrived from across the water? The atmosphere of fear and paranoia at Ethelred's court reached an unsustainable intensity in 1002. In that year the king 'and his councillors' decided again to attempt to buy off the attackers, and alderman Leofsige was sent to meet the fleet with an offer of 24,000 pounds and maintenance. The *Chronicle* then reports that the king received a warning that the Danes proposed to 'deprive him of his life by treachery and all his councillors after him, and then seize his kingdom'.[9] Roger of Wendover adds the detail that Ethelred's informant was a man named Huna, one of the king's leading military commanders. Huna, 'beholding the insolence of the Danes, who after the establishment of peace had grown strong throughout the whole of England, presuming to violate and insult the wives and daughters of the nobles of the kingdom, came in much distress to the king and made his doleful complaint before him'.[10] Roger seems to hint here that Huna may have been the instigator of what followed, the attempted genocide of Danes in England. From the fact that it took place on 13 November, the campaign became known as the St Brice's Day Massacre.

The documentary evidence for the massacre is slight. To the rumour of a Danish plan to kill him and take over his kingdom, the *Anglo-Saxon Chronicle* adds only that 'the king ordered to be slain all the Danish men who were in England – this was done on St Brice's Day'.[11] A retrospective reference occurs in a charter concerning St Frideswide's Abbey in Oxford.[12] In a striking inversion of the roles historically assumed in such encounters a terrified group of Danish 'Vikings' in flight for their lives from a violent mob of armed English 'Christians' had sought refuge in a Christian church. The Christian mob violated the sanctuary and set the church on fire. Those inside burnt to death. In 1004 an unrepentant Ethelred ordered that the church be repaired:

For it is fully agreed that to all dwelling in this country it will be well known that, since a decree was sent out by me with the counsel of my leading men and magnates, to the effect that all the Danes who had sprung up in this island, sprouting like cockle among the wheat, were to be destroyed by a most just extermination, and this decree was to be put into effect even as far as death, those Danes who dwelt in the aforementioned town, striving to escape death, entered this sanctuary of Christ, having broken by force the doors and bolts, and resolved to make a refuge and defence for themselves therein against the people of the town and the suburbs; but when all the people in pursuit strove, forced by necessity, to drive them out, and could not, they set fire to the planks and burnt, as it seems, this church with its ornaments and books.

To complain, as the king does, that in their search for sanctuary the Danes had broken the bolts on the church doors is an indication of the degree of hatred that lay behind Ethelred's order, as is the claim that those who set fire to the church did so only because they were 'forced by necessity'. A legacy of this hatred are the patches of what was alleged to be the skin of excoriated Danes that were still to be found in the late nineteenth century on the doors of churches at Hadstock and Copford in Essex, on the north door of Worcester Cathedral and the door of a chamber in the south transept of Westminster Abbey. Only one has been positively identified as human skin, though we might think one is enough.[13]

Those on the other side of the history of this relationship, like the Norman William of Jumièges, described horrors of a Hieronymous Bosch-like intensity, with Danish women buried to the waist only so that their breasts could be savaged by dogs, and Danish children who had their brains beaten out against door-posts. William insisted that Ethelred had ordered the massacre for no good reason at all, but was only a man 'transported by a sudden fury'. The twelfth-century cleric Henry of Huntingdon was also horrified:

I have heard in my youth some very old persons give an account of this flagrant outrage. They said that the king sent with secrecy into every town letters, according to which the English suddenly rose on the Danes, everywhere on the same day and at the same hour, and either put them to the sword, or, seizing them unawares, burnt them on the spot.[14]

Anonymity and unmarked graves are the characteristics of a genocide, which may explain why only two victims of the massacre are known by name, both of them aristocrats. One was Pallig, the Danish earl who had taken Ethelred's money in 1001 and then deserted him to join his fellow Danes. The other was his wife Gunnhild, a Christian and a sister of Sven Forkbeard, who had offered herself as a voluntary hostage to the English. Whether St Brice's really was a full-scale massacre involving a great many unrecorded deaths or, as seems more likely, a localized 'day of terror', with a handful of high-profile victims including a known traitor, that was intended largely to frighten Anglo-Danes away from any thought of collaborating with the invaders, it had no deterrent effect on the Danes in Denmark. In 1003 Sven returned at the head of an army that destroyed Exeter and the following year burnt Norwich. William of Jumièges tells us that a group of young men who had escaped made their way from London to

Denmark to inform Sven Forkbeard of the murders of members of his family. This has sometimes been proposed as the provocation behind Sven's return, but while the idea has strong narrative appeal it overlooks the equally compelling financial and political attractions of mounting a major assault on the country. The raiding that had softened up the south of the kingdom over the preceding years, the vast and debilitating payments demanded, the Danes' evident disdain for an enemy unable to defend itself, and the encouragement of the repetitive ease of victory against a thoroughly demoralized population, all these must have combined to make it clear to Sven that finally, after 200 years of pinching, hairpulling, punching, kicking and worse from Viking bands of various sizes, the English were ready to be taken.

There was a severe famine in 1005 and the Danes sailed back to Denmark, only to return the following summer. They recorded more triumphs against the levies of Wessex and Mercia, rested briefly at a safe base on the Isle of Wight and marched on through Reading, putting to flight an English force at East Kennet. At the conclusion of the campaign the inhabitants of Winchester were subjected to the humiliating spectacle of Danes marching past the gates of the city on their 50-mile trek back to the sea, burdened in their progress only by the amount of booty they had taken.

In 1007 another danegeld was offered, 36,000 pounds this time. In 1008 Ethelred ordered a massive programme of ship-building, but with the new fleet assembled at Sandwich and ready for action all its potential was dissipated by quarrelling and accusations of treachery among his military commanders. A Sussex alderman named Wulfnoth defected, taking twenty ships with him, and went off raiding and harrying along the south coast like any Viking. Eighty ships that set off to arrest the renegade took a terrible battering in a storm and those that survived were burnt by Wulfnoth. The remainder of Ethelred's 'great fleet' headed for London, 'thus inconsiderately allowing the effort of the whole nation to come to naught, so that the threat to the Danes, upon which the whole of England had set its hopes, turned out to be no more potent than this'.[15]

A ubiquitous demoralization had taken hold of the English. The *Anglo-Saxon Chronicle* resorts to cataloguing their woes, as though the act of numbering and listing might calm its agitation. Ethelred and his councillors had resigned themselves to offering the Vikings yet another danegeld in 1011, and the chronicler notes: 'By this time they had overrun (i) East Anglia, (ii) Essex, (iii) Middlesex, (iv) Oxfordshire, (v) Cambridgeshire, (vi) Herefordshire, (vii) Buckinghamshire, (viii) Bedfordshire, (ix) half of Huntingdonshire, and to the south of the Thames all Kent and Sussex, and the district around Hastings, and Surrey, and Berkshire, and Hampshire, and a great part of Wiltshire.'[16] 'In the end,' we learn, 'there was no leader who was willing to raise levies, but each fled as quickly as he could; nor even in the end would one shire help another.'[17]

England was reverting to a chaotic parody of the structure of several kingdoms that had obtained at the very outset of the insular Viking Age. One late incident in particular strikes a brutal echo of the anti-Christian violence that had been a keynote of the Viking raids in the late eighth and early ninth centuries. Early in August 1009 the people of Canterbury had been threatened by what the chronicler calls an 'immense army' under a Jutland earl, Thorkel the Tall. On that occasion they had bought themselves off with the payment of a local danegeld of 3,000 pounds. Two years later Thorkel's army returned and were admitted to the city by Abbot Ælfmær of St Augustine's. Bishop Godwine of Rochester was captured, as was an abbess named Leofrun and the Archbishop himself, Ælfeah or Alphege, the man who had sponsored Olaf Tryggvason's confirmation at Andover in 994. Ælfmær was permitted to escape, Alphege was taken back to the ships.

With a cruel precision the Vikings' demand for money had been rising incrementally by half each time, from the 16,000 paid in 994 through the 24,000 in 1002 to the 36,000 of 1007. A few months later, following the raid in Canterbury, they were camped in idle and arrogant triumph in Greenwich, just outside London, and awaiting a payment of 48,000 pounds. An additional 3,000 demanded as a personal ransom for the release of this most important of prisoners was almost enough to observe the symmetry of previous demands. The main payment had been handed over in April. The subsidiary demand had still not been met. According to Thietmar of Merseburg this was at the express command of Alphege himself, on the grounds of the 'dire poverty' of the see.[18] On the evening of Sunday 19 April, bored and angry with their prisoner for his intransigence, and drunk on imported wine, Thorkel's men turned on Alphege and made him their after-dinner entertainment, pelting him with bones, stones, blocks of wood and the skulls of cattle. *King Hrolf and his Champions*, one of the Icelanders' *fornaldarsögur*, or sagas set in mythical times, offers a fictional example of the attack as a form of rough humour,[19] and Cnut's own retainers were bound by a law that punished 'persistent audacity' among then by ostracizing the offender at mealtimes, when he might be 'pelted with bones at any man's pleasure'.[20] The attack on Alphege was savage and sustained. Finally, as an act of mercy it seems, someone struck him on the head with the back of an axe, and the spiritual head of the Christian Church in England was dead. To the English it must have seemed as though every dreadful millennial prophecy of the end of the world was about to come true.

Sven Forkbeard left Denmark for England with his conquest fleet in the summer of 1013 and went ashore at Gainsborough, in Lindsey. The people of Lindsey and of the Five Boroughs hailed him as king, and soon afterwards he received the submission of 'all the Danes to the north of Watling Street'. It marked a reversion to something like the state of affairs after the invasion of the Great Heathen Army, and was for Ethelred a bitter confirmation of his doubts about the loyalties of his Anglo-Danish subjects. Sven then headed south. Oxford surrendered, as did Winchester, seat of the ancient capital of the royal house of Wessex. The west country capitulated, and by the time Sven turned north again 'the whole nation accepted him as their undisputed king'.[21] In the year of the St Brice's Day Massacre, Ethelred had arranged a diplomatic marriage between himself and Emma, daughter of Richard I of Normandy and of the Countess Gunnor, and sister to the ruling Duke Richard II, who had succeeded his father in 996.[22] As a tactic it turned out to be as little successful as Christian baptism, danegeld payments, giant fleets or ethnic cleansing, for when Sven resumed his large-scale raiding in England in 1003 he had done so with the collusion of Duke Richard, whose reward for his involvement was that familiar Viking unit of wealth, a share of the booty.[23] This was in continuing and flagrant disregard of the 991 treaty that had promised a peace 'that should remain ever unshaken'.[24] But at such a time, perhaps only a flagrant regard of the treaty would have been worthy of note. With the arrival of Sven's conquest fleet Emma and her children fled for safety to her brother Richard's court in Normandy. Shortly afterwards they were joined there by Ethelred, a melancholy benefit of his marriage and not at all the one he had been looking for.

Then, on 2 February 1014, a matter of months after achieving the goal for which he had more or less consciously striven for over twenty years, Sven died. The Danes and Anglo-Danes chose his son Cnut to succeed him; but the reaction of the English was well-caught in the report of Sven's death in the *Anglo-Saxon Chronicle* as 'the happy event'.[25] In one last throw of the dice a group of English leaders invited Ethelred to return. He accepted and was duly restored to the throne. Cnut remained in Gainsborough until late April. The people of Lindsey agreed to provide him with horses and join him in his struggle with Ethelred, but for once Ethelred and the English army caught their opponents by surprise. Many of Cnut's supporters were killed and Cnut himself driven out to sea. Passing Sandwich on his way back to Denmark he put ashore the hostages who had been given to his father, having first cut off their ears, noses and hands.

It was at this juncture, in the brief hiatus of legal kingship that followed, and with the horrific martyrdom of his brother archbishop, Alphege, still vivid in the memory, that Wulfstan, archbishop of York, composed a sermon for the edification of his fellow-countrymen which, punning on his name, became known as 'The Sermon of the Wolf to the English'. The opening lines of it identify 1014 unequivocally as the year 'when the Danes persecuted them [the English] the most', and proceed straight to the point:[26]

Beloved men, realize what is true: this world is in haste and the end approaches; and therefore in the world things go from bad to worse, and so it must of necessity deteriorate greatly on account of the people's sins before the coming of Antichrist, and indeed it will then be dreadful and terrible far and wide throughout the world.

Wulfstan shared with Alcuin two centuries before him the almost heroically masochistic conviction that all the troubles that had befallen the English were of their own making. In so far as they mattered at all, the Vikings were important only as the instruments of God's punishment. In his sermon he even tried to shame his Christian audience by contrasting the degree of religious observance unfavourably with that of the worshippers of Heathen gods. Though much of his rhetoric was generalized he made several points that had a quite specific reference to the prevailing crisis. He lamented the decline in respect for God and the law that had taken place since the days of King Edgar, naming in the litany of woes the increase in stealing, killing, sedition, pestilence and 'wavering loyalties among men everywhere'. Traitors were to be found in both Church and state. He railed against the continuing sale of Christian slaves to foreign markets, and abominated in particular the practice of men banding together to buy a female slave for their sexual gratification before selling her on. He articulated the horror of the conservative at a world that was not merely changing but turning upside down, lamenting along the way the humiliations and dreadful demoralizations visited on the English by the conquering armies of the Vikings:

Though any slave runs away from his master and, deserting Christianity, becomes a viking, and after that it comes about that a conflict takes place between thegn and slave, if the slave slays the thegn, no wergild is paid to any of his kindred; but if the thegn slays the slave whom he owned before, he shall pay the price of a thegn. Very base laws and shameful tributes are common among us, through God's anger, let him understand it who can; and many misfortunes befall this people again and again ... The English have been for a long time now completely defeated and too greatly disheartened through God's anger; and the pirates so strong with God's consent that often in battle one puts to flight ten, and sometimes less, sometimes more, all because of our sins. And often ten or a dozen, one after another, insult disgracefully the thegn's wife, and sometimes his daughter or near kinswoman, whilst he looks on, who considered himself brave and mighty and stout enough before that happened. And often a slave binds very fast the thegn who previously was his master and makes him into a slave through God's anger. Often two seamen, or maybe three, drive the droves of Christian men from sea to sea, out through this people, huddled together, as a public shame to us all, if we could seriously and rightly feel any shame. But all the insult which we often suffer we repay with honouring those who insult us;

we pay them continually and they humiliate us daily; they ravage and they burn, plunder and rob and carry on board.[27]

He condemned opportunist apostates who had abandoned their Christian faith, and a time so out of joint that men were more ashamed of committing good deeds than bad, since the former only excited derision. Above and beyond the eloquence of his despair, what gives his sermon its peculiar interest is a paragraph close to the end, which is an almost literal translation of the Latin of one of Alcuin's letters written after the sack of Lindisfarne in 793:[28]

There was a historian in the times of the Britons, called Gildas, who wrote about their misdeeds, how with their sins they angered God so excessively that finally he allowed the army of the English to conquer their land and to destroy the host of the Britons entirely. And that came about, according to what he said, through robbery by the powerful, and through the coveting of ill-gotten gains, through the lawlessness of the people and through unjust judgements, through the sloth of the bishops and the wicked cowardice of God's messengers, who mumbled through their jaws where they should have cried aloud.[29]

Wulfstan was drawing some very long narrative lines here. He was asking his congregation to see a direct parallel between the Anglo-Saxon conquest of the Britons in the fifth and sixth centuries and the imminent Danish conquest of the Anglo-Saxons in the eleventh. Haunted by the similarities between the circumstances in 1014 and those under which Alcuin had written to King Ethelred of Northumbria, in the aftermath of 793, he was convinced that the hour of Alcuin's prophecy had come – 'Who does not fear this? Who does not lament this as if his country were captured?' – and now urged his listeners, if they wished to avoid a fate similar to the one they themselves had visited upon the Britons, to look to the lesson of history before it was too late.

Cnut was never likely to give up what his father had exhausted himself fighting for. Adam of Bremen numbered the fleet that he returned with in 1015 at over 1,000 large ships, a sure sign that it was a very large force indeed, probably larger even than the Great Heathen

Army.[30] The fleet sailed along the south coast of England until it reached the mouth of the Frome, and then the army went ashore and ravaged in Dorset, Wiltshire and Somerset. Thorkel the Tall, after a brief period of what some have seen as a guilty allegiance to Ethelred in atonement for the murder of Archbishop Alphege by men who were in his charge, changed sides and again joined Cnut. Ethelred, already a sick man, had to contend with a challenge for the throne by his son Edmund, known as the Ironside, which had gained some support in the north of the country. Eadric Streona, the Mercian alderman, raised an army and backed his campaign but then changed his mind and went over to Cnut's side, having persuaded the crews of forty of Ethelred's ships to join him.

Along with alderman Ælfric, Eadric Streona emerges as the other main villain on the English side in the *Anglo-Saxon Chronicle*'s account of these last years of the Wessex dynasty. His appointment as alderman of Mercia in 1007 put him in charge of the area between the Thames and the Humber and for the next eight years made him Ethelred's closest adviser. His marriage to one of Ethelred's daughters made him also the king's son-in-law. A consummate and unprincipled opportunist, he was more concerned with immediate threats to his position from rival English courtiers than the vastly greater threat of conquest posed by Sven's armies, and in 1006 and again in 1015 he arranged the murders of prominent English rivals.

Though a poor leader, on the evidence of the *Battle of Maldon* Byrhtnoth appears to have been a brave man. On the evidence of the *Anglo-Saxon Chronicle*, Eadric was neither. He shied away from confrontation with Thorkel the Tall's army of Danes in 1009 as they were making their way back to their ships. Ethelred had them surrounded with a large force and was all ready to attack: 'but,' says the Chronicler, 'as was always the case, it was alderman Eadric who prevented it'.[31]

Over the next six years, as the struggle for possession of the kingdom reached its climax and the prospects of the rival factions became harder to gauge, Eadric changed sides frequently. In 1016 he was with Cnut as they ravaged and burned their way through Warwickshire. The threat to the dynasty seems finally to have reconciled Edmund to his father and he raised an army and urged Ethelred in London to join him with all the men he could muster. But the large army thus assembled simply dissipated again, Ethelred was informed that none was willing to support him, and he made his way back to London. As the dark moral farce of English resistance played out, Edmund joined forces with Earl Uhtred in Northumbria and, according to the *Chronicle*, 'everyone thought that they would collect an army against King Cnut'. But by now everyone was a Viking and, instead of facing Cnut's Danes, this English army set off ravaging in parallel with Cnut's.

The death of Ethelred on 23 April must have greatly simplified the situation for all concerned. For several months Edmund fought on, engaging Cnut's armies in a series of six battles between April and October of 1016, and bravely enough to entice Eadric Streona back on to his side. Eadric marched with his men to Aylesford and Edmund, in what must surely indicate desperation rather than poor judgement, accepted his offer of support. 'No greater folly was ever agreed to than that was', was the *Chronicle*'s comment.[32] In the last of the series of battles, fought on a hillside on 18 October at Ashington in Essex, this Loki-like figure 'did as he had so often done before: he and the *Magesæte* [men from Herefordshire and South Shropshire] were the first to set the example of flight, and thus he betrayed his royal lord and the whole nation'.[33]

Eadric was one of Edmund's advisers at the negotiations which followed on the Severn island of Alney. There a payment to the Danes was agreed, hostages exchanged and the country divided between the two kings, with Edmund taking Wessex and Cnut Mercia. When Edmund died, assassinated at Minsterworth on the west bank of the Severn on 30 November the same year, Cnut, at the age of about twenty, was left the undisputed king of England. Indeed, it might seem as though the significant lay and ecclesiastical powers in the land had already accepted him as such, coming together after Ethelred's funeral at St Paul's and communicating their submission to Cnut at Southampton, as a final humiliation 'repudiating and renouncing in his presence all the race of King Ethelred'.[34] His formal accession took place in 1017 and he celebrated by raising what must now, despite its observing the customary incremental rise on the preceding demand, properly be called a *tax* rather than a danegeld. The 72,000 pounds that were raised represented the entire sum of created wealth in England in that year. Used to pay off his men, it shows more clearly than anything else the sheer size of the army Cnut had at his disposal.

Cnut was fortunate. As the first legitimate Viking king of a land outside Scandinavia he inherited from his Wessex predecessors a central administration, honed from the time of Alfred the Great to a remarkable efficiency, which he was able to continue using with a minimum of adaptation. Not least because of the financial demands made on the English by Viking raiders, it had become particularly adept at the imposing and gathering of taxes. The new king kept the four main regions of his new kingdom, making Wessex the seat of his power, allowing Eadric Streona to remain in Mercia and giving Northumbria to his Norwegian brother-in-law Erik, a son of Håkon the Great or Bad and himself a former earl of Lade. East Anglia was entrusted to the powerful Thorkel the Tall. The restoration of Eadric to Mercia may have been to lull this dangerous opportunist into a false sense of security. Better advised than Ethelred, Cnut carried out a selective purge of prominent Englishmen in 1017 that included the beheading of Eadric, 'so that soldiers may learn from this example to be faithful, not faithless to their kings'.[35] A son of Ethelred named Eadwig was exiled and then murdered, and the two infant sons of Edmund sent to Cnut's tributary king Olof Sköttkonung in Sweden to be killed. Olof mercifully sent them on to a king of the Hungarians, at whose court they found a safe refuge.[36]

Many of Cnut's most powerful and loyal thegns or followers were rewarded with gifts of land spread across almost every shire in England. Tofi the Proud was granted estates in Surrey, Somerset, Berkshire, Essex, Norfolk and Hertfordshire, Orc at Portishame in Devon, and Bovi at Horton in Dorset.[37] Cnut did not, however, as the Norman King William would do after his conquest of 1066, set about the wholesale replacement of what remained of the English aristocracy after the depletions caused by his own efforts and by those of his father. He dealt with the obvious problems of loyalty and security he faced as the violent usurper of a legitimate king by employing a large permanent guard or *thingalid*. The recurrence of the phrase '*harda godan thegn*', meaning something like 'stout-hearted fellow', on runic inscriptions on stones raised by relatives in Jutland, in south-eastern Skåne in Sweden, and in central Västergotland to commemorate the lives of these men indicates the degree to which Cnut's recruits came from these regions.[38] The presence of what may have been a large number of Swedes in his retinue has also been offered as an explanation for the claim, made in a document of 1027 addressed 'to the whole race of the English', to be 'king of all England, and of Denmark, and of the Norwegians, and of part of the Swedes'.[39] The care with which he specified 'Norwegians' and 'part of the Swedes', rather than 'Norway' and 'Sweden', is a reminder that, in these parts of Scandinavia, kingship was still a matter of personal loyalty to a leader and had little to do with modern notions of nationhood.

Though the England of which Cnut was now ruler went back in its current form only as far as the time of King Edgar in 959, in a dynastically obsessed age his accession had broken a line of West Saxon kings that went back to the middle of the sixth century. Very sensibly he wasted no time in signalling his intention to try to unite the Danish and Anglo-Saxon elements of the population into one people under his rule. Less than a year after Ethelred's death, Cnut sent for his widow Emma from Normandy and married her, supplementing his symbolic replacement of the dead king on his throne with his literal replacement in bed. Besides being Ethelred's widow she was also, of course, the sister of Duke Richard II of Normandy. Of the two children of this marriage her son, Harthacnut, became a king of England and her daughter, Gunnhild, the wife of a German emperor. The marriage did not spell the end of Cnut's long-term liaison with Ælfgifu, daughter of a Northumbrian alderman, who bore him two sons.

Cnut saw as the most important aspect of his new role the promotion of himself as not merely a Christian but an unusually pious Christian. Following the precedent of Guthrum in Alfred's time he is reported by Adam of Bremen to have rejected his Scandinavian 'Heathen name' and been baptized 'Lambert', though he seems to have made little official use of his Christian name.[40] His change of direction showed rapid results. Some time after 1020 he received a letter from Fulbert, bishop of Chartres, who, in thanking him effusively for his gift towards the rebuilding of the church there after it was burnt down in 1020, expressed himself all the more delighted at Cnut's piety, 'when we perceive that you, whom I had heard to be a ruler of pagans, not only of Christians, are also a most gracious benefactor to the churches and servants of God'.[41] Wulfstan, archbishop of York, was retained in office and until his death in 1023 remained an influential adviser. Aware that among the Danes who had decided to stay and invest their danegelds in England many were still Heathen, his was the guiding hand behind articles in the secular law codes known as II Cnut, issued in the early 1020s. In a country that had been Christian for 300 years these set out prohibitions new to English law against certain Heathen practices: 'It is heathen practice if one worships idols, namely if one worships heathen gods and the sun or the moon, fire or floods, wells or stones or any kind of forest trees, or if one practises witchcraft or encompasses death by any means, either by sacrifice or divination, or takes any part in such delusions.'[42] These strictures confirm, in passing, that the everyday practice of Heathendom had more to do with shamanism, animism and nature worship than with the pseudo-classicism of Snorri Sturluson's myths of the Aesir and the allusive world of the skaldic poets that was spun out of those myths. If our assumptions about the religious beliefs of this new wave of settlers are sound then these also cast doubt, by inference, on the boast made on the Jelling stone by Cnut's grandfather Harald to have made the Danes Christian. The introduction of these new prohibitions may also reinforce the impression created by Wulfstan himself in the 'Sermon of the Wolf', that belief in Christ was faltering even among the English themselves, perhaps as a result of Christ's apparent inability to defend his worshippers from Viking attacks.

There was a huge symbolic value in Cnut's response to a request in 1023 from the Church to translate the mortal remains of the martyred Archbishop St Alphege from St Paul's in London to Christ Church, Canterbury. The tomb was opened by members of the Canterbury community under the hostile gaze of the monks of St Paul's and a crowd of angry Londoners. Cnut not only provided a protective escort for the translation of the saint's remains but accompanied the body as it was carried across the Thames on a ship to Southwark before being handed over to the archbishop, Aethelnoth.[43] In the same year

Cnut made the richest of his gifts to the church of Canterbury, granting the port of Sandwich to Christ Church. His wife Emma also played her part in fostering the image of a pious royal house. After Alphege's body had lain three days at Rochester she arrived with her son Harthacnut to pay homage, and then accompanied the processional group to Canterbury. She was a patron of churches both in England and abroad and a collector of relics herself. In the year of St Alphege's translation she acquired a particularly powerful relic from Benevento in Italy, the arm of St Bartholomew, and made a gift of it to the Canterbury monks.[44]

On the death of his childless older brother Harold, in 1019, Cnut had inherited the throne of Denmark. He made a short journey home to claim the crown formally, and seems to have taken with him a number of bishops who had been consecrated in England, probably by the archbishop of Canterbury. As the close ties in Christian kingship between temporal and spiritual power became ever more apparent to Cnut in his new role, this may have been his way of trying to curb the influence of German rulers in Denmark, through their patronage of the Hamburg-Bremen archbishopric which, since the time of Louis the Pious and the missionary activity of St Anskar, had been the natural seat of ecclesiastical authority in the north, once the conversion of the Scandinavian peoples became an established political goal. Cnut's actions were certainly seen as an attack on the authority of the German see by its archbishop, Unway.

But if political thinking did lie behind Cnut's choice of Cantabrian rather than Hamburgian bishops, the situation changed after what was probably his most dramatic display of Christian piety. This was the pilgrimage made to Rome in 1027, to attend the coronation of the Emperor Conrad II of Germany. The invitation confirmed a wider degree of acceptance than any Scandinavian ruler had experienced before. With evident pride he related in his report of the pilgrimage that 'they all both received me with honour and honoured me with precious gifts', and that the emperor had paid him particular honour in the form of 'vessels of gold and silver as well as silk robes and very costly garments'.[45] The rhetoric is a clear statement of how fiercely this northerner now longed to enter the European political and cultural mainstream. Once he had returned from Rome he made no further attempts to promote the missionary claims of Canterbury above those of the German see.

On the practical side, he had obtained assurances that English and Danish merchants would be allowed to travel freely to and from Rome without being subjected to all manner of local tolls and taxes, and he obtained satisfaction over complaints from his archbishops at the large sums of money demanded of them when they journeyed to Rome to receive the pallium. The spiritual purpose of his journey had been 'to pray for the remission of my sins and for the safety of the kingdoms and of the peoples which are subjected to my rule', and in the letter of report he vowed to God 'to amend my life from now on in all things'. His reeves and sheriffs were enjoined to stamp out injustice and to ensure an adherence to the law so strict that it did not deviate, not even 'to amass money for me; for I have no need that money should be amassed for me by unjust exaction'.

A number of the Scandinavian rune-stones that commemorate men who took Cnut's geld ask God to have mercy on the souls of those who lost their lives attacking a Christian country in pursuit of nothing more elevated than power and money. It seems ironic, bearing in mind the effort made from the time of Charlemagne onwards by emperors, kings, bishops and missionaries to convert the Norsemen to Christianity. But if we turn the prism slightly we can see the bargain being struck here, with the English spiritual leadership eliciting these public expressions of piety from Cnut as the price of accepting his leadership. For him to have rejected the role of a good Christian king would have turned his reign into an enervating series of Christian-led insurrections. Acceptance of it paid off: at his death in 1035 Cnut was master, either directly or through his family and tributary relationships, of a compact maritime empire consisting of Denmark, Norway and England. The curious tale of how Cnut sat in his throne on the seashore and commanded the waves to go back is attested only 100 years after his death by Henry of Huntington, whose account makes it clear that the performance was designed solely to instruct his followers in the severe limitations God had placed on his powers. Homiletic tales concerning historical figures do not usually wander too far from their known characteristics. The lesson of this one must be that Cnut was a most talented, intelligent and pragmatic king.

*

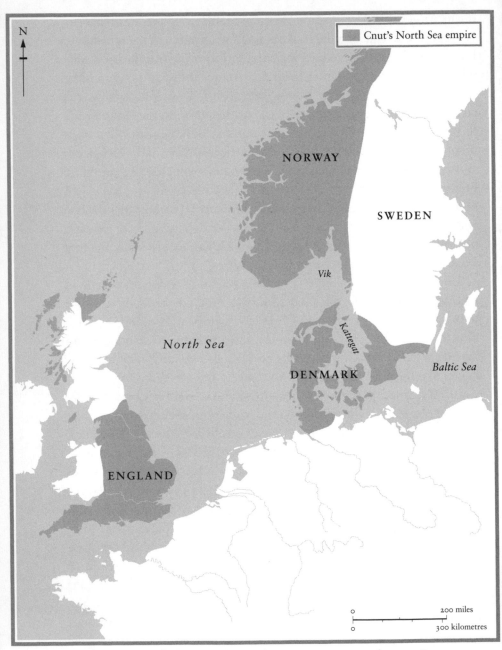

Cnut's North Sea empire at its greatest extent in 1028.

If this was all a credible and indeed creditable act of self-reinvention, at least one group of people were not seduced. Cnut's own idea of himself as king was expressed in the letter following his visit to Rome, which was addressed to 'the whole race of the English, whether nobles or *ceorls*', the lowest class of freemen in Anglo-Saxon England. To the eight Scandinavian court poets listed in the later Icelandic *Skáldatal* or 'List of Poets' who flocked to his court and for the duration of his reign made it a centre of patronage and composition, however, Cnut was and remained their great and triumphant Viking leader.[46] Roberta Frank's analysis of the verse made in honour of his achievements suggests that these skalds were singing not for Cnut alone but for a wider audience of people of Danish extraction living in England, using a syntax, words and idioms that together made up a language at times so distinct as to invite the term Anglo-Danish.[47] The incidental content of the poems reinforces the sense of separate cultural identities in England, with an assumption on the part of the Scandinavian poets that their listeners were Danes first and Englishmen second. Cnut's poets praised him for the benefits his expeditions and activities brought to Danes in Denmark and Danes in England. Their possible benefits to native Englishmen were of no interest to them.

We have noted on several occasions the innate conservatism of the skalds, well illustrated by the opposition of Hallfred the Troublesome Poet to the coming of Christianity. Religious conscience was a factor in this, but there was also the devastating effect on the skaldic art of being compelled to abandon the entire structural underpinning of Heathen myths and lore that lay behind it. In threatening Heathendom, Christianity threatened the cultural history of which the skalds were the oral custodians.[48] One poet who found solutions to these problems was the Icelander Sigvat Thordarson, regarded by Snorri Sturluson and by many later connoisseurs as the greatest skald of them all. 'Sigvat did not talk quickly in ordinary language,' Snorri writes, 'but skaldship came so naturally to him that he talked in rhymes as easily as if he were talking in the ordinary way.'[49] Without lessening it, he managed to reinvent skaldic poetry by reducing its reliance on a frame of reference that would have embarrassed the Christian sensibilities of kings such as Olaf Tryggvason and Cnut, and by rationalizing the complexity of its sentence structure.[50] Just as

Archbishop Wulfstan had shown an awareness of his own Anglo-Saxon roots in harking back to the start of the insular Viking Age in the 'Sermon to the English', so did Sigvat show what a high degree of historical awareness of themselves as Vikings these eleventh-century Scandinavians had. In the course of the 'Víkingarvísur', a praise-poem that enumerates the battles of Olav Haraldson, he invoked the name of the ninth-century Northumbrian king, Aella, to characterize the English as 'all the race of Aella' to whom Olaf had caused such suffering.

> It is true that the sixth attack was where Olav attacked London's
>   bridge.
> The valiant prince offered Ygg's strife to the English.
> Foreign swords pierced, but there the Vikings guarded the dike.
> A part of the host had their booths in level Southwark.
>
> Once more Olav brought about the meeting of swords
> A seventh time in Ulfcetel's land, as I relate.
> All the race of Aella stood arrayed at Ringmere Heath.
> Men fell in battle, when Harald's heir stirred up strife.[51]

We saw earlier how, in another context, he again invoked the memory of King Aella in a line from his praise-poem for Cnut called the 'Knútsdrápa': 'And Ivar, who dwelt in York, carved the eagle on Aella's back.'[52] The significance of these two references lies in the parallel Sigvat was drawing between the two Danish heroes, Ivar the Boneless, whose achievement as one of the leaders of the Great Heathen Army lay in his capturing York in 867 and giving the Vikings their first firm foothold in England, and Cnut, now undisputed king over all England. His long narrative line is clear: Cnut had finished the job started by Ivar. Cnut had brought to a successful conclusion a long-term military campaign pursued, with exemplary and unwavering patience, towards just this end. His was a poetic and not a political or historical analysis, but Sigvat's choice of image gives us a piercing insight into the historical self-awareness of the Vikings. Remarkably, Cnut's crowning as king of England in 1016 was figured in the poet's literary imagination as the heroic realization of a plan that had been fashioned by his Viking ancestors over 150 years earlier.

After so long a gestation, the only Viking empire that warrants the term turned out to be short-lived. As the Frankish empire had been after the death of Louis, Cnut's North Sea empire was plagued by succession problems. When he died at Shaftesbury, on 12 November 1035, he intended his son Harthacnut to inherit England and Denmark, the two most prestigious and wealthy components of the empire. But problems with the Norwegians detained Harthacnut in Scandinavia, and his half-brother Harold, known as Harefoot, Cnut's son by Ælfgifu, seized his opportunity, ruling first as regent, then as king from 1037. By 1040 Harthacnut had settled his business with the Norwegians and was preparing a fleet to sail to England and depose the usurper, when Harold died suddenly at Oxford.

As their new king, Harthacnut at once alienated his subjects with the imposition of a large tax to pay for the fleet. Coming at a time when a scarcity had caused the price of corn to soar, it provoked widespread hardship and unrest. Tax-collectors named Feader and Thurstan, in flight from an angry mob in Worcester, were cornered and killed in one of the monastery towers. Harthacnut's response was to raise an army, ravage in Worcester, and burn the city. Such an opening did not augur well for his reign, and there was general relief when, on 8 June, after less than two years on the throne, he collapsed and died while drinking at a wedding-feast, falling to the ground 'with fearful convulsions'.[53] So ended the short rule of the Jelling dynasty in England.

17

The Viking saint

Writing some two centuries after the conversion of Iceland and the reign in Norway of Olaf Tryggvason, Snorri includes in his biography a vignette from the latter days of that king's short life:

Once when King Olaf was at a feast at Avaldsnes he was visited by an old man who wore a broad-brimmed hat on his head. He was one-eyed, and very eloquent and had something to tell of every land. He entered into conversation with the king; and as the king found much pleasure in the guest's speech, he asked him concerning many things, to which the guest gave good answers: and the king sat up late in the evening. Among other things, the king asked him if he knew who the Avaldi had been who had given his name both to the ness and to the house. The guest replied, that this Avaldi was a king, and a very valiant man, and that he made great sacrifices to a cow which he had with him wherever he went, and considered it good for his health to drink her milk. This same king Avaldi had a battle with a king called Varin, in which battle Avaldi fell. He was buried under a mound close to the house; 'and there stands his stone over him, and close to it his cow also is laid'. Such and many other things, and ancient events, the king inquired after. Now, when the king had sat late into the night, the bishop reminded him that it was time to go to bed, and the king did so. But after the king was undressed, and had laid himself in bed, the guest sat upon the foot-stool before the bed, and still spoke long with the king; for after one tale was ended, he still wanted a new one. Then the bishop observed to the king, it was time to go to sleep, and the king did so; and the guest went out. Soon after the king awoke, asked for the guest, and ordered him to be called, but the guest was not to be found. The morning after, the king ordered his cook and cellar-master to be called, and asked if any strange person had been with them. They said, that as they were making ready the meat a man came to them, and observed that they were cooking very poor meat for the king's table; whereupon he gave them two thick and fat pieces of beef, which they boiled with the rest of the meat. Then the king ordered that all the meat should be thrown away, and said this man can be no other than the Odin whom the heathens have so long worshipped; and added, 'but Odin shall not deceive us'.[1]

The picture of Odin as a solitary old tramp wandering through the forest alone is very different from the one Snorri gave us at the beginning of *Heimskringla*, in the *Ynglingasaga*, where Odin was in the infancy of his godhood, the human at the centre of an adoring tribe: 'when he sat with his friends he was so fair and noble in looks'. It is part of Snorri's literary genius to present the persistence and the enduring power of the old faith in this way, showing us how even the passionately Christian king was loath to stop listening to the old man's stories. Of all the early post-Christian historians in Scandinavia, Snorri was the one most palpably nostalgic for the vanishing indigenous culture of the north. But this was not a noble appearance, and this Odin was clearly on the run.

Olaf contented himself in throwing away the horse-meat steaks that the wily old god had tried to slip him. He might have been better advised to hunt him down and kill him, for in the aftermath of his own death at the battle of Svold both the *Ágrip* and Theodoricus Monachus describe a Heathen revival in Norway. Politically, the results of the battle were that King Sven reasserted the direct rule of Danish kings over the Vik that they had exercised at least since the end of the eighth century. Olaf Sköttkonung of Sweden was allowed to control the eastern shores of the Vik. The long tradition of alliance between Lade earls and the Danish kings which had been disrupted during the reigns of Håkon the Bad and Olaf Tryggvason was revived. One of Håkon's sons, Sven Håkonarson, became effective ruler of the four eastern provinces of the Trondheim region. His brother Erik ruled in the west of the province.[2] The *Ágrip* claims that 'as much pain and effort as Olaf Tryggvason had put into forwarding Christianity – and he spared nothing which was to the honour of God and the strengthening of the Christian faith – so Eric and his son put all their strength into quelling it'.[3] All four rulers were, as far as we know, baptized Christians and a respectful deconstruction of this might lead us to suggest that Sven and Erik, aware how many enemies Olaf Tryggvason's coercion had made him, practised a tolerance that turned a blind eye to sacrificing, necromancy and the eating of horse-flesh. Theodoricus Monachus notes merely that under Erik's rule 'many Christians had turned aside from the true faith'.[4]

The medieval concern with the legitimacy of royal lines was inevitably largely a retrospective affair, and in view of King Olav Haraldson's huge subsequent historical and cultural importance for Norway, it became a cultural necessity for Norwegian and Icelandic historians to furnish him with an appropriately distinguished ancestry. Working in the twelfth century, both Ari and a younger contemporary Sæmund, known as the Learned, compiled genealogies for the Norwegian kings which reached back some thirty generations into the earliest times of the Heathen gods, along the way plotting in Olav as the great-great-great-grandson of Harald Finehair. The extant evidence adduced for their genealogies are the two stray references to a 'Harald' in poems by Ottar the Black and Sigvat, skalds who sang his praises during the period of his reign. It seems almost certain, however, that the 'Harald' they were referring to was not the architect of the first Norwegian unification but Harald Grenske, one of a number of tributary kings based in the Vik.[5] These are the origins Snorri gives him in his *Saga of St Olav*. After Harald Grenske's death, Olav's mother, Åsta, married another minor Norwegian aristocrat and produced a son, Olav's half-brother Harald. He later became a king himself and acquired the nickname Hardrada, or the Hard-Ruler. The date of Olav's birth is traditionally set at 995, though it may have been unknown and set at this by later historians as a way of establishing a narrative connection with Olaf Tryggvason, who came to power in Norway in that year. Accepting the dating means that he was no more than twelve years old at the time of the first Viking adventures in the Baltic that are referred to in the praise poems concerning him, and only fourteen when he came to England as a soldier in the army of Thorkel the Tall in 1009. Sigvat's 'Víkingarvísur', or 'Viking Verses' (the title is modern), celebrate nine battles from Olav's Viking days, of which the sixth was that attack on London Bridge which gave rise to one of the more surprising legacies of the Viking Age, the English nursery rhyme 'London Bridge is falling down'. The enormous gelds this army took from the English, including the 48,000 pounds in 1012, must have laid the foundations of Olav's fortune. The point is expressly made by Ottar the Black in the 'Head-Ransom', a poem of reparation composed after Ottar had angered his master by making a verse about Olav's wife:

> Lord wide-renowned, the people of the English race
> might not stand against you,
> undaunted one,
> when you took tribute.
> Not seldom
> did man pay gold to the gracious prince.
> I learn that great treasures went ever and again
> Down to the shore.[6]

The same poet in the same poem refers to Olav's participation in the taking of Canterbury, where 'fire and smoke played fiercely upon the dwellings,' and hails Olav as the destroyer of the lives of men. In the light of Olav's later beatification there is irony in the fact that, in his Viking youth, this saint-king was a member of the army responsible for the murder of St Alphege in 1012.[7]

Upon the break-up of this army, Olav's skalds praise him for the part he took in the raids in France and al-Andalus, along what is now the Atlantic coast of Portugal, which we looked at in an earlier chapter. It seems that, on his return, Olav made his way to the Norman court of Richard II, where Ethelred and other members of the English royal family had sought refuge after Sven Forkbeard's conquest in 1013. According to Theodoricus, Olav was baptized in Rouen,[8] though several Icelandic sagas, including Snorri's *Saga of Olaf Tryggvason*, savour the symmetrical possibility that he was baptized at the age of about three by Olaf Tryggvason himself, during a missionary trip to Ringerike, the home of Olav's stepfather. It seems that, during this visit to Normandy, he entered into some kind of alliance with Ethelred.

Olav's baptism in Rouen must have taken place at about the same time as Sven Forkbeard's death, and from this sudden change in the political scene he emerged as a pretender with serious designs on the crown of his native Norway. Two contrasting scenarios exist to describe what happened next. One takes its reasoning and psychology from the narrative in Snorri Sturluson's saga, in which Olav abandoned his alliance with the Danish kings and assisted at the restoration of Ethelred and in driving Cnut out of England in 1013. As we saw earlier, Cnut returned the following year, and the Lade earl Erik Håkonson fought alongside his Danish brother-in-law in his attempt to regain the crown of England from Ethelred and, after Ethelred's death, deal with the challenge of Edmund Ironside. Following the death of Edmund Ironside in 1016, Erik was rewarded for his loyalty with the earldom of Northumbria. From 1018 until 1023, when he bled to death after his uvula was cut,[9] his name appears regularly as a signatory of various of Cnut's charters granting lands to church institutions.[10] In Norway, he was succeeded as earl of Lade by his son, Håkon.

With Cnut and Erik fighting for the larger prize of England, this left the west coast of Norway vulnerable to attack. Olav Haraldson wasted no time and, in 1015, in a peculiarly low-key adventure that involved the use of only two ships that were not even longships but trading *knarr* and an army of as few as 200 men, he sailed to Norway. According to Snorri, this small force landed on the island of Selja. In keeping with the mysteriously low-budget nature of the whole enterprise, Håkon came against him with a single ship, and with some ease Olav captured it. Snorri invents dialogue for their encounter, in which Håkon explains the feebleness of his defence by describing himself as 'newly come out of my childhood', a curious excuse, bearing in mind that Olaf himself was probably only about twenty years old at the time. *Ágrip* gives Håkon's age as fifteen. Whatever the difference in years between them, it was enough for Olav to make an avuncular offer of release to the boy, on condition that he leave the country at once and make no attempt to reclaim it. Håkon agreed and sailed to England where, as his father's son, he found immediate favour and was given the earldom of Worcester.

The alternative scenario ignores Snorri's interpretation of events and looks instead to other sources for a rational and credible explanation for the remarkable ease of Olav's arrival in Norway – for it seems hardly appropriate to call his landing an invasion. *Ágrip* is unequivocal on the score: 'At this time Cnut ruled in England, which he had won with the help and support of St Olav.'[11] Adam of Bremen, William of Jumièges and the *Historia Norwegie* all take the same line. Claus Krag suggests that Cnut may have prised Olav away from any putative agreement entered into in Rouen with Ethelred by offering him power over all, or a large part, of Norway, with Erik, earl of Lade, being persuaded to agree to the plan by the offer of the much more wealthy English earldom of Northumbria. His son Håkon would likewise have been persuaded that a better future awaited him in the affluent west. In the *Hofudlausn* or 'Head-ransom' verses, Ottar the Black seems specifically to credit Olav with restoring Ethelred to the throne. Krag's suggestion is that the saga writers who made this assumption exaggerated Olav's role; in saying that Olav 'gave land' to Ethelred, the poet meant only to convey that Olav had won control of certain regions for him, not the whole country. This hypothesis of a deal struck between all the parties involved eliminates the anomalies in Snorri's story, from Olav's use of two trading vessels to the oddly amicable tone of the meeting between Olav and Håkon.[12]

The authentic opposition to Olav came in a battle fought on 25 March 1016, at Nesjar (now Brunlanes) in Vestfold, on the western shore of the Vik. In the *Nesjavísur*, or 'Nesjar Verses', Sigvat celebrated his master's victory over an army gathered by the last remaining of the three Lade earls, Sven, Erik's brother and uncle of the exiled boy-ruler Håkon. If Krag's hypothesis is correct, then Sven must have rejected the terms offered by Cnut and accepted by both Erik and Håkon. Though it may only be poetic licence, Sigvat attributes Olav's victory in part at least to his generosity as a gift-giver, which suggests that his danegeld fortune must have been still largely intact. Sven, by contrast, was miserly and so unable to attract support. The anonymous, thirteenth-century *Legendary Saga of St Olav* adds a credible account of Olav's visiting his parents' home in Ringerike before the battle, summoning all the petty kings to meet him there, and offering them the choice between abandoning their claims to descent from Harald Finehair and their allegiance to a Danish overlord and becoming his men, or being killed. Most chose the former.[13] Sven lost a great many men in the battle but escaped with his life and made his way to Russia.

In 1019 Olav had entered into an alliance with his neighbour in the east, King Olof Sköttkonung, and married his daughter Astrid. The alliance was not weakened when Olof died in 1022 and was succeeded by Astrid's brother, Anund Jakob. With the death in 1019 of his brother Harald, Cnut was now also king of Denmark, and from a political point of view Olav's marriage may have been a response to the alarm felt among Cnut's neighbours at the relatively sudden appearance among them of an emperor with the most powerful army in northern Europe at his disposal. If Olav did indeed come to power in Norway with the blessings and connivance of King Cnut, then we may be sure that Cnut intended any agreement between them to be along the traditional lines of the tributary relationship that had existed as long ago as 813, when Klak-Harald and his brother Reginfrid crossed the waters of the Vik to put down a rebellion in Vestfold, and one which Cnut's grandfather Harald Bluetooth had confirmed on the Jelling stone boast of a century and a half later, to have won for himself 'all of Norway'. In the ecclesiastical law code *I Cnut*, dated to before 1023, Cnut had described himself as 'king of the Norwegians', and as time passed it must have seemed to him that Olav was conducting himself with far too much independence for a tributary king.[14] At about this time he sent a letter to Olav in which he reminded him of the realities of their relationship and asserted his legitimate right to Norway. He assured Olav that he did not wish to assert his rights by force, but he was insistent that Olav should travel to England and formally accept Cnut as his lord.[15]

Olav declined the offer. He may have hoped that the demands of Cnut's empire were stretching him too far and that it would be possible to exploit this, for shortly afterwards he and Anund Jakob launched a strike against Denmark. Cnut sailed to meet them with a fleet and a major battle took place at a site on the Holy River in Skåne. The result appears to have been inconclusive. The *Anglo-Saxon Chronicle* reported heavy losses on Cnut's side and that the Swedes and Norwegians 'had control of the field', but Ottar the Black in the 'Knúts-drápa' praised King Cnut, 'bold in attack, you smote the Swedes in the place called Holy River, and there the she-wolf got much wolf's food. Terrible staff of battle, you held the land against two princes, and the raven did not go hungry there. You are swift to deal with the race of men.'[16] In his celebratory verses Sigvat, too, awarded the victory to Cnut.

Cnut was aware that Olav had made himself many enemies during his years on the throne and he seems to have sponsored the discontent of the chief among them, Erling Skjalgsson, from Sola in Rogaland. In an occasional verse, Sigvat lamented the fact that 'the king's enemies are walking about with open purses; men offer the heavy metal for the priceless head of the king'. But when Erling was defeated and killed in battle at sea off the south-west tip of Norway, Cnut took matters into his own hands, assembled a fleet of fifty ships and in 1028 crossed the North Sea himself. Olav had no chance against such a force and fled the country to Russia. Cnut was content to resume the traditional relationship and allow the next Lade earl, another Håkon, to rule in Norway for him. He took hostages to England with him, the conventional form of insurance. Håkon drowned in 1029, however, and with him the powerful line of Lade earls died out. Olav was encouraged to return from Russia and try his luck again. The popularity of his cause had not improved in his absence and at the battle of Stiklestad in 1030 he was defeated and killed.

From the start of his reign in 1015, Olav's task as a missionary king had been to complete the work begun twenty years earlier by Olaf Tryggvason. Olaf's successes had been mostly on the coastal fringes of Norway over which he had control; Olav made it his business to bring the men and the women of the remote interior to Christianity. As described by Snorri, his methods did not differ greatly from those of his predecessor, involving coercion and the threat and use of violence against those who resisted him. Adam of Bremen relates that he upset many by having their womenfolk killed as witches. The twin impositions of monarchy and monotheism angered local chieftains, who preferred the long-distance relationship with a Danish overlord that gave them greater autonomy. Snorri describes at length a rebellion against Olav's rule planned by five minor kings from the central district of the country known as Uppland. Their plans were betrayed and Olav surprised them in their sleep. One had his tongue cut out and another was blinded. The rest were sent into exile. Modern sensibilities are surprised, some perhaps even affronted, at the claim of such a man to be spreading the word of Christ, but where Olav was truly modern and Christian was in his law-making. He succeeded where Håkon the Good had failed in his attempt to introduce Christian law to Norway. The Kuli-stone inscription from Nordmøre dated itself to a time when 'Christendom had been twelve winters in the realm', and we mentioned earlier the possibility that the runemaster's reference point was the *Thing* meeting held at Moster in 1024, at which Olav introduced his revolutionary innovations, acting on the advice of his English bishop, Grimkel. Fragments of the contributions attributed to Olav and known as the 'Olav texts' dating from the end of the twelfth century are known, but the earliest surviving manuscript copy of the complete Gulathing Law dates from about 1250.[17] Section ten of this stated a communal obligation 'to maintain all the churches and uphold the Christian religion as St Olav and Bishop Grimkel laid down at the Moster *Thing*'. Section fifteen carried three important institutional stipulations: that 'our bishop shall have authority over the churches, just as St Olav promised bishop Grimkel at the Moster *Thing*'; that the people would 'provide the priests with a living as decreed by St Olav and Grimkel at the Moster *Thing*'; and that the feast and fast days introduced by Olav and Grimkel at Moster should continue to be observed. These new laws of Olav were then carried to the various assemblies throughout the country, read aloud and adopted with the assent of the communities.

Thus began the long and irreversible process of the institutional replacement by law of Viking Age, Heathen culture with modern, Christian culture. At the heart of the legislation lay the enforcement of certain crucial Christian practices: the fast and feast days that were to be observed; the baptism that would enrol all healthy, normal infants into the Church; the adoption of Christian rules concerning marriage, including regulations governing the degree of consanguinity permitted by the Church between the bridal pair; and the burial of the dead in Christian ground. The Church's urgent need was for a way of imposing these practices with only a rudimentary institutional clerical structure at its disposal. As the founders of Islam in the seventh century, the French Revolutionaries of 1789, and Josef Stalin in the Soviet era in Russia all show in their different ways, a reform of the calendar is a perennially popular way of announcing a revolution that at the same time facilitates the large-scale social control of people.

Across the Heathens' loose conception of a year that followed the seasons and rhythms of nature, Olav and his successors and their clerical advisers imposed a calendar that was as man-made as was practicable, austerely stamped throughout with the demand for discipline in the form of fasting. There was to be fasting during Lent, and the other Quadragesimal fasts that preceded Christmas, St John's Day and Assumption Day; the four, three-day fasts spread across the year known as the Quatember fasts were to be observed, as were the three Rogation Day fasts. The Church also required that each Friday be a day of fasting, and with the demand that Sunday be held a day of rest there remained hardly more than a hundred days in the calendar which had not, in one way or other, been requisitioned in the name of the new religion.[18] So that the demands should not be hollow, the law required priests to send out reminders of imminent fasts and feast days, in the form of a marked wooden calendar which was carried on a fixed round from farm to farm.

By embedding detailed aspects of Christian culture in the law in this way, these early legislators were able to ensure that it was manifest in every aspect of the daily lives of the individuals and families who made up the community. None of the laws specifically addressed the issue of Christian belief, but the numerous laws on fasting encouraged a resistance to the demands of appetite and instinct that was seen to be essential to the practice of Christianity at the individual level.

For five years following Olav's death Norway was ruled by Cnut's thirteen-year-old son Sven, with his English mother Ælfgifu acting as his regent.[19] The regime quickly revealed itself as a colonial exploitation. New laws were introduced that made the testimony of a single Dane enough to outweigh that of ten Norwegians. No one was allowed to leave the country without the king's permission, and anyone who did so would forfeit his or her possessions to the crown. New taxes were introduced. At Christmas a measure of malt was due to the king from every household, a ham from a three-year-old ox, and a unit of butter. Five fish from every catch were the king's part, and on each ship leaving the country a space was reserved for the king's use. For the levy seven men were to provide a complete set of equipment for one able-bodied man, defined as anyone over the age of five. Women were to contribute a separate tax, a measure known as a 'lady's tow' that was as much clean flax as could be held between thumb and forefinger.[20] The hostages held by the crown were enough to discourage any thought of revolt. To hard laws were added the burden of harsh seasons when people had to eat cattle fodder. Sigvat's poem easily conjures a syncretic connection between the good luck associated with the sacral kingship of Heathen times and Olav's Christian kingship:

> Ælfgifu's time
> long will the young man remember,
> when they at home ate ox's food,
> and like the goats, ate rind;
> Different it was when Olav,
> the warrior, ruled the land,
> then everyone could enjoy
> stacks of dry corn.[21]

As discontent with direct Danish-English rule grew, those farmers and chieftains who had opposed and killed Olav began to regret their actions. The burgeoning store of legends and miracles associated with the dead king added to their unease, and at some point word was sent to Bishop Grimkel. He obtained permission to open the grave and, having exhumed the body, declared, according to Snorri, with the assent of the king and the people, that Olav was a saint.[22] This was powerful medicine indeed, and the *Anglo-Saxon Chronicle* reported on these happenings in Norway with quiet bewilderment. The scribes who began the work in the reign of Alfred over a hundred years earlier can scarcely have imagined the development that was reported in the C version of the *Anglo-Saxon Chronicle* for 1030: 'In this year King Olav was killed in Norway by his own people, and was afterwards holy.'[23]

Among the enigmas of Olav's beatification are the fact that the men who defeated and killed him were themselves Christians; that they were neither Danes nor Englishmen but his fellow-Norwegians; and that his own army at Stiklestad was largely made up of foreigners, many of them Heathens. In the first instance, the cult fed on reports of miracles associated with his name. The evidence of the 'Erfidrápa', composed by his friend and skald Sigvat in about 1040 and so only about ten years after his death, is that the cult was already well established by that time. In the poem, Sigvat refers to a St Olav's mass, to the existence of a reliquary containing the saint's remains, and to a miracle said to have taken place almost immediately after Olav's death, concerning a blind man who stumbled and fell at the spot where the blood-tinged water used to wash the king's body had been thrown. The water splashed up into his eyes, and he regained his sight. A century later another skald, Einar Skulesson, enumerated fourteen miracles worked by Olav, and by the end of the century and the time of the *Passio Olavi*, a hagiography written in Norway around 1170, the number had risen to twenty-five.[24] Well before that date, there were churches dedicated to Olav in Iceland, England, Scotland, Ireland and the Isle of Man.[25] The reference on a memorial rune-stone from Sjusta in Uppland, Sweden, to a man who '*daudr i Holmgardi i Olafs kirkiu*' ('died in Holmgard in Olav's church') shows that, within decades of his death, his cult had established itself in the Byzantine east.[26] By succeeding in their efforts to present Olav's death on the battlefield at Stiklestad as a triumph, the Church was able to suggest a parallel with the death of Christ which, in time, was reinforced by a claim that Olav had faced his killers unarmed. To make a hero and an exemplar out of a beaten man who had refused even to defend himself at the moment of his death turned every tenet of Viking Age Heathen ethics on its head. In a later and final posthumous transformation, this remarkable Norwegian Viking adventurer became his country's patron saint and its *Rex Perpetuum Norvegiæ*, its king in all perpetuity.

In response to a groundswell of despair at the misrule of Sven and Ælfgifu and hope aroused by the fact that they now had a saint of their own to look to, a group of leading Norwegians made the journey to the court of Prince Jaroslav in Kiev, where Olav had taken his young son Magnus when he fled the country in 1028, and brought the eleven-year-old prince back with them to be their new figurehead. Even the boy's name was another sign that the Viking Age in Norway was over. It was given to him at his christening by Sigvat in honour of Charlemagne, *Karla Magnus* in Norwegian, the man who had once wept as he contemplated the trouble the inhabitants of this most northerly part of the known world would visit on his descendants and their peoples. With the same curious ease and dispatch with which Olav had taken power in 1015, Magnus found himself accepted as king of Norway in 1035. Sven and his mother fled to Denmark.

At the start of his reign Magnus almost compromised the large amount of good-will he enjoyed as the native son of a saint with a verbal attack on the men of the Trøndelag at the Nidaros assembly. The *Ágrip* conveys a vivid impression of the reception given to the eleven-year-old boy's speech: 'They all stuck their noses in their cloaks, and were silent and gave no answer. Then a man named Atli stood up and said no more words than these: "So shrinks the shoe on my foot that I cannot move"'. Sigvat, his godfather, rebuked the boy in verse:

> Dangerous is the threat
> – this must first be dealt with –
> when all the elders, whom I hear,
> would rise against their king.
> It is dangerous too
> when the assembled men bow their heads
> and stick their noses in their cloaks;
> the thanes are struck silent.

There were at least fifteen more of these *Bersoglisvísur*, or 'Plain-Speaking Verses'. The boy-king is said to have retired for the night, chastened by his godfather's words. In the morning he delivered a second and much more successful speech to the gathering in which he 'promised all men kindness and kept what he had promised, or better'.[27]

And yet he remained a boy. His own accession in 1035 and the death of Cnut in the same year created an unstable situation in the region which he and his advisers attempted to exploit. Though it offers no circumstantial detail, the thirteenth-century Icelandic collection of kings' sagas known as *Morkinskinna* describes a period with a 'great deal of strife and warfare' that preceded an encounter at the mouth of the Göta river between fleets led by Magnus and by Cnut's successor in Denmark, Harthacnut, who at fifteen years of age was about four years Magnus's senior.[28] Theodoricus Monachus offers a devastatingly clear analysis of how hostilities were avoided:

Whereupon the leading men, seeing that the two kings, still immature, could easily be swayed in any direction, and that they themselves would more likely bear the blame for anything the kings might do amiss, fell back on the more sensible plan of negotiating peace.[29]

As a result of these negotiations it was agreed that, if one of them died without leaving an obvious heir, the survivor of the pact should inherit both kingdoms. Twelve of the leading men on each side swore on oath to observe the terms of the agreement. According to the *Morkinskinna*, the treaty was modelled on that made between Cnut and Edmund Ironside at Alney in 1016.

Cnut's and Emma's son, Harthacnut, had added the crown of England to his Danish crown in 1040. Following his death just two years later the treaty came into operation, and Magnus of Norway was elected king of Denmark without opposition. Snorri tells us that this ready acceptance was in part because 'King Olav's saintliness and his miracles were then known all over the land.'[30] In a dramatically rapid inversion of a long-established tradition, it was now the turn of a Norwegian king to appoint a tributary ruler to run his affairs in Denmark. Snorri also claims that Magnus addressed a letter to Harthacnut's successor in England, Edward, later the Confessor, telling him that, as far as he was concerned, the treaty between Harthacnut and himself also made him the legitimate ruler of England: 'I will that you give up the kingdom to me or otherwise I shall seek it with forces from both Denmark and Norway.'[31] In 1044 the *Anglo-Saxon Chronicle* tells us that Edward 'sailed out to Sandwich with thirty-five ships'.[32] No reason is given for the mustering, but Florence of Worcester assumed that it was a response to this threat by Magnus to invade England.[33]

Though Magnus did not act on his threat, the existence of the Norwegian claim would prove a fateful element in the chain of events that led to the Norman conquest of England in 1066. It was at about this time that the late King Olav's half-brother Harald, later Hardrada or 'the Hard-Ruler', returned to the region. Having fought alongside Olav as a fifteen-year-old at Stiklestad, he had fled to Sweden and thence to Jaroslav's court at Novgorod, where he remained for three years before travelling south to join the Byzantine emperor's

Varangian Guard. During his ten years in Constantinople he had amassed a fortune, and by the time he returned to Scandinavia he was still only thirty years old. His first move was to strike up an alliance with Sven Estrithson, Magnus's tributary king in Denmark, who was not at all pleased at the humiliations imposed on him by the recent inversion of the status quo.

Harald played off his nephew Magnus and his ally Sven against each other. When Magnus asked for his help in bringing Sven back into line, Harald offered to do so on condition that Magnus cede half the kingdom to him, as he claimed was his hereditary right. After some hard and acrimonious dealings, an agreement was reached: Magnus would indeed share Norway with his uncle, but remain sole monarch of Denmark. Harald, content with his prospects, duly took a fleet to Denmark to re-impose Norwegian overlordship on Sven. Magnus was killed fighting in Jutland in the year following their agreement and Harald Hardrada inherited all of Norway.

Harald also inherited the Norwegian claim to Denmark, which Sven never ceased to dispute throughout the twenty years of Harald's reign. Finally, in 1064, Harald recognized him as king of the Danes. Turning his attention to another and richer prize he then resurrected the claim to England that derived from the earlier agreement between Magnus and Harthacnut. He spent the next two years preparing an invasion fleet, and in 1066 crossed the North Sea and sailed up the Humber. The army that came out to meet him was defeated at Fulford Gate, York was captured by a Norwegian king and for a moment it looked as though Viking history, this time with a cross rather than a hammer around its neck, might be about to repeat itself. Edward had died early in the year, to be succeeded by Harold Godwinson, and only a few days after the occupation of York Harald's men were surprised by Harold's English army at Stamford Bridge, some seven miles east of the city. Harald himself was killed, along with a huge number of his followers. Three hundred ships had been required to bring his army over; a mere twenty-four sufficed to take what was left of it back across the sea to Norway. On 27 September 1066, two days after Harold's victory, the Norman Duke William, later 'the Conqueror', landed with an army at Pevensey in Sussex. About four days later, news of his arrival reached Harold Godwinson in the north.

He at once turned his troops about and set off for the south again. Four days later, on 5 October, he was in London. After a week of rest the army was on the move again, still marching south, still tired, as they headed for Hastings to a confrontation that would lead to yet another cultural upheaval for the English – whoever 'the English' were by this time – with the introduction of the names, language and mores of William's Franco-Norman aristocrats. But that is another story, and it is not a Viking story.

18

Heathendom's last bastion

Harald Hardrada has a claim to be regarded as the last great leader of the age whose mode of living warrants the description 'Viking'. His adventures took him from the icy wastes of the Barents Sea to the sweltering heat of the Mediterranean. After the battle at Stiklestad and his sojourn at Prince Jaroslav's court he left Russia in 1034 and travelled to Constantinople at the head of a band of 500 men to join the emperor's Varangian Guard. For most of the following six years he fought against the Saracens, latterly on the island of Sicily. He was also in action against the Normans in southern Italy. In 1041 he helped the Emperor Michael IV against the Bulgars. Having amassed a personal fortune he returned in the following year to Kiev, where his machinations to gain a share of Norway began. Up until this point his 'Viking credentials' are impeccable. It is when these machinations prove successful and he emerges, first as joint ruler of Norway with Magnus the Good in 1046, and then as sole ruler on Magnus's death the year after, that he sheds his Viking skin to become a king, following the classic career trajectory outlined by so many of the subjects of Snorri Sturluson's *History of the Kings of Norway*. So it was as a king, about a king's business of trying to press his claim to a crown he genuinely believed he had a right to, that he died in battle at Stamford Bridge in 1066. A better candidate for the title of 'the last Viking' might be the Swedish adventurer Ingvar, known as the Far-Travelled, who led an expedition in about 1036 across the Baltic and all the way down through Russia to the Black Sea. On the way back disaster struck the group and only one man returned to tell their story. The surviving documentation of this ill-fated expedition is one of the most dramatic and remarkable monuments of the whole Viking

Age. Twenty-six rune-stones record the deaths of twenty named members of the expedition. Twenty-three are still standing, most of them in the Lake Mälaren region of Uppland in Sweden.[1] The most renowned of the 'Ingvar stones' is probably the Gripsholm stone, found by a Swedish runologist in 1827 in the basement of the castle at Gripsholm where, covered in tar, it was being used as a threshold.[2] The stone was cleaned and, in 1930, moved to stand by the driveway to the castle. Framed within the outlines of a coiled snake, the inscription gives a succinct picture of the standards of manhood associated with the Viking Age, and a proof of the persistence of these values:

Tola let ræisa stæin thennsa at sun sinn Harald, brothur Ingvars
(Tola had this stone raised in memory of her son Harald, Ingvar's brother).[3]

> *ThæiR foru drængila*
> *fiarri at gulli*
> *ok austerla*
> *ærni gafu,*
> *dou sunnarla*
> *a Særklandi*

> (Manly they travelled
> far for gold
> gave the eagle food
> in the east
> died south
> in Serkland.)

Ingvar himself died on this expedition, so it seems Tola either used the term 'brother' in the sense in which it often occurs on such memorials, as a 'brother-in-arms' or sworn companion in a joint enterprise; or else that Ingvar had the same father as Harald, but someone other than Tola as his mother. The six lines that follow the plain statement of names are in the verse form known as *fornyrdislag*, with recurring alliterations that bind the lines together. The adjective *drængila* is intimately connected with the Viking Age's ideal of a manly way of being. The reference to providing food for the eagle conveys Harald's valour by referring to the men he killed in the east as dead bodies upon which the eagle might feast. 'Serkland' was the name the Vikings gave to the area between the Black Sea and the Caspian, home of the Saracens, whose robes seemed to them like long, flowing shirts.

On an inscribed rune-stone at the church at Svinnegarn, in Uppland, the proud parents of a Viking named Banki remembered their lost son:[4]

Þialfi ok Holmlaug letu ræisa stæina þessa alla at Banka, sun sinn. Es atti æinn seR skip ok austr styrði i Ingvars lið. Guð hialpi and Banka/Bagga. Æskell ræist

(Þjalfi and Holmlaug had all these stones raised in memory of Banki, their son. He owned his own ship and sailed east with Ingvar's force. May God help Banki's spirt. Æskell carved.)

While no rune-stones commemorate peaceful journeys and trading expeditions, the self-consciously heroic tone of the Gripsholm memorial is absent from the brief Svinnegarn inscription. Only the word *lið* conveys the fact that this was a military expedition. Some of the 'Ingvar stones', like the one at Gredby, are classically concise: '*GunnulfR ræisti stæin þannsi at Ulf, faður sinn. Hann vaR i faru með Ingvari*'. ('Gunnulv raised this stone in memory of Ulv, his father. He travelled with Ingvar'.)[5] With just a change of names, the inscription on the Balsta stone is practically identical.[6]

Beyond telling us that it was in search of profit (gold), none of the inscriptions goes into detail about the purpose of the expedition, or the cause of death of its members. In a remarkable act of collaboration across the ages, an Icelandic saga, copied towards the end of the thirteenth century from a lost earlier manuscript, joins up the dots of these scattered stones to tell a coherent story which, despite the occasional presence of obviously fictional elements such as the appearance of a dragon and a giant, probably preserves a core of truth from an oral history of this ill-fated adventure until it could be written down.[7] According to his saga, Ingvar was a precocious child who left home at the age of nine to broker a peace between Øymund his father, and Øymund's old rival Olof Sköttkonung, king of the Swedes. He spent a few years in the *hird* of the Swedish king and distinguished himself in an action to restore Olof's tributary rights over a tribe in

Latvia. At the age of twenty he travelled away in search of a kingdom of his own. With thirty ships he crossed the Baltic and made his way to the Kievan court of Prince Jaroslav. Three years later he was on the move again, leading his men on a journey south in which he hoped to trace three unnamed rivers to their sources. This is a rare instance in saga literature of sheer curiosity being given as the motive for an adventure, and it sounds a faint echo of the Norwegian Ottar and the hazardous voyage he made around the northern tip of his country which was likewise motivated by curiosity alone. Along one of the rivers, Ingvar and his men came to a city of white marble over which a beautiful queen, named Silkisiv, ruled. She was a Heathen, like all the other women in the city, and Ingvar forbade his men to have anything to do with any of them. A few who disobeyed him were killed to re-establish his authority. Queen Silkisiv fell in love with Ingvar and offered him her kingdom and herself. No doubt promising himself he would see to her conversion first, he accepted her offer but postponed the marriage until he had first found the source of the river.

With the passing of winter he sailed on. A Greek king provided him with further information about the sources of the rivers, and about a year later his ships finally reached their goal, at a place called Lindibelti. The expeditionaries were attacked by local pirates who showered them with 'Greek fire'. The saga tells us that Ingvar took up his bow and shot back at them, using some kind of consecrated fire-arrows which successfully drove off the attackers. On their way back up the river, Ingvar's men were visited by a group of women. In defiance of Ingvar's warnings, eighteen of them lay with the women and in the morning were found dead in their beds. What remained of the party travelled on. Plague broke out among them and more died. Ingvar himself died. By now there were only twelve of the original fleet of thirty ships left. With the loss of their leader, disagreement broke out among the survivors about which direction to take for home. They split up but only one man, the Icelander Ketil, made it back to Gardarike. 'We don't know which way the others sailed,' says the storyteller, 'because most people think the ships sank.' Ketil eventually made his way home to Iceland, where he told his story and where, in due course, it came to be written down. The saga says that Ingvar was twenty-five years old when he died in 1041, and that this was eleven winters after the fall of Olav Haraldson at the battle of Stiklestad.

In the *Gesta Hamaburgensis*, Adam of Bremen tells a brief tale that has clear connections with the fate of Ingvar and his men. Citing as his source Bishop Adalward of Sigtuna, known as 'the Younger', in the same Lake Mälaren region as the main concentration of Ingvar stones, Adam writes of a military expedition sent by the Swedish king across the Baltic in search of territorial gain. The ships reached a territory Adam calls 'the land of women', where the leader and all his following were wiped out when the women poisoned the source of their drinking water.[8]

From the information given in the saga concerning Ingvar's time at the court of Jaroslav the Wise, he may well have been among the Varangians who helped Jaroslav drive away a huge army of Pechenegs that was laying siege to Kiev in 1036.[9] The saga also mentions the group's participation in a war in the more distant east, where they helped a king put down a rebellion led by his brother. This has been related to an entry in the old Georgian chronicle, *Kartlis tsovreba*, which describes the arrival, in the early 1040s, of a Varangian army at a place called Bashi, on the river Rioni, in Georgia. Seven hundred soldiers of the army joined a Georgian king, Bagrat, on his advance further into the country with the aim of putting down a rebellion led by his brother. There was a battle in the forest at Sasirethi, a few miles west of Tbilisi, now the Georgian capital, at which Bagrat's forces were defeated. The Varangians came to an agreement with the victors, set off westwards and disappeared from the record.[10] Though the river-journey as described does not correspond particularly well with the Volga, another possibility is that Ingvar and his men were Varangians sponsored by Prince Jaroslav to re-open trade routes along the lower reaches of the river which had become too dangerous to use because of the threat of nomadic tribesmen in the region.

In the final analysis all we know for certain is that twenty named men, from the Lake Mälaren region of eastern Sweden, died while on a journey through Russia under the leadership of a certain Ingvar. A cautious use of his saga as a source might allow us to add that Ingvar and his men left Sweden for Kiev and travelled on to the Black Sea. From there they probably sailed the Transcaucasian rivers until they reached the Caspian Sea. On their way home again the survivors of the journey fell victim to disease and poisoning, whether deliberate or accidental, and died. In its ambition, its obscurity and its ultimate failure, Ingvar's expedition is an appropriate symbol of the end of the large-scale, private-enterprise military activity that was perhaps the most significant defining characteristic of the Viking Age. In the words of the Gripsholm stone, 'they travelled far for gold'.

Of the three Scandinavian peoples in the Viking Age, it is the Swedes who most successfully remain hidden behind the swirl and chaos of history. Among the Svear and Gautar the art of skaldic poetry was not cultivated to anything like the extent it was among Norwegians and Icelanders; and in the centuries following the Viking Age no Swedish Snorri Sturluson or Saxo Grammaticus took it upon himself to write their early history. What the Swedes did have, by way of compensation, was a culture of raising rune-stones to commemorate the dead, and sometimes the living, to a degree that far exceeds anything in Norway or Denmark. The little we know of Viking Age Swedes derives largely from the histories and poems composed by other Scandinavians in which their kings and leaders play a part, from Rimbert's 'Life' of the ninth-century missionary Anskar, and from what can be gleaned from the inscriptions on these rune-stones. The dramatic flourishing of the fashion, from the middle of the tenth century to its decline around the beginning of the twelfth century, has been attributed to the renown of King Harald Bluetooth's Jelling stone, in Jutland in Denmark; but it was among the Swedes that the art reached its apotheosis. About 2,500 examples from the period have survived in Sweden, compared with some 220 in Denmark, a mere handful in Norway and none at all in Iceland.

Where the Ingvar stones are most evocative of our conventional ideas about the Viking Age is in their terseness and monumentality; the carving of an eagle's head on one stone intensifies its aura of Heathen exoticism. But it stands guard alone, heavily outnumbered by the references on at least eleven other stones to the Christian God, as well as the Christian crosses carved on several of them. The saga's depiction of Ingvar as an exceptionally pious Christian is an obvious exaggeration, but there is no reason to doubt that he and the majority of his party were baptized men. And yet, to a much greater degree than among either the Danes or the Norwegians, both of whom were by this time irrevocably members of the community of Christian peoples in Europe, Christianity among the Swedes was still struggling to establish the exclusive dominance which its dogma required. Perhaps it was that the territory was more remote; or that the spiritual centre of the whole cult of the Aesir was located at the temple in Gamla Uppsala (Old Uppsala) in Sweden.

The rapidity and scale of the conversions carried out under Harald Bluetooth in Denmark, and Olaf Tryggvason and Olav Haraldson in Norway, owed everything to the fact that they were native kings. Adam of Bremen quotes Sven Estridson, who succeeded Magnus the Good as king of Denmark in 1047, as advising the Hamburg-Bremen Bishop Adalbert against carrying out a plan to undertake a great missionary journey through the Scandinavian lands, on the grounds that 'the Heathens are more willing to be converted by someone who speaks their own language and who observes the same customs as themselves, than by foreigners who object to their way of life'.[11] By the middle of the eleventh century, no such determined, native, missionary king had yet risen among the Swedes, though there had been kings, like the Emund mentioned by Adam of Bremen, who were favourably disposed towards Christianity;[12] and Erik Segersäll, or 'the Victorious', whose victory in 988 over Styrbjørn Starke, in a battle near Uppsala, is referred to on rune-stones. Ingvar's saga makes the credible claim that Erik was the great-grandfather of Ingvar the Far-Travelled.

It is with Erik Segersäll that the more or less continuous history of the kings of Sweden begins. Adam tells us that he was baptized in Denmark, but reverted to the old religion on his return to Uppsala.[13] On his death in about 995 he was succeeded by his son Olof Sköttkonung. Olof was the first known king to rule over both the Svear and the Gautar of the Mälardalen and Västergötland regions of Sweden. He was also the first Swedish king to be baptized who did not later revert to Heathendom, and the first to practise the other major innovation associated with Christian modernity besides writing in Latin, the minting of coins to be used as coins and not as hack-silver to be judged by weight. He married Estrid, the Christian daughter of an Obodrite prince, who bore him a son, Jakob. He also had three children by his mistress Edla. His name 'Sköttkonung' probably derives from the fact that his profit from the battle of Svolder in 1000, at which Olaf Tryggvason of Norway was killed, was control over the Bohuslän district, on the eastern side of the Vik, which he ruled as Sven Forkbeard's tributary king. Other explanations on a stimulating roster of possibilities that depend upon different translations of the first element of his nickname include the 'sheet-' or 'lap-' king;[14] an interpretation that may suggest a caesarean birth; the possibility that he spent some time in Scotland; and that, as the first Swedish king to mint coins, he was remembered as 'the tax king'.

By the late 990s these coins, minted in his name by English moneyers in Sigtuna, bore Christian motifs, suggesting that King Olof was baptized earlier rather than later in his life, and almost certainly not as late as the 1008 given in the legendary 'Life' of St Sigfrid from the beginning of the thirteenth century, which ascribes his baptism to an English bishop Sigfrid, known as the apostle of Sweden. An intriguing suggestion that offers to settle a number of the problems connected to the dating of Olof's baptism, as well as the identity of the man who baptized him, proposes that the 'Anlaf' who raided in England with Sven Forkbeard in the early 990s, and whom the *Anglo-Saxon Chronicle* tells us was baptized at Andover in 994, was not the Norwegian Olaf Tryggvason at all but the young Olof Sköttkonung. Archbishop Sigeric of Canterbury was urgently involved in raising the money used to pay off the Viking armies in 994,[15] and it was very likely he that baptized 'Anlaf' at the ceremony in Andover that year. A subsequent confusion over the names 'Sigfrid' and 'Sigeric', as well as the 'Sigurd' mentioned by Snorri Sturluson in his reference to the event, may have become embedded in the traditions relating to Olof Sköttkonung's baptism. The uncertainties are entirely characteristic of Swedish history of the period.[16]

Adam of Bremen, who greatly admired Olof, tells us that at some unspecified point in his rule he proposed to pull down the temple at Uppsala as part of a campaign to convert the whole population of his regions, but that the Svear who formed the dominant majority in the coastal east remained as firmly attached to their Heathen beliefs as ever and would not allow it. In a solution that would probably not have appealed to Thorgeir Ljosvetningagodi in Iceland, Olof's authority was limited to control of the Götar of the Västergötland region in the west of the country, the region of present-day Gothenburg, which had been converted in the second half of the 990s and become a point of entry for missionary priests travelling in Sweden:[17] 'If he wished to be Christian himself he might choose the best part of Sweden and have full power there. He might build a church and introduce Christianity. But he must not force people to abandon the old faith. Only those who wished to should be converted.'[18] It seems that the arrangement was followed and as a possible result – for the chronology is uncertain – a bishopric was established at Skara in Västergötland in about 1013. Snorri adds that Olof's long and futile attempt to exploit the volatile situation in Norway at this time led him to neglect and finally lose his tributary rights over tribes on the other side of the Baltic, and that this was another factor in the dissatisfaction that led to his demotion.

For the last years of his reign, Olof ruled only over Västergötland, as a tributary king under his young son Jakob. As the name indicates, Jakob, too, was a Christian, but not one overly imbued with the missionary imperative. In an inversion of the practice we have become familiar with over the centuries of dealings between Christians and Heathens, Jakob adopted the local and traditional name 'Anund' at the request of his Heathen subjects, who made it a condition of his rule.[19] On his death in 1050 he was succeeded by his half-brother, Emund the Old, also called Emund the Mean, also a Christian. At about the same time, and as a reminder of how far Sweden still was from anything approaching a modern monarchy, Christianity was introduced into the province of Jemtland in north-central Sweden, with Norway on its western border, by a local chieftain about whom very little other than this is known.[20] The documentation is the inscription on the Frösö stone, the most northerly rune-stone in Sweden:

Austmaðr, Guðfastr's son had this stone raised and this bridge made and he made Jamtaland Christian. Ásbjôrn built the bridge, Trjónn (?) and Steinn carved these runes.[21]

Scholarly debate over the conversion of the Scandinavian peoples has long concerned itself with the competing claims to decisive involvement of German bishops associated with the archbishop of Hamburg-Bremen, and of missionary priests and bishops from England sponsored by Olaf Tryggvason and Olav Haraldson. Adam of Bremen writes that Emund the Old was baptized but that he was not much interested in religion, an ingenuous observation that may have been occasioned by the fact of Emund's open opposition to the German political influence in Sweden that the power of the Hamburg-Bremen see in Scandinavia entrained. He seems to have rejected the see's attempts to establish itself at Sigtuna, in Mälardalen, and to have driven its prospective bishop out of the country, on the grounds that there was already a bishopric in Mälardalen, complete with incumbent. Adam complains that this 'unofficial' appointee, Bishop Osmund, 'led the newly converted savages astray with his false teaching'.[22] Indeed, in the deaths of all the members of Ingvar's expedition Adam saw only God's just punishment for this particular effrontery.

Adam's condemnation of the 'false teaching' of both the king and his bishop may relate to a tradition that Emund provoked the German missionaries in Sweden with his attraction to eastern forms of Christianity, and a recent theory from Sweden on the origins, dating and significance of the so-called 'Lily-stones' suggests that the influence from Constantinople on the arrival of Christianity in Sweden may well have been underestimated.[23] These stone rectangles carved with stylized lilies, a familiar image of the resurrection, are among the earliest examples of Christian art known from Västergötland. Their original purpose is not known, but they are believed to have been used at some point as gravestones. The prevailing view is that they were influenced by English and German religious art and were carved in about 1100, at about the time the first stone churches were built. The radical hypothesis behind the new theory is that Viking Age Swedes who joined the Varangian Guard as the emperor's personal bodyguard were compelled to accept baptism before enrolment, and that the Christianity these returning Varangian mercenaries brought back with them when they returned to Sweden was accordingly neither the Hamburg-Bremen variety nor the Canterbury, but the Greek Orthodoxy of the Byzantine empire. The stones were then made to the commission of these homecoming warriors around 1000, thus a full century earlier than the date traditionally given for them, by local stonemasons whose influences were from the east. Finds of a number of other objects associated with eastern Christianity, such as resurrection eggs, as well as the occurrence of Greek crosses on rune-stones, can be used to support the theory. Its most dramatic proposal, however, is that Heathendom as a 'state religion' had effectively disappeared from Sweden as early as about 1000, and that when Adam of Bremen writes of conflict between 'Heathens' and 'Christians' and of attacks on 'Heathen temples', he is referring to a Swedish version of the conflict between the Catholic and the Orthodox Churches that was raging on the larger stage outside Scandinavia at this time. On this analysis, Adam's 'Heathen priests' were the Catholic Church's Orthodox competitors, and his 'Heathen temples', on the same analysis, the first churches to be built in the country in the late tenth and early eleventh centuries – rectangular wooden buildings, often elaborately decorated, with staves set directly into the ground. The break between the Catholic and the Orthodox Churches that occurred in 1054 finally compelled the triumph of Roman Christianity among Swedes and the theory proposes that a century of Greek Christianity in Sweden was thereafter edited out of Swedish history.[24] If further evidence emerges in support of this then the history of Christianity in Sweden will have to be rewritten. In the eleventh century that history has to be put together from some notoriously unreliable sources, but as things stand the general picture suggests that the Heathendom which Christianity struggled to overcome was the original, native version rather than imported, Byzantine Christianity.

Emund, son of Edla, a mistress of Olof Sköttkonung, proved to be the last of his line. Following his death in 1060, his son-in-law, a Västergötland earl named Stenkil, became king. Stenkil was an active promoter of Christianity who did not share his father-in-law's hostility to the archbishopric of Hamburg-Bremen, and it was probably he who established the see at Sigtuna, near the site of the great Heathen temple with its statues of Thor and Odin and Frey. Since at least the time of Anskar's mission in 829, the major trading centre in the east of Sweden had been Birka, but by the end of the tenth century its role had been taken over by Sigtuna, as rising land-levels made the old town increasingly inaccessible from the sea. Though Stenkil facilitated the work of Adalvard the Younger, the next German bishop to be appointed to the see, he prudently advised him against carrying out a plan to burn down the temple at Uppsala, predicting that he and his associate Egino would certainly be killed in revenge and he himself driven from the country as the sponsor of the men responsible for the act. Instead, the two bishops turned their attention to Götaland and the lesser violence of destroying Heathen images there. With Adalvard's death, however, the work of conversion was once again held up. Adam of Bremen tells us that his successor, a bishop named Tadiko from Ramelsloh, was a man too fond of his food who was more concerned 'to curb hunger at home than proselytize abroad'.[25]

Our knowledge of the events following the death of Stenkil in 1066 is, if anything, still more hazy than it is of events preceding it. Though Stenkil founded a dynasty that endured until the 1120s, it did not re-establish itself with any certainty until 1080 and the long reign of Inge the Old. The intervening twenty years see the appearance of a number of pretenders and phantom kings, whose existence is attested only in sagas with little claim to historical credibility. Even where doubt surrounds the very existence of these kings, the roles and actions ascribed to them in the legendary material seem to sound clear echoes of an intense phase of religious conflict in Sweden, in which Heathendom mounted a last and ultimately doomed campaign of defiance against the engulfing tide of Christian religious culture.

Rivals, both named Erik, engaged in a struggle for the succession so bloody that Adam of Bremen, our only reasonable source for the period, says that most of the leading men of the country were killed, including the two Eriks. The violence precipitated another crisis for the Christian Church as the bishops appointed to the sees at Skara and Sigtuna stayed in their homes in Germany in fear for their lives rather than travel.[26] Halsten, a son of King Stenkil, was then chosen as king; but nothing is known of his reign other than that it was brief and that he was driven out and replaced by a certain Anund, whom the Swedes had invited from Russia, and whose reign turned out to be equally short. Adam gives as the reason for his rejection his refusal, like Håkon the Good in Norway over 100 years earlier, to enact to the full the role of a Heathen king at the *Thing* meeting.[27] After so many decades of Christian influence and Christian institutional presence in the Mälaren region, the trenchant nature of the demands made of their king invites the suspicion that these Svear were still a largely syncretic people, who continued to ignore the Christian demand that the old gods be rejected as part of the acceptance of the new one. It may be eloquent of the tensions in the region that, in 1066, a Heathen reaction among the Obodrites, from the coastal region of what is now northern Germany, between Denmark and Poland, led to the killing of the Obodrite ruler and the destruction of all three Obodrite bishoprics, and that it took the institutional Church over fifty years to re-establish itself there.[28]

Håkon, known as the Red, as obscure as any of his immediate predecessors, seems to have succeeded Anund. We know nothing of his reign and can only presume that he was, if not Heathen himself, then at least tolerant enough of Heathen practices to go through the required motions at the sacrificial ceremonies. If, as seems likely, he remained in power for much of the 1070s, then a relatively long reign in such volatile times probably does indicate flexibility in the matter of religious faith and, most pertinently, in religious practice.

Of the circumstances of his death nothing is known, only that the succession of King Inge the Older saw the return of the Stenkil dynasty and a renewed attempt to impose Christianity or, equally, to eradicate Heathendom. A letter from Gregory VII, dated 4 October 1080 and addressed to 'the glorious king of the Svear', expresses the pope's satisfaction at the conversion of Inge's people to Christianity. A second letter in the following year addressing 'I and A' – only initials are used – as 'the glorious kings of the people of Västergötland' is a likely indication that there was a period of joint rule in which power was shared between Inge and his brother Hallsten. Ominously for the stability of the region, the letter concerned the payment of tithes to the Church. There seems to have been more turbulence, obscure but certainly of a religious nature, in which Eskil, the English bishop of Strängnäs in Södermanland, was stoned to death after an incident in which a Heathen ceremony was disrupted and the altar destroyed. The scene might have been Birka, the year 845, the murder that of Anskar's chaplain Nithard.

Now history, literature and myth once again dissolve into each other.[29] At the Assembly in 1084 Inge, like Anund before him – though confusion in the sources may well have conflated the two kings – is said to have refused to enact the king's part in the ceremonies. Sven, Inge's brother-in-law, who may only have been the fictional or symbolic creation of the compiler/author of the legendary, thirteenth-century 'Saga of Hervar and Heidrek' that tells the story, rose to address the enraged Heathens and promised that, if they would elect him king, he would carry out the sacrifices required of a king.[30] Sven was duly elected. The saga then describes a scene in which Sven led the Assembly in a ritual repudiation of Christianity as a horse was led out, sacrificed, cut up and its flesh passed around to be eaten. By common assent, the rituals of sacrifice to the old gods were re-introduced, and King Sven acquired a nickname – 'Blotsven', or Sven the Sacrificer.

Orkneyinga Saga turns aside from its main concern with the doings of the earls of the Northern Isles to describe Earl Håkon Paulson's visit to Sweden in the time of King Inge and offer a rapid résumé of what happened after Sven came to power. 'Inge was forced into exile and went to West Götaland, but eventually managed to trap Sven inside a house and burnt him there.'[31] Back on the throne again, Inge was able to press through the re-introduction of Christianity to the Svear. Finally, in about 1090, he presided over the long-postponed destruction of the great Heathen temple at Uppsala. With that, the last true refuge of Odin, Thor, Frey, Freyja and the rest of the Aesir was gone.[32]

Throughout the Viking Age, kings had founded towns. Hedeby's rise to prominence as an international trading centre began when the Danish king Godfrid compelled the tradesmen and merchants of Reric to relocate there in 808. Ribe, a little south of Jelling and on the west side of the Jutland peninsula, seems to have been founded at about the same time. Birka thrived for two centuries as the main trading centre in Sweden before the merchants moved their activities to Sigtuna. The cultivation of Kaupang, for a century and a half the major trading centre in southern Norway, and the goal of Ottar the merchant's long journey along the west coast of Norway, was probably the work of Danish kings such as Godfrid. Trondheim is believed to have been founded by Olaf Tryggvason in about 997, and Oslo's transformation from small settlement to large town began in the middle of the eleventh century and was the work of Harald Hardrada.

The origins of Lund in Skåne are obscure, but the church that was built there in about 990 was almost certainly the work of King Sven Forkbeard. By the turn of the century, Lund had a markedly cosmopolitan character, as a Christian centre, as the site of what would later become the largest mint in Scandinavia, and as the home of a large community of foreign artisans and craftsmen.[33] Both Sven and his son and successor Cnut conceived of Lund as a kind of ideally *modern* Scandinavian town. Paradoxically perhaps, in view of their military activities in the west, this involved for both the cultivation of a pronounced anglophilia. Sven's appointment of an English bishop to his church, Gotebald, was an early indicator of this.[34] After his death in England in 1014, Sven was buried in York. The author of the *Encomium Emmae Reginae* ('In Praise of Queen Emma') tells us, however, that he had previously chosen a burial site for himself in Lund, and in due course his remains were disinterred and taken over the sea to be reburied in the church built by himself. Recent excavations have revealed what seems to have been a grave beneath the floor of the church. It was empty, probably because Sven's remains were removed when the church was pulled down to make way for a stone church. The circumstances sound a poignant echo of the transfer, some fifty years earlier, of the remains of his grandfather, Gorm the Old, from the North Mound at Jelling to a Christian grave beneath the floor of the Jelling church. Pre-mortem funeral and burial arrangements may have been a family tradition among the Jelling kings. As we speculated earlier, the empty South Mound at Jelling was possibly intended by Harald Bluetooth as his own grave, with the circumstances of his death somehow making this impossible.

Following Sven's death, Cnut continued to develop and expand Lund. According to Adam of Bremen, it was Cnut's bold ambition to make the town 'as important as London'.[35] As well as employing English bishops in his church, he imported moneyers and designers from England, like the Leowin who signed the elegantly carved penholder found during the excavations of 1961. A moneyer with the same name was employed at the Lund mint around the turn of the tenth century and may well have been the same man. Also found was a walking stick, the intricate carvings on its handle in the form of a snake or dragon in the so-called Winchester style. Ulfkil, the maker's name, is etched on to the stick in runes, and the name is also found among the Lund moneyers active in the middle of the eleventh century. Across a large central area of the city, shards of Viking Age pottery have been found that are unique to Lund and to London.[36]

Lund's growing status presently demanded something more imposing than Sven's original wooden church and the larger stone church that replaced it was built by about 1050. In about 1060 the see of Lund was established, and its first incumbent was an English bishop, Henrik. Adam of Bremen who was, we must remember, writing a house-history of the archbishopric of Hamburg-Bremen, describes him as a drunken sybarite who choked to death on his own vomit. At about the same time as Lund was established, a German bishop named Egino was appointed to a second Danish see at nearby Dalby, and he took over at Lund on Henrik's death. By Adam's account a much more pious and learned man than his predecessor, Egino struck up an alliance with his colleague Adalvard at Sigtuna that, in the name of missionary Christianity, stretched right across geographical Sweden and ignored its political divisions. As we saw earlier, the two had to be dissuaded by King Stenkil from a plan to burn down the Heathen temple at Uppsala.

Back in 831, the see of Hamburg had been created to civilize the peoples of the north by bringing Christianity to them. We saw that, as a result of the Viking sack of the settlement in 848, Hamburg had been joined to Bremen and relocated there, with its missionary aims unchanged. Some two and a half centuries later, it would seem, the job was done, with the Danes, Swedes and Norwegians formally enrolled as members of the union of Christian peoples. And yet, in what should have been the hour of its greatest triumph, the see endured the bitter humiliation of having its authority over the region removed. The so-called 'investiture controversy' began when Pope Gregory VII, determined to reform a Church that turned a blind eye to clerical marriage and simony and to free it from the corrupting influence of the political world, neither notified nor sought the approval of the German King Henrik IV on the occasion of his consecration as pope in 1073. His reforming programme would put an end to royal control of the appointment of bishops, but Henrik defied him and continued to select bishops over whom he knew he had control. Rebuked by Gregory, he convened a synod of bishops at Worms in 1076, which obediently deposed his turbulent pope for him. Gregory responded by excommunicating Henrik, suspending his royal power and releasing his subjects from their oath of allegiance to him.[37] Henrik feared the move might precipitate a rebellion among his nobles, and in the extraordinary aftermath to this exchange walked barefoot across the Alps, wearing the hairshirt of a penitent, in search of an audience with Gregory at Canossa, and of his pardon. For three full days the pope kept him waiting and fasting in the snow outside the gates of the fortress where he was lodged before granting him an audience. Though Gregory revoked the excommunication, he upheld his deposition of the king as the lawful ruler of Germany. Henrik remained intransigent, and in 1080 Gregory lost patience with him and again excommunicated and deposed him, recognizing his rival Rudolf as the lawful king of Germany. Henrik's response was to appoint the first of that flock of anti-popes that would keep the institutional Church in a state of disarray for much of the next two centuries.

Gregory died in 1085, but Henrik had had himself crowned Holy Roman Emperor the year before by his anti-pope, Clement III, and the investiture controversy continued to sully the relationship between Henrik and Gregory's successors for years to come. For most of this crisis, Archbishop Liemar at Hamburg-Bremen had sided with the king against the reforming pope. In choosing to send his letter of congratulation and Christian welcome directly to King Inge in Sweden in 1080, Gregory had delivered a deliberate snub to the archbishopric on this account. His letter to Inge the following year, on the requirement to pay tithes to the Church, reflected his urgent need for both new friends and new sources of funds, and a feeling that both might be found among the newly converted peoples of the north.

For a long time Hamburg-Bremen had held the moral right to exercise institutional authority over the Church in Scandinavia, but with the support of its leaders for the German king and emperor in his struggle with the papacy it disappeared. Along with Lund's burgeoning status as a Christian and royal centre in the far north of

Europe, this led the papacy presently to take full account of the fact that the people of the north were now firmly committed to a modern, Christian civilization. Hamburg-Bremen was an irrelevancy and the Scandinavian Church could now be trusted to manage its own affairs. The first archbishopric with responsibility for all Scandinavia was established at Lund in 1103, with Asser as its first incumbent. New archbishoprics established at Nidaros in Norway in 1153 and Uppsala in 1164 moved the institutional Church ever further north. In St Olav, the Norwegians had had their patron saint since about 1034. The Danes, who had accepted Christianity at the monarchical level some sixty years earlier, had to wait a little longer for theirs. In 1086 Cnut II of Denmark was planning an invasion of William the Conqueror's England with a fleet which, somehow, never quite managed to leave the waters of the Limfjord. It was almost as though the memory of how such things were done was fading. Before it had returned he was dead, murdered by his enemies in the church of St Alban, in Odense. As St Cnut he was canonized in 1101. The canonization of the first saint-king of the Swedes was, in view of their enduring reluctance to join the fold, a suitably confused and ambiguous affair. In about 1155 Erik of Sweden, later known as 'the Holy', led an expedition into the southern tip of Finland. Brief and without discernible result, the spirit of the age nevertheless identified it as a crusade following his death in 1160 outside the church at Uppsala, allegedly against overwhelming odds and after a session at prayer inside the church. Erik was thereafter venerated as a saint by a local church anxious to achieve parity with its neighbours in the north, but his canonization was never official, for the papacy was persuaded by other stories that told of a drunkard who had met his death in a drink-fuelled brawl, so much so that in 1172 Pope Alexander III actively tried to forbid Erik's veneration.

But in the context of the Viking past of these Scandinavian kings, perhaps the starkest symbol of the demise of one culture and its replacement by another was the adventure of the Norwegian King Sigurd, known as Jorsalafarer, the Jerusalem Traveller, who led a crusade to the Holy Land in 1108 and was the first European ruler to do so.[38] When he returned to Norway three years later he brought back with him a splinter of the True Cross, given to him by Baldwin of Boulogne, first ruler of the Christian kingdom of Jerusalem. It was the most prized Christian relic of the age. We can be sure that Sigurd's Viking forefathers, had they come across it during a raid on a church, would have tossed it without a second thought into the flames of the fire they started on their way out.

Notes

ABBREVIATIONS USED IN THE NOTES

EHD   *English Historical Documents*, vol. 1, *c.*500–1042, 2nd edn, edited by Dorothy Whitelock, General editor David C. Douglas (London and New York 1979).

KHLNM   *Kulturhistorisk leksikon for nordisk middelalder fra vikingtid til reformasjonstid*, in 22 volumes. General editor John Danstrup (Copenhagen 1980–82).

Rundata   *Rundata* is the name of the joint Nordic database for runic inscriptions at http://www.nordiska.uu.se/forskn/samnord.htm. This was started at the University of Uppsala on 1 January 1993 with the aim of assembling in a single database every known Nordic runic inscription in the Scandinavian countries and beyond. The database currently contains some 6,000 inscriptions. References are given in the form A 123, where A indicates either the province of Sweden in which the stone was found or, if outside Sweden, the country, and 123 its serial number within the system. All inscriptions are given in transliterated and normalized forms, as well as in English translation. The database can be downloaded and is fully searchable.

AU   *The Annals of Ulster*. Corpus of Electronic Texts Edition: T100001 C. This is an Internet resource at http://www.ucc.ie/celt/published/T100001A. html.

A magazine called *Viking Heritage* is referred to several times in these Notes. For a number of years this exemplary mixture of the scholarly and the popular was published by the University of Gotland, Visby, under the editorship of Professor Dan Carlsson. Regrettably, it had to cease publication in 2005.

INTRODUCTION

1. Quoted in *Vikingtiden som 1800-tallskonstruksjon* by Jørgen Haavardsholm (Oslo 2004: 38).

2. 'The Viking Age – which period are we referring to?' by Sven Rosborn, in *Viking Heritage*, 1 (2005), p. 28.

3. 'Limits of Viking influence in Wales', by Mark Redknap, in *British Archaeology* 40 (December 1998, 40).

4. 'The Viking mind or in pursuit of the Viking', by Anthony Faulkes, in *Saga-Book*, journal of the Viking Society for Northern Research, vol. XXXI (University College, London 2007: 47).

5. Per Sveaas Andersen in *Forum Medievale*, no. 5, Oslo (June 2004: 51).

6. *Rundata* lists twelve.

7. Like most other Viking Age monuments, the stone takes its name from the place where it now stands, or where it was originally sited.

8. Finn Hødnebø in *Proceedings of the Tenth Viking Congress* (Oslo 1987: 50).

9. For a critique of the revisionist view, see David Dumville, *The Churches of North Britain in the First Viking Age* (Whithorn 1997: 9–14).

10. 'Traditionen om Gange Rolf' by Ebbe Hertzberg, in *Rikssamling og Kristendom*, ed. Andreas Holmsen and Jarle Simensen (Oslo 1967: 36–7).

11. *Skalk – Nyt om Gammelt*, 5 (October 2006), Cover text.

CHAPTER I THE OSEBERG SHIP

1. *Aftenposten* (28 October 2007). Report by Cato Guhnfeldt.

2. *Hva Oseberghaugen gjemte*, by A. Ljono (Oslo 1967: 11).

3. What follows is based on 'Gåten Oseberg', by Terje Gansum, in *Levende Historie* no. 6 (2004).

4. *Aftenposten* (2 April 2006: 2).

5. *Osebergdronningens grav, Vår arkeologiske nasjonalskatt i nytt lys*, ed. Arne Emil Christensen, Anne Stine Ingstad and Bjørn Myhre (Oslo 1992).

6. Although the fact that both had beds and were buried in the same chamber does not tally with the social status accorded the slave in Viking Age society.

7. Laszlo Berczelly in *Aftenposten* (9 April 2006: 2).

8. *The Saga of the Jomsvikings*, trans. Lee M. Hollander (Austin 1990: 109).

9. 'Risala: Ibn Fadlan's account of the Rus'. Internet resource at http://www.vikinganswerslady.com (accessed 16.02.2009).

10. Saxo Grammaticus, *The History of the Danes, Books I–IX*, ed. Hilda Ellis Davidson, trans. Peter Fisher (Cambridge 2002: 31).

11. *Hva Oseberghaugen gjemte*, op. cit., p. 19.

CHAPTER 2 THE CULTURE OF NORTHERN HEATHENDOM

1. *Fornnordisk mytologi enligt Eddans lärdomsdikter*, by Lars Magnar Enoksen (Lund 2004: 22).

2. A suggestive twist to Snorri's tale of tribal wandering from the south has been the identification of the DNA of the younger of the two Oseberg women as belonging to haploid group U7, which is rare in Europe but common in Iran and the region around the Black Sea ('Uskadd ut av kisten', Schrödingers katt, NRK 12.09.2007).

3. My interpretation of the basic structure outlined here owes much to Gro Stensland's *Eros og død i norrøne myter* (Oslo 1997).

4. *Poems of the Vikings*, trans. Patricia Terry (Indianapolis 1978: 64).

5. *Fornnordisk mytologi*, p. 133.

6. *The Poetic Edda*, trans. and introd. Carolyne Larrington (Oxford 1996: 34).

7. *Poems of the Vikings*, op. cit., p. 6.

8. 'Vikingenes stjernebildet', by Jonas Persson, in *Astronomi*, April 2004, p. 17.

9. *Star Names, their Lore and Meaning*, by Richard Hinckley Allen (New York 1963: 313).

10. *KHLNM*, vol. 20, p. 360.

11. ibid., vol. 6, p. 373.

12. *EHD*, p. 194.

13. *Poems of the Vikings*, op. cit., p. 29.

14. *Hávamál*, trans. and ed. D. A. H. Evans (London 1986: 123).

15. *Exodus* 24: 6–8.

16. *Saxo Grammaticus: The History of the Danes, Books I–IX: I. English Text; II. Commentary*, trans. and annotated by Hilda Ellis Davidson and Peter Fisher (Cambridge 2002: 172).

17. *Adam av Bremen. Beretningen om Hamburg stift, erkebiskopenes bedrifter og øyrikene i Norden*, trans. and ed. Bjørg Tosterud Danielsen and Anne Katrine Frihagen (Oslo 1993: 207) (Book IV, Chapters 26 and 27).

18. *KHLNM*, vol. 6, p. 254.

19. *The Poetic Edda*, op. cit., p. 167.

20. 'Vikinger fra Vestsjælland ofrede mennesker', by Anne Bech-Danielsen, in *Politiken*, 9 January 2009.

21. The pit and contents are on display in the Museum of Antiquities in Visby, Gotland.

22. Many of the surviving picture-stones are on display in the Museum of Antiquities, Visby, Gotland. The Hammars stone is in the open-air museum at Bunge, in the north of the island.

23. *The Viking Age in the Isle of Man. The archaeological evidence*, by David M. Wilson (Odense 1974: 26).

24. *Gulatingslovi*, trans. and ed. Knut Robberstad (Oslo 1952: 44).

25. 'Den gamla och den nya religionen', by Gustaf Trotzig, in *Gutar och vikingar*, ed. Ingmar Jansson (Stockholm 1983: 361).

26. *Møtet mellom hedendom og kristendom i Norden*, by Fredrik Paasche, ed. Dag Strömbäck (Oslo 1958: 115).

27. 'The communal nature of the judicial systems in early medieval Norway', by Alexandra Sanmark, in *Collegium Medievale*, Oslo 2006, pp. 31–64.

28. *Viking Age Iceland*, by Jesse Byock (London 2001: 225–6).

29. *Heimskringla, or The Lives of the Norse Kings*, by Snorri Sturluson, ed. with notes by Erling Monsen, trans. with the assistance of A. H. Smith (New York 1990: 11).

30. *Ynglingasaga*, trans. with notes by Carl Säve (Uppsala 1854: Chapter 7).

31. *The Poetic Edda*, op. cit., p. 89.

32. 'The *Historia Norwegie* as a shamanic source', by Clive Tolley. On-line resource at http://www.dur.ac.uk/medieval.www/sagaconf/tolley.htm (accessed 11.11.2007).

33. 'Oseberg-dronningen: hvem var hun?' by Anne Stine Ingstad, in *Oseberg-dronningens grav, Vår arkeologiske nasjonalskatt i nytt lys*, ed. Arne Emil Christensen, Anne Stine Ingstad and Bjørn Myhre (Oslo 1992). See also 'Viking-Age Sorcery' by Neil Price, in *Viking Heritage*, nos. 3/2004 and 4/2004.

34. 'Osebergkvinne var invalid', by Cato Guhnfeldt, in *Aftenposten*, 15 January 2009, p. 7.

35. *Poems of the Vikings*, trans. Patricia Terry (Indianapolis 1978: 22).

36. *Ville vikinger i lek og idrett* by Bertil Wahlqvist (Oslo 1980: 51).

37. *Ingimund's Saga. Norwegian Wirral*, by Stephen Harding (Birkenhead 2006: 75).

38. *KHLNM*, vol. 4, p. 157.

39. ibid., p. 158.

40. *The Topography of Ireland*, by Giraldus Cambrensis, trans. Thomas Forester, rev. and ed. with additional notes by Thomas Wright, ch. XXVI.

41. *Heimskringla*, op. cit., p. 6.

42. ibid., p. 7

43. *KHLNM*, vol. 20, p. 382.

44. *Kampen om Nordwegen*, by Torgrim Titlestad (Bergen-Sandviken 1996: 37).

45. 'Osebergskipets gåte løst', by Cato Guhnfeldt, in *Aftenposten*, 1 March 2009. The dendrochronological analyses reported on here were the work of Niels Bonde in Copenhagen and Frans-Arne Stylegar in Vest-Agder, Norway.

CHAPTER 3 THE CAUSES OF THE VIKING AGE

1. *The Anglo-Saxon Chronicle*, trans. and ed. G. N. Garmonsway (London 1990: 57).

2. *Vikingatiden i Skåne*, by Fredrik Svanberg (Lund 2000: 20).

3. *Alcuin of York*, c. AD 732 to 804 – *his Life and Letters*, by Stephen Allott (York 1974: 18).

4. *EHD*, p. 273.

5. *Alcuin of York*, op. cit., pp. 18–19.

6. *EHD*, p. 896. The meaning of 'blinded eyes' is obscure. It might refer to a hairstyle, or possibly to eye make-up.

7. Ingeld is a character in *Beowulf*, whose father was killed by Danes; see *Beowulf*, ed. and introd. Michael Swanton (Manchester 1978: 132–3).

8. *The Agricola and Germania* by Tacitus, trans. A. J. Church and W. J. Brodribb (London 1877). Internet resource from ORB: Internet Medieval Sourcebook at http://www.fordham.edu/halsall/source/tacitus1.html (accessed 02.07.2004).

9. *Roman Britain and Anglo-Saxon England 55 BC–AD 1066* by Richard Fletcher (Mechanicsburg 2002: 117).

10. *Karmøys historie – som det stiger frem fra istid til 1050*, by Per Hernæs (Stavanger 1997: 201). See also 'The archaeology of the Early Viking Age in Norway', by Bjørn Myhre, in *Ireland and Scandinavia in the Early Viking Age*, ed. H. B. Clarke, Máire Ní Mhaonaigh and Ragnhall Ó Floinn (Dublin 1998: 3–36).

11. *Namn og gard. Studium av busetnadsnamn på – land*, by Inge Særheim, Ph.D thesis, University of Bergen, 2000.

12. 'Government in Scandinavia around 1000 AD', by Carl Löfving, in *Viking Heritage*, 4 (2001: 27).

13. The most fully argued presentation of this point of view is in *Kampen om Nordvegen*, by Torgrim Titlestad (Bergen 1996).

14. *Carolingian Chronicles: Royal Frankish Annals* and Nithard's *Histories*, trans. Bernhard Walter Scholz with Barbara Rogers (Michigan 1972: 51).

15. *EHD*, p. 269.

16. *The Life of Lebuin*. Internet resource at *Medieval Sourcebook*, http://www.fordham.edu/halsall/basis/lebuin.html.

17. *Carolingian Chronicles*, op. cit., p. 61.

18. *Two Lives of Charlemagne*, by Einhard and Notker the Stammerer, trans. and introd. Lewis Thorpe (London 1969: 63).

19. 'Capitulary' was the term used for all legislative and administrative decrees issued by the Frankish court in the time of Charlemagne.

20. 'Violence against Christians? The Vikings and the Church in ninth-century England', by Sara Foot, in *Medieval History*, vol.1, no. 3 (1991: 12).

21. *EHD*, p. 397.

22. *Carolingian Chronicles*, op cit. p. 50.

23. *Two Lives of Charlemagne*, op. cit., p. 61.

24. *The Decline and Fall of the Roman Empire*, by Edward Gibbon, chapter XLIX. Internet resource at http://www.ccel.org/g/gibbon/decline/index.htm (accessed 2.11.2007).

25. *The Outline of History: Being a plain history of life and mankind* by H. G. Wells et al. (New York 1920: Part II, 32.4).

26. Musset's views are summarized in 'The Vikings in Frankia', in *Early Medieval History*, by J. M. Wallace-Hadrill (Oxford 1975: 223).

27. *EHD*, p. 180.

28. *Ecclesiastical History of the English People*, by Bede, trans. Leo Shirley-Price, revised by R. E. Latham (London 1990: 278).

29. *Møtet mellom Hedendom og Kristendom i Norden*, by Fredrik Paasche (Oslo 1958: 75).

30. See *Decolonizing the Viking Age 1*, by Fredrik Svanberg (Lund 2003), for a particularly articulate account of the viewpoint expressed here.

31. 'Roskipet som maktsymbol', by Bjørn Myhre, in *Borreminne 1996*, p. 5, Arkeologisk museum i Stavanger. Internet resource at http://borreminne. hive.no/aargangene/1996/03-roskipet.htm (accessed 12.11.2007).

32. 'The beginning of the Viking Age – some current archæological problems', by Bjørn Myhre, in *Viking Revaluations*, ed. Anthony Faulkes and Richard Perkins (London 1993: 182–199).

33. 'Myten om menneskets skapelse i Voluspå – en speiling av Adam og Eva i Genesis – et hedensk motsvar til den bibelske myten – eller noe midt i mellom?' by Gro Steinsland. Seminar lecture at Middelaldersenteret, University of Oslo, 27 May 2004.

34. 'På tvers av Nordsjøen – Britiske perspektiv på Skandinavernes senere

jernalder', by John Hines, in *Universitets oldsaksamling Årbok 1991–1992* (Oslo 1993: 103–24).

35. 'Kirkebesøg', by Maria Panum Baastrup, in *Skalk*, 5 (October 2007: 17).

36. 'Norse studies: then, now and hereafter', by Christine Fell, in *Viking Revaluations*, op. cit., p. 94.

CHAPTER 4 'THE DEVASTATION OF ALL THE ISLANDS OF BRITAIN BY THE HEATHENS'

1. *The Vikings*, by Johannes Brønstad (London 1973: 18).

2. 'Embla: a Viking ship has been reconstructed', by Gunilla Larsen, in *Viking Heritage*, 4 (1998: 1–4).

3. 'Tiller thriller', by Jörgen Johansson, in *Viking Heritage*, 2 (2005: 23–4).

4. Not to be confused with six different Viking Age ships, the 'Roskilde ships', discovered in 1996.

5. See http://www.vikingeskibsmuseet.dk/page.asp?objectid=290&zcs=402.

6. 'Jakter på DNA i Osebergskipet', by Cato Guhnfeldt, *Aftenposten*, 10 July 2006. An unexpected benefit of this has been to provide marine biologists with invaluable information about the DNA of whales in the Viking Age.

7. *Arkæologi Leksikon*, ed. Lotte Hedeager and Kristian Kristiansen (Copenhagen 1985: 224).

8. 'Paviken – a Viking-age port and shipyard', by Malin Linquist, in *Viking Heritage*, 4 (2004: 17).

9. *KHLNM*, vol. 12, p. 261.

10. 'The wooden disc from Wolin', by Blazej M. Stanislawski, in *Viking Heritage*, 2 (2002: 10–11).

11. *KHLNM*, vol. 12, p. 260.

12. 'Fine prehistoric optics or just finery?' by Malin Lindquist, in *Viking Heritage*, 3 (2000: 3–4).

13. *EHD*, p. 182.

14. ibid., p. 273.

15. ibid., p. 281.

16. 'Pict and Viking: settlement or slaughter?' by Sigurd Towrie. Internet resource at http://www.orkneyjar.com/history/vikingorkney/takeover.htm (accessed 13.11.2007).

17. *AU* 794.7.

18. *The Anglo-Saxon Chronicle*, trans. and ed. G. N. Garmonsway (London 1990: 57, n. 5).

19. 'The Vikings in Ireland and Scotland in the ninth century', by Donnchadh

Ó Corráin. Internet resource in 'Chronicon: An electronic history journal' at http://www.ucc.ie/chronicon/ocorr2.htm (accessed 02.02.2004).

20. *Orkneyinga Saga*, trans. and ed. Hermann Pálsson and Paul Edwards (London 1978: 26–7).

21. 'Genocide in Orkney? The fate of the Orcadian Picts', by Julie Gibson and Tom Muir, in *Viking Heritage*, 3 (2005: 26).

22. *The Conversion of Europe*, by Richard Fletcher (London 1997: 169).

23. 'Before the Vikings: pre-Norse Caithness', by Robert B. Gourlay, in *The Viking Age in Caithness, Orkney and the North Atlantic*, ed. Colleen E. Batey, Judith Jesch and Christopher D. Morris (Edinburgh 1993: 115).

24. *Viking Orkney: Did Vikings kill the native population of Orkney and Shetland?*, an essay by Brian Smith, quoting John Steward. Internet resource at http://www.orkneyjar.com/history/vikingorkney/warpeace/ (accessed 26.02.2006). See also 'Explorers, raiders and settlers. The Norse impact upon Hebridean place-names', by Arne Kruse, in *Cultural Contacts in the North Atlantic Region: The evidence of names*, ed. P. Gammeltoft, C. Hough and D. Waugh, published by NORNA, Scottish Place-name Society and Society for Name Studies in Britain and Ireland (2005: 141–56).

25. 'Central places in Viking Age Orkney', by Frans-Arne Stylegar, in *Northern Studies*, no. 38 (2004: 6).

26. *Viking Scotland*, by Anna Ritchie (London 2001: 28).

27. *Viking Orkney*, op. cit.

28. See http://www.orkneyjar.com/history/vikingorkney/genetics.htm.

29. 'Viking genetics survey results', by Nicola Cook (December 2001), BBC History. Online resource (accessed 3.3.2003).

30. *Historia Norwegie*, ed. Inger Ekrem and Lars Boje Mortensen, trans. Peter Fisher (Copenhagen 2003: 67).

31. ibid., p. 65.

32. See 'An ethnic enigma – Norse, Pict and Gael in the Western Isles', by Andrew Jennings and Arne Kruse, in *Proceedings of the Fourteenth Viking Congress*, ed. Andras Mortensen (Tórshavn 2001: 251–63).

33. 'Genetic evidence for a family-based Scandinavian settlement of Shetland and Orkney during the Viking periods', by S. Goodacre, A. Helgason, J. Nicholson, L. Southam, L. Ferguson, E. Hickey, E. Vega, K. Stefánsson, R. Ward and B. Sykes, in *Heredity*, no. 95 (2005: 129–35). Published online, 6 April 2005, at http://www.nature.com/hdy/.

34. *Sunday Times*, 5 January 2003.

35. *AU* 798.2.

36. Quoted in 'The Viking towns of Ireland', by Liam de Paor, in *Proceedings*

of the Seventh Viking Congress, ed. Bo Almqvist and David Greene (Dublin 1976: 29).

37. 'The Irish Church, 800–*c*.1050', by Kathleen Hughes, in *A New History of Ireland*, ed. Daibhi Ó Cróinín (Oxford 2005: 637).

38. *Ireland before the Normans*, by Donncha Ó Corráin (Dublin 1972: 28–32).

39. *AU*, 807.9.

40. *AU*, 831.5.

41. *AU*, 830.6.

42. 'The Irish Church, 800–*c*.1050', op. cit., p. 636.

43. CELT Corpus of Electronic Texts at http://celt.ucc.ie/irllist.html, *AU*, 828.3.

44. ibid., *AU*, 800.6.

45. 'The Viking Age', by F. J. Byrne, in *A New History of Ireland*, ed. Daibhi Ó Cróinín (Oxford 2005: 612).

46. *KHLNM*, vol. 13, p. 440.

47. 'The Irish Church, 800–*c*.1050', op. cit., p. 638.

48. 'Short report on a recent Viking find in Norway', by Ragnar L. Børsheim, in *Viking Heritage*, 1 (2000: 22).

49. 'Insular finds in Viking Age Scandinavia and the state formation of Norway', by Egon Wamers, in *Ireland and Scandinavia in the Early Viking Age*, ed. H. B. Clarke, Máire Ní Mhaonaigh and Ragnhall Ó Floinn (Dublin 1998).

50. *AU*, 853.2.

51. 'Viking genetics survey results', op. cit.

52. 'Nordisk innvandring, bosetning og samfunnsdannelse på Isle of Man i middelalderen', by Per Sveaas Andersen, in *Collegium Medievale*, vol. 8.1 (1995: 5–49).

53. *The Viking Age in the Isle of Man*, op. cit., p. 41. See also http://www.gumbley.net/churches.htm.

54. *Orkneyinga Saga*, op. cit., pp. 74–5.

55. 'Viking Age Faroe Islands and their southern links', by Steffen Stummann Hansen, in *The Viking Age in Caithness, Orkney and the North Atlantic*, op. cit., p. 475.

56. *The Vikings in History*, by F. Donald Logan (London 1992: 61).

57. *Skalk*, 2 (April 2007: 24–5).

CHAPTER 5 THE VIKINGS IN THE CAROLINGIAN EMPIRE

1. *Two Lives of Charlemagne*, by Einhard and Notker the Stammerer, trans. and introd. Lewis Thorpe (London 1969: 159).
2. *The Annals of Fulda*, trans. and annotated by Timothy Reuter (Manchester 1992: 122).
3. 'Study into the socio-political history of the Obodrites', by Roman Zaroff, *Collegium Medievale* vol. 16 (2003: 7).
4. *Carolingian Chronicles: Royal Frankish Annals* and Nithard's *Histories*, trans. Bernhard Walter Scholz with Barbara Rogers (Michigan 1972: 59).
5. *Two Lives of Charlemagne*, op. cit., p. 72.
6. ibid., p. 68.
7. The origin and meaning of the nickname Klak are uncertain. See *The Works of Sven Aggesen*, trans. with introd. and notes by Eric Christiansen (London 1992: 116–17).
8. *Carolingian Chronicles*, op. cit., p. 96.
9. 'Haugbrott eller gravplyndring i tidlig kristentid?' by Bjørn Myhre, in *Fra hammer til kors. 1000 år med kristendom. Brytningstid I Viken* (Oslo 1994: 85).
10. *Carolingian Chronicles*, op. cit., p. 114.
11. ibid., p. 114
12. 'Rimbert: *Life of Anskar*, the Apostle of the North, 801–865', trans. Charles H. Robinson, ch. 7. Internet resource at *Medieval Sourcebook*, http://www.fordham.edu/halsall/basis/anskar.html (accessed 17.02.2004).
13. 'The medieval theory of empire', in *Lectures in the History of Political Thought*, by Michael Oakeshott (Charlottesville 2006: 288–9).
14. 'Study into the socio-political history of the Obodrites', by Roman Zaroff, *Collegium Medievale*, vol. 16 (2003: 25).
15. *Adam av Bremen. Beretningen om Hamburg stift, erkebiskopenes bedrifter og øyrikene i Norden*, trans. and ed. Bjørg Tosterud Danielsen and Anne Katrine Frihagen (Oslo 1993: 37–8) (Book 1, Chapter 15).
16. *Two Lives of Charlemagne*, op. cit., pp. 168–9.
17. Rimbert: *Life of Anskar*, op. cit., ch. 7.
18. *The Annals of St-Bertin*, trans. and annotated by Janet L. Nelson (Manchester 1991: 51) (s.a. 841).
19. ibid.
20. *Saxo Grammaticus: The History of the Danes, Books I–IX: I. English*

Text; II. Commentary, trans. and annotated by Hilda Ellis Davidson and Peter Fisher (Cambridge 2002: 291).

21. *The Annals of Fulda*, op. cit., p. 33.

22. Rimbert: *Life of Anskar*, op. cit., ch. 9.

23. ibid., ch. 11.

24. ibid., ch. 12.

25. ibid.

26. ibid.

27. *Carolingian Chronicles*, op. cit., p. 108.

28. 'The foreign policy of Horik I, king of Denmark 814–54', by Nils Lund. Internet resource from *Historisk Tidskrift*. At http://www.historisktids skrift.dk/summary/102_21.html (accessed 02.06.2004).

29. 'Ex Ermentarii miraculis sancti Filiberti'. Extracts trans. and printed in *The History of Feudalism*, ed. David Herlihy (London 1971: 9).

30. *The Annals of St-Bertin*, op. cit., p. 60.

31. 'The defence of Birka – this year's excavation at the Garrison', by Lena Holmquist Olausson, in *Viking Heritage*, 5 (1998: 6–8).

32. Bj 854: 'Rikaste kvinnan i Birka', on CD-ROM *Vikingarnas Birka: Utstillingen 1998*. Produced by Statens Historiska Museum, Stockholm, 2000.

33. Rimbert: *Life of Anskar*, op. cit., ch. 19.

34. ibid., ch. 17.

35. ibid., ch. 19.

36. *The Annals of St-Bertin*, op. cit., p. 65.

37. Rimbert: *Life of Anskar*, op. cit., ch. 31.

38. *Adam av Bremen*, op. cit., p. 46 (Book 1, Chapter 28).

39. 'Pagan and Christian in the age of conversion', by Anne-Sofie Gräslund, in *Proceedings of the Tenth Viking Congress* (Oslo 1987: p. 85).

40. See, for example, *Encyclopaedia of the Viking Age*, by John Haywood (London 2000: p. 24).

41. 'The Frankish tribute payments to the Vikings and their consequences', by Simon Coupland, in *Francia*, 26, 1 (1999).

42. *The Annals of Fulda*, op. cit., p. 30.

43. ibid., p. 91.

44. *The Annals of St-Bertin*, op. cit., p. 224.

45. *The Annals of Fulda*, op. cit., p. 92.

46. Abbo's *'Wars of Count Odo with the Northmen in the Reign of Charles the Fat*. Quoted in *A Source Book of Medieval History*, ed. Frederic A. Ogg (Chicago 1907: 168).

47. 'The Vikings in Francia', in *Early Medieval History*, by J. M. Wallace-Hadrill (Oxford 1975; 208).

48. 'Three sources on the ravages of the Northmen in Frankland, *c.*843–912: Abbo's '*Wars of Count Odo with the Northmen in the Reign of Charles the Fat*'. Internet resource at *Medieval Sourcebook*, http://www.fordham.edu/halsall/source/843bertin.html (accessed 21.07.2006).

CHAPTER 6 ACROSS THE BALTIC

1. For a full discussion of these and other possible goals see *The Emergence of Rus, 750–1200*, by Simon Franklin and Jonathan Shepard (Eastbourne 2002: 31–41).
2. *Aschehougs Norges Historie b.2: Vikingtid og rikssamling 800–1139*, by Claus Krag (Oslo 2005: 14).
3. *Heimskringla, or The Lives of the Norse Kings*, by Snorri Sturluson, ed. with notes by Erling Monsen, trans. with the assistance of A. H. Smith (New York 1990: p. 23).
4. ibid., p. 9.
5. *Stones, Ships and Symbols*, by Erik Nylén and Jan Peder Lamm (Stockholm 1998: 144).
6. 'Saxo Grammaticus on the Balts', by Tomas Baranauskas, in *Saxo and the Baltic Region. A symposium*, ed. Tore Nyberg (Odense 2004: 71).
7. 'Grobin – Anskars-krönikans Seeburg?' by Agneta Lundström, in *Gutar och vikingar* (Stockholm 1983: 325).
8. 'Gotland och Ostbaltikum', by Lena Thunmark-Nylén, in ibid., pp. 306–22.
9. 'The first Scandinavians in northern Rus', by E. N. Nosov in *Viking Heritage*, 2 (2001: 11).
10. *The Islamic World, Russia and the Vikings 750–900: the numismatic evidence*, by Thomas S. Noonan (Aldershot 1998: 333).
11. *The Eastern World of the Vikings. Eight essays about Scandinavia and Eastern Europe in the early Middle Ages*, by E. A. Melnikova (Gothenburg 1996: 33).
12. *The Russian Primary Chronicle*, trans. and ed. Samuel H. Cross (Cambridge, Mass. 1930: 130).
13. 'Rus', by P. B. Golden, in *The Encyclopedia of Islam. New Edition*, vol. 7, ed. C. E. Bosworth, E. van Donzel, B. Lewis and Ch. Pellat (Leiden 1986: 624).
14. *The Hoard from Spillings*, ed. Gun Westholm (Gotland 2005: 12–13).
15. *The Eastern World of the Vikings*, op. cit., p. 40.
16. *The Russian Primary Chronicle*, op. cit., p. 122.

17. 'Saxo Grammaticus on the Balts', op. cit., p. 75.

18. *The Russian Primary Chronicle*, op. cit., p. 145.

19. 'Rimbert: *Life of Anskar*, the Apostle of the North, 801–865', trans. Charles H. Robinson, ch. 30. Internet resource at *Medieval Sourcebook*, http://www.fordham.edu/halsall/basis/anskar.html (accessed 17.02.2004).

20. *The Russian Primary Chronicle*, op. cit., p. 121.

21. ibid., p. 123.

22. *The Emergence of Rus*, op. cit., pp. 53–7.

23. Photios, quoted in *The Emergence of Rus*, op. cit., p. 51.

24. *The Russian Primary Chronicle*, op. cit., p. 149.

25. ibid., p. 150.

26. *Kievan Russia*, by George Vernadsky (New Haven and London 1976: 22).

27. *The Russian Primary Chronicle*, op. cit., p. 154.

28. *Kievan Russia*, op. cit., p. 54.

29. ibid., pp. 39–40.

30. *Vikingenes Russland*, by Halvor Tjønn (Stavanger 2006: 47).

31. *The Emergence of Rus*, op. cit., p. 150.

32. *Chronicles of the Viking. Records, Memorials and Myths*, by R. I. Page (London 2000: 95).

33. ibid., p. 96.

34. 'Gotländska runinskrifter', by Thorgunn Snædal Brink and Ingmar Jansson, in *Gutar och vikingar* (Stockholm 1983: 427).

35. 'The Antipodes – a little something about two ocean trades that never met, or . . .', by Malin Lindquist, in *Viking Heritage*, 3 (2002: 16).

36. *Stones, Ships and Symbols*, op. cit., pp. 90–97.

37. *Rundata*, G 116.

38. Public Lecture given at the Länsmuseet in Visby, Gotland, in 2005.

39. *The Hoard from Spillings*, ed. Gun Westholm (Gotland 2005: 15).

40. *Kievan Russia*, op. cit., p. 58.

41. *The Russian Primary Chronicle*, op. cit., p. 180.

42. *The Emergence of Rus*, op. cit., p. 158.

43. *The Russian Primary Chronicle*, op. cit., p. 159.

44. *The Emergence of Rus*, op. cit., p. 142.

45. ibid., p. 159.

46. 'Rus', op. cit., p. 627.

47. *The Russian Primary Chronicle*, op. cit., p. 200.

CHAPTER 7 THE DANELAW I: OCCUPATION

1. *Fact and Fiction in the Legend of St Edmund*, by Dorothy Whitelock, in *Proceedings of the Suffolk Institute of Archaeology*, 31 (1969: 233, note 17).
2. Book review by Matthew Innes, in *Saga-Book* of the *Viking Society for Northern Research*, vol. XXVI (2002: 126).
3. *England: An Oxford Archaeological Guide to Sites from Earliest Times to AD 1600*, by Timothy Darvill, Paul Stamper and Jane Timby (Oxford 2002: 184–5).
4. 'Boundaries and cult centres', by Julian D. Richards, in *Select Papers from the Proceedings of the Thirteenth Viking Congress* (Oxford 2001: 99–100).
5. *EHD* p. 194.
6. ibid., p. 277.
7. ibid., p. 195.
8. ibid., p. 194.
9. *The Poetic Edda*, trans. and introduced by Carolyne Larrington (Oxford 1999: 20).
10. *Alfred the Great: Asser's Life of King Alfred and other contemporary sources*, trans. and introd. by Simon Keynes and Michael Lapidge (London 1983: 83).
11. ibid.
12. ibid., p. 197.
13. ibid., p. 203.
14. ibid., p. 85.
15. ibid., p. 87.
16. *EHD* p. 199.
17. ibid., p. 416.
18. ibid.
19. *Íslendingabók and Kristni Saga*, trans. Siân Grønlie (London 2006: 3 and 14).
20. *Norrøne Gude- og Heltesagn*, by P. A. Munch. Revised edition by Anne Holtsmark (Oslo 1981: 266).
21. *Saxo Grammaticus: The History of the Danes, Books I–IX: I. English Text; II. Commentary*, trans. and annotated by Hilda Ellis Davidson and Peter Fisher (Cambridge 2002: 281 and 292).
22. *Orkneyinga Saga*, trans. and ed. Hermann Pálsson and Paul Edwards (London 1978: 29–31).
23. See, for example, the exchanges in the *Saga Book (Notes and Reviews)*

of the *Viking Society for Northern Research*, vol. XXII, 1 (1986: 79–82); vol. XXII, 5 (1988: 287–9); vol. XXIII, 2 (1990: 80–83).

24. *Adam av Bremen, Beretningen om Hamburg stift, erkebiskopenes bedrifter og øyrikene i Norden*, trans. and ed. Bjørg Tosterud Danielsen and Anne Katrine Frihagen (Oslo 1993), p. 50 (Book 1, Chapter 37).

25. *EHD*, p. 192.

26. *Abbo of Fleury: The Martyrdom of St Edmund, King of East Anglia, 870*, trans. K. Cutler in *Sweet's Anglo-Saxon Primer* (Oxford 1961: 81–7).

27. 'Repton and the "great heathen army", 873–4', by Martin Biddle and Birthe Kjølbye-Biddle, in *Select Papers from the Proceedings of the Thirteenth Viking Congress* (Oxford 2001: 83).

28. 'Kings and kingship in Viking Northumbria', by Rory McTurk. Pre-print of conference paper, Thirteenth International Saga Conference, Durham and York, 2006. Internet resource at http://www.dur.ac.uk/medieval.www/saga conf/mcturk.htm (accessed 13.10.2006).

29. J. de Vries, quoted in *Saxo Grammaticus*, op. cit., pp. 281 and 154.

30. 'Vikingerne i Vasconia', by Anton Erkoreka, in *Vikingerne på Den Iberiske Halvø* (Madrid 2004: 22).

31. 'Repton and the "great heathen army", 873–4', op. cit., p. 77.

32. ibid., p. 67.

33. 'Boundaries and cult centres', op. cit., p. 100.

34. 'Repton and the "great heathen army", 873–4', op. cit., pp. 82–4.

35. *EHD*, p. 202 (s.a. 893).

36. ibid., p. 203 (s.a. 893).

37. ibid., p. 205.

38. ibid., p. 200.

39. *Early Medieval History*, by J. M. Wallace-Hadrill (Oxford 1975: 226–7).

40. *The Vikings: a very short introduction*, by Julian D. Richards (Oxford 2005: 72).

41. Fitzwilliam Museum, Coins and Medals – The Normans, 5.1. 'Finds from the Viking Wintercamp at Torksey'. Internet resource at http://www.fitz museum.cam.ac.uk/gallery/normans/chapters/Normans_3_5.htm#c51 (accessed 4.11.2007).

42. *Ottar og Wulfstan. To rejsebeskrivelser fra vikingetiden*, ed. Niels Lund (Roskilde 1983: 20).

43. *Alfred the Great*, op. cit., p. 103; see also Fulco's letter to Alfred, ibid., p. 182.

44. *Vikings: Fear and Faith*, by Paul Cavill (Michigan 2001: 272).

45. ibid., p. 272.

46. *Ottar og Wulfstan*, op. cit., p. 14.

CHAPTER 8 THE SETTLEMENT OF ICELAND

1. *The Book of the Settlements*, in *The Norse Atlantic Saga*, by Gwyn Jones (Oxford 1986: 157).

2. ibid., p. 159.

3. ibid., p. 158.

4. *Historia Norwegie*, ed. Inger Ekrem and Lars Boje Mortensen, trans. Peter Fisher (Copenhagen 2003: 71).

5. *Viking Age Iceland*, by Jesse Byock (London 2001: 89).

6. *Íslendingabók and Kristni Saga*, trans. Siân Grønlie (London 2006: xiv–xviii).

7. ibid., p. 4.

8. *The Norse Atlantic Saga*, op. cit., p. 35, n. 7.

9. ibid., p. 33.

10. See 'The Papar Project'. Internet resource at http://www.rcahms.gov.uk/papar/introduction.html (accessed 4.11.2005).

11. 'Cave culture in South Iceland', by Florian Huber, in *Viking Heritage*, 4 (2001: 8).

12. *Historia Norwegie*, op. cit., p. 67.

13. *Íslendingabók and Kristni Saga*, op. cit., p. 17.

14. *Heimskringla, or The Lives of the Norse Kings*, by Snorri Sturluson, ed. with notes by Erling Monsen, trans. with the assistance of A. H. Smith (New York 1990: 43–77).

15. ibid., p. 46.

16. See *Ynglingatal og Ynglingesaga: En studie i Historiske Kilder*, by Claus Krag (Oslo 1991).

17. See, for example, 'Storhaugene i Vestold – riss av en forskningshistorie', by Einar Østmo, in *Gokstadhøvdingen og hans tid* (Sandefjord 1997: 55–7).

18. 'Islands forfatning', by Ólafur Lárusson, in *Rikssamling og kristendom*, ed. Andreas Holmsen and Jarle Simensen (Oslo 1967: 219).

19. *Heimskringla*, op. cit., p. 46.

20. *Historia Norwegie*, op. cit., p. 196.

21. *The Little Ice Age: How climate made history 1300–1850*, by Brian Fagan (New York 2002: 7).

22. *Vikings: Fear and Faith*, by Paul Cavill (Michigan 2001: 273).

23. *The Little Ice Age*, op. cit., pp. 8–9.

24. *Aftenposten Aften* (29 Feb. 2004: 18). Article by Frede Vestergaard.

25. 'Climate and history: the Westviking's saga', by John and Mary Gribbin, in *New Scientist* (20 Jan. 1990: 52–5).

26. 'Utflytterne i Vest', by Claus Krag, in *Aschehougs Norges Historie v.2* (Oslo 2005: 46).

27. *The Icelandic Saga*, by Peter Hallberg, trans. with notes and introduction by Paul Schach (Lincoln, Nebraska 1962: 5).

28. *The Norse Atlantic Saga*, by Gwyn Jones (Oxford 1986: 162).

29. ibid., p. 163.

30. *The Saga of King Olaf Trygvasson*, trans. J. Sephton (London 1895: 337).

31. *The Vikings: a very short introduction*, by Julian D. Richards (Oxford 2005: 100).

32. 'Utflytterne i Vest', op. cit., p. 46.

33. *mtDNA and the Islands of the North Atlantic: Estimating the Proportions of Norse and Gaelic Ancestry*, by Agnar Helgason, Eileen Hickey, Sara Goodacre, Vindar Bosnes, Kári Stefánsson, Ryk Ward and Bryan Sykes, in *American Journal of Human Genetics*, 68 (2001: 723–7).

34. *The Book of the Settlements*, op. cit., p. 172.

35. *Viking Age Iceland*, op. cit., p. 84.

36. ibid., p. 75.

37. *The Book of the Settlements*, op. cit., p. 165.

38. Quoted in *A Piece of Horse Liver and the Ratification of the Law*, by Jón Hnefill Adalsteinsson (Reykjavík 1998: 45).

39. 'Pingnes by Ellidavatn: The first local assembly in Iceland?', by Gudmundur Ólafsson, in *Proceedings of the Tenth Viking Congress*, ed. James E. Knirk (Oslo 1987: 344).

40. *Íslendingabók and Kristni Saga*, op. cit., p. 4. Teit was Ari's foster-father and one of his most important sources.

41. Martina Stein-Wilkeshuis and Stefan Brink, quoted in 'The communal nature of the judicial systems in early medieval Norway', by Alexandra Sanmark, in *Collegium Medievale* (Oslo 2006: 32).

42. The origin of the name is not known.

43. *The Viking Achievement*, by Peter Foote and David M. Wilson (London 1974: 371).

44. For a discussion on *Rigsthula* as a historical source see, 'The Historical worth of Rígsthula', by Fredric Amory, in *alvíssmál 10*. Online resource at http://userpage.fu-berlin.de/~alvismal/alvinh.html.

45. *Mennesket i Middelalderens Norge: Tanker, tro og holdninger 1000–1300*, by Sverre Bagge (Oslo 1998: 20).

46. 'Sagas and Society III: How credible is the picture of slavery in Icelandic literature?' by Michael Neiss, in *Viking Heritage*, 1 (2001: 8–9).

47. *The Saga of Gisli*, trans. George Johnston, with notes by Peter Foote (London 1978: 30).

48. *Eyrbyggja Saga*, trans. with notes by Hermann Pálsson and Paul Edwards (London 1989: 100–101).

49. *The Viking Achievement*, op. cit., p. 70.

50. *KHLNM*, vol. 19, p. 14.

51. *Chronicles of the Vikings*, by R. I. Page (London 2000: 63).

52. *The Sagas of Icelanders*, ed. Jane Smiley (London 2000: 457–9).

53. *Konungs skuggsjá*, Chapter XV. Online translation by Laurence Marcellus Larson at http://www.mediumaevum.com/75years/mirror/ (accessed 25.11.2007).

54. 'Utflytterne i Vest', op. cit., p. 47.

55. *The Icelandic Saga*, op. cit., p. 9.

CHAPTER 9 ROLLO AND THE NORMAN COLONY

1. *Source Book of Medieval History*, ed. Frederic A. Ogg (London 1907: 174).

2. *The Normans in Europe*, trans. and ed. Elisabeth van Houts (Manchester 2000: 14).

3. See, for example, 'Rollo as historical figure', by Robert Helmerichs. Internet resource at www.mm.com/user/rob/Rollo/HistoricalRollo.html (accessed 01.01.2004).

4. This identification has been made previously in *Dudo of St-Quentin: History of the Normans*, trans. and ed. Eric Christiansen (Woodbridge 1998: xiv).

5. ibid., p. 40.

6. ibid., p. 39.

7. *Heimskringla, or The Lives of the Norse Kings*, by Snorri Sturluson, ed. with notes by Erling Monsen, trans. with the assistance of A. H. Smith (New York 1990: 59).

8. ibid., p. 60.

9. *The Normans in Europe*, op. cit., p. 54.

10. So called to distinguish it from the saga in *Heimskringla*.

11. *The Saga of King Olaf Trygvasson*, trans. J. Sephton (London 1895: 223).

12. *The Normans in Europe*, op. cit., p. 15.

13. *Heimskringla*, op. cit., p. 230.

14. 'Le Prétendu Rollon et la Normandie', by Jean Renaud, in *Les Vikings, premiers Européens. VIII–XI siècle*, ed. Regis Boyer (Paris 2005: 183).

15. 'Saga om Gange-Rolv', in *Sagalitteraturen*, vol. 4 (Oslo 1984: 180).

16. *Historia Norwegie*, ed. Inger Ekrem and Lars Boje Mortensen, trans. Peter Fisher (Copenhagen 2003: 67).

17. *Dudo of St-Quentin*, op. cit., p. 46.

18. Not to be confused with Lothar II's daughter Gisela, who was given in marriage to the Viking Godfrid in 883. See p. 105.

19. *The Normans in Europe*, op. cit., p. 25.

20. ibid., p. 43.

21. *The Vikings in Brittany*, by Neil Price (London 1989: 83).

22. *Dudo of St-Quentin*, op. cit., p. 51.

23. *Normandy before 1066*, by David Bates (London 1982: 22).

24. 'Le Prétendu Rollon et la Normandie', op. cit., p. 194.

25. *Dudo of St-Quentin*, op. cit., p. 16.

26. 'La conversion des Normands peu après 911', by Olivier Guillot, in *Cahiers de civilisation medievale: Xe–XIIe siècles*, no. 2 (Poitiers 1981, April–June: 110).

27. ibid., p. 109.

28. *The Vikings: a very short introduction*, by Julian D. Richards (Oxford 2005: 56).

29. *The Viking Achievement*, by Peter Foote and David M. Wilson (London 1974: 407).

30. *The Vikings: a very short introduction*, op. cit., p. 56.

31. Dudo makes no mention of this, commenting merely that Rollo, 'full of days, migrated to Christ'.

32. Quoted in *The Norsemen in the Viking Age*, by Eric Christiansen (Oxford 2002: 268).

33. 'Brief presentation of a thesis on the Viking presence in France from the 9th to the 11th century: sources and sets of problems', by Jean-Christophe Guillon, in *Viking Heritage*, 4 (1998: 5).

34. *The Vikings in Brittany*, op. cit., p. 56.

35. *Viking Heritage*, article by Jean-Christophe Guillon, op. cit., p. 6.

36. 'Some aspects of Viking research in France', by Anne Nissen Jaubert, in *Acta Archaeologica*, vol. 71 (2001).

37. Le Prétendu Rollon et la Normandie', op. cit., p. 190.

38. *KHLNM*, vol. 12, p. 339.

39. *Kampen om Nordvegen*, by Torgrim Titlestad (Stavanger 1996: 16), quoting Lucien Musset.

40. *Dudo of St-Quentin*, op. cit., p. 49.

41. ibid., p. 36.

42. Quoted in *The Normans in Europe*, op. cit., p. 53.

43. 'William Longsword', by Robert Levine. Internet resource at http://www.bu.edu/english/levine/longsword.htm (accessed 27.11.2007).
44. *Normandy before 1066*, op. cit., p. 14.
45. 'Normandy, 911–1144', by Cassandra Potts, in *A Companion to the Anglo-Norman World*, ed. Christopher Harper-Bill and Elisabeth van Houts (Woodbridge 2003: 27).

CHAPTER 10 THE MASTER-BUILDER: HARALD BLUETOOTH AND THE JELLING STONE

1. *The Penguin History of Europe*, by J. M. Roberts (London 1997: 130–32).
2. *Adam av Bremen. Beretningen om Hamburg stift, erkebiskopenes bedrifter og øyrikene i Norden*, trans. and ed. Bjørg Tosterud Danielsen and Anne Katrine Frihagen (Oslo 1993: 61) (Book 1, Chapter 55).
3. ibid., p. 62 (Book 1, Chapter 59).
4. *The Heroic Age of Scandinavia*, by G. Turville-Petre (London 1951: 92).
5. *The Viking Achievement*, by Peter Foote and David M. Wilson (London 1974: 377).
6. *Skalk*, 1 (Feb. 2005: 18).
7. *A Source Book of Medieval History*, by F. A. Ogg (New York 1907: 199).
8. The scene on the seventh bronze is too badly mutilated to identify.
9. *Rundata*, DR 42.
10. 'Crucifixion iconography in Viking Scandinavia', by Signe Horn Fuglesang, in *Proceedings of the Eighth Viking Congress*, ed. Hans Bekker-Nielsen, Peter Foote and Olaf Olsen (Odense 1981: 87–9).
11. *Gods and Myths of Northern Europe*, by H. R. Ellis Davidson (London 1976: 148).
12. *Aschehougs Norgeshistorie*, b. 1, *Fra jeger til bonde – inntil 800 e.kr*, by Arnvid Lillehammer (Oslo 2005: 246).
13. 'Runeinnskrifter som kilde til historiske hendelser i vikingtiden', by James E. Knirk, in *Nytt Lys på Middelalderen* (Oslo 1997: 87).
14. *Rundata*, Sö 333.
15. ibid., Sö 179.
16. ibid., Ö 11.
17. ibid., DR 216.
18. 'Oseberggraven-Haugbrottet', by A. W. Brøgger, in *Viking Tidsskrift for norrøn arkeologi*, vol. IX, (Oslo 1945: 20–21).
19. *Rundata*, DR 26.
20. *Vikingarnas egna ord*, by Lars Magnar Enoksen (Lund 2003: 178).

21. *The Viking-Age Rune-Stones: custom and commemoration in early medieval Scandinavia*, by Birgit Sawyer (Oxford 2000); see also *Chronicles of the Vikings*, by R. I. Page (London 2000: 74–6).

22. *Vikingarnas egna ord* op. cit., pp. 139–48.

23. *The Works of Sven Aggesen*, trans. with introduction and notes by Eric Christiansen (London 1992: 56).

24. *The Saga of the Jomsvikings*, trans. Lee M. Hollander (Austin 1990: 34).

25. *De Kongelige Monumenter i Jelling*, by Steen Hvass (Jelling 2000: 17).

26. *The Saga of Grettir the Strong*, trans. G. A. Hight (London 1982: 45).

27. *The Book of the Settlements*, in *The Norse Atlantic Saga*, by Gwyn Jones (Oxford 1986: 161).

28. 'Oseberggraven-Haugbrottet', op. cit., p.5.

29. *Fra Hammer til Kors*, ed. Jan Ingar Hansen and Knut G. Bjerva (Oslo 1994: 85).

30. *Vikinger i Vestfold 2006* (Sandefjord 2006: 10).

31. 'Myth and reality: the contribution of archaeology', paper delivered by John Hines at the Eleventh International Saga Conference, Sydney 2000. Internet resource at http://www.arts.usyd.edu.au/departs/medieval/saga/pdf/165-hines.pdf (accessed 25.07.2008).

32. *De Kongelige Monumenter i Jelling*, op. cit., p. 26.

33. *The Russian Primary Chronicle* says that, in 1044, Jaroslav the Wise had the remains of Svyatoslov's sons Jaropolk and Oleg baptized and moved to the Church of the Holy Virgin. *The Russian Primary Chronicle*, ed. Samuel H. Cross (Cambridge, Mass. 1930: 228).

34. *Vikingetidens Jelling*, by Hans Ole Matthiesen (Jelling 2004: 22).

35. *The Works of Sven Aggesen*, op. cit., p. 61.

36. 'Cnut's Scandinavian Empire', by Peter Sawyer, in *The Reign of Cnut: King of England, Denmark and Norway*, ed. A. R. Rumble (London 1994: 12).

37. *Vikingatiden i Skåne*, by Fredrik Svanberg (Lund 2000: 77).

38. Recent satellite images of the area around Rygge in the Norwegian Østfold reveal a structure that in shape and size suggests another ring-fort. See Frans-Arne Stylegar's article at http://arkeologi.blogspot.com/2005/03/en-trelleborg-i-rygge.html.

39. 'Water routes in pre-Mongol Rus', in *The Eastern World of the Vikings*, by E. A. Melnikova (Gothenburg 1996: 43).

40. *Skalk*, 5 (2001). Article by Kåre Johannessen.

41. Poul Nørlund, extract printed in *Danmark i vikingetiden*, ed. Carl og Esben Harding Sørensen (Århus 1980: 127).

42. *De Kongelige Monumenter i Jelling*, op. cit., p. 32.

43. *The Works of Sven Aggesen*, op. cit., p. 61.

44. *Adam av Bremen*, op. cit., p. 83.

45. 'Facts and fancy in Jomsvikinga saga', by Leszek P. Slupecki. Pre-print of a conference paper delivered at the Thirteenth International Saga Conference, 6–12 August 2006, Durham and York. Internet resource at www.dur.ac.uk/medieval.www./sagaconf/sagapps.htm (accessed 29.11.2007).

46. *The Saga of the Jomsvikings*, op.cit., p. 63.

47. ibid., p. 110.

48. 'The Vikings bare their filed teeth', by Caroline Arcini, in *American Journal of Physical Anthropology* (December 2005, 128 (4): 727–33).

CHAPTER 11 THE DANELAW II: ASSIMILATION

1. *EHD*, p. 416.

2. ibid.

3. 'Defining the Danelaw', by Katherine Holman, in *Viking and the Danelaw: Select papers from the Proceedings of the Thirteenth Viking Congress*, ed. J. Graham-Campbell, Richard Hall, Judith Jesch and David N. Parsons (Oxford 2001: 2).

4. ibid., p. 5.

5. *Viking Treasure from the North West – the Cuerdale Hoard in Context*, ed. James Graham-Campbell (National Museums and Galleries in Merseyside 1992).

6. *Ingimund's Saga: Norwegian Wirral*, by Stephen Harding (Birkenhead 2006: 21).

7. *Dagbladet*, 27.11.2007.

8. *The Medieval Foundations of England*, by G. O. Sayles (London 1950: 105).

9. *EHD*, p. 214.

10. *Who's Who in Roman Britain and Anglo-Saxon England*, by Richard Fletcher (Mechanicsburg 2002: 146).

11. *EHD*, p. 217.

12. *The Formation of England 550–1042*, by H. P. R. Finberg (St Albans 1976: 147).

13. ibid., p. 142.

14. *EHD*, p. 38.

15. *Who's Who in Roman Britain and Anglo-Saxon England*, op. cit., p. 153.

16. Internet resource at http://www.lse.co.uk/ShowStory.asp. (accessed 24.07.2007).

17. *Ingimund's Saga*, op. cit., pp. 121ff.

18. *EHD*, p. 37.

19. ibid., p. 219.

20. ibid., p. 38.

21. *Heimskringla, or The Lives of the Norse Kings* by Snorri Sturluson, ed. with notes by Erling Monsen, trans. with the assistance of A. H. Smith (New York 1990: 72).

22. *EHD*, p. 308.

23. *Egil's Saga*, trans. and introd. by Hermann Pálsson and Paul Edwards (London 1976: 164).

24. *Historia Norwegie*, ed. Inger Ekrem and Lars Boje Mortensen, trans. Peter Fisher (Copenhagen 2003: 83).

25. *The Early History of the Church of Canterbury*, by Nicholas Brooks (Leicester 1984: 222).

26. *Who's Who in Roman Britain and Anglo-Saxon England*, op. cit., p. 159.

27. *EHD*, p. 344.

28. *The Early History of the Church of Canterbury*, op. cit., p. 223.

29. *Egil's Saga*, op. cit., p. 248.

30. On stylistic grounds it has been argued that Snorri Sturluson was the author. See *The Sagas of Icelanders*, ed. Jane Smiley (London 2000: 7).

31. *Egil's Saga*, op. cit., p. 118.

32. *Egil's Saga* trans. and ed. by Christine Fell (London 1975: 76–8). The 'King Olaf' of the saga is not to be confused with the later kings of Norway Olaf Tryggvason and Olav Haraldson.

33. ibid., p. 73.

34. *Egil's saga*, trans. and introd. by Pálsson and Edwards, op.cit., p. 148.

35. 'The Saga of the People of Vatnsdal', trans. Andrew Wawn, in *The Sagas of Icelanders*, op. cit., p. 243.

36. For a description of the terms of the Lesser Outlawry see pp. 280–81.

37. 'Monstrous allegations: an exchange of ýki in Bjarnar saga Hítdoela-kappa', by Alison Finlay, in *alvíssmál*, 10 (2001: 21).

38. *Nid, ergi and Old Norse moral attitudes*, by Folke Stiröm (London 1974: 6).

39. ibid., p. 15.

40. Preben Meulengracht Sørensen suggested that the threat may be one of castration, in *Norrønt Nid. Forestillingen om den umandige mand i de islandske sagaer* (Odense 1980: 102).

41. For a good general survey, see 'In the steps of the Vikings', by Gillian Fellows-Jensen, in *Viking and the Danelaw: Select papers from the Proceedings of the Thirteenth Viking Congress*, op. cit.

42. *Place Names in the Landscape*, by Margaret Gelling (London 2000: 52).

43. ibid., p. 10.

44. ibid., p. 11.

45. W. H. F. Nicolaisen, quoted in ibid., p. 210.

46. 'In the steps of the Vikings', op. cit., p. 284.

47. ibid., p. 283.

48. *The Formation of England 550–1042*, op. cit., p. 158.

49. *Dictionary of English Place-Names* by A. D. Mills (Oxford 1998).

50. *The Formation of England 550–1042*, op.cit., p. 158.

51. 'In the steps of the Vikings', op. cit., p. 280.

52. 'Norse in the British Isles', by Michael Barnes, in *Viking Revaluations*, ed. Anthony Faulkes and Richard Perkins (London 1993: 69).

53. 'Settlement and Acculturation', by David Griffiths, in *Land, Sea and Home*, ed. John Hines, Alan Lane and Mark Redknap (Leeds 2004: 133).

54. 'Defining the Danelaw', op. cit., p. 7.

55. *Ingimund's Saga: Norwegian Wirral*, op. cit., p. 24.

56. ibid., p. 4.

57. *KHLNM*, vol. 8, p. 647.

58. *EHD*, p. 439.

59. *KHLNM*, vol. 8, p. 647.

60. 'Defining the Danelaw', op. cit., p. 3.

61. *EHD* 1, p. 435.

62. ibid., p. 435.

63. C. Neff, quoted in 'Defining the Danelaw', op. cit., p. 3.

64. *The Early History of the Church of Canterbury*, op. cit., p. 227.

65. *Encyclopedia of the Viking Age*, by John Haywood (London 2000: 214).

66. *Who's Who in Roman Britain and Anglo-Saxon England*, op. cit., p. 158.

CHAPTER 12 WHEN ALLAH MET ODIN

1. *Nordens historie i middelalderen etter Arabiske kilder*, by Harris Birkeland (Oslo 1954: 5–6).

2. ibid., p. 111.

3. ibid., p. 100.

4. 'Vikingerne i Vasconia', by Anton Erkoreka, in *Vikingerne på Den Iberiske Halvø* (Madrid 2004: 11).

5. 'Al-Madjus', by Arne Melvinger, in *The Encyclopedia of Islam*, vol. 5, ed. C. E. Bosworth, E. van Donzel, B. Lewis and Ch. Pellat (Leiden 1986: 1118).

6. *Les premières incursions des Vikings en Occident d'après les sources arabes*, by Arne Melvinger (Uppsala 1955: 44).

7. ibid., p. 9. See also pp. 51–5, where further possible evidence is explored.

8. ibid., pp. 179–80.

9. *The Encyclopedia of Islam*, op. cit., p. 1120.

10. 'Vikingerne i Vasconia', op. cit., p. 10.

11. Mauritania is in North Africa, present-day northern Morocco and west and central Algeria. It was conquered by the Arabs in the seventh century.

12. CELT (Corpus of Electronic Texts) *Fragmentary Annals of Ireland*, FE 330. Internet resource at http://www.ucc.ie/celt/published/T100017/text017. html (accessed 4.12.2007). This online edition is based on *Fragmentary Annals of Ireland*, ed. and trans. by Joan Radner (Dublin 1978).

13. *Nordens historie i middelalderen etter Arabiske kilder*, op. cit., p. 111.

14. Not until the early fourteenth-century geographer ad-Dimasqi, who refers to Scandinavia as a 'large island, inhabited by very tall people with white skin, fair hair and blue eyes, who understand no one else's language', do we find a reference to the familiar racial stereotype of present-day Scandinavians. See *Nordens historie i middelalderen etter Arabiske kilder*, op cit., p. 114.

15. *Nordens historie i middelalderen etter Arabiske kilder*, op. cit., p. 16.

16. ibid.

17. 'Eastern Connections at Birka', by Björn Ambrosiani, in *Viking Heritage*, 3 (2001: 7).

18. ibid.

19. *Nordens historie i middelalderen etter Arabiske kilder*, op. cit., p. 17.

20. ibid., p. 104.

21. This accounts for its disappearance from Europe throughout the era of Christian culture until it was reintroduced by seamen in the eighteenth century. The word was borrowed from the Tahitian and brought to Britain by the explorer Captain Cook.

22. *Poems of the Vikings. The Elder Edda*, trans. Patricia Terry (Indianapolis 1978: 167–8).

23. The '*disir*' were female gods.

24. *Kroppen som lerret*, by Terje Gansum (Midgard Historisk Senter, undated, no page number).

25. ibid.,

26. *Nordens historie i middelalderen etter Arabiske kilder*, op. cit., p. 84.

27. A. Fabricius, quoted in ibid., p. 154.

28. ibid., p. 87.

29. ibid., p. 86.

30. *The Muslim Discovery of Europe*, by Bernard Lewis (London 1982: 286).

31. *Adam av Bremen. Beretningen om Hamburg stift, erkebiskopenes bedrifter og øyrikene i Norden*, trans. and ed. Bjørg Tosterud Danielsen and Anne Katrine Frihagen (Oslo 1993: 189) (Book 4, Chapter 6).

32. Évariste Lévi-Provencal, in *Un échange d'ambassades entre Cordue et Byzance au IXième siècle*, quoted in *Les premières incursions des Vikings en Occident d'après les sources arabes*, op. cit., p. 61.

33. 'San Isidoro-æsken i León', by Eduardo Morales Romero, in *Vikingerne på Den Iberiske Halvø* (Madrid 2004: 118ff).

34. 'Vikingerne i Vasconia', op. cit., p. 32.

35. 'The Vikings in the Iberian Peninsula: questions to ponder', by Jose Manuel Mates Luque, in *Viking Heritage* 3 (1998: 8).

36. 'Vikingerne i Galicien', by Vicente Almazán, in *Vikingerne på Den Iberiske Halvø*, op. cit., p. 46.

37. 'The Vikings in the Iberian peninsula', by Manuel Velasco. Internet resource at http://www.scandinavica.com/culture/history/iberian.htm (accessed 5.12.2007).

CHAPTER 13 A PIECE OF HORSE'S LIVER: THE PRAGMATIC CHRISTIANITY OF HÅKON THE GOOD

1. *Heimskringla, or The Lives of the Norse Kings*, by Snorri Sturluson, ed. with notes by Erling Monsen, trans. with the assistance of A. H. Smith (New York 1990: 159).

2. Quoted in *A Piece of Horse Liver and the Ratification of Law*, by Jón Hnefill Adalsteinsson (Reykjavík 1998: 63).

3. *Narratives of Veøy* by Brit Solli (Oslo 1996: 187).

4. *De temporum ratione*, by the Venerable Bede, Chapter XV. Internet resource at http://www.nabkal.de/beda/beda_15.html (accessed 7.12.2007).

5. *KHLNM*, vol. 18, p. 271.

6. *Heimskringla: Norrøne tekster og kvad*. Internet resource at http://www. heimskringla.no/original/skaldekvad/haraldskvaedi.php (accessed 6.12.2007).

7. *Heimskringla, or The Lives of the Norse Kings*, op. cit., p. 87.

8. *KHLNM*, vol. 8, p. 7.

9. From *Fagrskinna/Nóregs konunga tal*, quoted in *A Piece of Horse Liver*, op. cit., p. 65.

10. *Heimskringla, or The Lives of the Norse Kings*, op. cit., p. 90.

11. ibid., pp. 86–90. Snorri spreads these developments over two years.

12. ibid., p. 92.

13. *A Piece of Horse Liver*, op. cit., p. 62.

14. *Historia Norwegie*, ed. Inger Ekrem and Lars Boje Mortensen, trans. Peter Fisher (Copenhagen 2003: 85); *The Ancient History of the Norwegian Kings*, by Theodoricus Monachus, trans. and annotated by David and Ian McDougall (London 1998: 61).

15. *A Piece of Horse Liver*, op. cit., p. 64

16. ibid., p. 64.

17. *Heimskringla, or the Lives of the Norse Kings*, op. cit., pp. 100–101.

18. The 'sampling' of the 'Hávamál' may account for Eyvind's nickname, 'the Plagiarist'. The interpretation of the last two lines as a comment on 'king's luck' is based on a reading by the Danish translator, Martin Jensen.

19. *Aschehougs Norges Historie, b. 2, Vikingtid og rikssamling 800–1139*, by Claus Krag (Oslo 2005: 151).

20. *Den Norsk-Isländska Poesien*, by Erik Noreen (Stockholm 1926: 219).

21. *Heimskringla, or The Lives of the Norse Kings*, op. cit., p. 104.

22. *The Ancient History of the Norwegian Kings*, op. cit., p. 63.

23. ibid., p. 8.

24. *KHLNM*, vol. 19, p. 641.

25. *Kampen om Norvegen*, by Torgrim Titlestad (Bergen-Sandviken 1996: 63).

26. *Aschehougs Norges Historie, b. 2*, op. cit., p. 134.

27. Translated from *Blot: Tro og offer i det forkristne Norden*, by Britt-Mari Näsström (Oslo 2001: 27).

28. *Aschehougs Norges Historie, b. 2*, op. cit., p. 134.

29. *Historia Norwegie*, op. cit., p. 89.

30. Such a statement of relationship was necessary for the legitimation of Olaf's later kingship. Norwegian historians increasingly doubt the validity of the genealogical links to Harald Finehair of both Olaf Tryggvason and of the later saint-king, Olav Haraldson.

31. *Historia Norwegie*, op. cit., p. 91.

32. *The Formation of England 550–1042*, by H. P. R. Finberg (St Albans 1976: 182). For a different assessment of the importance of the battle, see *The Return of the Vikings: The Battle of Maldon 991*, by Donald Scragg (Stroud 2006).

33. *EHD*, p. 319.

34. *A Choice of Anglo-Saxon Verse*, ed. and trans. by Richard Hamer (London 1972: 51–2).

35. *EHD*, p. 234.

36. ibid., p. 439.

37. *EHD*, p. 234.

38. ibid., p. 438.

39. *The Return of the Vikings*, op. cit., p. 61.

40. *The Ancient History of the Norwegian Kings*, op. cit., p. 13.
41. *Heimskringla, or The Lives of the Norse Kings*, op. cit., pp. 155–7.
42. *Ágrip: A Twelfth-Century Synoptic History of the Kings of Norway*, edited and translated, with an introduction and notes by M. J. Driscoll (London 1995: 31).
43. *The Conversion of Iceland*, by Dag Strömbäck (London 1975: 33).
44. *Heimskringla, or The Lives of the Norse Kings*, op. cit., p. 176.
45. *The Ancient History of the Norwegian Kings*, op. cit., p. 15.

CHAPTER 14 GREENLAND AND NORTH AMERICA

1. Quoted in *Icelandic Culture*, by Sigurdur Nordal, trans. with notes by Vilhjálmur T. Bjarnar (New York 1990: 91).
2. *The Vinland Saga. The Norse discovery of America*, trans. and introduced by Magnus Magnusson and Hermann Pálsson (London 1978: 76).
3. *KHLNM*, vol. 4, p. 605.
4. ibid., p. 604.
5. ibid., vol. 3, p. 537.
6. It is not clear from the saga whether Erik had been exiled for life or only for another three years, and there may have been flexibility in such matters. Given his avowed intention to settle in Greenland it is possible he was permitted to return for the purposes of organizing the colonization.
7. *The Vinland Saga*, op. cit., p. 78.
8. *Islendinga Saga*, by Jon Jóhannesson, trans. by Haraldur Bessason (Winnipeg 1974: 95).
9. 'Far and yet near: North America and Norse Greenland', by Kirsten Seaver, in *Viking Heritage*, 1 (2000: 3).
10. *KHLNM*, vol. 8, p. 651.
11. *Eirik den Rødes Grønland*, by Knud J. Krogh (Odense 1967: 52).
12. *The Vinland Saga*, op. cit., pp. 32–3.
13. ibid., p. 86.
14. *Eirik den Rødes Grønland*, op. cit., p. 71.
15. 'The fate of Greenland's Vikings', by Dale Mackenzie Brown, in *Archaeology. A Publication of the Archaeological Institute of America*. Internet resource at http://www.archaeology.org/online/features/greenland/ (accessed 12.12.2007).
16. What follows is based on an article in *Viking Heritage*, 4 (2001: 3–7), by Joel Berglund, of the Greenland National Museum, who was one of the leaders of the excavation.

17. 'Far and yet near', op. cit., p. 3.
18. 'A "Northern Periphery" project: The Viking Trail', in *Conservation of an Early Norse Farm at Narsaq, South Greenland*, by Hans Kapel and Rie Oldenburg. Internet resource at http://www.narsaq-museum.org/common-doc/viking-trail.pdf (accessed 24 July 2008).
19. 'Reconstructing the costume of the Viking Age', by Viktoria Persdotter, in *Viking Heritage*, 3 (1999: 3).
20. *Eirik den Rødes Grønland*, op. cit., p. 74.
21. *KHLNM*, vol. 8, p. 657.
22. *The Norse Atlantic Saga*, by Gwyn Jones (Oxford 1986: 99).
23. Both letters are in the *American Journeys Collection* of the Wisconsin Historical Society Digital Library and Archives, Document No. AJ-060. Internet resource at www.americanjourneys.org/aj-060/ (accessed 11.12.2007).
24. *KHLNM*, vol. 5, p. 405.
25. *Viking Heritage*, 4(2003: 35).
26. 'Inuit and Norsemen in Arctic Canada AD 1000 to 1400', by Robert McGhee, in *Archaeological Survey of Canada: Oracles*. Internet resource at www.civilization.ca/cmc/archeo/oracles/norse/40.htm (accessed 11.12.2007).
27. 'Viking Navigation', by Søren Thirslund, in *Viking Heritage*, 4 (1999: 6).
28. *Eirik den Rødes Grønland*, op. cit., p. 71.
29. ibid., pp. 127–34.
30. *Konungs skuggsjá (The King's Mirror)*, online translation, by Laurence M. Larson, Chapter XVII (1917). Internet resource at http://www.medium aevum.com/75years/mirror/ (accessed 12.12.2007).
31. *The Vikings and America*, by Eirik Wahlgren (London 2000: 15).
32. 'Vikingerne tidligere i Amerika end vi troede', article in *Berlingske Tidende*, 23 September 2008.
33. *The Vinland Saga*, op. cit., pp. 52–4.
34. 'L'Anse aux Meadows and Vinland: The Norse in the North Atlantic', by Birgitta Wallace, in *Viking Heritage*, 3 (2004: 26).
35. For a discussion of the differences between the sagas as literature and history, see *The Vinland Saga*, op. cit., pp. 35–9.
36. 'Far and yet near', op. cit., p. 4.
37. The name is an example of the pitfalls of modern mapmaking when written encounters oral culture. What looks like a mixture of French and English is probably a misrendering of the all-French L'Anse aux Méduse, 'the bay of jellyfish'.
38. 'L'Anse aux Meadows and Vinland', op. cit., p. 28.
39. *The Vikings and America*, op. cit., p. 124.

40. 'Norse Greenland on the eve of Renaissance exploration', by Kirsten A. Seaver, in *Voyages and Exploration in the North Atlantic from the Middle Ages to the XVIIth Century*, ed. Anna Agnarsdóttir (Reykjavik 2001: 30).

CHAPTER 15 RAGNARÖK IN ICELAND

1. *Íslendingabók and Kristni Saga*, trans. Siân Grønlie (London 2006: 36).
2. ibid., p. 23.
3. *The Tale of Thorvald Chatterbox*, collected in *Viga-Glum's Saga*, trans. John McKinnell (Edinburgh 1987).
4. *Íslendingabók and Kristni Saga*, op. cit., p. 40.
5. *Adam av Bremen. Beretningen om Hamburg stift, erkebiskopenes bedrifter og øyrikene i Norden*, trans. and ed. by Bjørg Tosterud Danielsen and Anne Katrine Frihagen (Oslo 1993: 216) (Book IV, Chapter 36, scholium 156).
6. *Íslendingabók and Kristni Saga*, op. cit., p. 40.
7. ibid., pp. xxxii, 42–43.
8. ibid., p. 44.
9. ibid., p. 8.
10. *The Ancient History of the Norwegian Kings*, by Theodoricus Monachus, trans. and annotated by David and Ian McDougall with an introduction by Peter Foote (London 1998: 15).
11. ibid., p. 16.
12. Ari writes that the mission took place in the same summer as Olaf Tryggvason was killed, but that Olaf met his death in the year 1000. The apparent discrepancy arises because Ari began his year on 1 September and Olaf is believed to have died on 9 September. Starting the year on 1 January as we now do gives a date for both the conversion mission and Olaf's death of 999. See *The Conversion of Iceland*, by Dag Strömback (London, 1975), esp. footnote 1 on page 2, summarizing a 1964 paper *Studier i kronologisk metode i tidlig islandsk historieskrivning* by Dr Ólafiá Einarsdottir.
13. *Íslendingabók and Kristni Saga*, op. cit., p. 8.
14. 'On the conversion of the Icelanders', by Peter Foote, reviewing *Under the Cloak* by Jón Hnefill Adalsteinsson, in *Aurvandilstá: Norse Studies* (Odense 1984: 62).
15. J. H. Adalsteinsson, *Under the Cloak: The acceptance of Christianity in Iceland with particular reference to the religious attitudes prevailing at the time* (Uppsala 1978: 99).
16. ibid., p. 99.

17. *Íslendingabók and Kristni Saga*, op. cit., p. 49.

18. ibid., p. 9.

19. There is no evidence that Runolf and Hjalti were related. The implication that Runolf took the prosecution upon himself as someone outside the family would bear strong witness to his opposition to Christianity's progress.

20. *Norrøne Gude- og Heltesagn*, by P. A. Munch, revised by Anne Holtsmark (Oslo 1981: 143).

21. 'Fimbulvinteren, Ragnarök och Klimatkrisen år 536–537 e. kr.', by Bo Gräslund, in *Saga och Sed 2007* (Uppsala 2008).

22. *Heimskringla, or The Lives of the Norse Kings*, by Snorri Sturluson, ed. with notes by Erling Monsen, trans. with the assistance of A. H. Smith (New York 1990: 6).

23. *Saxo Grammaticus: The History of the Danes, Books I–IX: 1. English Text; II. Commentary*, trans. and annotated by Hilda Ellis Davidson and Peter Fisher (Cambridge 2002: 290).

24. *Íslendingabók and Kristni Saga*, op. cit., p. 50.

25. *EHD*, p. 435, Law 2.1.

26. 'The fantastic future and the Norse Sybil of Völuspå', by Gro Steinsland. Internet resource at http://www.dur.ac.uk/medieval.www/sagaconf/steins land.htm (accessed 25.09.2007).

27. 'The last Viking in Iceland', by Steinunn Kristjánsdóttir, in *Viking Heritage* 3 (1998: 5).

28. *The Ancient History of the Norwegian Kings*, op. cit., p. 16.

29. *Icelandic Culture*, by Sigurdur Nordal (New York 1990: 178).

30. See Jón Hnefill Adalsteinsson's doctoral thesis *Under the Cloak: The acceptance of Christianity in Iceland with particular reference to the religious attitudes prevailing at the time* (Uppsala, 1978), for a full exposition of this theory and further examples of this practice.

31. 'Sjamanisme i norske sagn fra middelalderen', by Ronald Grambo, in *Forum Mediævale*, 4/5, no. 1/2 (1983: 9).

32. 'Rimbert: *Life of Anskar*, the Apostle of the North, 801–865', trans. Charles H. Robinson, chapter 27. Internet resource at *Medieval Sourcebook*, http://www.fordham.edu/halsall/basis/anskar.html (accessed 17.02.2004).

33. *The Agricola and Germania*, by Tacitus, trans. by A. J. Church and W. J. Brodribb (London 1877: ch. 10: 'Auguries and methods of divination'. Internet resource at *Medieval Sourcebook*, http://www.fordham.edu/halsall/source/tacitus1.html (accessed 18.12. 2007).

34. 'Rimbert: *Life of Anskar*' op. cit., chapter 27.

35. *Íslendingabók and Kristni Saga*, op. cit., p. 50.

36. 'Gunnlaug Wormtongue' is included in *Eirik the Red and Other Icelandic Sagas*, trans. by Gwyn Jones (London 1961).

37. *Fornskandinavisk religion*, by Britt-Mari Näsström (Lund 2002: 297).

38. *KHLNM*, vol. 1, p. 349.

39. 'Children's graves – status symbols?' by Malin Lindqvist, in *Viking Heritage*, 2 (2003: 28).

40. *Viking Age Iceland*, by Jesse Byock (London 2001: 50).

41. *ibid.*, p. 375.

42. *The Saga of Hallfred*, trans. and introduced by Alan Boucher (Reykjavik 1981: 37).

43. These tenth-century verses question a popular assumption, deriving from Stendhal's 1822 treatise 'On Love', that romantic love was invented at some point after 1100. Some years ago an American scholar joked that the most frequent cause of death among young men in the Saga Age was the composing of love poetry. See 'Jeg elsker deg', by Bjørn Bandlien in *Klassekampen*, July 2007, p. 9.

44. *Íslendingabók and Kristni Saga*, op. cit., pp. 45–7.

45. The complicated structure of skaldic poetry makes these effects impossible to convey in translation. For a complete exposition of how close Hallfred sails to the wind see 'The Reluctant Christian and the King of Norway', by Cecil Wood, in *Scandinavian Studies*, Vol. XXXI, 2 (May 1959: 65–72).

46. Based on the circumstances of its composition, valid but not fatal objections to the authenticity of this last verse have been raised. See 'The Last Hour of Hallfredar vandrædaskald', by Bjarni Einarsson, in *Proceedings of the Eighth Viking Congress* (Odense 1981: 217–223).

47. *The Saga of Hallfred*, op. cit., p. 51.

48. *Ágrip: A Twelfth-Century Synoptic History of the Kings of Norway*, ed. and trans. with an introduction and notes by M. J. Driscoll (London 1995: 34)

49. *Adam av Bremen*, op. cit., p. 216 (Book IV, Chapter 36).

50. *The Icelandic Saga*, by Peter Hallberg, trans. and introduced by Paul Schach (Lincoln 1962: 31–4).

CHAPTER 16 ST BRICE, ST ALPHEGE AND THE
WOLF: THE FALL OF ANGLO-SAXON ENGLAND

1. *The Kings and Queens of Britain*, by John Cannon and Anne Hargreaves (Oxford 2001: 72).

2. *EHD*, p. 234.

3. ibid., p. 895.

4. *The Anglo-Saxon Chronicle*, trans. and ed. G. N. Garmonsway (London 1990: 57).

5. ibid., p. 133.

6. *EHD*, p. 894.

7. *The Anglo-Saxon Chronicle*, op. cit., p. 133.

8. *EHD*, p. 132.

9. *The Anglo-Saxon Chronicle*, op. cit., p. 135.

10. Roger of Wendover's is one of a number of accounts of St Brice's Day collected at http://www.havhingsten.dk/index.php?id=925&L=I&id=925& type=98. Internet resource (accessed 24 July 2008).

11. *EHD*, pp. 238–9.

12. *Anglo-Saxon Charters: An annotated list and bibliography*, by P. H. Sawyer (London 1968: 277) (Charter no. 909).

13. *The Vikings*, by Magnus Magnusson (Stroud 2003: 274).

14. A version of Henry of Huntingdon's account can be read on the website cited in note 10 above.

15. *The Anglo-Saxon Chronicle*, op. cit., p. 139.

16. ibid., p. 141.

17. ibid.

18. *The Early History of the Church of Canterbury*, by Nicholas Brooks (Leicester 1984: 285).

19. *Erik the Red and other Icelandic Sagas*, selected and trans. by Gwyn Jones (London 1961: 279–80).

20. *The Works of Sven Aggesen*, trans. with introduction and notes by Eric Christiansen (London 1992: 35).

21. *The Anglo-Saxon Chronicle*, op. cit., p. 144.

22. It was this marriage between his great-aunt and Ethelred, followed after Ethelred's death by her marriage to Cnut of Denmark, that would give William of Normandy his slender claim to the throne of England in 1066.

23. *The Normans in Europe*, trans. and ed. Elisabeth van Houts (Manchester 2000: 20).

24. *EHD*, p. 894.

25. ibid., p. 246.

26. ibid., p. 928.

27. ibid., p. 932.

28. ibid., p. 933, n. 6.

29. ibid., pp. 933–4.

30. *Adam av Bremen. Beretningen om Hamburg stift, erkebiskopenes*

bedrifter og øyrikene i Norden. Trans. and ed. Bjørg Tosterud Danielsen and Anne Katrine Frihagen (Oslo 1993: 99) (Book 1, Chapter 52).

31. *The Anglo-Saxon Chronicle*, op. cit., p. 139.

32. *EHD*, p. 250.

33. *The Anglo-Saxon Chronicle*, op. cit., p. 153.

34. *EHD*, p. 249, n. 3.

35. *Encomium Emmae Reginae*, trans. and ed. Alistair Campbell, with a supplementary introduction by Simon Keynes (Cambridge 1996: lx).

36. *EHD*, p. 312.

37. *Who's Who in Roman Britain and Anglo-Saxon England 55 BC–AD 1066*, by Richard Fletcher (Mechanicsburg 2002: 204).

38. 'Who were the thegns of Cnut the Great?' by Carl Löfving, in *Viking Heritage*, 2 (2005: 14–17).

39. 'Cnut's Scandinavian empire', by Peter Sawyer, in *The Reign of Cnut: King of England, Denmark and Norway*, ed. Alexander R. Rumble (London 1994: 19–20).

40. *Adam av Bremen*, op. cit., p. 98 (Book 2, Chapter 52).

41. *EHD*, p. 896.

42. ibid., p. 455.

43. *The Early History of the Church of Canterbury*, op. cit., p. 292.

44. ibid., p. 292.

45. *EHD*, p. 477.

46. 'Contextualising the Knútsdrápur: skaldic praise-poetry at the court of Cnut', by Matthew Townend, in *Ango-Saxon England* (2001, 30: 145–79). Internet resource at http://journals.cambridge.org/action/displayAbstract?fromPage=online&aid=123937 (accessed 19.12.2007).

47. 'King Cnut in the verse of his skalds', by Roberta Frank, in *The Reign of Cnut*, op. cit., p. 108.

48. Writing in the thirteenth century, Snorri Sturluson glossed the word *skáld* as *frædamadr*, meaning someone learned, knowledgeable and possessed of essential information, rather than simply a 'poet' in the modern sense of a maker of verse. See 'Memorials in speech and writing', by Judith Jesch, in *Hikuin*, ed. Gunhild Øeby Nielsen (Århus 2006: 101).

49. *Heimskringla, or The Lives of the Norse Kings* by Snorri Sturluson, ed. with notes by Erling Monsen, trans. with the assistance of A. H. Smith (New York 1990: 402).

50. *KHLNM*, vol. 15, p. 237.

51. *EHD*, p. 333.

52. ibid., p. 337.

53. ibid., p. 260.

CHAPTER 17 THE VIKING SAINT

1. *Heimskringla, or The Lives of the Norse Kings*, by Snorri Sturluson, ed. with notes by Erling Monsen, trans. with the assistance of A. H. Smith (New York 1990: 167).

2. *Ágrip: A Twelfth-Century Synoptic History of the Kings of Norway*, ed. and trans. with an introduction and notes by M. J. Driscoll (London 1995: 96).

3. ibid., p. 35.

4. *The Ancient History of the Norwegian Kings*, by Theodoricus Monachus, trans. and annotated by David and Ian McDougall, with an introduction by Peter Foote (London 1998: 21).

5. *Aschehougs Norges Historie, b. 2, Vikingtid og rikssamling 800–1139*, by Claus Krag (Oslo 2005: 179); see also *Heimskringla*, op. cit., p. 218.

6. *EHD*, p. 333.

7. ibid.

8. *The Ancient History of the Norwegian Kings*, op. cit., p. 17.

9. *Ágrip*, op. cit., p. 35.

10. *Regestica Norvegica I 822–1263*, ed. Erik Gunnes (Oslo 1989: 28–32).

11. *Ágrip*, op. cit., p. 39.

12. For a full account of this hypothesis, see *Aschehougs Norges Historie, b. 2*, op. cit., pp. 185–8.

13. ibid., p. 185.

14. *EHD*, p. 454.

15. *Heimskringla*, op. cit., pp. 356–7.

16. *EHD*, p. 336.

17. *KHLNM*, vol. 5, p. 559.

18. 'Fast and Feast: Christianization through the regulation of everyday life', by Alexandra Sanmark, in *Viking Heritage*, 4 (2005: 3–7).

19. Florence of Worcester reports the rumour that Ælfgifu deceived the king and presented as his own the son of a priest. *EHD*, p. 315

20. *Ágrip*, op. cit., p. 41.

21. ibid., p. 45.

22. In 1031 the Church's bishops could confer sainthood on the dead on their own initiative. By Snorri's time the Pope alone had this power.

23. *EHD*, p. 255.

24. *Aschehougs Norges Historie, b. 2*, op. cit., p. 165.

25. 'Anglo-Saxon saints in Old Norse sources and vice-versa', by Christine E. Fell, in *Proceedings of the Eighth Viking Congress* (Odense 1981: 95–6).

26. *Rundata*, U 687.

27. *Ágrip*, op. cit., pp. 47–9.

28. *Morkinskinna: The earliest Icelandic chronicle of the Norwegian Kings (1030–1157)*, trans. with an introduction and notes by Theodore M. Andersson and Kari Ellen Gade (Ithaca and London 2000: 66 and 101).

29. *The Ancient History of the Norwegian Kings*, op. cit., p. 34.

30. *Heimskringla*, op. cit., p. 489.

31. ibid., p. 502.

32. *The Anglo-Saxon Chronicle*, trans. and ed. G. N. Garmonsway (London 1990: 165).

33. *Heimskringla*, op. cit., p. 503, note 1.

CHAPTER 18 HEATHENDOM'S LAST BASTION

1. There are fewer names than stones because a number of the stones and inscriptions are fragments without names.

2. *Rundata*, Sö 179.

3. This is of course not Harald Hardrada.

4. *Rundata*, U 778.

5. *Rundata*, Sö 108.

6. *Rundata*, Sö 107.

7. A small body of opinion prefers to identify the 'Ingvar' of this saga as the Kievan prince Igor, who attacked Constantinople in 941. See above, Chapter 6. See also *Vikingar i Österled*, by Mats G. Larsson (Stockholm 2003: 24).

8. *Adam av Bremen. Beretningen om Hamburg stift, erkebiskopenes bedrifter og øyrikene i Norden*, trans. and ed. Bjørg Tosterud Danielsen and Anne Katrine Frihagen (Oslo 1993: 132) (Book 3, Chapter 16).

9. *The Russian Primary Chronicle*, trans. and ed. Samuel H. Cross (Cambridge, Mass. 1930: 225).

10. 'Runestones tell about mercenaries going east,' by Mats G. Larsson, in *Viking Heritage*, 2 (2001: 18–19).

11. *Adam av Bremen*, op. cit., p. 178 (Book 3, Chapter 72).

12. ibid., p. 80 (Book 2, Chapter 25).

13. ibid., p. 89 (Book 2, Chapter 37).

14. *The Viking Achievement*, by P. Foote and D. Wilson (London 1974: 32).

15. *The Early History of the Church of Canterbury*, by Nicholas Brooks (Leicester 1984: 283).

16. *Olof Skötkonung och kristnandet*: http://www.tacitus.nu/svensk

historia/kungar/vikingatid/oskristnandet.htm. Internet resource (accessed 26.10.2007).

17. A clear division of geographical Sweden into regions dominated by separate tribes known as the Svear and the Gautar at this time is not universally accepted by historians.

18. *Adam av Bremen*, op. cit., p. 102 (Book 2, Chapter 58).

19. *Hedenskap og Kristendom*, by Fredrik Paasche (Oslo 1948: 41).

20. *Kristninga i Norden 750–1200*, by Jón Vidar Sigurdsson (Oslo 2003: 33).

21. *Rundata*, J RS1928;66 $.

22. *Adam av Bremen*, op. cit., p. 131 (Book 3, Chapter 15).

23. 'The Lily Stones: research findings shed new light on the history of Christianity', by Christen Åhlin in *Viking Heritage*, 3 (2002: 28).

24. Populär Historia: 'Til hvilken tid hör liljestenarna?' http://www.popu larhistoria.se/o.o.i.s?id=170&vid=509&template=.print.t. Internet resource (accessed 26.10.2007). See also *Viking Heritage*, 3 (2002: 28).

25. *Adam av Bremen*, op. cit., p. 209 (Book 4, Chapter 30).

26. ibid., p. 161 (Book 3, Chapter 53).

27. The rituals were those at Uppsala described by Adam and mentioned earlier, involving the sacrifice of nine males of different genus over a period of nine days. *Adam av Bremen*, op. cit., p. 207 (Book 4, Chapter 27).

28. 'Study into the socio-political history of the Obodrites', by Roman Zaroff, in *Collegium Medievale*, vol. 16 (2003: 27).

29. Örjan Martinsson's website (http://www.tacitus.nu) is a good guide to this obscure but important period of the history of the Swedes.

30. *Hervarar saga ok Heidreks* was an important source for Tolkien's *The Lord of the Rings*.

31. *Orkneyinga Saga*, trans. and ed. Hermann Pálsson and Paul Edwards (London 1978: p. 80).

32. *Kristninga i Norden*, op. cit., p. 33.

33. *Vikingatiden i Skåne*, by Fredrik Svanberg (Lund 2000: 87).

34. *Adam av Bremen*, op. cit., p. 91 (Book 2, Chapter 41).

35. ibid., p. 189 (Book 4, Chapter 7).

36. *Vikingatiden i Skåne*, op. cit., p. 93.

37. *Oxford Dictionary of Popes*, by J. N. D. Kelly (Oxford 2003: 154).

38. *Aschehougs Norges Historie, b. 2, Vikingtid og rikssamling 800–1130*, by Claus Krag (Oslo 2005: 240).

Index

Characters found only in Scandinavian alphabets are interfiled with their nearest equivalents in the English alphabet; Scandinavian personal names using patronymics rather than surnames are indexed under first name; the prefixes 'al-' and 'ar-' are ignored (e.g. 'al-madjus' is filed as if it were 'madjus').